THE
CREATURE
IN THE MAP

The Chemical Theatre
A Cup of News: The Life of Thomas Nashe
The Fruit Palace
Borderlines
The Reckoning: The Murder of Christopher Marlowe

Ralegh's Guiana chart, 1595

THE
CREATURE
IN THE MAP

A Journey to El Dorado

Charles Nicholl

THE UNIVERSITY OF CHICAGO PRESS

Published by arrangement with William Morrow and Company, Inc.

The University of Chicago Press, Chicago 60637

Library of Congress Cataloging-in-Publication Data

Nicholl, Charles.
  The creature in the map : a journey to El Dorado / Charles
Nicholl. — 1st U.S. ed.
      p.   cm.
  Includes bibliographical references and index.
  ISBN 0-226-58025-3 (paper : alk. paper)
  1. El Dorado.   2. Raleigh, Walter, Sir, 1552?–1618—Journeys—
Guiana.   3. Guiana—Description and travel.   4. South America—
Description and travel.   5. Nicholl, Charles—Journeys—South
America.   I. Title.
E121.N53   1997
918.804'1—dc21   96-45631
                                                              CIP

⊗ The paper used in this publication meets the minimum
requirements of the American National Standard for
Information Sciences—Permanence of Paper for Printed
Library Materials, ANSI Z39.48—1984.

This book is printed on acid-free paper.

FOR
SASHA

ACKNOWLEDGMENTS

My foremost thanks are to those I traveled with in Venezuela: Ron Orders, Maggie Ellis, Frank Battersby, Uwe Neumann, María Teresa Poza, Trevor Davies, Eulogio Rossi, Anita Castro and Lobo Loffler. I am also grateful to Heinz Dollacker, Tomás Bernal, Alexander Laime, Rudy Truffino, and Parchita Floresta; to the Warao people of Pedernales and Wakahara; and to Jorge Calcaño and his many relations among the Kamerakoto Pemón. Also, to our deliverer at Puerto Chicanán, Victor; to our hosts in El Dorado, Jim and Allen; and to the voice of Neptune Central, Lorna.

All these people helped to make a difficult journey possible and, for the most part, tremendous fun.

In Caracas I was generously received by the then British ambassador Giles Fitzherbert and his wife Alexandra, and received assistance from staff at the British embassy, especially Carlos Villalobos; staff at the *Caracas Daily Journal*, especially Mitch Chase; and John Dickenson and John Coope.

I would also like to thank John Willis and Marie Thomas of Channel 4, Julian Sabath, Patricia Díaz, Jacqui Timberlake, Verena Henman, Dan Franklin, Euan Cameron, Jacqueline Korn, Elizabeth Cree, and Serena Sapegno. My thanks also to Simon Wingfield-Digby, current owner of Sherborne Castle; to the archivist, Ann Smith, and the caretaker, Harold Smith; and to Reg and Jean Wood.

Expert and scholarly advice was provided by Malcolm Deas of the Latin America Centre at St. Antony's College, Oxford; Paul Henley of Manchester University; Michael Glenn at the Springfield-Greene County Library, Missouri; Joan Thirsk; and Raymond Skinner, whose work on the early explorer John Ley demands to be published.

I have been helped throughout by staff at the British Museum, the Public Record Office, and the London Library.

I am indebted to the late Stella Sparry for her researches into the Sparry family, and to her husband, Erle, for permission to use unpublished material collected by her.

CONTENTS

CONTENTS

Thinking to get at once all the gold that the goose could give, he killed it, and opened it—only to find nothing.

—AESOP, "The Goose That Laid Golden Eggs"

Introduction

✳   ✳   ✳

I N THIS book I want to reconstruct, as nearly as possible, a single journey that took place in South America four hundred years ago.

It was not a long journey. The nub of it, the "expedition" proper, lasted less than six weeks, in May and June 1595. It is not remembered for any great contribution to early geography, nor for any extremes of distance or endurance in the making of it. Its fame belongs more to the realm of legend than achievement. This journey involves not one but two legends: Its purpose was to locate the "golden city" of El Dorado, which is certainly a legend; and its leader was Sir Walter Ralegh, who is also—in a rather looser sense—a legendary figure.

I would say my purpose is to find the reality that lies behind the legend, though I am aware that these are difficult commodities to deal in, and that the one may not lie quite so snugly "behind" the other.

I SHALL call the protagonist of this story Ralegh. I do not like to call him Sir Walter: As such he seems no more than a cliché, a posture, an adornment of English Heritage biscuit tins and humorous No Smoking signs. He is caught in the dead space of recurrence. He is forever having to lay down his cloak in the mud, to parley with red-skinned Indians, to puff elaborately on a long clay pipe. The pipe is his trademark, as familiar as Florence Nightingale's lamp and Nelson's empty sleeve. They always have a prop, these famous personages.

"Sir Walter" is, in short, the Ralegh legend. It is in part authentic—his own creation, his own publicity—and is of interest to that extent, but four hundred years later this way of remembering him is largely a way of forgetting the complex, flawed, and occasionally somewhat crazy man who first generated the legend.

Queen Elizabeth called him Water. The nicknaming of courtiers was one of her little routines: a coquettish in-joke. It was a mode of possession, like the naming of regions in America. Sir Robert Cecil, a small man deformed by scoliosis, was sometimes her Elf and sometimes her Pygmy. Sir Christopher Hatton was Mutton, and Walsingham was the Moor, and even Archbishop Whitgift was her "little black husband." A royal nickname was the ultimate status symbol.

Perhaps Ralegh liked to think that Water conveyed a sense of his elusive temperament, his fluent discourse, his gift of refreshment, his dangerous depths. Perhaps it did, but it was more specifically a joke at his own expense (of course, with her it was always at your own expense). It was a joke about his modest origins, the thick provincial brogue of his accent. Even at the height of courtly success, he refused to affect those punctilious new vowels: "He spake broad Devonshire to his dying day."

Water was nothing more than Walter said in a yokel accent. War-ter. Wore-uh. It made of him a clown, in the particular sense they used the word: a clumsy rustic. He is reminded that he is an *arriviste,* a made man, and that he could therefore be unmade whenever she pleased.

To the Spanish, who have trouble with *w*s, he was Gualtero, and Ralo, and most often a hybrid of the two: Guaterrale. It is as such that he features in the Spanish accounts of his El Dorado venture—at one point he is El Conde Guaterrale, a piratical count appearing over the horizon with his fleet of three-masters.

It might be attractive to call him Guaterrale but I shall stick to Ralegh. There are many variant spellings of the name—an assiduous biographer has counted more than seventy—but this is the one he used most consistently.

The name is nowadays usually pronounced as "Rahley" or "Ralley," but there is no doubt that he himself said it as "Rawley," and so did those who knew him. Most of the spellings indicate this. On his first venture into print—some verses in praise of the soldier-poet George Gascoigne, published in 1576—he was "Walter Rawley of the Middle Temple." When soldiering in Ireland he is plain Captain Rawlye. Contemporary puns also turn on this pronunciation, as King James's sour comment, on first meeting him in 1603: "I have heard rawly of thee." It is not obligatory to follow the Elizabethan usage—we do not need Shagspur's *Hamlet* or Marley's *Faustus*—but I personally favor "Rawley" on the grounds of sonority as well as authenticity. There is a toughness in the timbre of it.

So let Ralegh stand for all these—for Water Rawley, and Count Guaterrale, and even for that pantomime knight Sir Walter—as we place him in this highly particular context of his South American adventure.

THIS BOOK is in part a historical reconstruction, based as much as possible on original documents. My chief source is Ralegh's own account of the expedition, *The Discoverie of Guiana,* written within a few weeks of his return to England and published early in 1596.

But this is not, as his biographers might lead us to believe, the only source. There exists another firsthand account by a young man who was part of the expedition, Francis Sparry or Sparrow. This document, written in a Madrid prison in about 1600, is given here for the first time in English translation (Appendix 1), together with some related papers. Sparry adds fresh information on the journey, as do other sources—Spanish newsletters, Admiralty Court documents, etc.—not usually consulted. Other early English expeditions in the area are also useful: Dudley in 1595; Keymis in 1596; Harcourt in 1609; and Ralegh's own second attempt, the tragic Last Voyage of 1617–18. Using all these, one can expand on the narrative of Ralegh's *Discoverie,* and sometimes modify it, and in doing so learn more of its complexity as a text.

There is also some visual evidence to consider. There are two separate sets of engravings. These illustrate later editions of the *Dis-*

THE
DISCOVERIE
OF THE LARGE,
RICH, AND BEVVTIFVL
EMPYRE OF GVIANA, WITH

a relation of the great and Golden Citie
of Manoa *(which the Spanyards call* El
Dorade) And of the Prouinces of *Emeria,*
Arromaia. Amapaia , and other Countries, with their riuers, ad-
ioyning.

Performed in the yeare 1 5 9 5. by Sir
W. ℞*alegh* Knight, Captaine of her
Maiesties Guard, Ln. Warden
of the Stanneries, and her High-
nesse Lieutenant generall
of the Countie of
Cornewall.

Imprinted at London by ℞*obert* ℞*obinson.*
1 5 9 6.

1. Title page of Ralegh's Discoverie *(1596)*

Kurtze Wunderbare Beschreibung.

Deß Goldreichen König:

reichs Guianæ in America/oder newen Welt/ vnter der
Linea _AEquinoctiali_ gelegen: So newlich Anno 1594. 1595.
vnnd 1596. von dem Welgebornen Herrn / Herrn Walthero Ra=
legh einem Englischen Ritter/besucht worden: Erstlich auß befehl seiner
Gnaden in zweyen Büchlein beschrieben / darauß _Iodocus Hondius,_ ein
schöne Land Taffel/mit einer Niderländischen erklärung gemacht,
Jetzt aber ins Hochteutsch gebracht/vnd auß vnter=
schiedlichen _Authoribus_ erkläret.

Durch

Levinum Hulsium.

Noribergæ, impensis Levini Hvlsii.
M D XCIX.

2. Title page of the Hulsius edition (1599)

coverie, by Theodore de Bry and Levinus Hulsius, both published in Germany in 1599. Their documentary status is questionable—they belong more to the legend than the reality of the journey—but they are still interesting.

And then there is, most tantalizing of all, the "large charte": Ralegh's map, drawn up under his instructions in late 1595, and now preserved at the British Museum.

I am also drawing throughout the book on more personal experiences of South America, and in particular on notes and tapes brought back from a journey I made in late 1992, tracing the route of Ralegh's expedition through present-day Venezuela. (The region he called Guiana is now mostly part of Venezuela; only the easternmost part lies in modern Guyana.)

I am certainly not comparing my own journey to Ralegh's. The scale of difficulty, of expectation, of the unknown, is quite different. I see it more as an ambulant gloss on that earlier journey, made in the belief that history should be learned by foot—or, in this case, mostly by boat—as much as by studying books and documents. One sees a landscape in parts unchanged from what those early travelers saw; one meets people who pass their days and decades in it; one hears certain stories or indeed legends that are still going around in the area. These are also a kind of data. They are different from the evidence of the documents: This is evidence you have felt on the surface of your skin.

Thus this reconstruction of Ralegh's El Dorado journey of 1595 is made out of materials collected in part from historical sources and in part from my own experiences and encounters upriver.

PART ONE

THE GUIANA VOYAGE

Let sea-discoverers to new worlds have gone,
Let maps to others worlds on worlds have shown . . .

—JOHN DONNE, "The Good Morrow"

[1]

Mapping El Dorado

* * *

THE PURPOSE of Ralegh's Guiana Voyage was to locate El Dorado, and so a question immediately arises: Where *was* El Dorado?

The first and sensible answer is, nowhere. El Dorado did not exist. There never was a "great and golden city" (as Ralegh put it) lost in the South American jungle, and that is why it could not, and cannot, be found. There have been remarkable discoveries in Latin America this century—Machu Picchu, Buritaca, Akakor: genuinely lost cities, or anyway settlements, that lay undisturbed for centuries. There are probably others still waiting to be found, but El Dorado will not be among them. (I am aware of recent reports in the Brazilian press that a site being excavated near Boa Vista "is" El Dorado. It has certain constituents—a mountain lake, evidence of early gold-working—but as such it joins a longish list of places that may have contributed to the El Dorado legend.)

In another sense, of course, El Dorado certainly did exist. It existed, during a period that can be defined quite precisely, as an idea in people's minds, as a destination of their journeys, as a vividly specified desire. From the late 1530s, and for about a hundred years after, El Dorado—by which I mean this *idea* of El Dorado: the probability that it was there, the possibility of finding it, the untold riches it contained—was a craze that gripped people. It has the force field of a cultish religion. There are sudden converts and hostile skeptics; an intense rhetoric of signs and revelations. There are joyful glimpses of the promised land, though always—as the skeptics point out—at second hand.

These are two answers to the question: Where was El Dorado? It

9

was nowhere; it was in people's heads. There is a third answer, which is that it was in different places at different times. This is a story of people searching for something, and when they failed to find what they were looking for, they explained their failure by saying that it must be somewhere else, and so the location changes.

During the sixteenth century, the location of El Dorado shifted by stages, in a generally eastward direction, across the subcontinent. The story began in the late 1530s. It was in part a refraction of rituals performed by an Andean tribe, the Chibcha or Muisca, at the sacred lake of Guatavita. The protagonist of this ritual, mixed in with other rumors, came to be known as *el dorado,* "the golden man" (also *el indio dorado,* "the golden Indian," and *el rey dorado,* "the golden king"). The place El Dorado was the empire, or kingdom, or city of this legendary golden king. To begin with, the Spanish searched for it near the Andes of present-day Colombia, where the Chibcha were first located by the *conquistador* Jiménez de Quesada. Later the search moved east, to the headwaters of the Amazon: This is the El Dorado of the Omagua sought by Von Hutten and others. In northern Peru they searched for it in the guise of Lake Paititi, a legendary Inca location. By the end of the century, when Ralegh came on the scene—the first English expedition in search of El Dorado—its location had moved nearly a thousand miles from its original site, to the rugged Guiana Highlands south of the Orinoco River. The chief explorer of Guiana, the nominal Governor of this trackless region, was a man named Antonio de Berrio.

So this would be Ralegh's answer to the question. El Dorado stands, he would tell you, in the mountainous heart of Guiana, on the shores of a huge inland lake, the Lake of Manoa. This belief was mostly based on Spanish information obtained by Ralegh: It came from seized papers and seized people, notably Antonio de Berrio himself, whom Ralegh captured at Trinidad in April 1595. There was, at the time of his departure, no printed information about this latest siting of El Dorado. This was part of the excitement. Manoa was a secret, privileged superseding of those other known, printed, failed Dorados. Thus Thomas Harriot, Ralegh's chief adviser, writing to Sir Robert Cecil in 1596: "Concerning the Eldorado which hath

been showed your Honour, out of the Spanish book of Acosta [i.e.,
José de Acosta, *Historia Natural y Moral de les Indias,* 1590] . . . I shall
show you it is not ours, that we mean, there being three." Guiana
was not the only Dorado, but is "our" Dorado. It is what we mean
when we say those magic syllables.

In one sense, I suppose, the location of El Dorado remains constant; it was always farther on. It is a few days' march away; it is in
the next range of mountains. In the account of one Guiana expedition, led by Domingo de Vera in 1593, they seem to be only *half
a league* away from it, less than two miles, practically close enough
to smell the woodsmoke and see the first glint of solid gold spires
rising up above the trees. But they are tired, and frightened of the
fierce resistance they will encounter. They move away from the area.
This near encounter is subsumed into the reservoir of rumors.

The last, synaptic gap is never bridged. No one ever gets there.
There is only the journey, the approach toward something that you
cannot reach, something—one might infer from De Vera's curious
retreat—that you dare not reach.

WE SEE already two aspects to this search for El Dorado: the geographical and the psychological. We have to hold both in mind to
understand the nature of this enterprise. I am interested in Ralegh's
journey as just that—an actual physical journey—but I am interested also in the peculiar mental ambience that pervades the El
Dorado quest.

It is conventional to describe those who went looking for El Dorado as people gripped by an obsession. This seems true but vague.
I think of El Dorado more precisely as a *projection.*

Early maps of South America show the literally marginal knowledge that Europeans had of the continent. By the mid-sixteenth
century there are small settlements all around the coast, mostly
Spanish, some Portuguese. There are expeditions up the rivers, over
the mountains, into the jungles and savannas. But the travel was
hard, and they never got very far. These are nibblings of reconnaissance around the coastal margins. The center, the core, of South

America remained untouched. The great transverse rivers were navigated—the Orinoco by Diego de Ordaz in 1531, the Amazon by Francisco de Orellana ten years later—but what lay between them and beyond them no one really knew.

This is always where El Dorado is: somewhere farther in, in this unknown landmass at the center of South America. It is placed in the empty spaces of the map, like the axiomatic dragons of medieval cartography. This is what I mean by projection. Onto the blank screen of *terra incognita* is projected this image of the golden city (or really these twin images, of the golden king and his golden city). These images embody desires that are quite conscious and recognized—for wealth, for power, for possession—but also convey, as projections do, other more buried meanings, other fantasies and desires. There are analogies here with two other tenacious legends of the region, the Amazons and the cannibals. These are also to some extent projections, embodying European fantasies and, in this case, fears. Ralegh will have something to say about them as well.

This is a simple but necessary observation: that El Dorado is something that proceeds from the mind of the searcher, and from his European culture, but is externalized from it, placed out there in the unexplored hinterlands, the still-imagined landscapes, of the New World.

El Dorado is an image, but it is also very much a story. These descriptions and imaginings of El Dorado are a kind of early oral tradition in South America. The story is carried from place to place. Details are added and subtracted. It is smoothed and modified and reiterated. It travels like a folk tale, and has in itself something of the imagery and narrative of folk tales: a golden king, a lake in the mountains, a quest. This is perhaps useful as a slight modifying of the word "legend," which suggests something dim and distant, whereas to those involved in these journeys it was the story of the day, and they were the latest episode of it. It almost begins to sound like a soap opera.

So we understand El Dorado as something constructed—an icon, a projected fantasy, an American folk tale—but we cannot consign it completely to the world of imagination, since the search for it involved real journeys that had many real and practical results.

Geographically, that shifting location of El Dorado is also the shifting frontier of exploration in South America. El Dorado, lying just beyond the known frontier, draws people on, forges the trails that will later convey settlers and soldiers and traders. In this sense, the quest for El Dorado is synonymous with the whole process of European exploration in tropical America. Those four syllables acted as a superb kind of slogan, a piece of publicity, a recruitment drive. It was something with the power to draw together these unwieldy and hugely expensive caravans of soldiers, adventurers, and press-ganged natives, and propel them off to reconnoiter new corners of the continent.

The typical charter, or "patent," to an El Dorado searcher charged him to "discover and people" (*descubrir y poblar*) the lands all around. For the native tribes, the "peopling" of regions by Spanish settlers meant expropriation and enslavement, and sometimes extinction. This is a bleaker reading of El Dorado—a colonial propaganda, the gloss on a policy of genocide, the first logging roads.

ON FIRST unrolling Ralegh's chart at the Department of Manuscripts at the British Museum—it is stiffened with preservative chemicals, and has to be held down with scuffed leather-bound paperweights—I was immediately struck by this mingling of the psychological and the geographical.

The map is remarkably legible. The ink is grayish but still clear; the lines of latitude and longitude are drawn in green and red ink respectively; a small spillage of red ink north of Santa Marta has dried to the color of clotted blood. And there is El Dorado itself, on the edge of the vast and equally imaginary Lake Manoa. It is represented by a small huddle of buildings with pointy roofs. It looks more like a street-row in Elizabethan London than the capital of a lost American civilization.

But though clear the map is curiously arranged: first, because it

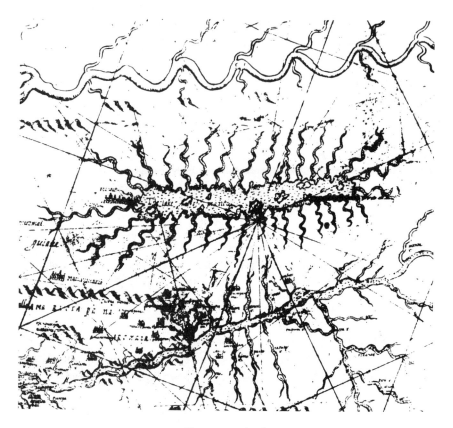

3. The creature in the map

is orientated to the south, and has to be read upside down to make geographic sense; and, second, because the upper (or southern) half of it is almost entirely blank. I cannot explain the first, except to say that orientation to the north was not insisted on at this time. The second I can explain. It is made necessary by a single decision, which is to place the Lake of Manoa—the site, Ralegh believed, of El Dorado—at the exact center of the map. This is where your eye goes, straightaway: to this mythical, strangely formed lake at the center of the paper.

It was a trick of the magnifying glass that made it seem suddenly to move. I had for a moment a vivid recollection of looking at a dead daddy longlegs under a schoolboy microscope—those worrying, alien features, those sculpted limbs, those hitherto undisclosed bristles—and scaring myself with the thought that it would wake, and start to stir, as I watched.

There is no doubt about it. The lake at the center of Ralegh's Guiana chart is quite unequivocally something animate. It looks like a monster, a creepy-crawly, some nightmare *cucaracha*. Its torso is the body of the lake, its legs are the wriggling rivers that pour into its shores—thirty-two in all—and its small, rudimentary brain is, of course, the city of El Dorado. I am not being facetious. I consider it rather extraordinary that the central icon of Ralegh's quest should be this creature, this swamp worm from hell.

This is precisely the blank space of the map, the *terra incognita*. What exactly is this thing we see projected here?

ELSEWHERE—ESPECIALLY in the area where he had traveled—Ralegh's map is purely geographical. It is, in fact, a mostly accurate representation of the eastern Caribbean coast, the Orinoco estuary, and the immediate surroundings of the lower Orinoco. It is based on the hard-won, firsthand information of the Guiana Voyage. It would be possible (if pretentious) to follow Ralegh's route using this map alone. The arterial routes through the region are still, as they were in 1595, the rivers.

This empirical part of the map, I soon established, has a fairly consistent scale. Taking some bearings from the text of the *Discoverie,* which gives certain distances—or rather Ralegh's estimates of certain distances, which is what I needed—I concluded that where the map is based on his own observations, it is drawn to a scale of approximately 1 inch to 50 miles. (I give my computations in Appendix 2.)

With this key, it seemed, one could say quite precisely where Ralegh thought El Dorado was. As we know, and as he shows on the map, he thought it stood on the shores of Lake Manoa. According to the map, the lake lay south of, and roughly parallel to, the Orinoco River. If you traveled due south from the mouth of the Caroní River— the largest tributary of the lower Orinoco, and the farthest point of Ralegh's expedition—you would arrive at the northern shores of Lake Manoa. The distance from the mouth of the Caroní to the lakeshore is represented on the map as about 3 inches.

In this case, Ralegh believed that the magical lake, the site of El Dorado, lay about 150 miles south of the confluence of the Caroní and the Orinoco. This speculative distance seems to tie in with Spanish information that Ralegh had, which stated that Manoa was eleven days' march from the Orinoco. The rule of thumb employed in these Spanish expeditions is that a day's march covers 5 leagues (i.e., 15 miles). Thus an eleven-day march would be expected to cover—or would be described as covering—55 leagues, or 165 miles.

This is only Ralegh's opinion, encoded in the map. It is an estimated distance to a place that did not exist. Nevertheless, I was curious to see what sort of place *actually* lay 150 miles south of the mouth of the Caroní. That night I spread out Tactical Pilotage Chart K-27-C, purchased from Stanford's of Long Acre, London. This is a 1:500,000 map of eastern Venezuela: a modern version of Ralegh's "large charte."

At the mouth of the Caroní there is now the new Venezuelan city of Ciudad Guayana. From there my ruler led me down through a swathe of unpopulated river, forest, and mountain, across an area of blankness ("Relief Data Incompatible"), to an area of high land near the Carrao River, a tributary of the upper Caroní. There were two small airfields not far away. One, to the east, was marked Campo Carrao; the other, to the west, was marked Canaima. The place I

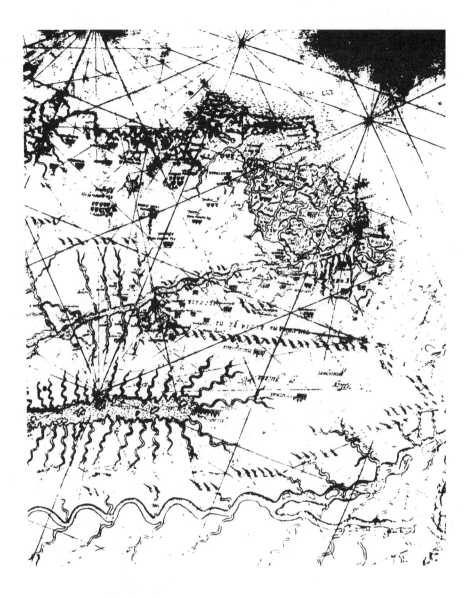

4. Detail from Ralegh's chart

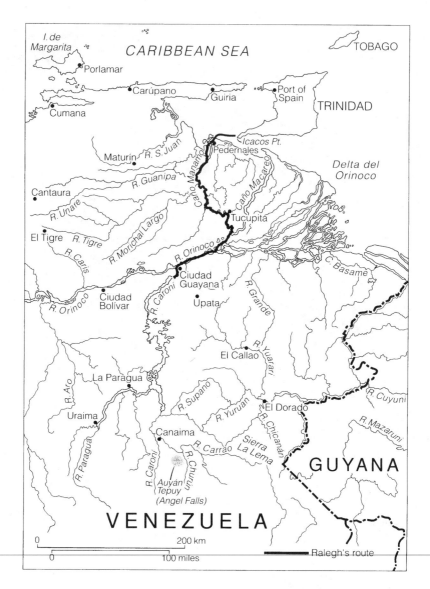

5. Modern map showing Ralegh's route

had arrived at, the spot where I marked my X, was not actually named on the Pilotage Chart. But I knew where I was. I had landed more or less slap-bang on the top of Auyán Tepuy, otherwise known as Devil Mountain.

Strictly speaking, this was pure coincidence, but it led me straight from the story of Ralegh's El Dorado expedition to another story entirely—or perhaps, as I now tend to think, to the same story told in another way. But this is not yet the place to go into it.

LOOKING AT Ralegh's chart—in part a piece of genuine, scientific cartography, in part an almost mandala-like document, with this strange emblem of the lake at its heart—I am reminded of the map in the opening scene of *King Lear:* how Lear's hand moves across it in a grand, ritualistic sort of gesture, "even from this line unto this"; how his daughters see it quite differently, as a scientific measuring of land, an apportioning of property. This sort of double reading, this oscillation between the symbolic and the physical, is essential to the story of El Dorado and is seen in graphic form in Ralegh's own chart.

This is what I have always found fascinating about the El Dorado story: It is this marvelous fiction that actually happened. The whole thing has the lineaments of a fairy tale; these are people stepping through a frame, into a picture they have themselves created. But then there comes that point of dangerous intersection, where the fantasy of the golden city shades into the reality of the South American jungle.

The Spaniards called these early expeditions *entradas,* entrances. You left the margin, the settled, the known, and made your "entrance" into that unmapped interior, where just about anything was possible.

[2]

Ralegh's America

*   *   *

IN THIS year 1595, the year of his El Dorado expedition, Ralegh was forty years old. Nowadays the whole business might be put down to "midlife crisis," though an Elizabethan would be optimistic to count forty as midway. He was a tall, dark-complexioned man, with brown curling hair swept back, and now appreciably thinning on top. John Aubrey, one of his earliest biographers, says, "He had a most remarkable aspect: an exceeding high forehead, long-faced and sour eye-lidded, a kind of pig-eye." His mustaches, it was said, curled up *naturally*.

He was a noted dandy even by Elizabethan standards, but the portrait believed to date from around the time of the Guiana Voyage shows him in austere mood. The pearl earring has gone; he wears a dark doublet, a finely woven but modest belt, and a sword. There is in his gaze the mood of *contemptus mundi* that we find in his poems. The painting—sometimes attributed to Federico Zuccaro—is undated, but Ralegh is clearly younger than he is in the "Cádiz portrait" of 1598. It is a portrait from his time of disgrace, his seclusion from public gaze, which was also the time of his preparation for Guiana. He rests his right hand on a globe, touches the coast of Greenland with thin scholarly fingers. It seems almost a caress, but also he is pointing; the geography perhaps suggests an allusion to the chimerical Northwest Passage, and so to his dead half-brother Humphrey Gilbert, who was his first mentor in American affairs. Gilbert had searched in the frozen north, but Ralegh is heading south.

He threw into this venture the full force of his prodigious energy—"he can toil terribly," said Sir Robert Cecil, no sloth himself.

6. Portrait of Ralegh, attributed to Federico Zuccaro

He reveled in the contrasts and conjunctions of his different pursuits: the philosopher and the man of action, the soldier-poet, the plain-speaking courtier, and now the discoverer. In his speech from the scaffold in 1618, he said, "I have long been a seafaring man, a soldier and a courtier, and in the temptations of the least of these there is enough to overthrow a good mind and a good man."

Ralegh at forty was a man in the ebb of his fortunes. The last few years had not been good for him. In the early 1590s he was increasingly overshadowed at court by his younger rival, the Earl of Essex. In 1592 he fell spectacularly from the Queen's favor when she discovered he had secretly married one of her vestal entourage, Elizabeth Throckmorton, and had a son by her. The erring couple was dispatched to the Tower during the plague summer of 1592, and then sent off in disgrace to Ralegh's estates in Dorset.

He was also under investigation for holding heretical opinions. Durham House, his London home on the Strand, was said to be a veritable "School of Atheism." Two of his followers—Christopher Marlowe and Thomas Harriot—were brought before the Council on charges of atheism; Marlowe was mysteriously stabbed to death during the investigation. This hue and cry pursued Ralegh into exile, and in early 1594 he had to appear before a special commission held at Cerne Abbas, and answer such questions as "Whom do you know to have spoken against the being or immortality of the soul of man, or that a man's soul should die and become like the soul of a beast?" Nothing was proved, but the smear of atheism stuck, and becomes oddly entwined with his American adventures.

With all this went money problems. His ill-fated attempts to colonize Virginia in the 1580s had cost him over £40,000; his attempts to profit from the Irish lands he had been given were unsuccessful. Even his fleet of privateering vessels operated on credit, at crippling interest rates. He borrowed £11,000 to fit out his fleet for the foray that brought in the *Madre de Dios* in 1592, and was promptly sequestered from his profits by the furious, jilted Queen. Status and influence are everything. His "fall" from favor presaged a financial collapse.

There are many possible readings of his El Dorado quest, but let us not forget the simple ones: for instance, that he was, or was going, broke.

THE SEA was in Ralegh's blood. It was the sound of his Devon childhood, and the passion of an extended family that included among his "cousins" Sir Francis Drake and Sir Richard Grenville, as well as the three Gilbert brothers (the sons of his mother Katherine by her first marriage). Humphrey Gilbert, twenty years his senior, was an important early influence. He was a strange, saturnine man, a friend of the occultist Dr. Dee, a brave but unlucky explorer. It was under Gilbert that Ralegh had his first command at sea, as captain of the one-hundred-ton *Falcon* in the abortive Northwest Passage expedition of 1578. He roamed the Atlantic for six months, but got no farther than the Cape Verde Islands.

After Gilbert's death at sea in 1583—he reportedly went down with the words "We are as near to heaven by sea as by land"— Ralegh stepped into his role as chief promoter of the English interest in America. In the coming years he was to draw around him almost everyone associated with the New World mood of the 1580s—Richard Hakluyt, the tireless propagandist, editor and translator; the scientists Thomas Harriot, already a "steward" in Ralegh's household, and Adrian Gilbert, the youngest of Ralegh's half brothers; the artists John White and Jacques le Moyne de Morgues (alias James Morgan); the navigator John Davis; the globe maker Emery Molyneux; the publisher Theodore de Bry. Ralegh was also a friend of Dr. Dee, who held fervent and arcane views on the subject of America. Dee was absent from England during this period, on his obscure six-year mission to Bohemia, but his influence is felt through Harriot and others, and will later be of interest to us. All these one might call the Elizabethan Americans, and Ralegh was their undisputed figurehead.

There was a sense of urgency. The English were late on the scene, had been content to skim off a bit of New World wealth by piracy and plunder. "I marvel not a little," wrote Richard Hakluyt,

that since the first discovery of America (which is now full fourscore
and ten years), after so great conquest and plantings of the Spaniards
& Portingales there, that we of England could never have the grace
to set fast footing in such fertile and temperate places as are left
unpossessed by them.

Ralegh's interest lay not in the inhospitable wastes of Labrador,
which Gilbert and Frobisher and Parkinson had explored in the
1570s. He did not fancy himself hacking up frozen creeks with a
mastiff and an eel spear. His interest focused on a little-known part
of the American seaboard, which lay between the two settled areas
of Newfoundland to the north and Florida to the south. It was then
vaguely referred to as Norumbega, but was now renamed, in honor
of the Virgin Queen, Virginia. It is not certain, but very likely, that
this name was Ralegh's idea: his "conceit," as they would put it.

On March 25, 1584—New Year's Day according to the old calendar still widely in use—the Queen signed Ralegh's letters patent
for the "discovering and planting" of Virginia.

> Know ye that of our especial grace, certain science and mere motion,
> we have given and granted to our trusty and well-beloved servant,
> Walter Ralegh Esquire, free liberty and license from time to time to
> discover, search, find out and view such remote, heathen and barba-
> rous lands, countries and territories not actually possessed by any
> Christian prince nor inhabited by Christian people; the same to have,
> hold, occupy and enjoy to him, his heirs and assigns forever.

In a sense, the "Virginia" of 1584 was as much an idea, a legend,
as "El Dorado" would be for Ralegh a decade later. It is nothing
more than a heavily associative name, given to an area by people
who have not yet visited it (and in Ralegh's case, never did). It
describes a place as yet fictional. The apportioning of vast amounts
of putative land to investors and colonists adds to the sense of un-
reality. In the year before his death, Gilbert built up a vast paper
scheme for the distribution and exploitation of Norumbega, dispos-
ing of nearly nine million acres, on paper, to intending colonists.

Within a few weeks of his patent, Ralegh's reconnaissance fleet was dispatched: two barks, captained by Philip Amadas and Arthur Barlowe, both Devon men. They landed on one of the islands now called the Outer Banks, off the coast of North Carolina. They parleyed with the natives, Algonquians; they noted the luxuriance of the land; they brought back pearls and skins, and two Indian braves named Manteo and Wanchese.

Ralegh's courtly career was then at the height of its arc. Knighted in January 1585, he described himself on his new seal, now at the British Museum, as DOMINUS & GUBERNATOR VIRGINIAE, the Lord and Governor of Virginia. In June of that year, after tireless organization and with heavy investment from his own pocket, he sent out the first wave of English settlers. Among them were Thomas Harriot and John White, the "discoverer" (in the sense of researcher) and the "artist" of the expedition: a formidable team of reporters. Harriot's observations were published as *A Brief and True Report of Virginia* in 1588; John White produced a series of watercolors, engravings of which illustrated de Bry's sumptuous second edition of the *Brief Report* (1590). Between them they provide a meticulous and often idyllic account of Algonquian life; this, more than any, is the image of America that is implanted in Ralegh's mind.

The story of the two Virginia colonies of 1585 and 1587 is too well known to repeat here: the founding of the "Cittie of Ralegh" among the pines of Roanoke Island; the birth of the first English person in America, Virginia Dare, daughter of Ananias and Eleanor Dare, and granddaughter of the painter White; the disappearance of the entire second colony, or "Lost Colony"—a hundred men, women, and children, and no trace of them left except for some letters scratched on a tree.

These Virginia voyages will be of interest for the parallels they offer—both practical and thematic—with the Guiana Voyage, but one thing to say straightaway is that Ralegh did not travel with them. It is often erroneously stated that he did, but in fact the Guiana Voyage of 1595 was the first and only time he ventured into the continent of America (on his last voyage of 1617–18 he was sick, and remained on the coast with his ships while others went inland). Until the Guiana Voyage, America was wholly in his imagination. He had sent hundreds of men there, but was himself—apart from a few brief naval forays—quite landlocked. They had gone out over the horizon, and he had stayed behind, in the damp, tawdry, pettifogging confines of England: the court, the city, the country, one tiny round of backbiting and envy, suspicion and surveillance, the creak of the floorboards, the listener at the door.

IT IS impossible to say exactly when Ralegh first turned his thoughts toward Guiana and El Dorado. This was an area of America—generally referred to as the Eastern Main—largely unknown to Englishmen. English activities in South America at this time (writes Joyce Lorimer) "concentrated in two distinct thrusts into the South Atlantic and the Caribbean, leaving the equatorial regions of the Atlantic coastline in limbo." By the 1580s the number of English privateers in the Caribbean "had reached epidemic proportions," but the nature of their activities—brief raids and piracies—contributed nothing to creating an English presence in South America. This is certainly one of the overt, patriotic motives of Ralegh's Guiana Voyage: to insert a wedge into the Spanish dominance of the region.

An early interest in the area is reflected in a passage written by Ralegh's publicist Richard Hakluyt in 1584. In his *Discourse of Western Planting,* issued to promote the Virginia expeditions, Hakluyt wrote:

> All that part of America eastward from Cumaná unto the River of St Augustine in Brazil containeth in length along the sea-side 2100 miles; in which compass and reach there is neither Spaniard, Portingale nor any Christian man, but only Caribs, Indians and savages; in which places is great plenty of gold, pearl and precious stones.

Here are the seeds of the El Dorado dream—the emptiness and the riches therein—though not yet focused on the talismanic name of El Dorado.

At about the same time, we learn from the *Discoverie,* Ralegh was gathering information about the "gold and rarities" to be found around the Amazon River: "I spake with a captain of a French ship that came from thence, his ship riding in Falmouth."

Ralegh also knew the story of Lope de Aguirre, the Basque mutineer who left a swath of blood and mayhem during a year-long *entrada* up the Amazon. This is the most notorious of the searches for El Dorado: an archetypal downward spiral into brutality and craziness. The expedition set out from Lima in September 1560, led by a young nobleman from Navarre, Pedro de Ursua. Already there is a frisson in the story, for Ursua was accompanied—against all advice, against the protocol of the *entrada*—by his lover, Inez de Atienza, a half-caste said to be "the loveliest woman then remaining in Peru." On January 1, 1561, at their camp on the Putamayo River, Ursua was stabbed to death, Caesar-like, by thirteen mutineers led by Aguirre. There followed one of those strange, comic-opera ceremonies in the middle of nowhere. Another leader, Don Fernando de Guzmán, was sworn in. He was named General of El Dorado and Omagua, with Aguirre as *maestro de campo.* A document to this effect was drawn up. At the foot of it he signed himself "Lope de Aguirre, traitor."

The journey now becomes a bloodbath: Singly or in groups, men were stabbed, hanged, garroted, or drowned by Aguirre and his henchmen. His chief sidekick was a sadistic Portuguese shoemaker named Llamoso. Out of 370 Europeans on the expedition, about 150 were murdered or marooned, Guzmán and the beautiful Inez among them.

In the midst of these horrors emerges a kind of political theme. It is there in Aguirre's strange formalization of himself as a "traitor," and it is recorded in other speeches he made. "We must renounce our allegiance to Spain," he announced. He used the word *desnaturar:* a renouncing of vassalage. The King was no longer "our natural lord." Historians have discerned in this the first airing of the idea of an independent America. In the depths of the jungle he styles himself "Lope de Aguirre, Wrath of God, Prince of Freedom, King of Tierra Firme."

All thoughts of El Dorado had long been jettisoned. "The reports are false," he says. "There is nothing on the river but despair."

They reached the Atlantic Ocean on July 4, 1561. Whether they came down the entire length of the Amazon, like Orellana twenty years before, or whether they debouched at the mouth of the Orinoco is uncertain. If the latter they must have come via the Casiquiare Canal, which connects the Río Negro to the Orinoco, and which was otherwise unknown to Europeans until the mid-eighteenth century. After a few months of ransacking the coast, Aguirre was killed, near Valencia in present-day Venezuela, on January 9, 1562. He had just murdered his own daughter, Elvira, to prevent her falling into enemy hands: one last act of lunacy, performed with that strange lucidity that is perhaps the most frightening aspect of the whole business.

Ralegh tells Aguirre's story in some detail in the *Discoverie*. His account is based partly on printed sources, but it is also underpinned with the personal, anecdotal knowledge that Elizabethan travelers valued so highly. Referring to Aguirre's ransacking of Caracas and Riohacha in 1561, Ralegh adds:

> I remember it was in the same year that John Hawkins sailed to San Juan de Lua in the *Jesus of Lubeck;* for himself told me that he had met with such a one upon the coast, that rebelled and had sailed down the River of Amazon.

A laconic synopsis of Aguirre's trail of destruction: "one that rebelled." Ralegh knew Hawkins well, and must have heard of Aguirre early on. He must also have read garbled stories of El Dorado in the many texts on the New World that he knew. Some are quoted in the *Discoverie,* and some occur in the catalog of his Tower library, drawn up in about 1606—works like Pedro de Cieza León's *Crónica del Peru* (Seville, 1553); Francisco López de Gomara's *Historia General de los Indias* (Zaragoza, 1552); André Thevet's *Singularitez de la France Antarctique* (Paris, 1558)—though as already mentioned, none of these printed sources discussed the latest siting of El Dorado in Guiana.

Guiana itself was, at this stage, just a shimmering rumor. Stories of this mysterious gold-rich land were brought back by English sailors who had been to the coast of Brazil to trade with the Portuguese, and to Trinidad to buy tobacco from the Indians. It was known that the Caribs brought gold from the interior to trade. It was known that the Spaniards were searching the area—one in particular, Don Antonio de Berrio.

Berrio is the chief key to Ralegh's conception of El Dorado—the ardent proponent of Guiana, the coiner of the name Manoa. He was born in Segovia in about 1526. He was a soldier for Spain in Italy, Africa, and the Low Countries, and rose to the rank of captain of the Guardia Vieja of Granada. Then, in 1579, at an age when most *hidalgos* were ready to hang up their swords, came the news that his wife's uncle, the old *conquistador* Gonzalo Jiménez de Quesada, had died, childless, and that he was now the inheritor of Quesada's distant legacy. As well as estates in the highlands of New Granada, now Colombia, he inherited the governorship of Pauto y Papamene, a huge, notional province that stretched for nine hundred leagues east of the Andes, and which Quesada believed to contain El Dorado.

In early 1581, with his wife and three children, Berrio set out for the New World. "I judged," he later wrote, "that it was no time to rest." (Indeed not. Doña Maria gave birth to no fewer than seven more children during the ten years she spent in America. This says much for the tonic air of the Colombian Andes, and something perhaps for the fevers and passions aroused by El Dorado.)

It took Berrio over two years to equip his first *entrada*. He set out in September 1583. "May it please God," he wrote, "to let this concealed province be discovered." And so he descended, along the trails first opened by his mentor Quesada, from the chilly spaces of Tunja, where everything seems clear in the rinsed mountain air, and into the long, disorientating vistas of the *llanos*. He had eighty men, five hundred horses, and an itinerant farmyard of cattle and pigs. They hacked their way east of the Meta River, deep in the humid lowlands, until, on Palm Sunday 1584, from a distance that he later estimated as twenty-eight leagues, Berrio caught sight of the Guiana Highlands, "the *cordillera* so ardently desired and sought for seventy

7. *Autograph of Antonio de Berrio from a letter of 1595*

years past, and which has cost the lives of so many Spaniards." They were on the upper Orinoco, not far from where Puerto Ayacucho now stands. The peaks Berrio could see were probably Cerro Paraque and Cerro Yavi, in the northwestern corner of the Guiana shield.

He was back in Tunja, with his late-blooming family, by April 1585. He had been away for over eighteen months. In May he was writing direct to the King in Spain, announcing his "certain knowledge" of El Dorado, "the object of so many years' search, which by the grace of God I have found." It became his project now to settle the land. He reckoned he needed three hundred men to enter El Dorado, and more than three thousand to "people" it, and from the moment of his return in mid-1585 he was possessed with a frenzy of fund raising, rent raising, and recruitment driving. Soon the news of this new Dorado was percolating through the continent, was spoken of at dusty crossroads and riverside depots, and so passed across the "Ocean Sea" to Europe and to England.

Some of Berrio's exploits must have reached Ralegh's ears, but there is no documentation of what he learned and when. He gives a detailed account of Berrio's first *entrada* in the *Discoverie*. Much of this he got from Berrio himself, after capturing him at Trinidad in 1595, but it is likely that Ralegh heard about it at the time, through the travelers' tales and dockside gossip, still the primary sources of Elizabethan knowledge of America.

These are the rumors and hints and half-understood motifs of El Dorado that began to stick in Ralegh's mind in the mid-1580s, though at first only a footnote to his more pressing concern with Virginia, only one of the seemingly infinite possibilities of the New World.

[3]

A Gentleman of Spain

*   *   *

WHATEVER VAGUE interest Ralegh had in El Dorado was particularly sharpened in the late summer of 1586, during conversations he held with a certain "gentleman of Spain," Don Pedro Sarmiento de Gamboa.

Sarmiento was an old American campaigner. He had been in the New World continuously for nearly thirty years, and was currently governor of a small Spanish colony on the coast of Patagonia. He had been in Lima back in the 1550s, the days of the Aguirre expedition. He was later on the voyage that discovered the Solomon Islands. In the early 1570s he served with the military expedition sent to root out Inca rebels from Manco Capac's mountain retreat at Vilcabamba. On this he served alongside Juan Alvarez Maldonado and Gasparo de Sotello, both veterans of the search for Paititi. Paititi (or "Paipite," as Sarmiento calls it) was the Peruvian El Dorado, believed to be a lost Inca empire. Sarmiento was himself a scholar of Inca history and mythology, and wrote what is thought by many to be the most authoritative contemporary study of the subject, *La Historia de las Incas.* This work, dedicated to Philip II in 1572, remained unknown to historians until the manuscript was rediscovered by chance, in the library of Göttingen University, in 1893.

In early August 1586, returning across the Atlantic to Spain, Sarmiento's ship was taken by two English pinnaces, the *Mary Sparke* and the *Serpent.* They had left Plymouth a month earlier, under the command of Captain Jacob Whiddon, on a roving foray into Spanish waters. Both ships were owned by Ralegh.

As the English ships bore down, Sarmiento's first thought was to get rid of his American papers: "secrets of navigation and discoveries, tidings, warnings, narratives," and most notably a "great book" full of paintings and maps of Patagonia—a cargo of New World knowledge more precious to the enemy than actual treasure. The whole lot went overboard, with the exception of a few papers written in cipher. The jettisoning was seen from the English ships, as described by one of the crew, John Evesham: "They . . . cast their ordinance and small shot, with the draft of the Straits of Magellan, into the sea."

What happened after the Spaniards were taken—as later described by Sarmiento—makes grim reading. Some of them were "stripped naked, and put to such torture by fire and stripes, and the knuckles and tips of their fingers being crushed, to make them confess whether they had any hidden silver or moneys." This may be an exaggeration, to blacken the English enemy, but I doubt it. It is probably a true and unpleasant glimpse of methods used aboard Ralegh's privateering vessels. One should not be surprised: Torture was routinely applied to captives. But this is a kind of beginning to the story of Ralegh's Dorado, and it starts with the harsh realities of war and piracy. The crews of the *Serpent* and the *Mary Sparke* were the kind of men who would travel with Ralegh to South America. Their commander Jacob Whiddon became a key figure in the Guiana expedition, praised by Ralegh as a "man most honest and valiant," but here we meet him supervising the torture of Spanish sailors to get "silver and moneys" out of them.

They failed to find any, but in Sarmiento himself they had a catch—a Spanish *hidalgo,* a mine of information, a pot of ransom money. Sarmiento duly returned with the English ships as a prisoner of war. They reached Plymouth at the end of August. For a while Sarmiento remained there, not apparently under close arrest, since he managed to smuggle out a message to King Philip, on a Venetian ship bound for Lisbon.

Eventually word was sent to bring him to court, and he was escorted, first to Hampton Court and then to Windsor, where he was met by Ralegh himself.

There seems to have been an immediate personal rapport between the two men. From the moment of his arrival at Windsor, he was treated more like an honored guest than a prisoner. Ralegh greeted him personally, and seated him next to him at dinner. They conversed in Latin. He was provided with comfortable lodgings, and a Spanish-speaking "gentleman" to attend on him. This was in part the protocol of dealing with a high-ranking prisoner of war, but seems to have gone further. This special treatment caused comment, not least from the rather volatile clique of Portuguese exiles headed by Don Antonio de Ocrato. Portugal had been annexed by Spain in 1580; Don Antonio was a pretender to the Portuguese throne, and was courted by the English, though considered rather a pest. Sarmiento soon clashed with him. Don Antonio complained to the Queen "that Pedro Sarmiento called him bastard" (accurately enough), and asked her to "avenge the slight." The Queen demanded Sarmiento's punishment, but Ralegh spoke so winningly in his favor that "the hatred she harboured against him was turned against Don Antonio." Shortly after this she gave a personal audience to Sarmiento: They spoke in "cordial converse" for an hour and a half.

RALEGH HAD doubtless heard of El Dorado before, but this chance Atlantic encounter in August 1586 seems to have precipitated the idea in his mind. It was almost certainly from Sarmiento that he got one of his strongest convictions about El Dorado—that it was originally an "empire" of Inca refugees, founded by Manco Capac.

"Many years since," he wrote at the beginning of *The Discoverie of Guiana,*

> I had knowledge by relation of that mighty, rich and beautiful Empire of Guiana, and of that great and golden city which the Spaniards call El Dorado, which city was conquered, re-edified and enlarged by a younger son of Guainacapa [i.e., by Manco, son of Huana Capac], Emperor of Peru, at such time as Francisco Pazaro [i.e., Pizarro] and others conquered the said empire.

By "relation" he means a personal communication: what was related to him, as opposed to what he learned from books and other written material. Plenty was related to him by Berrio, but that was a few months, rather than "many years," before. I do not think there is much doubt that the man who "related" this Inca-slanted version of El Dorado was the Inca expert Pedro Sarmiento.

Ralegh does not mention him by name in the *Discoverie,* but more than twenty years later the memory of their conversations was still fresh in his mind, and in his *History of the World* he relates a brief but telling anecdote—"a pretty jest of Don Pedro Sarmiento," as he calls it. They were discussing Sarmiento's "enterprise" in the Straits of Magellan. Ralegh asked him some questions about a certain island there. Sarmiento laughed.

> He told me merrily that it was to be called the 'Painter's Wife's Island', saying that whilst the fellow drew that map, his wife sitting by, desired him to put in one country for her, that she, in imagination, might have an island of her own.

This is revealing of the atmosphere between the two men: relaxed, genial, curious. They are poring over a map (not the actual map drawn by Sarmiento's "painter," which had gone overboard before his capture, but another one). And it is a pertinent "jest": an ironic comment on the colonial venture, with its emphasis on naming as a form of possession.

There is also in it a sense of deflection. Ralegh's questions are not exactly answered, rather parried, by this "pretty jest." Sarmiento was aware of the delicacy of his position, and unlikely to give away strategic details. It may have been in a spirit of deflection, also, that he began to interest Ralegh in his own belief in a lost Inca empire.

There is nothing in Sarmiento's writings to suggest he was an El Dorado fanatic, but he certainly believed in Lake Paititi. He gives a glowing account of Maldonado's expedition in search of it. Maldonado had "penetrated more deeply than anyone else into that country," he writes, and "received full and certain tidings of the River and Lake of Paipite." Sarmiento would also have plenty of stories about Manco Capac's fastness at Vilcabamba, which the Spaniards never found, and which was supposed to have the usual Inca accoutrements of temples and virgins, and, of course, gold.

Ralegh is insistent, almost strident, on the Inca origin of Manoa and the other cities of Guiana.

> Because there may arise many doubts how this Empire of Guiana is become so populous, and adorned with so many great cities, towns, temples and treasures, I thought good to make it known that the Emperor now reigning is descended from those magnificent Princes of Peru. . . .
>
> The Empire of Guiana is directly east from Peru towards the sea, and lieth under the equinoctial line, and it hath more abundance of gold than any part of Peru, and as many or more great cities than ever Peru had when it flourished most. It is governed by the same laws, and the Emperor and people observe the same religion, and the same form and policies in government as was used in Peru, not differing in any part.

This states the matter unequivocally. The city of Manoa or El Dorado was in all respects an Inca city. It also states the error that caused Ralegh problems when drawing up his map. The Guiana Highlands are not "directly east" of Peru, but northeast; and they are not "under" (i.e., on) the equator, but several degrees north of it. Ralegh's geography wrests Guiana southward and nearer to Peru. By a complementary movement, he stretches Manco's flight from Cuzco northward and into Guiana.

> [He] fled out Peru, and took with him many thousands of those soldiers of the Empire called *oreiones* [i.e., *orejones,* or "big ears," the Spanish word for high-ranking Inca, who wore disc-shaped lobe-plugs], and with those and many others which followed him, he vanquished all that tract and valley of America which is situate between the great rivers of Amazones and Baraquona, otherwise called Orenoke.

Here the Inca diaspora, which in fact remained within the boundaries of present-day Peru, is exaggerated by Ralegh into a process of conquest and colonization stretching far into the "tract and valley" between the Amazon and the Orinoco. Thus, with these rearrangements to geography and history, "El Dorado . . . was conquered, re-edified and enlarged" by Manco, the son of "Guainacapa." Ralegh's spelling—"Guainacapa" for Huana Capac—seems to underscore this link he is forging between the Inca and Guiana.

Ralegh read other writers on the subject of the Inca—Cieza León and López de Gomara are both quoted in the *Discoverie*—but the initial impetus comes firsthand, by "relation," from Sarmiento. It is possible that Sarmiento also related the more recent news of Berrio's *entradas* and of his trumpeted claims for the city of Manoa. Sarmiento had been on the coast of Brazil for two years before setting out for Europe: well placed to learn news of expeditions in the Amazon and Orinoco regions.

There are conflations and blurrings in Ralegh's account of the Inca origin of El Dorado. These are probably his rather than Sarmiento's. There is the merging of Manco Capac's hidden stronghold at Vil-cabamba—a historical fact—with the legendary Inca site of Lake Paititi, and a separate merging whereby this becomes the same as Berrio's lacustrine city of Manoa. By these imaginary links, these blurrings, Ralegh's El Dorado acquires a spurious historical pedigree, and its riches acquire a historical precedent. They are comparable to, a part of, the documented riches of the Inca.

SARMIENTO IS a live source. Unlike those authors whom Ralegh consulted, his conversation draws on that substratum of current rumor and folklore that is the true repository of the El Dorado story.

He is, perhaps, more than just a source. Ralegh finds something magnetic about this "gentleman of Spain." He seems the epitome of the American explorer: the man of experience, the hard-bitten traveler with tales of voyages and shipwrecks, giant thigh bones and fantastical fauna. We have glimpses of him deep upcountry: trekking across the freezing tundras of Patagonia, scouring the pampas for ostrich eggs, hunting *guanaco* deer, "which we then cooked in a stewpot carried for this purpose by Pedro Sarmiento, who knew what was needful in unexplored lands."

He was an old-style *conquistador* who had lived and breathed the New World for a quarter of a century. But he was also a scholar and *littérateur*—a man of discernment, a writer with a vigorous prose style that would appeal to Ralegh, though given to Spanish prolixity. He had earned his living in Lima as a teacher of Latin. He even turned his hand to verse. Some sonnets remain: complimentary verses to a volume of Spanish translations of Petrarch by his friend, Enrique Garces. He would also edit—as official censor—the *Elegías* of Juan de Castellanos, taking the opportunity to suppress certain material therein that glorified an old enemy of his in Peru, Alvaro de Mendana.

Ralegh's encounter with Sarmiento introduces us to one of the curiosities of the new English interest in America, which is that it entailed a curious rapprochement with the idea of "Spanishness"— a sense that the Spaniards were the only role models for American exploration, and that Englishmen bound for America must emulate them, must in a sense *become* Spanish. This is a surprising but entirely clear message one finds in the writings of Richard Hakluyt, who frequently urges Ralegh to emulate the spirit of Hernán Cortés, the *conquistador* of Mexico, "a mirror and an excellent precedent of glory, renown and perfect felicity."

Ralegh himself wrote, in *The History of the World,* in a passage that seems controversial unless understood in this American context:

I cannot forbear to commend the patient virtue of the Spaniards. We seldom or never find that any nation hath endured so many misadventures and miseries as the Spaniards have done in their Indian discoveries; yet persisting in their enterprises with invincible constancy, they have annexed to their kingdom so many goodly provinces to bury the remembrance of all dangers past. Tempests and shipwrecks, famine, overthrows, mutinies, heat and cold, pestilence and all manner of diseases both old and new, together with extreme poverty and want of all things needful, have been the enemies wherewith every one of their most noble discoverers at one time or another hath encountered.

Sarmiento is perhaps a model for this. In one of his last supplications to King Philip, written in the early 1590s, he summed up his long life of service to Spain,

by land and sea; in times of war and times of peace; with sword and with pen; amidst most grave events and occurrences; with prosperous results and perils safely past; all thanks, honour and glory to God.

This has something of the tone of extremity and endurance that Ralegh champions in the Spanish Americans.

Explorer, soldier, scholar, colonist: This was the "gentleman of Spain" who first introduced Ralegh to the idea of El Dorado, and perhaps to the rather unsettling ambiguity of allegiances it entailed—that the man who is nominally his enemy now becomes his pattern of behavior, a role model, a hero even. The adventurer in America floats dangerously free. He begins to understand those notes of desperation and anarchy, of severance from authority, that cluster round the Aguirre story: "one that rebelled."

RALEGH'S NEW interest in Guiana is perhaps highlighted in a little-known episode early the following year, though it is ironically Sarmiento's enemy, the Portuguese pretender Don Antonio, who appears in the leading role.

In January 1587, at Le Havre, an unnamed Italian boarded a French ship bound for the Caribbean. With him were four young Englishmen. According to a later deposition by the captain of the ship, Jean Retud, this Italian belonged to the retinue of Don Antonio. He came with the special recommendations of the French Admiral, who had in turn been "requested through many letters from England" to support him. Retud was ordered to take him along, to disembark him wherever he wished, and if necessary to wait for him, "because he was a person who was worthy of it."

This well-introduced Italian and his English companions duly sailed with Retud's little fleet, having first loaded aboard "a certain cargo of axes, knives, jew's harps, blue and white beads and coloured cloths"—the usual trifles for trade with the Indians. The next we hear of them they are at Trinidad. Two of the Englishmen were left there, "under the care of an Indian chief," to learn the language. Crossing the Gulf of Paria, Retud continues, the fleet came to the mouth of the Orinoco. Here the Italian embarked in a "brigantine," and ventured inland with the other two Englishmen and a party of twenty-two harquebusiers. They "went upriver, and remained for three days on an island in the middle of the river where an Indian chief lived." He then departed, leaving the two Englishmen, and the remainder of the trading goods. Retud states that the Italian had specifically been sent by Don Antonio "to see the nature of this land of the Orinoco, and to see if it was possible to settle it upriver, because it was known that thither there was to be discovered the Yeguana." The latter is clearly a garbled form of Guayana or Guiana.

The fate of these four English scouts and their Italian captain is unknown. Retud himself was captured at Jamaica in April 1587, delivered his *declaración* to the Spanish authorities on June 27, and was hanged by them shortly afterward.

There is no documentary evidence of Ralegh's involvement in this scouting party. It is possible that he was a patron of the Italian, who brought "letters from England." Alternatively, it might be seen as a rival move by Don Antonio, whose dislike of Pedro Sarmiento was well known. Either way, it shows the new interest in the Orinoco hinterland, an interest quite distinct from the privateering agenda: a desire to reconnoiter, to settle, and to find the way into "the Yeguana," or Guiana. This is an early, tentative survey of the way that Ralegh would travel eight years later.

[4]

Love and Exile

*　　*　　*

 I T MAY be chronological coincidence but I do not think so. The time when Ralegh's Dorado changes from a pipe dream to a plan of action is precisely the time of his "disgraces" and his withdrawal from courtly life. There are many reasons why this might be so: He had the leisure time to work on it; he had the financial problems to prompt it; and he needed to do something big and dramatic to recoup the Queen's favor. It was his "fall" that enabled him actually to *go* to America, whereas before Elizabeth had always required his presence at home.

There was one particular cause of his disgrace or fall, so in a sense you could say that his El Dorado adventure began this process of realization on that fateful summer's day or night in 1591 when he bedded one of the Queen's maids of honor, Mistress Throckmorton. A child was conceived, a clandestine marriage followed, and when the Queen got to hear of it his life changed overnight.

This is not an entirely frivolous connection, because it is a very Elizabethan one. The conquest and colonization of the New World was habitually linked, in metaphors and jokes, to a sexual "conquest," as in Donne's famous words to his mistress:

> O my America, my new-found-land,
> My kingdom, safeliest when with one man mann'd.

And though the court wits of the day could not foresee how his liaison with Bess Throckmorton might one day lead to the Guiana Voyage, they certainly had a field day with leering puns about continents and continence, and the "discovery of the discoverer." The

8. Elizabeth Throckmorton

sexuality of exploration, the femininity of America, becomes a theme in this story, so it is not quite out of bounds to say that the whole business began in the arms of his mistress and future wife.

ELIZABETH THROCKMORTON was a tall, angular, forceful-looking woman. At the time of the marriage she was about twenty-seven—ten years younger than Ralegh. Her face cannot be called beautiful: rather long and horsey, and framed with frizzy hair, but it is strong. Her family, of Norfolk origin, was wealthy, numerous, and politically active. Her father, Sir Nicholas Throckmorton, was a top-level civil servant: He had been the Queen's ambassador in France. The younger generation, Bess's generation, had a wilder streak. Among her cousins were Francis, executed in 1584 for his part in the infamous plot to put Mary Stuart on the English throne; and Thomas, a Catholic exile in Paris; and—at the other end of the spectrum—the Puritan agitator, Job Throckmorton, believed by some to be the true author of the ribald, anti-episcopal "Martin Marprelate" pamphlets.

In these dangerous cousins, rather than in Bess's careerist father, one finds the trait that corresponds to the sharpness of her looks, and to the attraction she exerted over Ralegh.

In 1584, just out of her teens, she was "sworn of the Privy Chamber" at Hampton Court. She became, in other words, one of that decorative circle of acolytes known as the Queen's maids of honor. Drilled by the aged Welsh spinster, Blanche Parry, they attended to the Queen's personal and female needs, and added glamour to the constant round of dances and entertainments. They hover gorgeously at the periphery of early court performances of plays like *Twelfth Night,* imparting to the scene the air of a candlelit nightclub.

Ralegh must have known her from her first arrival at court: He was then Captain of the Queen's Guard. When they became lovers is unknown. All that we know is that sometime in the summer of 1591 they conceived a child, and on November 10 they were secretly married.

Right up to the time of Bess's confinement, the liaison remained secret, but inevitably there were rumors. One piece of courtly tattle is often quoted:

> S. W. R., as it seemeth, have been too inward with one of Her Majesty's Maids. All think the Tower will be his dwelling, like hermit poor in pensive place, where he may spend his endless days in doubt. It is affirmed that they are married, but the Queen is most fiercely incensed and, as the bruit goes, threateneth the most bitter punishment to both the offenders. S. W. R. will lose, it is thought, all his places and preferments at court, with the Queen's favour. Such will be the ending of his speedy rising, and now he must fall as low as he was high, at the which many will rejoice.

The authenticity of this document is not certain, but it is too good to resist. It concludes with a pun that suggests the metaphorical link between sexual and colonial conquest: "All is alarm and confusion at this discovery of the discoverer, and not indeed of a new continent but of a new incontinent."

As late as March 1592, Ralegh was angrily denying the rumors. He was down at Chatham, fitting out a privateering voyage. He writes to Sir Robert Cecil:

> I mean not to come away, as they say I will, for fear of a marriage, and I know not what. If any such thing were, I would have imparted it unto yourself before any man living, and therefore I pray believe it not, and I beseech you to suppress, what you can, any such malicious report. For I protest before God, there is none on the face of the earth I would be fastened unto.

This is a lie, or a series of lies, but it arrives at a truthful moment of disquiet about the marriage he is embarked on. There is no one he wishes to be *fastened* to. The figure is one of imprisonment, quite the opposite to the metaphor of freebooting sexual conquest and "discovery."

Bess meanwhile was at Mile End, well out of the public gaze. She was living with her brother, Arthur. She had a nurse in attendance, who was paid two shillings a week. Between 2:00 and 3:00 P.M. on Wednesday, March 29, 1592, she gave birth to a son. Her brother's footman, Dick, carried the news to Ralegh at Chatham.

On April 10 the baby was christened. The boy was named Damerei—a piece of arrogant bravura on Ralegh's part, recalling a medieval prince, D'Amerey de Clare, whose daughter had married a Ralegh in the thirteenth century. On May 19 the marriage was "solemnized," and by the end of the month the new Lady Elizabeth and her two-month-old baby had moved in to Durham House. In a letter to Cecil she signs herself for the first time "E.R.," which seems both a cool assertion of her new marital status and a piece of spectacular effrontery toward that other "E.R.," the jilted Elizabeth Regina.

The courtly tatler quoted above proved accurate in his forecasts. By early June the Raleghs were under house arrest, and on August 7 they were dispatched to the Tower. They were released after about four months. Ralegh is briefly glimpsed, on December 13, at Durham House, but shortly after this they retired down to his new country estate at Sherborne. They were probably there for Christmas. Ralegh's long "disgraces" had begun.

RALEGH THUS begins 1593 as an entirely new chapter in his life. His career is in ruins; he has a wife and a child. In political and psychological terms he is a man in exile, though as befits one of his rank it is a well-appointed exile.

His new home is Sherborne Castle, on the banks of the Yeo River in western Dorset. He had a ninety-nine year lease on it, at a giveaway rent of £200 per annum. This was a gift from the Queen— her "bon," as Aubrey puts it. The transaction was finally signed by her in July 1592, shortly before his dispatch to the Tower. She did not withdraw this last favor, one infers, because she *meant* Sherborne to be his place of exile.

Sherborne Castle was a huge, drafty, twelfth-century fortress surrounded by fourteen thousand acres of wood, park, and farmland. To the south of the castle, across the other side of the river, stood a small Tudor hunting lodge. This was to become their home. Extension work began almost immediately, in early 1593. Aubrey says:

> He built a delicate lodge in the park, of brick; not big but very convenient for the bigness; a place to retire from the court in summertime, and to contemplate, etc. In short and indeed, 'tis a most sweet and pleasant place and site as any in the West, perhaps none like it.

This elegant three-story house was among the first in what Girouard describes as the seventeenth-century "lodge tradition"—a summer home: informal, pastoral. The tall facades and curly eaves show a Dutch influence. The brick walls are rendered with dressings of Ham Hill stone, now a rich honey color.

In its first form the Raleghs' house was only the centerpiece of the present building. The four hexagonal corner-towers were added later, in or soon after 1600; the architect for this was Simon Basil. (You can still see parts of an exterior wall inside the line of the towers.) The wings, which give the house its H shape, were added by the Digbys in the early seventeenth century. The now-derelict room at the top of the northeastern tower, thought to be Ralegh's study, is post-1600, and was not his study while he was plotting El Dorado.

He became a keen gardener. The Lodge stood on rough land above a boggy stretch of the Yeo known as Black Marsh. The area outside the parlor was cleared and planted: It is marked on Simon Basil's plot as "ye garden syde." Black Marsh itself was turned into a water garden. Sir John Harington chided Ralegh's extravagance at Sherborne, one of the chief expenses being "drawing the river through rocks into his garden." Ralegh's chief adviser on landscaping was his youngest half brother, Adrian Gilbert, a neglected but interesting figure.

The river garden is now a lake, and beyond it—below the curtain of the old castle—is a line of tall, wind-blasted red cedars "said to have been" grown from seeds brought back from Virginia. A couple of them were felled not long ago. I did an informal ring count on the stumps: I would say they are about 250 years old, and perhaps therefore second generation.

9. Sherborne Lodge: a view of the south front

The feel of Sherborne Lodge was one of managed rusticity. This is Ralegh's get-away-from-it-all gesture; the new Elizabethan pastoralism in action. He disappears from public view, down to his well-appointed *dacha* in the Dorset woods. He is licking his wounds; he is getting back to the land. He hawks, he hunts, he dines with bluff country gents with pepper-and-salt beards and kersey hose. His brother Carew lives nearby, employed none too arduously as governor

of Portland Bill and warden of Gillingham Forest. Sir George Tren-
chard and Sir Ralph Horsey are guests. There are legal disputes with
the farmer John FitzJames, philosophical disputes with the Reverend
Ironside, visits to Longleat to see his nephew, Charles Thynne.

He has his Irish estates to think of also, and in this year devises
a scheme to send Cornish miners to Munster. Iron ore has been
discovered on his land. In 1595 he licensed the building of a smelt-
ing works, and the felling of timber to fuel it. Here, in the absence
of "places and preferments," we see the new, necessary obsession with
tangible riches, from Irish bog-iron to South American gold.

Of Damerei Ralegh nothing more is heard after his tempestuous
birth in March 1592. He may have died when still a baby; he was
certainly dead by 1597, for Ralegh makes no mention of him in the
early draft of his will. Their second son, Walter or Wat, was born
in November 1593, and christened at Lillington church near Sherborne.

This is his new chapter: the country gent, domestic bliss. But all
the while, virtually from the *moment* he is down there, his mind is
reaching out for somewhere else. From the earliest months of 1593
he was beginning his preparations for the Guiana Voyage.

The search for El Dorado begins, like all journeys, at home. In
this paradoxically domestic setting of parlors and water gardens, the
grandiose distant plans begin to unfold. On his desk, among the
bric-a-brac of estate papers, there appear the charts and atlases and
portolanos and "excellent sea-cards done in hand" that would guide
him to America, and the tomes of the Spanish chroniclers that he
quotes in the opening sections of the *Discoverie*. These are probably
notes written down before the voyage, and later co-opted into the
text.

The separation now begins in him between the real things of his
life—the family and the home he loves—and the illusory but irre-
sistible quickening of tempo inside him as he turns the globe and
touches its shapes, his fingers moving down from Greenland, down
past Virginia, to touch the fruitlike shape of South America.

[5]

Preparations

*   *   *

T HE EARLIEST practical sign of Ralegh's new commitment to the search for El Dorado was the sending out of reconnaissance fleets. There were two sent out early in 1593.

The larger of the fleets went out under the command of Sir John Burgh. The flagship was Ralegh's own vessel, the *Roebuck.* Burgh was a close associate of Ralegh's, and of his scholarly friend, the Earl of Northumberland. He had captained the *Roebuck* the previous year, in the privateering raid that took the great carrack *Madre de Dios;* and now he has charge of her again on this expedition to the West Indies.

Admiralty Court documents show that this voyage was already being planned in the earliest days of 1593. The preliminary warrant requesting "letters of reprisal" was signed by Lord Admiral Howard on January 27. This grants Burgh the catch-all privateer's charter, "to go to the seas with certain ships, to be employed by him against the King of Spain and his subjects . . . [and] for the recovery of goods detained by the said King of Spain and his subjects." On March 3 bonds totaling £12,000 were posted by Burgh and others, this representing £3,000 for each of the four ships of the expedition—the *Roebuck*, the *Golden Dragon,* the *Prudence,* and the *Virgin* (the last two perhaps inviting some ribaldry given the events of the previous summer).

They probably sailed in April. They are next sighted at Margarita Island off the Caribbean coast of South America. There, in July or August, they attacked the Spanish garrison, but were repelled, suffering casualties. Spanish accounts of the raid survive, Burgh featur-

49

ing as "Don Juan de Amburgo," a Hispanicized corsair like "Guaterrale."

In the *Discoverie,* Ralegh mentions in passing that Burgh had landed on Margarita and "attempted the island." Later, in the *History of the World,* he gives a fuller account:

> Sir John Borrowes [i.e., Burgh] also, with a hundred English, was in great danger of being lost at Margarita, in the West Indies, by having the grass fired behind him; but the smoke being timefully discovered, he recovered the seashore with the loss of sixteen of his men.

In neither case does he say that Burgh's voyage entailed a reconnaissance of the Guiana coast, but an informed contemporary reference by Sir William Monson, later Admiral of the Narrow Seas, makes the connection explicit. In a memorandum he writes: "1595: Sir Walter Ralegh to Guiana, no profit at all; and the year before Sir John Burgh, with the like success." This is inaccurate as to the date of Burgh's voyage, but shows that it was connected in Monson's mind with the later Guiana Voyage.

What happened after the abortive attack on Margarita is not clear. The only information is that one of the ships, the *Golden Dragon,* was back in England, in a very battered state, by early December. On December 10 the ship, together with its "tackle, apparel & furniture," was valued by a team of Admiralty appraisers. The total valuation of the ship and its contents came to less than £300, a very low figure for a ship of this burden. We do not know what compensating profits there were from the voyage.

Spanish reports in February and March 1595 claimed that Burgh was "fitting out" for a new expedition against Margarita. In fact Burgh was dead, killed at the age of about thirty-two in a duel with Ralegh's nephew, John Gilbert. The expedition heading toward the Caribbean was actually Ralegh's.

*   *   *

BURGH'S WEST Indies voyage brings back news and information about Spanish activities on the Eastern Main, and perhaps topographical research on the Guiana coast. These are now fed into Ralegh's fattening dossier on El Dorado. It seems possible that Burgh's attack on Margarita was specifically aimed at someone who knew all about El Dorado—the redoubtable old *doradista* Don Antonio de Berrio.

As we saw, it was Berrio—the heir of Quesada—who first placed the city of Manoa, or El Dorado, in the Guiana Highlands. Since that first *entrada* of 1583–85, which Ralegh probably heard of from Sarmiento, Berrio had been twice more down the Orinoco in search of Manoa. In late 1591, at the end of his last and most heroic journey, he emerged out of the Orinoco Delta, into the Caribbean, and arrived in a fever of exhaustion at Margarita. There he was lodged by the Governor, though there was soon distrust between them.

Berrio remained at Margarita until January 1593, vigorously recruiting for one last triumphant *entrada*. Thereafter he moved across to Trinidad, to the newly founded capital of the settlement, San José, and from there, in April, his henchman Domingo de Vera set out to take formal possession of El Dorado. These later movements would not yet have reached England when Burgh's fleet sailed in March or April. I suspect that at least one of the motives for the attack on Margarita was Burgh's belief that Berrio was there. He may also have known that the Governor of Margarita was engaged in slave-trading expeditions to the Orinoco-Caroní area, and had privileged information on the region. Burgh's foray into Margarita was made in hope of capturing precious information as much as booty.

Another reconnaissance voyage was undertaken by Captain Jacob Whiddon, a trusted captain of Ralegh's privateering fleet, and the man who captured Pedro Sarmiento at the Azores in 1586. No documentary record remains of this reconnaissance, but Ralegh refers to it frequently in the *Discoverie,* and we can reassemble his remarks into a brief report of Whiddon's expedition.

> I sent my servant Jacob Whiddon the year before, to get knowledge of the passages [i.e., the entrances to the Orinoco]. . . .

> [At Trinidad] there stole aboard us in a small *canoa*, two Indians; the one of them being a *cacique* or lord of the people called Cantyman, who had the year before been with Captain Whiddon, and was of his acquaintance. . . .

> I sent Ja. Whiddon the year before to get intelligence, with whom Berrio himself had speech at that time, and remembered how inquisitive Ja. Whiddon was of his proceedings and of the country of Guiana. . . .

From this one gathers that Whiddon had been in the Caribbean to gather "intelligence" for Ralegh, and that he had found Berrio at Trinidad, had parleyed with him, and had pressed him inquisitively on the subject of Guiana. He thus accomplished what Burgh perhaps hoped to do in Margarita—though Burgh's was a military expedition, while Whiddon's fleet seems to have been a small, unthreatening presence in Trinidad: perhaps a lone ship. While there, Whiddon also made contact with Trinidad natives—the chief Cantyman, who later remembered him—and reconnoitered the "passages" into the Orinoco.

Three times Ralegh says that Whiddon had been there "the year before." It is therefore always said that Whiddon made his reconnaissance in 1594. But this is directly contradicted by another passage in the *Discoverie*, which dates his presence in Trinidad to mid-1593. Ralegh describes how Berrio attacked Whiddon's men— a moment of Spanish perfidy that he later vowed to "revenge." Berrio had given his word to Whiddon that the English could "take water and wood safely," but

> he [Berrio] betrayed eight of Captain Whiddon's men, and took them while he [Whiddon] departed from them to seek the *E. Bonaventure*, which arrived at Trinedado the day before from the East Indies; in whose absence, Berrio sent a *canoa* aboard the pinnace only with Indians and dogs, inviting the company to go with them into the woods to kill a deer. . . . But Berrio's soldiers lying in ambush had them all.

According to this, Berrio killed the eight English while Whiddon and most of the crew were absent, seeking "the *E. Bonaventure,*" which had arrived in the area the previous day. The *Edward Bonaventure* was one of three ships that set out for the East Indies in 1591. Her captain was James Lancaster. On the return journey, in the early summer of 1593, the crew threatened to mutiny. Captain Lancaster set course for Trinidad, where "we should be sure to have refreshing," but "not knowing the currents we were put past it in the night, into the Gulf of Paria, in the beginning of June." They were struck by currents and suffered a "great leak," but after eight days they "beat out of" the gulf and headed northward. This is from the journal of one of her crew, Edward Barker. There is no indication that they returned to Trinidad after this.

Thus the *Edward Bonaventure* was off Trinidad, in the Golfo de Paria, for a specific period of eight days, described in Barker's journal as at the beginning of June 1593. She was swept away from the island by the treacherous Paria currents, which is why Whiddon went off to "seek" her.

It is likely that the killing of Whiddon's men marks the end of his stay at Trinidad. It certainly happens later than his cordial questioning of Berrio: It is seen as a betrayal of that earlier rapprochement. I conclude that Ralegh's scout, Jacob Whiddon, was conversing with Berrio at Trinidad some time around the end of May or the beginning of June 1593. He must have left England, therefore, by mid-April at the latest. This is about the time that Sir John Burgh set off, in Ralegh's *Roebuck*.

Whiddon is not part of Burgh's fleet according to Admiralty records, but these can now be seen as two closely linked voyages. They have the usual privateering agenda, no doubt, but their purpose is also to reconnoiter and investigate this corner of the Eastern Main—the Spanish outposts of Margarita and Trinidad where Berrio has his den; and the coastal "passages" of the Orinoco Delta that lead into the mainland. These are, in the troubled summer of 1593, Ralegh's first serious soundings for the journey to El Dorado.

He was also gathering specialist information about the coast of South America from other sources. Among the papers of Thomas

Harriot is a navigational tract, or "rutter" (French *routier*), specially compiled for the Guiana Voyage. It is a fattish manuscript, headed "A Rutter or Course to be kept for him that will sayle from Cabo Verde to the coast of Brasilie and all alongst the coast of Brasilia." It gives computations, instructions, landmarks, bearings, etc., under such headings as "How to know Cape Augustine" and "Marks of all the coast from Santa Marta to Cartagena." It is actually two separate rutters, in different hands, with annotations and cross-references by Harriot. As his scribbled end note explains:

> This whole rutter hath been examined with a copy of John Douglas's, which was written out of Sir Walter Ralegh's had of Captain Parker. Those notes that are written on the blank pages are such readings as are in that copy, & where lines are stroked [i.e., crossed out] without note of diverse readings they are words of my copy more than in his. My copy was had of E. M. 1590, & this was examined 1595, & the last part from page 35 was more than was in my copy.

We have here a fascinating geology of how information of this sort was built up. There is an earlier rutter, communicated to Harriot in 1590 by "E.M." This is Captain Edmund Marlowe, who may or may not be a distant cousin of the dramatist. Then, in early 1595, shortly before Ralegh's departure, Harriot compares and intercalates this with another document belonging to John Douglas, who is about to sail with Ralegh as the master of his flagship. This is a copy of a rutter owned by Ralegh, who in turn "had" it from Captain Parker. William Parker was an associate of Ralegh's in the privateering business, and a frequent visitor to the Caribbean in the early 1590s. He is mentioned in the *Discoverie* as someone who had spoken of El Dorado—"I had some light from Captain Parker . . . that such a place there was to the southward of the great Bay of Charuas or Guanipa"—but whose information had proved faulty. The rutter he gave to Ralegh was probably a captured Spanish document.

*   *   *

10. Thomas Harriot, Ralegh's chief scientific adviser

THE TWO chief backers of Ralegh's El Dorado project were the Lord Admiral (Charles Howard, Lord Effingham) and Sir Robert Cecil. In dedicating his account of the voyage to them, Ralegh writes: "For your honours' many honorable and friendly parts I have hitherto only returned promises, and now for answer of both your adventures I have sent you a bundle of papers." The bundle of papers is, of course, the text of the *Discoverie,* ironically presented as the return on their investment. This is the meaning of "adventures" here: They have ventured or invested in the expedition.

In the case of Lord Admiral Howard, the investment consisted of a ship, the *Lion's Whelp;* in the case of Cecil it was probably capital. But both men were important to Ralegh as more than just investors. They were political backers, his representatives at court at this time of his isolation. He had, he says, "trial of both your loves, when I was left of all but of malice and revenge." They have been steadfast, "knowing what little power I had to perform aught." (This note of impotence seems to belong with the nexus of sexual metaphors mentioned earlier.)

These were two men at the peak of their professions. Howard had been involved with Ralegh on a practical maritime level for years. As Lord Admiral he was the nominal director of all matters relating to passports, letters of marque and reprisal, partition of prize moneys, and so on: the daily language of the privateering business. The post was enormously profitable. In June 1594, from Sherborne, Ralegh wrote to Howard (passing on intelligence sent by his brother Carew) about the gathering of Spanish ships on the Breton coast, recommending prompt action to "assail" them.

For aught I hear, your fleet will be far too weak. I hope you will take my remembrance in good part, and if you will vouchsafe to move Her Majesty for me to attend you privately [i.e., as a privateer] in her service, I hope I shall stand your Lordship in the place of a poor mariner or soldier. I have no other desire but to serve Her Majesty, and seeing I desire nor place nor honour nor reward, I hope it will be easily granted, if I be not condemned to the grave, and no liberty nor hope left.

The shift from the gruff, man-in-the-know tone of the opening remark to the melodramatic abasement at the end suggests the oscil-
lations of Ralegh's character at this time. The rather overplayed irony
of offering himself as a "poor mariner or soldier" is also typical. This
image of himself as a worker, a freelancer, a gun for hire, recurs in
other letters. It is an affirmation of physicality and solidity after the
fantasy of court life.

He signs this letter to Howard, "evermore your most assured poor
kinsman to serve you"—the kinship referred to is probably through
Lady Ralegh and her Norfolk connections.

Sir Robert Cecil, the sickly but brilliant son of Lord Burghley,
was a powerful guide and ally in the jungle of courtly politics.
Groomed for years as Burghley's successor, involved in a whole range
of shady political operations as Burghley's spymaster, Cecil was
shortly to be named Secretary of State and already held the post in
all but name. He had been a careful associate of Ralegh's: always in
touch, always ready to deal on his behalf. But for Cecil, friendship
was always expendable in the interests of political advantage, and
all who dealt with him knew this.

So events would prove, in the days of the new century, but for
now Cecil was an ally in those corridors of power from which Ralegh
was barred, and an enthusiastic promoter of the Guiana Voyage.

Ralegh also had an important backer in the City, a merchant and
broker named William Sanderson. Sanderson was family of a sort—
his wife was the daughter of Ralegh's half sister Margaret Snedall—
and he had played a part in the finances of Virginia, and in
supporting some of the "scholars" involved in the new American
studies, among them the globe maker Emery Molyneux and the
mathematician Thomas Hood.

By a stroke of good fortune some of the financing of the Guiana
Voyage has survived—not the original accounts, but certain details
that emerge from a lawsuit, filed by Sanderson against Ralegh and
others, nearly twenty years later. From this it appears that the total
sum of £60,000 was raised, and this served to equip both Whiddon's
scouting expedition of 1593 and Ralegh's voyage of 1595. This was a
tremendous sum—say £25 million in modern money. These are major

projects: high capital, high risk, and potentially astronomic returns.

In raising this sum, Sanderson himself "stood bond" for loans of £50,000 "and upwards," as well as investing about £750 of his own money. According to Sanderson, Ralegh repaid him with dishonest and high-handed dealing, hence the acrimonious legal dispute of 1613.

Howard, Cecil, Sanderson, and other backers (whom one could guess at but are unnamed in the suit) expected to reap dividends, but everyone from the Queen to the ship's cat had some kind of stake in the voyage. The customary division of prize money (i.e., the value of captured shipping, cargo, ransom, etc.) gave 10 percent of the gross to the Admiralty and 5 percent to Her Majesty's Customs. The remainder was divided between the investors (i.e., shipowners, victuallers, etc.) and the crew, at a ratio of two to one. Thus each £100 of profit from a voyage would be distributed as follows:

Investors	£56	13s	4d
Crew	£28	6s	8d
Lord High Admiral	£10	0s	0d
H.M. Customs	£5	0s	0d

However, the Queen's automatic percentage was often increased: She expected, and usually obtained, a fifth of all gold, silver, and jewels taken on the voyage. This was on top of the 5 percent customs duty. It is referred to as "Her Majestys fyfte."

ON FEBRUARY 8, 1594, Elizabeth Ralegh wrote a touching letter to Sir Robert Cecil, urging him to dissuade her husband from his intended American voyage. She writes: "I hope, for my sake, you will rather draw Sir Walter towards the east than help him forward towards the sunset." This refers quite specifically to the dangers and uncertainties of the El Dorado venture—a westward journey, a voyage "towards the sunset," an omen of decline. By early 1594, then, Ralegh's plans are advanced enough, his obsession visible enough, for his wife to be alarmed. Cecil remains deaf to her entreaty, and continues to promote the Dorado voyage at court.

The year of 1594 for Ralegh was one of almost unbearable frustration and tension. Toward the end of it, he summed it up gloomily:

> This unfortunate year is such as those that were ready and at sea two months before us are beaten back again and distressed. This long stay hath made me a poor man, the year far spent, and what shall become of us God knows. The body is wasted with toil, the purse with charge, and all things worn.

By the beginning of the year he was ready, in his mind, to go. He had the information: from his reconnaissance fleets, from the captured reports, from the gossip of returning captains. He had the momentum. Lady Ralegh's letter, written in February, shows him already hell-bent on this journey "towards the sunset," but it is a whole year before he will finally set off.

Another letter among the Cecil papers suggests that Ralegh's fleet may have been prepared to leave in the summer of 1594, though this is not conclusive. It is from Captain John Troughton to Sir Robert Cecil, and it was written "from aboard the *Lion's Whelp.*" This was the Lord Admiral's ship that later took part in the Guiana Voyage. According to this, the *Whelp* had sailed down from Deptford in June 1594 (suggesting some refit or rebuilding at the shipyards there). Somewhere west of Dover, she sprang a leak, "such as every glass we pumped 300 strokes by the least." Due to this, and also a "bad wind," they were forced to put in at Portsmouth on June 20. On June 24, Troughton writes to Cecil; they have been "furnished of all wants," and are now "determined to touch no more England shore, till God give us a safe return, and to you and others good content."

This may be an entirely separate voyage that the *Whelp* was about to embark on, with the backing of Cecil; or it may be the El Dorado voyage, optimistically seen as imminent in late June 1594.

A letter of Ralegh's to Sir John Gilbert, unfortunately not dated, probably relates to the recruitment of crew for the voyage. It too speaks of delays.

Where by my last letters directed unto you concerning the levying of sailors and mariners, I gave direction that they should be ready against the 15th of this month at Dartmouth, which I am now through many urgent occasions constrained to defer; hereby praying you to have special care that they be levied from places least infected, and to be ready at Dartmouth the 20th day of this present month, to take shipping.

What exactly the delays were it is hard to say—money problems, probably; perhaps a difficulty in getting authorization—but they are the theme of this year.

Aggravating the frustration was the fact that other English expeditions were getting off, some of them bound for the very same area. He grumbles:

It is more than time that there be a restraint of all shipping bound out to the wars, for there are multitudes going for the Indies. If any men be taken (as some every year are) the Queen's purpose will be frustrate; and if Eaton's ships go, who will attempt the chiefest places of my enterprise, I shall be undone, and I know they will be beaten and do no good.

Who Eaton was, and what came of his expedition to the Eastern Main, is unrecorded. Ralegh complains that the delays he is experiencing will "forewarn the enemy" of his intentions. He means the Spanish, but the "enemy" right now, as he paces the parlor at Sherborne, is those other Englishmen who are sailing off over the horizon toward the "chiefest places" of his own stymied enterprise.

Chief among these—and the one who actually beat him to the finishing post: the first English *entrada* up the Orinoco—was Robert Dudley's expedition. Dudley was the illegitimate son of the Earl of Leicester—or so Leicester said. Dudley himself consistently claimed that his mother, Lady Douglas Sheffield, was formally betrothed to Leicester. His claim for recognition finally came to court in 1604, and was rejected, whereupon he stormed off to Italy. He lived there in exile for thirty years. His navigational masterpiece, the *Arcanum del Mare,* was published in Florence in 1647. Its intricate pop-ups and volvelles still move with perfect smoothness in the copy at the British Museum.

It is often said that Dudley was not actually intending an expedition into Guiana and that he only stopped there as part of a more general, speculative roaming. I am not sure that this is true. It certainly appears that Dudley had specialist documents about the Guiana coastline—a "discoverie" of the coast, he calls it—and that this was given him, *before* he left England, by Captain George Popham.

Dudley's expedition sailed from Plymouth, after the usual delays, on November 22, 1594. His fleet was the *Bear* of two hundred tons, admiral or flagship; the *Bear's Whelp,* under Captain Munck, vice-admiral; and two small pinnaces, the *Frisking* and the *Earwig.* (The naming of Elizabethan ships, as of jazz tunes and racehorses, has a poetry of its own.) Fifty leagues out they met a storm, the fleet was scattered, and they returned to port. When he set out again, on December 1, he was without the *Bear's Whelp.* Another storm soon sank his pinnaces. So, in early December, "all alone I went wandering on my voyage." He had a crew of nearly 140 men, who were extremely "pestered"—cramped—owing to the loss of the pinnace. At Tenerife he captured a pair of Spanish caravels. These "amended my company, and made me a fleet of 3 sails."

"Thus cheered, as a desolate traveller, with the company of my small and new-erected fleet, I continued my purpose for the West Indies"—and, Ralegh would have bitterly added, for Guiana.

AT LAST, in December 1594, Ralegh received the Queen's letters patent, granting official permission for the voyage. A draft survives at the Public Record Office, with some corrections in Cecil's hand; the docket accompanying it is dated December 6. It addresses Ralegh simply as her "servant," contrasting bleakly with the "trusty and well-beloved" terminology of the Virginia patent ten years earlier. It says:

Upon his desire to better his knowledge by further experience, and do us service in offending the King of Spain and his subjects, we give him leave to prepare and arm two ships and two small pinnaces. As his own ability is not sufficient to furnish out such vessels, and he is driven to use the assistance of friends to adventure with him, we for his satisfaction and the assurance of such persons, further promise that he and they shall enjoy to their own use all such goods and merchandise, treasure, gold, silver and whatever else shall be taken by him or his associates, either by sea or land, from the subjects or adherents of the King of Spain, paying such customs and duties as appertain. For the better ruling of such of her subjects as shall go with him in this service, as also of any other shipping that may voluntarily join with him at sea or at the Indies, and for the better effecting of any such enterprise, we hereby charge and command all captains, masters, mariners and others so consorted, to be wholly directed by him and . . . both by land and sea to submit themselves and give him due obedience.

This is mostly formulaic, but has one or two interesting touches. The opening phrase, for instance—his "desire to better his knowledge by further experience"—is not conventional. It probably echoes Ralegh's own phrasing in a preexistent letter or petition. It has the precise empirical temper of Ralegh as discoverer. The passage about his lack of "ability" (i.e., money) and the involvement of "friends to adventure with him" is probably Cecil's work, a careful formalizing of his investment in the enterprise. Thus brusquely, Ralegh's quest for El Dorado becomes official, at least insofar as it contributes to the annoyance of the King of Spain.

It is probably around this time that Thomas Harriot delivered a series of lectures to the captains and masters of Ralegh's Guiana crew. The surviving notes suggest there were six or seven lectures in all. They are a digest of Harriot's research on new navigational techniques, covering such topics as the use of astrolabes, sea rings, and cross-staves; "how to find the declination of the sun"; "how to find the elevation of the pole by the meridian altitude of the sun"; and so on. Some of this was based on his *Arcticon*, a navigational textbook compiled in the early 1580s and now lost, and some on "mine own experience & trial at sea" during the Virginia voyages. It also incorporated new techniques pioneered by Tycho Brahe, Erasmus Rheinhold, and "one Nicolaus Copernicus of Cracow," as well as Harriot's own astronomical observations made "upon Duresme leads"—in other words, from the roof of Durham House, Ralegh's London residence.

Historians of mathematics wax lyrical here about Harriot's innovational use of trigonometry, logarithmic tangents, stereographic projections, etc. I am sure they are right. I discern also a sense of Ralegh himself: the importance to him of intellectual prowess, of expertise, of modernity. His captains are here being drilled by the foremost mathematician in the country. They will be using the newest techniques, the "precise & late observations." They will proceed "with more exactness than hath been used heretofore." Against this, I place the curious erroneousness of Ralegh's location of Guiana—his determined clinging to the idea that Lake Manoa lay on the equator (as in his map), and the consequent dislocation of other latitudes (both Trinidad and the Caroní are given erroneous latitudes in the *Discoverie*). Here again is that oscillation between the actual and the symbolic that is such a feature of the El Dorado quest, as seen in Ralegh's map, where "precise & late" cartography bumps up against a more nebulous and ancient imagery, and does not quite displace it.

These lectures were probably delivered, toward the end of 1594, at Durham House, where Harriot then resided. They are a genuine counterpart to those scare-mongering rumors about Durham House as a "School of Atheism," of which Harriot was said to be the "master" and to which Marlowe was said to have delivered an "atheist lecture."

A snatch of verse is found among Harriot's lecture notes, and seems to be a little personal flourish to conclude the course. He sums up the doctrine of his lectures as the "three sea marriages"—between the staff and the astrolabe, the sun and the stars, the chart and the compass—and concludes, on a note that brings the imminent hopes and perils of the journey into sudden focus:

> If you use them well in this your journey
> They will be the King of Spain's attorney

To bring you to silver & Indian gold
Which will keep you in age from hunger & cold.
God speed you well & send you fair weather
And that again we may meet together.

NOW ALL that held them back was the weather, immune alike to the Queen's command and the mathematician's theories.

On December 21, at Sherborne: "I stay but for the wind to bring about the ship."

On December 26, in tetchy mood: "This wind breaketh my heart; that should carry me hence now stays me here, and holds my ships in the river of Timeis [i.e., Tamar]." He is on the brink, a coiled spring waiting for release: "As soon as God send them hither I will not lose one hour of time."

On January 1, 1595, still at Sherborne: "Only gazing for a wind to carry me to my destiny."

And then at last it is happening. It is early February, the ships are loading, and Ralegh and his wife are down in Plymouth preparing for his departure.

At its grandest, the El Dorado fleet was envisioned as eight ships: four under Ralegh, and four under the command of Captain Amias Preston. However, not everything was going according to schedule down in Plymouth. Only three of Preston's ships were ready. They were waiting for Captain Jones, who "in all that time, through the bad dealing of those which he put in trust, could not make his ship in readiness, according to his appointment." This is later given as the reason why Preston's contingent did not sail with Ralegh, though there is evidence also of ill will between the two men. Preston did not actually leave until mid-March, failed to keep certain rendezvous with Ralegh, and did not meet up with him until July, off Cuba, by which time Ralegh was preparing for the homeward leg.

Ralegh cannot wait. If these ships cannot or will not sail, he will sail without them.

Thus Ralegh's expedition was actually accomplished with just four ships. There is a maddening absence of documentation on this

11. Ships of the Guiana Voyage (details from De Bry)

fleet. From the *Discoverie* one gleans the following. The flagship, unnamed, was one of Ralegh's own ships: It was probably the *Bark Ralegh*. The vice-admiral was the *Lion's Whelp*, a frigate belonging to the Lord Admiral. There were also a "small bark of Captain Cross's," and an old *gallego*, or galliot, of Spanish origin, probably a privateering prize. The total burden of the fleet, according to Francis Sparry's estimate, was 440 tons. (Further details of these ships, and of Sparry's information relating to them, are given in Appendix 3, "The Fleet.")

Thomas Harriot is down there with him in Plymouth—the old Virginia hand, the adviser, the unseen philosophical backer of the enterprise. So too is the financier, Sanderson. Those later litigations about the Guiana accounts provide us with a sudden, oddly intimate glimpse of the three men in a room in Plymouth, on the night of Wednesday, February 5.

[Ralegh] at the very instant upon his departure in his intended voyage, in the night time, under pretence of a desire he had to see the release delivered many days before unto Sanderson, and Sanderson nothing doubting of any ill meaning of Ralegh's, gave the release unto Ralegh, who perusing the same a while, presently gave the release unto Thomas Harriot, willing him not to deliver the same to Sanderson unless he [Ralegh] should miscarry in his said voyage.

At this dealing, Sanderson was "much moved" and "broke out into great discontentment, for that Sir Walter did deal so unkindly and violently with him."

This is Sanderson's version of it (verbatim except that I have substituted names for legal formulas like "the said plaintiff"). In his wording he seems to recall the mood of the incident as much as the strict legalities. In other words, Ralegh's behavior at that time, the night before he left for South America, was violent and impatient. He was a man under severe stress, as this sudden access of "ill meaning" toward the financier shows.

This is the disappointed, somewhat harassed man who left for South America in 1595. Every morning, he feels, he looks, a little older and cares a little less for people and things he once held dear. He leaves in the depths of winter, his wife returning up the icy tracks to Sherborne. The Guiana Voyage is his big gamble, his "game of hazard." He stakes his reputation on this wild surmise—given the nature of these journeys he stakes his health and his life.

The "fruit" of his former life, he wrote in the preface to the *Discoverie,* "was long before fallen from the tree." He sets off for the tropics, for the distant glories of El Dorado, in a mood of bitter, almost nonchalant despair.

> I did therefore even in the winter of my life undertake these travels, fitter for bodies less blasted with misfortunes, for men of greater ability, and for minds of better encouragement.

He is a man with nothing left to lose—or that, at least, is how he would play it, for the benefit of his readers, when he got back home.

[6]

The Crew

*　　*　　*

WE CAN surmise the dockside scene: the rowdy soldiers, the fond farewells, the loading of beer and bacon and gunpowder. But what of the faces that populate the scene? Who were these men who sailed off with Ralegh to South America? The evidence is sketchy, but a few of them—their careers and characters, if not their faces—can be discerned.

At its fullest complement, when the fleet assembled off Trinidad in early April, Ralegh's expeditionary force numbered about 250 men, perhaps a little more. Roughly half of these were the ships' crews, and half the soldiers, adventurers, and specialists of the expedition proper. When they raided Cumaná in July, the Spanish numbered the landing force as 210 men. There would have been others back on the ships. The number of men who actually traveled with Ralegh up the Orinoco was 100. This was dictated by the room available in their small boats, and by the need to leave the fleet "well garrisoned" at their backs.

We can salvage from the record the names of just twenty-four— less than 10 percent—of the Englishmen who accompanied Ralegh in his search for El Dorado. All but four of them are named in an interesting manuscript list in the British Museum. This is dated 1618; it was written, therefore, at the time of Ralegh's second, tragic venture to South America. It lists the "diverse Captaines and Gentlemen" who accompanied him on the First Guiana Voyage "by him performed in Anno Domini 1595." It does not, unfortunately, add any names to those mentioned in Ralegh's *Discoverie;* in fact the compiler has the *Discoverie* in front of him, and sometimes writes the name down exactly as it appears there (e.g., "my nephew John Gil-

12. Soldiers of the Guiana Voyage (details from De Bry)

bert"). However, the names are not listed in the order they appear in Ralegh's text, so this is a little more than a mechanical compilation.

It is, at any rate, a useful contemporary list of the first English searchers for El Dorado, and it reads as follows:

Capt George Gifford, Vice Admirall
Captain Calfeild
Captain Amiotts Preston
Captain Thynne
Captain Laurence Keymis

Captain Eynos
Captain Whiddon
Captain Clarke
Captain Crosse
Captain Facy
My cousin Butsheade George
My nephew John Gilbert
John Dowglass, Master of myne owne shipp
Mr Edward Porter
Lieutenant Hewes
My cousin Greeneveile
———— Connock
Anthony Wells
———— King, Mr of the Lions Whelpe
Jerom Farrar
Thomas Upton
Nicholas Mellechapp, surgeon (he is now, 1618, dwelling in Ludlow)

The last note serves to date the manuscript. It rounds off this rather functional document with an unexpected biographical flourish. Clearly the list was compiled by someone who knew Nicholas Mellechapp—or quite possibly by Mellechapp himself, refreshing the memory of his South American adventure over twenty years earlier.

For whatever reason, the compiler considered the list now complete, and omitted three further names that appear in the *Discoverie.* These are Francis Sparry or Sparrow, whom I would be sorry to miss; Hugh Godwin or Goodwin, who was Ralegh's cabin boy on the voyage; and Edward Hancock, who is heard of elsewhere as a servant and secretary of Ralegh's. (It is not impossible that Hancock was the compiler of the list, though whether he was still alive in 1618 I do not know.) There is also a certain "Vincent," who appears neither in the list nor in the *Discoverie,* but who is later named as one of the casualties of the journey. This gives us twenty-six names in all, but two of the men listed above—Captains Preston and Cross—did not actually accompany Ralegh. Preston's ships were intended to be part of the fleet, but never were, while the single reference to Captain

Cross in the *Discoverie* suggests he was the owner of one of the ships, the unnamed "small bark," but not that he was aboard it when it sailed from Plymouth.

Of seven of these twenty-four men—Eynos, Facy, Porter, Wells, King, Farrar, and Vincent—I can find no documentation at all. Three others belong to identifiable families—the Uptons of Devon, the Connocks of Cornwall and the Mellechapps of Shropshire—but are otherwise untraced. We know that Hugh Godwin was sixteen at the time of the voyage, but nothing of his origins. Lieutenant Hewes is possibly a relative of the geographer Robert Hues, author of the *De Usu Globorum* (1593) and friend of Thomas Harriot, but the name is too common to be sure. Just twelve of the voyagers, therefore, can be described in any detail.

THE FIRST on the list is George Gifford, the captain of the *Lion's Whelp,* and nominally Ralegh's second-in-command. Here, straightaway, is a fascinating character completely overlooked by Ralegh's biographers. He steps straight out of the Elizabethan *demi-monde:* a man of squandered wealth and shady political connections. It is something of a surprise to find him out there, wading through the swamps of the Orinoco. He brings a complex note of adventurism to the scene.

He has a family connection with Lady Ralegh, but his presence on the expedition relates more particularly to Lord Admiral Howard: He is the captain of Howard's ship, and is elsewhere described as "serving" the Lord Admiral. He is a power faction within the expedition, though also a man desperate to remedy his losses.

There are three George Giffords on record. Our man is not the Protestant parson and minor author of that name. Nor is he George Gifford of Chillington, Staffordshire, a Catholic seminarian at Rheims in 1583–84 and a brother of the notorious spy, Gilbert Gifford, then also at Rheims, who became one of Walsingham's chief agents against Mary, Queen of Scots.

The George Gifford who traveled with Ralegh was a cousin of the Chillington Giffords, and like them was born into a family of a strong Catholic stamp. He was the eldest son of John Gifford of Ithell, Hants; his mother was Elizabeth, née Throckmorton, an aunt or cousin of her namesake, Lady Ralegh. He was born in 1552. He was two years older than Ralegh and was in his early forties when he arrived in South America.

His younger brother, William, pursued the Catholic cause, became reader in theology at the English seminary at Rheims, and was a constant target of English intriguers, notably his cousin Gilbert Gifford.

George's father died when he was ten. His wardship was sold to relatives of his mother, Kenelm and Thomas Throckmorton. As well as the Hampshire estates, he inherited the manor of Weston-under-Edge in Gloucestershire. He was granted livery on his lands in 1573, at the age of twenty-one. His inheritance was valued at £116 8s 8d. At about this time, according to his own later statement, he began to "serve the Crown." He also married Eleanor Brydges, stepdaughter of Sir William Knollys and a relation of Lord Burghley. In 1578 he was made a "gentleman pensioner"—this showed favored status at court and provided a modest salary. In the early 1580s he is living at Eltham, in Kent. He is said to be a favorite of Sir Christopher Hatton, the Queen's dandified Captain of the Guard. He perhaps meets the future Captain of the Guard, Walter Ralegh, around this time.

A prospering career so far for George Gifford: a fortunate elder son, a promising courtier, building himself patiently into the networks of Elizabethan power. It seems conventional enough. Then suddenly we learn of a wild side. In April 1583 he is named as one of a gang of men assisting in the escape of a highwayman named Nix from the White Lion prison in Southwark. He bragged that his standing with Hatton would protect him, and it seems it did. On another occasion he is charged with involvement in a gang of housebreakers. We have come through to another part of Gifford's life: the *demi-mondain.*

But these underworld leanings are only part of the story: George was now preparing a sting more complex and dangerous—and, if it worked, more profitable—than Nix had ever dreamed of. In late

April or early May 1583, he engineers a clandestine meeting in Paris with the Catholic exiles, Thomas Morgan and Charles Paget, agents of the imprisoned Mary Stuart. He is a secret Catholic, he tells them; he is close to Queen Elizabeth; he offers, for a sum of money, to assassinate her. Morgan promises to get money and support for the project from the Duke of Guise, head of the Catholic League in France, and—as is his way—soon boasts of having done so to other conspirators. This is first documented in a report from the Papal Nuncio in Paris, Castelli, dated May 2, 1583. There is talk, he says, of a plot [*maneggio*] to assassinate Queen Elizabeth.

> One of her household, who conceals his Catholicism, hates the Queen because she has executed some of his relatives. He made proposals to the Queen of Scots, who would not listen to them. He was sent here [Paris] and it has been agreed that the Duke of Guise shall give him a bond for 50,000 francs.

The news was noted. A Catholic mole within striking distance of the hated Jezebel: an assassin in her household. There is a flutter of interest in various Catholic dispatches. The Cardinal of Como asserts that the Pope would support such an action, with hard cash if necessary. But soon the doubts creep in. Castelli cools: "The design against the person of the Queen of England will, I believe, come to nothing." It is decided that the man was working for "private interests." There will be "no further dealing with it."

The same story is told by Father Persons, with his dry Jesuit wit. Morgan and Paget, he relates, petitioned the Duke of Guise "to deliver a certain sum of money to a young *caballero* in England, who had promised the said pair to kill the Queen of England." However, the Duke had "learned that the said *caballero* was a reprobate [*perdito*] who would do nothing, as the effect proved."

This letter from Persons is written in Spanish, and in the margin beside the words "a young *caballero* in England" are written the initials "J.G."; in other words, Jorge Gifford.

It was not until 1586 that Gifford was actually charged on this matter. He was denounced by one of the Babington plotters, John Savage. Under interrogation in early August, Savage stated:

> that George Gifford promised to have slain Her Majesty, for the furtherance whereof he received 800 crowns or pounds sent to him by the Duke of Guise . . .

> that the Duke of Guise protested if he ever caught him [Gifford] he should die for it, for that he performed it not before this . . .

> that Richard Gifford, brother to George Gifford, was privy to this vowed attempt by his brother George against Her Majesty . . .

Gifford was duly arrested, and was examined in the Tower on August 23. He was questioned about his dealings with the Jesuits in Paris, particularly Father Persons, and with the outlaw priest John Ballard, alias Captain Fortescue, now under arrest at Wood Street; and about his receipt of money and intelligence from the "Duke of Gwyse." He denied it all. His elegantly carved graffiti can still be seen on the walls of the Beauchamp Tower: DOLOR PATIENTIA VIN-CITUR—patience conquers sorrow.

He was free by the end of the year. This was a very brief spell in the Tower, and confirms what is obvious enough, that the assassination offer of 1583 was nothing more than a lure, a casting in the waters of sedition. Gifford was working as a "projector," or agent provocateur: an infiltrator into Catholic conspiracy. There is the element of the con man: He stings Morgan there in Paris. The sum mentioned by Castelli as the price for murdering the Queen is 50,000 francs (at current exchange rates, £5,000: something like £2 million today—"Day of the Jackal" prices). It was never likely that Gifford would get his hands on that, but according to Savage he did get something: 800 crowns or pounds. (Savage cannot remember which: He had been under torture for some days.) But the con man is covered by the cloak of semiofficial sanction. It is probable Gifford had some kind of backing for this charade, perhaps as an agent of Sir Christopher Hatton, with whom he is associated at this time, and who dabbled in secret politics; or perhaps under Sir Francis

13. Gifford's Tower graffiti, August 1586

Walsingham, the spymaster himself, even now beginning to thread together the web of the Babington plot.

We see Gifford here as the political opportunist, walking that thin line between treason and government service. It was a dangerous business: The Welshman William Parry, another courtier with a sideline in burglary, played the same regicidal game. He was hanged for treason at Westminster, in 1585, claiming to the last that he had been working for the Queen all along.

After his release from the Tower, George Gifford disappears from view. In 1586 he is said to be going to Constantinople. In 1590 he is again given leave to travel abroad. And in 1595 he is given charge of the *Lion's Whelp,* and sails for South America as the Vice-Admiral of Ralegh's El Dorado fleet.

* * *

LAWRENCE KEYMIS, who captained the old *gallego,* or galliot, on the Atlantic crossing, was the scholar of the expedition. A close associate of Thomas Harriot, he has in Guiana something of Harriot's status on the Virginia Voyage ten years earlier: The scientific observer, the mathematical adviser. One would call him the "discoverer" of the expedition, were it not that Ralegh counted himself to fill that role. He was the natural choice to lead the smaller, subsequent expedition of 1596, which attempted Manoa from a more easterly route, and he was there again with Ralegh on his last voyage of 1617–18. From that last voyage we have a glimpse of him, as seen by a captured Spanish soldier: "He was a tall, slim man, with a cast in one eye."

Keymis was a native of Wiltshire, aged thirty-three at the time of the Guiana Voyage. He had a brilliant Oxford career behind him. Matriculating at Balliol in 1581, at the late age of nineteen, he was almost immediately elected to a fellowship because of his proficiency in mathematics. He was a contemporary and friend of Harriot, then a student at St. Mary's Hall. He proceeded to his M.A. in 1586 and by 1588—though still nominally a fellow at Oxford—he is found in London. A year later, probably through the influence of Harriot, Keymis resigned his fellowship and became a member of Ralegh's household: part of his scientific team.

Already a noted mathematician, he had also gained a reputation in another part of the rambling mansion of late Elizabethan science—alchemy. As such he was highly praised by Dr. Gabriel Harvey. On his copy of a distiller's broadsheet, dated 1588, Harvey writes: "Now M. [i.e., Master] Keymis, the great Alchymist of London." The broadsheet advertises the wares of the chemist John Hester, trading at the Sign of the Furnaces on Paul's Wharf. Hester himself had earlier dedicated a book of chemical recipes to Ralegh. We glimpse here an early coterie—Keymis, Hester, Harriot, Adrian Gilbert—which suggests that Ralegh's famous interest in chemistry was already advanced.

One inference from this is that Keymis's prominence in Ralegh's South American projects derives in part from mineralogical expertise relating to his studies and experiments as the "great alchymist" of Ralegh's circle.

Keymis performed various administrative duties for Ralegh. He had a clerk's post in the Wine Office and a military post in Jersey, both worth £100 per annum, and was a secretary-cum-bailiff in Ralegh's household. His small, neat, self-effacing signature appears at the bottom of various deeds and documents at Sherborne. A suit of 1610 shows him as a tobacco broker: a grocer named Axtell owed Keymis £53 "for tobacco bought by the said Axtell of [i.e., from] Sir Walter Rawleigh." In his early will (1597) Ralegh bequeathed him £100 from the sale of his ship, the *Roebuck.*

Keymis remained doggedly faithful to Ralegh after the attainder of 1603, and was probably his chief business-agent during his imprisonment in the Tower. It was Keymis who would negotiate as well as he could the confiscation of Sherborne, and its transfer to James's favorite Carr, for which Ralegh would receive £8,000. Under the shadow of the ax in 1603, Ralegh wrote to his wife: "Be good to Keymis, for he is a perfect honest man."

GIFFORD AND Keymis are two sides of the Guiana Voyage—the adventurer and the intellectual. The third important figure was the military chief of the expedition, Captain Robert Calfield. Calfield had been part of Ralegh's privateering crew of 1592 that took the Portuguese land carrack, the *Madre de Dios.* He was aboard the *Roebuck,* under the command of Ralegh and then, after a royal summons forced Ralegh's return, under Sir John Burgh. He took part in the unauthorized plundering of the carrack, though was not one of the chief culprits. (He had "two cods of musk" in his possession.) In his deposition concerning the stolen booty, he is described as "Capt Cawefield of the *Roebuck,* a Lieut-Col by land." He was, in other words, a high-ranking soldier, and it is as such that he features in the *Discoverie.* He is the leader of the expedition's military "companies." In Spanish documents, he is described as the "Commander-in-Chief" of the English troops when they raided Cumaná toward the end of the voyage.

Calfield is associated with Captain Robert Cross, who was also part of the *Madre de Dios* foray, and he was the captain of the ship that Ralegh describes as a "small bark of Captain Cross's." Cross himself was not on the expedition; naval documents show that he was in command of the Queen's ship *Swiftsure* in the summer of 1595. (I have considered the possibility that this *is* the "small bark" of the Guiana Voyage, but I do not think it can be.) Ralegh did not have a high opinion of Cross, as one gathers from his comments about the *Madre de Dios* engagement: "Cross was most to blame, and dealt lewdly to leave the carrack and steal away from Sir Martin [Frobisher]. I have always served him to my power, but his mad behaviour is too insolent in this action."

Calfield is one of the trusties of the expedition. Another is Jacob Whiddon. In 1586, as we saw, he captained Ralegh's privateer, the *Serpent,* and brought home the "gentleman of Spain," Pedro Sarmiento. In 1588 he commanded the *Roebuck,* which was employed as a scout and service-ship in Lord Admiral Howard's fleet against the Armada. In 1593, he was sent to Trinidad to scout out the Orinoco estuary and to parley with Antonio de Berrio, both of which he accomplished. Whiddon is the grizzled master seaman of the Guiana Voyage. Nothing is known of him other than his maritime career and Ralegh's estimation of him as "most honest and valiant." He may well be a Devonian, and is perhaps one of the six sons of Sir John Whiddon of Chagford, a justice of the peace and minor court official who died in 1576.

There is a death roll at the end of the Guiana Voyage. Neither Calfield nor Whiddon made it back to England.

Another experienced sea captain on the list is Captain Clarke, almost certainly the Captain John Clarke who held commands in Gilbert's Newfoundland fleet of 1582 and in Grenville's Virginia fleet of 1585. The following year he was captain of Ralegh's privateer the *Golden Noble,* with a crew that probably included the poet Thomas Lodge. In an Admiralty Court deposition dated June 1592, "Johannes Clercke, gentleman" states that he was born in Saffron Walden, that he had lived in London for twenty years, and that he had known Lord Thomas Howard (the Lord Admiral's brother) since he was a teenager. He was about thirty-six years old at the time of the Guiana Voyage.

Among the trusties I would also place John Douglas and Edward Hancock. Douglas is mentioned as a "ship-master" in 1589, when he appraised the "tackle & furniture" of the *Black Dog* for the Admiralty. He was involved with Harriot in the compiling of that navigational "rutter" used for the Guiana Voyage. He sailed as the master of Ralegh's flagship, and appears in the *Discoverie* as a staunchly dependable figure: the kind of man it was useful to have around. Edward Hancock was a "servant" of Ralegh's both before and after the voyage. In April 1594 Ralegh "very earnestly" urged his suitability for the office of "Clerk of the Peace" in Devon: an important judicial post. Back home from Guiana, Hancock personally delivered letters from Ralegh to Cecil, carrying Ralegh's seal with him so that he could close up some other letters after Cecil had read them. He is a trusted employee, an amanuensis, rather piquantly out of place in the tropics of Guiana.

ALSO AMONG the personnel was a batch of eager young relatives, all members of that extended, intermarried family of Devonian landowners and shipping magnates of which Ralegh was part. These were his nephew John Gilbert; his "cousin Greeneveile"; another cousin, the oddly named Buttshead Gorges; and Captain Thynne.

John Gilbert was the eldest son of Sir Humphrey and his wife Anne, née Archer. His portrait, painted in his early thirties, shows a handsome, thin-faced, saturnine man (he has an almost Spanish cast; some of the portraits of his father show the same). The mood is melancholy, aloof; the gaze seems filled with some bitterness. This is not the rather wild young man of the Guiana Voyage; time has altered but not exactly mellowed him. He was born in the early 1570s, and was still a minor when his father drowned aboard the *Squirrel*. He did not inherit wealth until the death of his uncle, Sir John, and was, as Ralegh later reminded him, a young man "of no ability"—in other words, no means—when he sailed for Guiana.

In his teens, as was de rigueur in this sort of circle, he signed up

14. John Gilbert

as a soldier. He had "a command under Sir John Norris" in Brittany, probably on the 1591 expedition in support of Henry of Navarre. The following year he was part of Ralegh's privateering foray that brought in the *Madre de Dios*. The next we hear of him is in London in early 1594. He is living in rented chambers near Tower Gate; he is preparing to leave for the Low Countries; he is challenged to a duel by Sir John Burgh, who demands to meet him at dawn between Charing Cross and Hyde Park. It is not clear what the cause of the duel was: Gilbert himself affects not to know. It may have been some dispute over the *Madre de Dios* plunder. At any rate, the quarrel was not a new one, since Burgh says Gilbert should not "use any boyish excuses or delays, as he did the last time." He calls him a "young puppy," and threatens to "beat him like a boy" if he refuses the challenge.

Gilbert replies resolutely: "Whichever of us shall be the first to go one foot back shall be held to be the boy." He chooses the weapon (as is his right, as the defendant in the challenge): a single rapier. Burgh is in such a temper that he stabs and wounds Gilbert's messenger.

The last of the letters, written from court on a Tuesday, has Burgh about to ride hotfoot to London, through the night if necessary, to fight the duel. According to a funeral tablet formerly at St. Andrew's Chapel, Westminster, Burgh's untimely death (MORTE IMMATURAE PRAEREPTUS) occurred on March 7, 1594, a Thursday. He was just thirty-two. The cause of death is assumed to be Gilbert's rapier.

Burgh was a tough customer; John Gilbert, one infers, even tougher. A year after the voyage, he was with Ralegh in the action at Cádiz, where he was knighted. Not long after this, however, there was a falling-out between them. An angry letter from Ralegh survives, in a fragmentary transcript by the eighteenth-century historian, Thomas Birch; the paper was already mutilated when Birch saw it. It is undated, but the address, "to my nephew, Sir John Gilbert," shows it was written in or after 1596, when he was knighted. It concerns a dispute over some privateering venture, in which Gilbert, Ralegh, and the Lord Admiral all had shares, but it also touches bitterly on remarks Gilbert has made about the Guiana

Voyage. One can broadly guess what these were from Ralegh's stung response.

> For your command under Sir John Norrice, it is not unknown to me what it was, or if it might have been more, in whose respect it had been. For Sir John Norrice himself ever needed me; I never needed him or his help. And the private journey to Guiana had as much honour as the public journey of Britayne [i.e., Brittany], and you was [*sic*] as private in Britayne as in Guiana. . . .

> Where you say you followed the worst of my fortunes in despite of envy, I pray forget not yourself, nor do not so much mistake my fortunes. . . . It were a strange conceit to think that a nephew should be envied for going to the wars with his uncle.

Ralegh speaks of Gilbert as motivated by "passion" and "ingratitude." He is "ashamed" of his behavior. He also reminds him:

> I pray you forget not that first I saved your parsonage from Cari, in your brother's time, and next from Thynn, in your time. And but in respect of me I know how your aunt had dealt with you well enough. Again, by your pardon, do not believe that how ill soever my fortune was, but for me and by the help of your friends, you were discharged in despite of a strong opposition.

This is obscure in detail—it is tempting to read "parsonage" as personage, but the context suggests property disputes rather than physical quarrels. "Cari" is presumably Carew Ralegh, and "Thynn" is one of the Thynnes of Longleat. Ralegh concludes sternly:

> For your fortunes otherwise, fear not that I will labour to lessen them; as I will not hereafter look after them. And when mine shall be at worst, yet they shall never need your help, whatsoever yours have done mine.
>
> > Your uncle,
> > W. Ralegh

John Gilbert emerges as a volatile, abrasive, rather uppity young man; an inheritor of his father's hot temper but not necessarily of his more visionary side. He has that Elizabethan swagger that verges on the unhinged, and which, judging from his later portrait, is not to be confused with *joie de vivre.* This later squabble need not affect Gilbert's standing in the Guiana venture—he is often mentioned in the *Discoverie,* a young man in the thick of things—but it does perhaps lend some sympathy to the aggrieved John Burgh.

Captain Thynne is obviously a connection of the Thynnes of Longleat, though which one is harder to say. They were nearish neighbors of Ralegh at Sherborne, and the families were linked when Sir John Thynne's widow married Ralegh's brother Carew.

Sir John, who died in 1580, had eight sons, five of them by his second wife, Dorothy, who became Ralegh's sister-in-law. Of these, Ralegh was especially close to Charles Thynne. He is probably the "Mr Thynne of Wiltshire" who was among those questioned at Cerne Abbas during the official inquiry into Ralegh's "atheism." He was still a friend of Ralegh's at the end. A snatch of death-cell conversation between the two men is recorded: "Sir," said Thynne, fearing Ralegh appeared too nonchalant about his execution, "take heed you go not too much upon the brave hand, for your enemies will take exception to that." Ralegh replied, "Good Charles, give me leave to be merry, for this is the last merriment that ever I shall have in this world."

It is conceivable that Charles was the Thynne of the Guiana Voyage, but a more plausible candidate is his brother Henry. In 1593 or early 1594 Henry was involved in a privateering venture with Carew Ralegh that drew protests from French fishermen. A letter from Ralegh to Sir Robert Cecil, dated February 25, 1594, asked his lenience on "this gentleman, Henry Thynne," who "was an adventurer in that journey and lost all," and who now "is come up to answer the complaint of the Frenchmen." The tone of the letter is one of instinctive patronage: "I shall think myself much bound to you for any favour you can afford him." The endorsement, written by one of Cecil's secretaries, describes the bearer as Captain Henry

Thynne, which is the rank invariably given to Thynne in the *Dis-coverie*.

I think it likely that this gentleman-adventurer is the Thynne who accompanied Ralegh. If so, one has to discount the evidence that the Thynne of the Guiana Voyage was—like Calfield, Whiddon, and others—one of the casualties of the expedition, since Henry Thynne was alive and well for some years after. In about 1597 he married the elder Sir John Gilbert's widow, Elizabeth, and was later in dispute with the younger John Gilbert concerning the estates at Compton Castle (probably the dispute referred to in Ralegh's letter to Gilbert above). The casualty evidence is debatable, certainly, and on balance I think it likely that the Thynne of the Guiana Voyage was Henry Thynne.

Buttshead Gorges was a younger brother of Ralegh's friend Arthur Gorges. His name is actually a version of—doubtless the pronunciation of—Budockshide. His mother, Winifred, was the daughter of Roger Budockshide of St. Budeaux, Devon.

John Grenville was the son of Sir Richard Grenville, who had carried Ralegh's colonists to Roanoke, and whose death in action aboard the *Revenge* in 1591 is described in Ralegh's pamphlet, *A Report of the Truth of the Fight About the Isles of Azores,* which tract—rather snappier than its title—is the literary precursor to the *Dis-coverie*.

THESE ARE some of the "Captaines and Gentlemen" who accompanied Ralegh: spies, scholars, soldiers, sailors, and well-born young blades. And there is another young man. He arrives on the scene with George Gifford; he is described variously as Gifford's "servant" and his "man." He is a shadowy but engaging figure, an unsung Elizabethan American: Francis Sparry. (The name is also spelled Sparrow—the same indeterminate final syllable as Christopher Marley or Marlowe—but his own spelling is Sparrey or Sparry.)

Francis Sparry is frequently mentioned in accounts of the voyage, but for one thing only: He was actually left there in Guiana, along with Ralegh's cabin boy Hugh Godwin, when the rest of the expedition returned home. He remained among the Indians for some months, but was captured by Spanish soldiers. After many years he made it back to England and penned a brief account of his experiences. This was later published by Samuel Purchas, from Hakluyt's papers, in *Purchas His Pilgrims* (1625).

I was tantalized by this man whose experience of South America was so much fuller, and more extreme, than all the others: the marooned Englishman watching the last boat leave round a bend in the river. Nothing seemed to be known of him except what I relate above. I can now add a few details on his early life, thanks largely to the researches of the late Stella Sparry, the wife of a collateral descendant, Erle Sparry. She also led me to that neglected cache of documents from Sparry's period of imprisonment in Madrid.

Francis Sparry was baptized at St. Margaret's, Westminster, on January 8, 1569. In a Spanish report of his capture in Guiana, it is said he was twenty-five years old when left by Ralegh in mid-1595; he was in fact twenty-six. He was the son of Francis Sparry senior, and the grandson of William Sparry of Moneyhill Hall, Worcs. This family seat survives today, near King's Norton. Little trace of the Elizabethan building remains; the house is now a mental hospital. There was also a Devon branch of the family: a Richard Sparry, M.P. for Totnes, whose first wife's niece married Ralegh's cousin, Charles Champernowne; and whose second wife was Prothesia Bodley, the daughter of Sir Thomas who founded the Bodleian Library. There was also an Arthur Sparry in Devon, whose will was destroyed during a Luftwaffe raid on Exeter. In his Madrid deposition, Sparry states that he is a "kinsman" (*deudo*) of Ralegh's. He is presumably referring to the tenuous Champernowne connection mentioned above.

There is a strong legal tradition in the Tudor Sparrys. Francis's grandfather William was a lawyer, and profited hungrily from the distribution of church lands during the Reformation. His father Francis (a younger son) also followed the law, in Westminster and London, and had business partners among the Hanseatic merchants of the Stillyard. An uncle, John Sparry, was at the Inner Temple. It would be plausible if young Francis also studied at the Inns, but no record remains, nor of university.

It is possible he traveled abroad, for he is almost certainly the Francis Sparry whose translation of a French book of fortune-telling was on sale in London in 1591. Entitled *The Geomancie of Maister Christopher Cattan,* it is trailed on the title page as "a book no less pleasant and recreative than of a witty invention, to know all things past, present and to come." The printer of it was John Wolfe. The Stationers' Register records Wolfe's entry for copyright on "the Geomantye" on September 26, 1590. The book was sold at the shop of his neighbor and partner Edward White, trading at the sign of the Gun in St. Paul's Churchyard.

Nothing of Sparry's own composition is found in the text. The prefatory epistles and the dedication to "Lord Nicot" are all translated from the original French text, *La Géomance due Seigneur Christofe de Cattan.* This was itself a translation from Italian, made by Gabriel du Preau. It was published in Paris in 1558, with at least three subsequent editions in the next twenty years. Sparry's English version proved popular enough to merit a second edition, in 1608, printed for White by E.A., probably Edward Allde.

Initially I was disappointed at finding no jaunty note from the translator, no fragments of autobiography to play with. There is nothing. Sparry's name is not even on the title page. It is tucked away on the last page before the index: "Thus endeth the third book of Geomancie, translated by Francis Sparry." But I came to see that this very facelessness is itself biographical. The printer John Wolfe ran a stable of hack translators to churn out the French news-pamphlets that were one of his stocks-in-trade. Among these were John Eliot, author of the *Survey of France* (1592) and *Ortho-Epia Gallica* (1593); and Anthony Chute, author of *Shore's Wife* (1593): all Wolfe publications. On the same day that Wolfe registered the *Geomancie* at Stationers' Hall, he also entered for two French pamphlets, one referred to as "The True News from France brought by post 23 September" and the other as a *"Discours des Horribles Meurtres Comis par le Duc de Savoy."* This is the milieu of Sparry's book: hack translation work for the booksellers of St. Paul's. The translator is seldom named in these tracts; there may be others from Wolfe's press that are Sparry's work.

This presses Francis Sparry into interesting company. John Eliot was a writer of great verve. He had the satirical, slightly surreal comic touch of Thomas Nashe, whom he knew and admired. Others who worked for Wolfe—Chute and the disreputable poet Barnabe Barnes—came under the blanketing effect of Nashe's chief enemy, Dr. Gabriel Harvey, and contributed to his "ink-squittering" tirade against Nashe, *Pierce's Supererogation* (1593), also published by Wolfe. Sparry, at work for Wolfe a couple of years earlier, brushes obliquely against these noted denizens of Elizabethan Grub Street.

The book's professional context tells us something of Sparry's circumstances. Its contents tell us less, though one assumes a certain bent in him to be given this assignment. This is not a work of sophisticated occultism, despite its attempt to sound so: "This science is no art of inchantry, as some may suppose it to be, or of divination, which is made by diabolic invention, but it is a part of natural magic, called of many worthy men the daughter of astrology." It mostly consists of diagrams—"points, pricks and lines"— and laborious interpretations thereof. It is soothsaying stuff: how and when to search for lost things, to treat afflictions, to expose unfaithful servants, to ensnare a heart. His fellow voyagers would be interested in such questions as "if the voyage which one would take in hand be long or short," "whether the wind will cause a shipwrack or not," and "the gain or profit to be done in a strange country."

We start to fix on Sparry in the early 1590s: a French speaker, a scholar of sorts, a dabbler in the fashionable hocus-pocus of "magick." He is one of those young "scholars about this city," a member of that louche fraternity living off penny-a-line work for the printers and playhouses, frequently going supperless ("dining with Duke Humphrey"), and containing among them some of the great names of Elizabethan literature.

Sparry is part of a literary element among the Elizabethan voyagers, a type exemplified by the poet and romance writer Thomas Lodge. Lodge's career, from Oxford to Inns of Court to sea voyaging, follows Ralegh's course a couple of years after him. In the mid-1580s

Lodge sailed on a privateering expedition, under a Captain Clark, to the Canaries. It was on this voyage that he wrote his romance *Rosalynde,* which he describes as "hatcht in the storms of the ocean, and feathered in the surges of many perilous seas." This was published in 1590, and supplied the plot line for Shakespeare's *As You Like It.* Lodge's captain was probably John Clarke, and the ship the *Golden Noble,* owned by Ralegh. She was off privateering in 1586, taking valuable prizes of sack, ginger, and raisins. Clarke is almost certainly the "Captain Clarke" of the Guiana expedition. In 1591 Lodge set sail once more, with Cavendish's voyage to South America. He later recalls conversing, in Latin, with a friendly sugar planter in Brazil, a Genoese named Giuseppe Adorno. At Santos he took from the Jesuits' library a religious tract in the Guaraní tongue; he later donated this literary plunder to the new Bodleian Library, his inscription noting that he "brought it from Brazil in his own hand." After his return he published a romance featuring an Inca princess, *A Margarite of America.* This appeared in 1596, probably cashing in on the Guiana craze.

And then there is John Donne, who a year after the Guiana Voyage was part of Ralegh's squadron at Cádiz, and whose presence on the Azores Voyage of 1597 is wonderfully recorded in his two verse-letters, "The Storm" and "The Calm."

And then there is the unnamed young gentleman whose literary tastes are described in an account of the Earl of Cumberland's voyage to Puerto Rico in 1596. In the Atlantic off southern France, "while we were at morning prayer, his Lordship happened to see a gallant of the company (purposely I name him not) reading of *Orlando Furioso.*" This was the hugely popular romance by Ariosto, doubtless in the translation by Sir John Harington first published in 1591. (Perhaps he was reading the passage describing the Amazons.) The Earl told the offender, in front of the entire company, that "God would serve us accordingly if we served not him better," and that "if again he took him in the like manner, he would cast his book overboard, and turn himself out of the ship."

There were poets, scribblers, and bookworms aboard these ships.

15. Autograph of Francis Sparry

Ralegh said of Sparry that he "could describe a country with his pen," ostensibly the reason for leaving him in Guiana. One can now see the context of this remark. I like this chipper, minor young Elizabethan whose career flits from the bookstalls of St. Paul's to the banks of the Orinoco to the dungeons of Madrid. His handwriting, in the Madrid papers, is elegant, fluid, and unfussy. We will hear more of him in this story.

[7]

Atlantic Crossing

*   *   *

E ARLY ON the morning of Thursday, February 6, 1595, the
ships of the First Guiana Voyage sailed out of Plymouth
Sound and into the English Channel. Just three ships set
off. Preston's fleet remained in harbor. So too did the *Lion's Whelp,*
for reasons unknown; she left a few days later and is next sighted by
Ralegh off Trinidad in early April. It is a depleted fleet that sets off
in search of El Dorado: three wooden vessels—the flagship, the
"small bark," and the *gallego*—packed with soldiers and prospectors. The embarkation is not included among De Bry's engravings
for the *Discoverie.* I do not see it as one of those proud maritime
scenes that so stirred the Elizabethans: more as a kind of gold rush
scene.

On February 9 they sighted Cape Finisterre. They sailed south
past the Berlenga Islands and "the Rock" (Cape Roca, off Lisbon).
Somewhere off the coast of Portugal they lost sight of Keymis's
gallego. The fleet was now down to two ships.

On February 17, after eleven days at sea, they reached the Canary
Islands. They put in at Fuerteventura. Here they rested for a couple
of days, and "relieved our companies with some fresh meat." ("Com-
panies" here refers specifically to the companies of soldiers aboard.)
They then moved on to Tenerife. They stayed there for about a week,
waiting—Ralegh says—for the remainder of the fleet: the *Lion's
Whelp* and the ships of Captain Preston, delayed at Plymouth; and
Keymis's galliot, blown off-course en route.

When none of these showed up, Ralegh and Calfield set off on
the longest leg of the crossing. The date of their departure from
Tenerife must be about February 28. The voyage from the Canaries

to Trinidad took a little over three weeks, therefore, for they arrived at "the Trinedado" on March 22.

THE CROSSING takes half a paragraph in Ralegh's *Discoverie,* written in brisk ship's-log style. Other documents, however, disclose some incidents he does not mention. The first is a report, dated March 20 and forwarded to Cecil by Arthur Gorges on April 1. It concerned a Portuguese fishing vessel brought into Plymouth by "one Rowe," who had captured it off Cape San Vicente on February 27. "The Portingales of this ship," the report says,

> affirmed that their ship, with 5 other Portingales of the same lading and from the same place, were all taken before by Sir Walter Ralegh, the 24 February, betwixt the Cape and the Islands; and that he had some of the principal men aboard him for two days; and finding their lading to be but fish, as mullets, bonitoes and purgose, he took some small quantity out of every ship, also a pipe of wine and a pipe of water, and so let them pass.

The authorities at Plymouth had heard a yarn or two. Here were some Portuguese fishermen, nervous and disorientated, claiming to have met the legendary Sir Walter, and to have been treated by him in this chivalrous, Robin Hood style. Was it true? They were soon convinced that it was:

> One of these Portingales, John Gonzalicis, boatswain of the prize, affirmed that he had served Don Antonio at London, and there knew Sir Walter Ralegh very well; who by divers descriptions gave sufficient testimony of knowledge of him. He also affirmed that when he was prisoner aboard him, he saw a pinnace in two halves, with other particular tokens of his ship; whereby we doubt not but he saw him.

This information is good. We learn that on February 24 Ralegh's ships, skulking off Tenerife, encountered a flotilla of six 80-ton Portuguese fishing vessels; that he took them in typical privateering style;

and that he spent two days questioning the "principal men," including a former servant of Don Antonio, the troublesome Portuguese pretender who had squabbled with Ralegh's prisoner Sarmiento.

What is curious is that Gonzaliques describes Ralegh's fleet as having *seven* ships.

> He was in all 7 sail, of which two were carvels that they [the Portuguese] deemed he had taken before them; and when Sir Walter had put them off, they observed he with his fleet set their course South South West.

This seems quite at odds with Ralegh's own account, which expressly states that he left the Canaries with just two vessels, "mine own ship" and the "small bark."

According to Gonzaliques, two of the fleet were prizes that Ralegh had taken earlier: They were "carvels," or caravels, small light ships much used by the Spanish and Portuguese. This suggests there was another unrecorded incident on the voyage, sometime before February 24, which resulted in the capture of these caravels.

This gives us four of the seven ships seen by Gonzaliques. What about the other three? It is possible that one was the pinnace, seen in halves aboard the flagship but now, perhaps, assembled and afloat, to ease congestion aboard the bigger ships. The remaining two are either exaggerations, or they are yet more "prizes" seized by Ralegh en route.

Further incidents are described in a letter to Lady Ralegh from a certain Captain White. Dated May 10, it contains the following news from the Canaries:

> My Lord [i.e., Ralegh] came thither, and rode before Garycherby [?] three days, sending the boat and pinnace ashore for water. A Spaniard ran away from them, and told that it was Sir W. R., not Sir Fras Drake, and with four ships in his company. On March 6 my Lord landed, but by reason of the great ordinance he drew aboard again, out of the reach of shot. In riding there he took a Spanish ship laden with fish, and sent the Captain ashore to fetch wine, sugar and bread, promising to restore him his ship and company, which was accord-

ingly done. He also took twenty butts of wine from a Fleming, and
then left Garycherby.

This seems to add one more, the "Fleming," to the list of ships taken
by Ralegh (the Spanish fishing vessel referred to is probably one of the
Portuguese ships of the earlier report). It also adds news of a brief and
unsuccessful foray onto the island. The date given for this landing,
March 6, seems faulty. It is probably continental dating; by English
reckoning (ten days behind) this would be February 24.

THESE REPORTS give us a fascinating glimpse around the edge
of the "frame" of the *Discoverie.* Ralegh rattles through the outward
voyage, makes it as routine as a local bus ride, but in fact it was
quite full of incident. If all these reports are true, he was involved
in at least three aggressive encounters in the Atlantic (the Spanish
caravels, the Portuguese fishermen, and the Flemish ship) and at least
one exchange of fire with the Spanish troops at Tenerife.

All this is erased from his own account of the voyage. Such omission is at odds with the style of the narrative, which is so clearly (at
this point) that of the ship's log or journal. Ralegh says as much in
his dedication to Howard and Cecil. He asks them to forgive the
roughness of his "discourse." He has written it "without the defence
of art." He has "neither studied phrase, form nor fashion." It is
deliberately presented as a rough-and-ready account, one of those
"true and faithful reports" that are the staple of Elizabethan travel
writing. Here, though, the style serves as a concealment, disguising
what is actually a rather unfaithful report.

Why does he suppress these incidents? They are not very glorious,
certainly. His loot consisted of nothing more than some fish and
some wine: faintly comic as plunder, perhaps. But I think there is
another, more central point, which is that Ralegh wished to disso-
ciate his voyage from any taint of privateering. (Or, at least, that by
the time he came to write the *Discoverie,* that was what he wished
to do.) Other fudgings and omissions in the narrative will bear this
out. It is, in Ralegh's mind, a different kind of adventure entirely.

[8]

Trinidad

* * *

THEY ARRIVED at Trinidad on Sunday, March 22, and anchored off the southwestern corner of the island, called Curiapan by the natives and Punto de Gallo by the Spanish: now known as Icacos Point. They "abode" there four or five days, seeing neither Spaniard nor native. It was a time of recuperation and reconnaissance.

Coasting up to La Brea, they found a black lake with "abundance of stone pitch." This is the celebrated pitch lake, a mile and a half in diameter, still in use as a source of asphalt.

> This Terra de Bri [i.e., Brea] is a piece of land of some two leagues long and a league broad, all of stone pitch or bitumen, which riseth out of the ground in little springs or fountains; and so running a little way, it hardeneth in the air and covereth all the plain.

According to Carib legend, the Chayma Indians once lived here. They angered the gods by eating the sacred hummingbird (*iere*), and in revenge their entire village was swallowed up in this lake of darkness. (Ralegh does not mention this legend, though he is aware of the "Sayma," or Chayma.)

Here they "trimmed" their ships. They found the pitch "excellent good." It "melteth not with the sun, as the pitch of Norway, and therefore for ships trading the south parts very profitable." According to Sir Robert Schomburgk, traveling the region in the 1830s, the pitch is "well-adapted for preserving the bottoms of ships against the destructive worm, the *teredo navalis*," but he also notes that Admiral Lord Cochrane, the hero of South American independence, "made several experiments" with it, and found so much oil was needed to render it pliable "that it far surpassed the price of common pitch."

The pitch lake can be visited today, though the *South American Handbook* warns, "it has been described by disappointed tourists as looking like a parking lot."

At Trinidad, Ralegh makes his first personal appearance in his story of the voyage, detaching himself from the fleet, taking his barge and a few men armed with muskets, and throwing himself wholeheartedly into an excited reconnaissance of the island.

> I myself coasted it in my barge, close aboard the shore, and landed in every cove the better to know the island, while the ships kept the channel. . . .
>
> I left the ships and kept by the shore, the better to come to speech with the inhabitants, and also to understand the rivers, watering places and ports of the island. . . .
>
> Three parts [of the island] I coasted with my barge, that I might the better describe it.

He is the energetic, inquisitive explorer: the "discoverer" in the sense that the term was used on these expeditions—the gatherer of data. He is close in to shore, "aboard" the island.

Slowly the little English fleet coasted northward toward their first objective: Puerto de los Hispanioles, or Port of Spain. They were now entering enemy territory. They looked daily for the remainder of the fleet, but in vain. On April 4, according to Spanish sources, they were off Port of Spain.

Here, at last, they saw some Spaniards: a small company guarding the "descent," or landing stage. They made "a sign of peace," and Ralegh dispatched Captain Whiddon to speak with them (he presumably spoke Spanish). They seemed "desirous to trade with us, and to enter into terms of peace," and some of them came on board. That evening, the Indian chief Cantyman, whom Whiddon had met on his reconnaissance voyage of 1593, came aboard. From him they learned the strength of the Spanish and the distance to their "city," San José (or Josef) de Oruña, the Spanish garrison founded by Berrio in 1592. This lay about ten miles inland from the port.

As important as this strategic information, Ralegh learned that Berrio himself was at San José. It was relief to learn that Berrio was alive at all. There had been rumors: he "was said to be slain in his second attempt of Guiana, but was not." (As Ralegh knew that Berrio was alive and well in 1593, when Whiddon met him, he cannot be referring to one of Berrio's actual *entradas*. The rumors probably arose from the 1594 expedition, under Berrio's sidekick De Vera, when ten Spaniards were killed by Orinoco Indians.)

Over the next few days Ralegh wound the Spanish into his confidence. They came aboard "to buy linen of the company, and such other things as they wanted, and also to view our ships and company." The mood is relaxed: détente. The Spaniards are "entertained kindly" and "feasted after our manner." The captured butts of wine are broached. Tongues are loosened, and Ralegh listens.

> I learned of one and another as much of the estate of Guiana as I could, or as they knew; for those poor soldiers having been many years without wine, a few drafts made them merry, in which mood they vaunted of Guiana and of the riches thereof, and all what they knew of the ways and passages. . . .
>
> I daily learned more of Guiana, the rivers and passages, and of the enterprise of Berrio, by what means or fault he failed, and how he meant to prosecute the same.

He appears casually interested, nothing more. He said nothing of his own purpose to enter Guiana, "but bred in them an opinion that I was bound only for the relief of those English which I had planted in Virginia, whereof the bruit was come among them."

From this time—the arrival of Ralegh's ships off Port of Spain in early April—we begin to get an independent (but by no means impartial) view of events from the Spanish side. There are two authoritative reports, both sent to Spain from the neighboring island of Margarita. The first, by the governor Pedro de Salazar, can be dated to late June 1595; the second, by the *licenciado* Pedro de Liaño, is a year later, but uses sources (including Berrio himself) that were not available to Salazar. These are, like those earlier snippets of documentation on the outward journey, a second camera, turned on the action from the opposite angle.

The group of Spaniards they met with at Port of Spain, we learn, was a detachment led by Rodrigo de la Hoz, Berrio's nephew. He came with eight soldiers and twenty-five Indians, and brought provisions: "fowl, venison and fruits of the country." When he arrived at the shore, "there presently came from the flagship a boat with a white flag of truce." This is clearly Captain Whiddon, coming to parley. He assures them that "they had not come with intention of doing harm, but only in search of refreshment." Don Rodrigo and the others are invited on board the flagship, "to amuse themselves and drink one another's health." Here is the carousing that Ralegh exploited to get them to talk. The soldiers onshore were not forgotten: "There on land food and drink were produced." As he conversed with the Spaniards,

> Guaterrale . . . mentioned that he had founded a town in Canaveral on the coast of Florida, and that he only came to the port to get wood which he needed, and to carry weapons and ammunition to the English who were in the Canaveral.

Here, in garbled form, is the "bruit" he put around, that he was only passing through en route for Virginia.

All this corroborates Ralegh closely, and fleshes out the brusque tones of the *Discoverie.* According to Liaño, Ralegh also conveyed a "message" to Berrio, saying that he came in peace, and "was his friend," and wished to meet him. In token of this friendship,

> he sent him [Berrio] a gold ring, with a letter, in which he said that if he needed men or ammunition, or anything else to pacify the country, he would give them to him; and that his men were conquerors of the Indies.

This is additional information, not mentioned in the *Discoverie:* dangerous promises, empty brags.

THIS INITIAL contact—trading, drinking, conversing—lasted for about three days. Then, on the evening of April 7, the decision was made to attack San José. This was swiftly and ruthlessly accomplished.

Here is Ralegh's account:

> Taking a time of most advantage, I set upon the *corp du guard* in the evening, and having put them to the sword, sent Captain Calfield onwards with 60 soldiers, and myself followed with 40 more, and so took their new city which they called St Joseph by break of day. They abode not any fight after a few shot, and all being dismissed but only Berrio and his companion, I brought them with me aboard, and at the instance of the Indians I set their new city of St Joseph's on fire.

Here is Governor Salazar's:

> It now being late . . . [there] came another boat from the flagship, which joined the others [i.e., at the shore]. And a signal was made from the flagship to the four soldiers with Berrio's nephew, and also to the fourteen who were busy eating. These were stabbed with poignards and halberds. Thus they were killed without being able to help or defend each other. Presently there landed from the fleet about 120 men, and that night, accompanied by Indians and guided by those they had brought from England, they set out by the land road, in the direction of the place where Governor Berrio was, about three leagues distant. Without the slightest warning, they fell upon the place at daybreak, and slaughtered all the Spaniards they could lay hands on.

There is one notable difference in these accounts. According to Ralegh, the Spaniards of San José fled or were "dismissed"; according to Salazar, they were slaughtered. He is quite insistent: The English "did not spare one Spaniard on whom they could lay hands." Liaño also says, dramatically: "At sunrise . . . they entered the place, crying out with a loud voice: 'Peace! Peace!' And saying these words they went on, killing and wounding those whom they met." The actual figures given by the Spanish are thirty-six men dead—nineteen killed at the beach (the *"corp du guard"* under Rodrigo de la Hoz) and seventeen in the town itself. As with the suppressed mention of his piracies in the Canaries, Ralegh appears to soften the harsher side of his expedition.

Thus the English enter San José, the capital of Trinidad, though in reality nothing more than a little wood-built encampment of huts, a church, and a Franciscan convent. Among those who escaped were sixteen soldiers and a friar—perhaps Fray Carillo, who had been in Guiana with De Vera in 1593—who hid themselves in the forest. Some of them found their way to La Brea, and from there crossed to Margarita by canoe. They arrived on April 12. It is their accounts—"the said maltreated Spaniards"—that are the basis of Salazar's report.

There was also a French soldier at San José, "Juan de Mumpabila" (perhaps Jean de Montpelier?). He too escaped, and found his way to Caracas, "where he reported what had occurred."

After two days, during which they remove "cloth and goods," the town is razed. Ralegh leads his true prize—the captured *conquistador* Berrio and his lieutenant Alvaro Jorge—back down the "land-road" to the harbor, and conducts him aboard the flagship. This very same day, the *Lion's Whelp* and Keymis's galliot hove into view, "and in them divers gents and others, which to our little army was a great comfort and supply."

This was undoubtedly a high point for Ralegh. He had captured Berrio, sacked the Spanish garrison, established relations with the natives, and he had, for the first time, the full complement of his fleet (and still, no doubt, expected the arrival of Preston's ships).

It is this moment of triumph, on about April 10, 1595, that is depicted in the first of Theodore de Bry's engravings of the expedition. At the center of the picture is Berrio, a gaunt figure in a tall Spanish hat; beside him his companion, Jorge. Both have their hands bound in front of them. Behind them is an escort of four musketeers.

16. The capture of Berrio at Trinidad

The English three-masters wait offshore, and Ralegh—dressed to the nines and armed to the teeth—points the prisoner peremptorily into the ship's boat. Elsewhere on the shore are Indians in feather head-dresses talking genially with a group of English soldiers. Farther in the distance a column of soldiers marches along the land road. This is stylized but generally authentic.

THE ENGRAVING focuses on the capture of Berrio, but at least as important is the friendly alliance with the Indians, as expressed in that background group.

In San José, Ralegh had seen evidence of atrocities suffered by the natives. He found five Indians chained together, "almost dead from famine, and wasted with torments." Among other tortures, the Spaniards had "dropped their naked bodies" with burning bacon fat. They were *caciques,* local chieftains ("lords or little kings" is Ralegh's graceful translation of *cacique*). He solemnly names them: Wanna-wanare, Carroaori, Maquarima, Tarroopana, Aterima. The exotic syllables roll out like some lost line from Marlowe's *Tamburlaine.*

Ralegh gives good information about the Indian tribes of Trinidad, predominantly Carib and Arawak. The *Discoverie* is still cited in modern ethnological studies. Island tribes suffered far worse, numerically, than on the mainland, having no hinterland to retreat to. In 1831, Schomburgk noted, the "remnant of those numerous tribes who inhabited Trinidad when Ralegh visited amounted to 762," and now they are virtually extinct. Ralegh's acute interest in them contrasts with the Spanish settlers', who left no comparable documentation. He correctly gives the indigenous name of the island, "Cairi." This is from the Carib *iri* or *iere,* and means "place of the hummingbird."

Ralegh's rapprochement with the American Indians will become a major theme in this story. His respect for them is remarkable, against the backdrop of standard European attitudes, though it is also, of course, politically expedient.

Before leaving Port of Spain, Ralegh "called all the captains of the island together," and delivered a speech to them, through an interpreter.

> I made them understand that I was the servant of a Queen, who was the great *cacique* of the north, and a virgin, and had more *cacique* under her than there were trees in their island; that she was an enemy of the *Castellani* in respect of their tyranny and oppression, and that she delivered all such nations about her as were by them oppressed; and having freed all the coast of the northern world from their servitude, had sent me to free them also, and withal to defend the country of Guiana from their invasion and conquest.

This is probably more or less verbatim. He gives a message the Indians wish to hear, and even uses a language that would appeal to them: The "more than all the trees in Trinidad" trope tallies with an Indian phrase later recorded by Ralegh, where a *cacique* speaks of losing as many warriors "as there were leaves in the wood upon all the trees."

With these words ringing in their ears, the Indians were treated to the next part of the show: "I showed them Her Majesty's picture, which they so admired and honoured, as it had been easy to have brought them idolatrous thereof." He also (according to a Spanish report) "erected a high pole with the Queen's coat of arms on it."

This speech, and some of the ceremony accompanying it, was to be repeated many times during his *entrada* up the Orinoco. He gave it, he says, "to the rest of the nations [i.e., tribes], both in my passing to Guiana, and to those of the borders," with the result that "in that part of the world Her Majesty is very famous and admirable, whom they now call *Ezrebeta Cassipuna Aquerewana,* which is as much as Elizabeth the Great Princess." (*Aquerewana,* elsewhere written by Ralegh as *acarewana,* is a Carib word for chieftain.) He also distributed her image in the costly form of gold sovereigns.

> I gave among them many more pieces of gold than I received, of the new money of 20 shillings with Her Majesty's picture to wear, with promise that they would become her servants thenceforth.

Ralegh presents himself as imperial envoy, rather than invader, and the Virgin Queen as the *"cacique* of the North," the liberator from Spanish oppression, the godlike creature whose talisman the natives now "wear" in place of the old false images. It is the terminology of crusade, and has some of the ideological duplicity one associates with that word.

The Trinidad ceremony is also, though Ralegh does not specify it as such, a ritual of possession, and can be compared with other English ceremonies in America. In Newfoundland, for instance, Sir Humphrey Gilbert took possession of the "harbour of St. John and two hundred leagues every way" in the name of the Queen, and to signify this "had delivered unto him, after the custom of England, a rod and a turf of the same soil, entering possession also for him, his heirs and assigns for ever." He then "caused the Queen's image to be graved in lead, and fixed upon a pillar of wood," as did Ralegh in Trinidad. A similar ritual was observed by Domingo de Vera in Guiana, taking possession on behalf of Berrio in 1593. A cross was erected, and

> the Captains and soldiers kneeled down and did due reverence unto the said cross, and thereupon the Master of the Camp [i.e., de Vera] took a bowl of water and drank it off, and took more and threw it abroad on the ground. He also drew out his sword, and cut the grass of the ground and the boughs of the trees, saying, "I take this possession in the name of the king, Don Philip, our master, and of his governor Antonio de Berrio."

These rituals of expropriation, this one-sided discourse enacted by Europeans on the shores of the New World, have been much anatomized in the "new historicist" analysis of the conquest, notably in Stephen Greenblatt's *Marvellous Possessions*.

ON ABOUT April 13 the fleet left Port of Spain and headed back south. They anchored in a harbor at or near Icacos Point. There—Salazar learns from his spies on the island—they are "busy felling trees, and making defences and a fort." They land pieces of artillery; they erect once more the arms of Queen Elizabeth on a "pole." The nature of this fort can be guessed from John White's meticulous depiction of the English fort built at Puerto Rico by the Virginia voyagers of 1585. It would not be as large as that one, but nonetheless quite sizable. The full complement of men was probably about 250 now (Ralegh had 100 soldiers when he attacked San José, and doubtless other men back at the ships; the *Whelp* and the galliot arrived later, bringing more).

This was Ralegh's base: a garrison against the Spanish, a base for reconnaissance of the mainland opposite, the Eastern Main, the gateway to El Dorado. From here they were, at its closest, about ten miles from the coast of South America.

Here also begins in earnest the grilling of Antonio de Berrio: "I gathered from him as much of Guiana as he knew."

Berrio was now nearly seventy years old. He was Old Spain through and through, a soldier, a Captain of the Guard; this doubtless impressed Ralegh, who was himself—though now only nominally—the Queen's Captain of the Guard. There is a note of undisguised admiration in Ralegh's description of him.

This Berrio is a gent well descended, and had long served the Spanish king in Millain, Naples, the Low Countries and elsewhere, very valiant and liberal, and a gent of great assuredness and of a great heart.

He admires Berrio in much the same way he had admired Sarmiento: a Spanish *hidalgo,* a veteran explorer, a repository of coveted American secrets. Here again that element of rapprochement, of the Hispanicization of Ralegh: "Guaterrale." The New World is the place where enmities are forgotten, where the boundaries dissolve.

And so they talk. Berrio tells of his grueling *entradas,* of the Indians of Guiana, of the richness of Manoa, of the many branches of the Orinoco River, which is the highway thither. They discuss the story of Juan Martínez, a chimerical figure who (Berrio asserted) had actually visited Manoa.

The atmosphere is cordial. "I used him according to his estate and worth in all things I could, according to the small means I had," says Ralegh, rather primly.

Once again there are glimpses from the Spanish angle. Salazar has spies in Trinidad (presumably Indians). To begin with they confirm the note of cordiality. On May 8 they report that Ralegh has "treated the Governor Berrio very well, entertaining him with banquets." But there is already a note of threat. Ralegh has been "persuading" Berrio

to divulge the letters which he had written to His Majesty [i.e., Philip II], saying that copies of them had been taken among his papers, describing the journey and the riches of Guayana, because

Her Majesty the Queen wished to conquer the same, and she would be disappointed if he did not do it.

A week later, the persuasion has grown more drastic, for Salazar learns that Ralegh

> intended to deliver up the said Governor Berrio to the Indians to be slain by bow-shot, and Capt Alvaro Jorge to be hanged, if they did not declare the way to Guayana, dragging them ashore with much fusillading.

Once again, this is not mentioned by Ralegh. A cordial converse or a rather rougher interrogation? (One recalls the torture of Spaniards by Whiddon's men aboard the *Serpent* in 1586, as recorded by Pedro Sarmiento.) We cannot really choose between these accounts. Each version is self-serving, each partly true.

As Ralegh relates it, it was only after he had pumped Berrio for information that he at last revealed his own intentions.

> After I had thus learned of his proceedings past and purposed, I told him that I had resolved to see Guiana, and that it was the end of my journey and the cause of my coming to Trinedado, as it was indeed. . . . Berrio was stricken into a great melancholy and sadness, and used all the arguments he could to dissuade me, and also assured the gentlemen of my company that it would be labour lost.

He told them the rivers were impassible to boats, the region too "low, sandy and full of flats." Even the Indians were "daily grounded in their *canoas* which drew but twelve inches of water." He told them the natives would flee at first contact, and would burn their towns rather than surrender them. He said "that the way was long, the winter at hand, and that the rivers beginning once to swell, it was impossible to stem the current." And—"which indeed most discouraged my company"—he said the chieftains of Guiana had "decreed" that none should trade with any Christians "because the same would be their overthrow," and that "for the love of gold the Christians meant to conquer and dispossess them of all."

Ralegh recites these formidable obstacles that lie ahead of him, then coolly says: "Many and the most of these I found to be true, but yet I resolved to make trial of all, whatsoever happened."

This is the key mood of the *Discoverie,* and of the journey that is now just beginning: to "make trial of all"—in other words, to test it out, to observe and experience at first hand what has hitherto been received as theory. It is the watchword of the empiricist, the skeptic. The idea of "trial" belongs to the theme of gold: Ore is "tried" by the goldsmith to establish its worth. The technical term for this is an "assay." This in turn is related to the literary form, the "essay," which tries and tests and analyzes a particular subject. (Both these come from French *essayer,* "to try.") The paradigm of the essayist for Elizabethans was Montaigne, whose *Essais* were published in 1580: Ralegh undoubtedly knew and admired his work, and I will look later at the influence of Montaigne's essay, *Des Canibales.* Perhaps "essay" is the best word for Ralegh's *Discoverie,* with its medley of approaches to an elusive central subject.

Making "trial" of El Dorado: we are at that dangerous point of intersection that all *doradistas* face, where the dreamed-up image of a golden city becomes the harsh reality of a journey through wilderness.

Now, at last, the journey begins: Ralegh's "trial" of America, his *entrada* into the unknown. "We then hastened away towards our purposed discovery."

PART TWO

THE
ENTRADA

―――――――――

Quien se va al Orinoco
O se muere o vuelve loco

―VENEZUELAN BOAT SONG

[9]

The Gulf of Sadness

*   *   *

THE JOURNEY begins in a boat, in the rain, with the taste of vomit not quite sluiced away by halves of lime. We are on a squally stretch of water that the early explorers called Golfo Triste, the Gulf of Sadness. There is land ahead, perhaps half a mile away, but there is nothing you can call a landmark. The coastline is low, darkish, a leisurely hedge of vegetation between the clouds and the sea. Sometimes the hedge opens, and oblique vistas of swampland stretch away. Sometimes there are colonies of birds: white egret, red ibis. They scatter as we pass, then settle back down. The eye finds nothing to hold on to; it is this, more than the weather, that makes the scene so inhospitable.

We pitch in the rain; the boatman is disgruntled. Empty cans of beer and tuna rock gently in the bilge at our feet. We might as well be lost, and it soon transpires that we are.

We have two maps with us. One is the 1:500,000 Tactical Pilotage Chart (TPC) of the area. It shows that we are at a latitude of about 10 degrees north, in the Gulf of Paria, working southeastward along the coast of Venezuela toward Boca Bagre, or Catfish Bay. The other is a photographic copy of Ralegh's "charte," according to which we are at the very gateway of the trail to El Dorado.

I have pored and puzzled over these maps. But now we're actually here. We're sitting in this boat, in this indeterminate region of gray air and brown water: water the color of ersatz milk chocolate. Everything looks the same as it did an hour ago, and both maps are for the moment quite useless.

Thus unpromisingly begins the journey to the promised land of El Dorado.

*   *   *

ON A date that cannot be precisely determined, but that I estimate to be Sunday, May 17, 1595, Sir Walter Ralegh led a small flotilla of rowboats across these sullen waters of the Golfo de Paria. The mood was one of intense expectation—he was about to touch the mainland of America for the first time in his life, as were most of the men with him—but was laced with the usual concomitants of fear, distrust, and discomfort.

It was a rough crossing: "We had as much sea to cross over in our wherries as between Dover and Calais, and in a great billow, the wind and the current being both very strong."

He had with him a hundred men, less than half the full complement of the voyage. He needed to leave mariners to man the ships, and soldiers to guard the newly built fort at Icacos Point, but the number he went with was mainly dictated by space available in the boats. A "poor troupe," he calls them: "a handful of men, being in all about 100 gentlemen, soldiers, rowers, boat-keepers, boys, and of all sorts." You can read that last phrase simply to mean et cetera, or you can read it as meaning there were some pretty desperate characters among the crew. This is not to be doubted: At its lower ranks this sort of expedition attracted, as Ralegh once phrased it, a "scum of men"—criminals, fugitives, malcontents, mercenaries. It was something recommended by his friend Richard Hakluyt in his propaganda for the Virginia expedition: The "prisons and corners of London" are full of "decayed" merchants and debtors, and "others that hide their heads." Such men, "schooled in the house of adversities," can be "employed to great uses in this purposed voyage."

Even the gentlemen, as we have seen, were rather "of all sorts." There was George Gifford, effectively Ralegh's second-in-command on the expedition: a man with an extremely checkered career, a man not always to be trusted. There was the scholar Keymis, and the scribbler Sparry, and the hot-blooded young "puppy" John Gilbert, and the surgeon Nick Mellechapp. There were the sailors Whiddon and Douglas, long-term employees in Ralegh's privateering service.

And there was Ralegh's "boy," sixteen-year-old Hugh Godwin, whose subsequent story has itself become a minor legend, one I will reluctantly disperse.

They had with them a native pilot—an "Arwacan" (i.e. an Arawak or Arhuaco) from Barima, on the southern stretch of the Orinoco Delta. The English had captured him on his way to Margarita, with canoes full of *cassava* to trade. He promised to guide the English boats "into the great river of Orenoque," in other words the Orinoco, which was their destination as they crossed the gulf.

There was also aboard a black, probably an escaped slave: a "very proper young fellow," according to Ralegh. He was to be the first of the expedition's casualties. On about day twelve of the *entrada,* jumping into the river for a swim, he was "taken and devoured" by those "ugly serpents" of the region, alligators.

OVER THE past weeks, from their base at Icacos Point, Ralegh had sent out small reconnaissance parties, across the Golfo de Paria and along the coast, looking for an "entrance" into the mainland. At first he hoped to find an inlet deep enough to allow some of the larger ships of the fleet to pass, but his searchers found none, because there are none. It was as Berrio had gloomily predicted: they "could not enter any of the rivers with any bark or pinnace." The decision was taken to use only smaller boats. Even then it was difficult to find a suitable entrance, but some time in early May, John Douglas, the master of Ralegh's flagship, set out in a barge, together with an Indian guide—"an old *cacique* of Trinedado"—and reconnoitered a part of the coast that Ralegh calls the Bay of Guanipa. There Douglas "found four goodly entrances, whereof the least was as big as the Thames at Woolwich." There were the usual problems of access in these shallow waters—"in the bay thitherward it was shoal, and but six foot of water"—but if these could be negotiated the rivers would be navigable.

The bay reconnoitered by Douglas, it can easily be established, was that which is now called the Boca Bagre, or Catfish Bay, and the "four goodly entrances" were the mouths of the Caño Bagre, the Caño Manamo (two separate channels), and the Caño Pedernales. These are indeed the biggest of the many labyrinthine branches at this end of the Orinoco Delta. They are called *caños* (channels) or *brazos* (arms), but they are in themselves sizable rivers.

It was up one of these—perhaps the larger channel of the Caño Manamo—that the expedition finally entered the mainland. They were driven by the winds, but managed to reach "the bottom of the bay," and "from thence to enter the mouth of some one of those rivers which John Dowglas had last discovered." Ralegh does not name the river at this point, but later, describing the return journey, he says:

> By the way we entered it was impossible to return, for that the river of Amana, being in the bottom of the Bay of Guanipa, cannot be sailed back by any means, both the breeze and the current of the sea were so forcible.

This seems to be clear: They entered the Orinoco Delta by a river that Ralegh called the Amana. This is undoubtedly the Manamo, and they were certainly on it later in the *entrada*. On his "charte," however, Ralegh identifies all four mouths in the bay as the mouths of Amana, so we cannot say for certain which one they entered, and probably Ralegh couldn't either.

They traveled in five rowboats. The largest of these is the vessel usually described by Ralegh as a *gallego*—in other words, a small Spanish galleon, or galliot. Francis Sparry estimated its burden at sixty tons. This vessel had crossed the Atlantic under the captaincy of Lawrence Keymis. At their base in Trinidad, Ralegh ordered it to be "cut down" and "fashioned like a galley" for the ascent upriver:

> I caused all the carpenters we had to cut down a *gallego* boat, which we meant to cast off, and to fit her with banks to row on, and in all things to prepare her the best they could, so as she might be brought to draw but five foot, for so much we had at the bar of Capuri at low water.

Her upperworks removed, and her hull reequipped as a galley, the ship was ready to be rowed upstream if winds were unfavorable. Thus stripped she had room for sixty men, though Ralegh's phrasing—"the bottom of the *gallego,* in which we thrust 60 men"—suggests it was a pretty tight squeeze, and elsewhere he speaks of men being "close pestered" together. In the *gallego* also they carried weapons and provisions: "We had no other means but to carry victual for a month in the same, and also to lodge therein as we could, and to boil and dress our meat." This "old" *gallego* has a rickety feel—a "bad *galiota,*" an "old cast *gallego.*" They were thinking of scuppering it in Trinidad, but it survives, and plays a leading part in the *entrada* up the Orinoco.

Together with the *gallego* were four smaller boats—two wherries, a barge, and the cockboat (or ship's boat) of the *Lion's Whelp.* Each of these carried ten men.

IN PURSUIT of these phantom adventurers, I crossed the Golfo de Paria in a thirty-foot, wood-built fishing boat. It was undoubtedly very similar in most respects to the smaller boats of Ralegh's party, except that it was powered not by Elizabethan "rowers" but by a pair of Yamaha 40 outboard motors. There were ten of us in the boat: the same number as traveled in Ralegh's boats.

I did not contrive these similarities. If you need to cross the Paria Gulf, this is how it's done.

We hired the boat in Guiria the previous day, not from the quiet boatman whose name was Fon and who turned out to be half Japanese, but from a scowling man called Milano. It is painted in the typical Caribbean colors: orange and blue. It is called *Yo Vine,* "I came," which seems an appropriate—or perhaps just a sarcastic—echo of Julius Caesar's famous imperial slogan.

It is a mongrel crew aboard, of which I am—nominally, alarmingly—the captain. There are three English (a Channel 4 film crew) and three Venezuelan (the boatman, Milano; and two officers of the Guardia Nacional). There is our fixer, Uwe, who is a German now living in Caracas; and our interpreter, María Teresa, a Chilean; and

Trevor, a half-caste Guyanese ("half Indian, half Indian" is how he describes himself, his father an immigrant from India, his mother an indigenous Maicatari). Trevor is, I suppose, our *maestro de campo* or camp master: a plump, genial young man with an Indian Hollywood mustache.

We were not sorry to leave Guiria, a small port on the Paria Peninsula. The place has the appurtenances of a Caribbean fishing town—a mainly black population, a dilapidated boatyard, a few scruffy palm trees, a series of almost indistinguishable provisions stores—but somewhere along the line it lost its Caribbean gaiety, its *alegría,* and succumbed to an indolent, sullen mood.

The eve of departure, we dine on swordfish and beer at the Hotel Paradise. The swimming pool is empty and scattered with big leaves. The moon is up and full, bringing surf. A few miles along the beach—exact location unknown but identified for convenience with the village of Macuro—Columbus's Spanish crew made the first recorded European landing on the American mainland. The date was August 5, 1498. They took "formal possession" the following day. The Florentine navigator Amerigo di Vespucci later claimed to have landed on the mainland earlier than Columbus. This is undoubtedly spurious, a publicity hoax, but it is he rather than Columbus who is remembered in the name America.

At the waterfront in the early gray light: boat hulls the color of washed inks, nets strung out under the almond trees, a café with bars at the front like an old-style jailhouse. Milano the boatman, dressed for the occasion in shorts and torn vest, scowls as he supervises the loading of our gear: Arriflex 16-millimeter camera, film stock in silver cans, tripods, lights, DAT sound equipment; cases called Pelicans, bags called Billinghams; a two-way radio, a kerosene stove, a first aid kit, a shotgun; hammocks, mosquito nets, machetes, fishing rods; rice, spaghetti, *arepa* flour, canned foods, cigarettes, six bottles of Pamplona rum, and several twenty-four packs of Polar beer—in short our "furniture" and "victuals."

Milano gets angry, ups the price of the crossing by two thousand bolivars. Maggie, the sound recorder, whispers in her soft Yorkshire accent, "Ooh, I bet he's a wife beater."

On the jetty we are impressed when Officer Wilves of the National Guard stoops down, and a handgun falls out of his beach shorts with a dull thud on the duckwalk. His sidekick is called Flaco—"skinny"—and has a high-pitched, somewhat sneering voice. He is from Merida, in the Andes, on the other side of the country. They say they have business over in Tucapita, but we suspect they have been sent along to keep an eye on us. No one makes this crossing for fun.

A rainstorm soaks us before we even start. An old-timer on the beach says the rain is a good sign: It keeps the winds down. The gulf is a funnel of winds and currents coming through the narrow straits between Trinidad and the mainland, known as La Boca de la Serpiente, the Snake's Mouth.

The crossing, we were told, would take *tres horas y pico:* three hours and a bit. The "bit" in this case proves as long as the rest. Once we are out of the bay, the water is choppy. The engine cuts out and we pitch violently in the swell. I have not had any breakfast, just a slug of Pamplona rum, and after a few minutes I am retching over the side. They film me, of course. Flaco slices a lime in half and passes it over to me: a remedy for nausea. Excellent for the scurvy too, no doubt.

The rain comes again, driving in across the gray water, soaking us in an instant. We huddle under waterproof ponchos and sheets of British Airways polyethylene. Uwe is sleeping, nothing visible except his hawklike nose and his absurd straw hat: a Fitzcarraldo figure. María Teresa's thick black hair is straggly in the rain. I see how Indian she looks (she is part Mapuche).

I comment on this. She laughs and says, *"Más ancestral, no?"*

Not far from the shoreline we run aground. The propeller grates and churns up a pale brown mud. Milano cuts the engine, growls for rum. We must wait, he says. Wait for what? We must wait for the tide to lift us off.

The rain has stopped. We lunch on a mulch of tuna and onion and sweet corn, mixed up in a tin pan, and looking—we inescapably conclude—like vomit.

I notice that we all have white, wrinkled hands.

Later, five hours out, bedraggled and beginning to get agoraphobic, it becomes apparent that Milano the boatman is uncertain where we are. We are looking, as Ralegh was, for a particular entrance into the Orinoco Delta, one of the mouths that he called Amana. We are finding, as he doubtless did, that everything looks the same.

Then we spy, off to our left, a small *curiara,* or canoe, with a couple of bare-chested men aboard. It has no engine; we are in paddling distance from somewhere.

Milano speeds toward them, shouts questions. He is asking them the best way in to the Caño Pedernales. They stand easily in their tiny bobbing craft, and in answer each one points in a precisely opposite direction. It was the perfect gesture; we have it on film. Then one of the men says something. I didn't catch it, but Uwe did.

"Did you hear what this guy said? He said, 'You go to the end of the sky and then turn right.'"

IN THE absence of any more reliable data, I take this as the approximate point at which our course across the Gulf, heading more or less due south from Guiria, intersects with Ralegh's, rowing westward from Icacos Point on the tip of Trinidad. I feel that the trip is at last beginning, that all that went before was a prelude. The maps ancient and modern lie damp and crumpled on my lap. I have a sense that we have entered some space between the maps: a space navigated by metaphors rather than directions. We must cross the Gulf of Sadness until we reach the end of the sky.

From now on we are on their trail. We will see much of what they saw, and perhaps feel a little of what they felt. We have not come here to find a lost city, but at this point we share with them the discomforts of the crossing, the uncertainties of direction that so easily become, under the blank gaze of the mangroves, a more pressing uncertainty about why we are here.

It was somewhere here, on this desolate stretch of the Venezuelan coast, that Sir Walter Ralegh first set foot on the mainland of America. It sounds pretty grand but I doubt it was. Very likely he went *into* America, straight up to his knees. Most of the land around here is not really land at all, just a thin, shifting crust of mud, silt, and mangrove root: an illusory land that collapses beneath your feet as you step out onto it.

To judge from De Bry's engravings in the Latin edition of the *Discoverie,* he managed to look spruce and courtly throughout his trip up the Orinoco. Experience prevails against this, as does Ralegh's own account of conditions in the boats. They lived "most sluttishly," he says,

> being all driven to lie in the rain and weather, in the burning sun, and upon hard boards; and to dress our meat and to carry all manner of furniture in them; wherewith we were so pestered and unsavoury, that what with the victuals being mostly fish, with the wet clothes of so many men being thrust together, and the heat of the sun, I will undertake there was never any prison in England that could be found more unsavoury and loathsome, especially to myself, who had for many years before been dieted and cared for in a sort far differing.

It was not heroic in the big-gestured, rhetorical way that De Bry depicts: Sir Walter the warrior lording it over Berrio; Sir Walter the statesman conversing with Chief Topiawari. It was muddy, sweaty, and smelly, and after years of easy living he was not really ready for it.

[10]

The Delta

*   *   *

THE ORINOCO Delta covers an area of nearly sixteen thousand square miles in the extreme northeast of Venezuela. Here the great eastward flow of the Orinoco falters and splits into a tangle of smaller branches. The mainstream continues eastward and debouches into the Atlantic at Boca Grande, not far from the border with modern Guyana, but northward the river sends off a mass of meandering channels that terminate in the *bocas chicas,* or "little mouths," of the Orinoco. The Boca Bagre, Ralegh's Bay of Guanipa, is the most westerly of the *bocas chicas.*

At the time of Ralegh's expedition the area belonged to the largely notional Spanish province of Nueva Andalucia. It was of little intrinsic interest to European explorers, except as a corridor to the richer lands of the interior. The region was also called Caribania, though this usage is not documented before the seventeenth century; this name suggests the "country of the Caribs," and hence by popular implication, the country of cannibals. Venezuela—or as Ralegh spells it, "Vensuello"—was then a much smaller area to the west, around Lake Maracaibo. It derives its name from the stilted houses of the lake-dwelling Indians of Maracaibo, which the first Spanish visitors compared to a "little Venice."

Ralegh does not use the term "delta," which in his day referred exclusively to the mouth of the Nile, whose triangular shape was compared, at least as early as Herodotus, to the *delta* of the Greek alphabet. According to the *Oxford English Dictionary,* the term was not used as a general geographical description before 1790, when Gibbon writes of the "delta of Mesola" at the mouth of the Po River.

Ralegh doesn't really name the area at all; it is simply the way he must go to get to the "great river of Orenoque" and the golden lands beyond. It is the gateway to El Dorado; its difficulties are only to be expected.

WE FINALLY find our way into the Boca Bagre, between Isla Venado and Isla Cotorra (Deer Island and Parakeet Island), and dock at the wharf of Pedernales. This is the only place on the whole of the delta coast that can be called a town. *Pedernal* means "flint," and perhaps refers to quarry produce shipped out of here. The soil of the region, where it manages to struggle above flood level, has a strong presence of hematite, the brittle brown ore sometimes called bog iron.

Pedernales is a small, single-story town straggled along the bay, population 1,500. There is not a single car in town, only boats and bicycles: a new mountain bike is the status symbol here. At the edge of town the roads peter out into swamp bush. The lowland extends from the coast twenty or thirty miles into the interior and is inundated during eight months of the year. A few small elevations, seldom more than thirty feet high, are the only habitable areas. On the TPC the whole area is white and blue: contour-free. Ralegh sums up the topography as "broken islands and drowned lands."

Small birds swoop across the bay. They flock like sandpipers: a low, arcing flight. They settle on a spar of sand, strut there awhile, then set off on another fast swing across the water. The man on the jetty calls them *tiwing.*

We have a welcoming committee of Guardia Nacional. They say we have come in at the wrong wharf. The correct way to enter Pedernales, it seems, is to come around east of Cotorra Island. This irregularity warrants a full search: everything opened up, unscrewed, peered at. Pedernales is a smuggling conduit. Consumer goods from Trinidad come down, drugs and guns from Brazil and Colombia go up. A hard-faced man with a mustache hangs back from the search and seems to be in charge. He gives me savage flashbacks of a run-in with Panamanian soldiers five years ago. He makes María uneasy, too. A Chilean has always memories: friends who disappeared, the horrors of the Stadium.

It starts to rain again.

Our gear is taken by handcart a few blocks to our hotel—a nameless hotel, the only hotel. The streets are surfaced in concrete, with a line of grass down the middle. The hotel is a dark wooden house. The rooms are windowless and there is no electricity. The backyard is piled with rubbish. "Instant cholera," says Ron, the film director.

Dusk falls on the waterfront. There's a dank smell of river mud, the sound of water slapping the pilings. The mosquitoes muster; they will stay with us now. Inside open doorways I see the flare of hurricane lamps, the indolent sway of hammocks.

We dine on chicken stew at the house of a plump, friendly woman named Doris. In the front room her daughter is making a mobile. There is a clock on the wall in the shape of an enormous gold wristwatch. The kitchen is made of corrugated tin painted a vivid turquoise.

Doris's baby grandson is called Anthony Quinn. There's a curious crossover of English names here. We are closer to Trinidad and Guyana than to the rest of Venezuela. Guyanese Trevor's three children sound like a lineup of West Indian fast bowlers. I ask one of her sons, a curly-headed man, if he is Anthony's father.

"No," he says. "I'm a eunuch." The family laughs, slightly embarrassed. *Qué bromista!* What a joker.

Out in the street a generator kicks into action. The street is lit with a single light, white and harsh. At the town "cinema"—a large TV set—there's a kung fu video showing. They talk of Indian Green, a local man (real name Andrés Cooper) who had a part in the film *Murphy's War.*

The only place to go drinking is a pool hall a few blocks away: Cantina Recreaciones de Pedernales. There's a kind of tapestry on the wall that shows pool players with bulldog heads, Zap Comic style; and a jukebox with a cast-iron frame around it that makes it look like a little shrine. They are mostly *mestizos* in here, with one or two Warao Indians in a state of trancelike drunkenness. The *guar-*

dia who had searched us earlier are there, in T-shirts and stone-washed jeans. The young one is called Noel Robinson. In the courtyard out back the evil mustachioed one is playing cards.

Frank and I play pool with a *mestizo* in a MAS baseball cap, and a muscular half-caste with the hairstyle of an English footballer and the demeanor of a young Charles Bronson. We lose, pay the table.

We stay to close the place. The barman chalks up the tab on the wooden counter. By the end of the night everyone's paid off except for us. We are listed under the name "Gringo."

We tack back to the hotel beneath the Orinoco moon. The water churns restlessly in the darkness. We sense its power. From now on we are at its command.

The following day, Uwe is down early on the waterfront fixing up boats for the first leg of our delta journey. I write up my notes while rain spits on the concrete strip outside the door. Schoolgirls scurry past. There is schooling up to tenth grade here; the nearest secondary school is Tucapita, five hours by speedboat.

At midday we are shooed out of the hotel, which doubles as a canteen for thirty schoolchildren. We stroll down to the wharf to meet our new boatmen. The western end of Pedernales is inhabited by Warao Indians in their wooden *rancherías.* We are introduced to the chief of the village, Simon Medina. (The chief is *wataka tekane* in Warao, generally called the *capitán* by the Creoles.) He's a polite, quiet man in a straw hat. We come upon him in a clearing by the river, reflectively hammering at the lid of an empty 200-liter gasoline drum. Children beside him blink with each hammer blow. He is taking the lid off so it can be used as a water barrel. He makes these barrels for other Warao villages inland that do not have a source of fuel drums.

It is, of course, contaminated water that causes cholera, which is spreading here as everywhere in South America, and there is plenty of rain to fill the barrels as an alternative to drinking delta water. Eating raw mud-crabs is another cause of waterborne cholera.

María asks if the people still use the traditional medicine men for treating cholera. The *capitán* says they will use anything they can. The larger Warao settlements have an *enfermero,* or nurse—a member of the village, usually of the chief family, who has responsibility for distributing "Western" medicine to the village. In practice this means long journeys to Tucapita and an unreliable supply of medicine, so of course the people turn to the old traditions of the medicine man, or *wasiratu.*

The wind gets up. A lone palm tree bends on the dirty shoreline. There's a spooky light over the jetty that walks out into the brown water on long spidery legs.

Uwe has hired two *curiara* (long Indian canoes) for the first leg of our journey through the delta. There are four boatmen. Each boat has a pilot up front and the *motorista* astern working the outboard. They are under the command of the chief's son, Rómulo, who answers to Trevor, who is in turn the sidekick of Uwe, who supposedly takes his instructions from Ron the film director, who is filming my journey, which is dictated by Sir Walter Ralegh's. This is the expedition.

Uwe instructs the boatmen that the *gente de filmación*—the "film people"—must be allowed to do whatever they wish, however bizarre it may seem. His manner with the Indians is chummy but brusque. *"Coño,* you have to know how to handle them." Uwe sees everything as something to be "handled," or—his favorite word, which we could not bear to correct—*"organizized."*

At the wharf they are drying and salting fish, as we load our gear once more. It is stashed in the middle of the boats and wrapped in polyethylene tarps. We leave around 3:00 P.M. Hugging the shoreline for a while, heading southwest along the bay, we enter the delta system—as Ralegh probably did—via the easterly channel of the Caño Manamo, the largest of the "four goodly rivers" that debouch into the bay.

THE DELTA is a strange, shifting landscape. It sucks you in. It is profuse and luxuriant, but also seems like a desert or a prairie in that you travel for hours, for days, and nothing much changes. When locals give you directions they do so with odd scooping gestures expressive of a circular, repetitive journey. Once off the main flow of the large *caños,* each of them a sizable river in itself, it is easy to get lost. The side channels, or *cañitos,* look wide to begin with, then suddenly narrow into these weird alleys of foliage and birdsong.

The mangroves grow tall like a woodland of young ash trees. Clumps of young mangrove drift in the main channel of the river, looking for new sites to colonize. They move upstream with the tide, then back down again when the tide turns. This far-reaching tide made for very slow travel for Ralegh and his oarsmen. They could only proceed when the tide was coming in: "We passed up the river with the flood, and anchored the ebb, and in this sort we went onward." It was four days before they were "past the ebbing and flowing."

Ralegh's pilot, the Arawak they called Ferdinando, proved useless. He was, says Ralegh, "utterly ignorant" of the area, and was eventually forced to admit that he had last been in the area twelve years ago, "at which time he was very young, and without judgement."

Soon enough, with no guide, they got sidetracked into that intricate maze of channels and streams, the *cañitos.* Ralegh calls them "by-creeks." Without a doubt, their first experience in the delta was of being hopelessly lost. "We might have wandered a whole year in that labyrinth of rivers, ere we had found any way either out or in," he wrote,

> for I know all the earth doth not yield the like confluence of streams and branches, the one crossing the other so many times, and all so fair and large and so like one to another, as no man can tell which to take. And if we went by the sun or compass, hoping thereby to go directly one way or other, yet that way we were also carried in a circle amongst multitudes of islands, and every island so bordered with high trees, as no man could see any further than the breadth of the river or length of the breach.

This expresses the disorientations of delta travel.

We see flocks of red ibis—*corocoro* in the native tongue—brilliant against the deep green hedge of trees. They are sometimes scarlet, heraldic, and sometimes a more muted red like brushed silk. A colony of egrets in a spreading tree looks from a distance like a profusion of magnolia flowers. These are the same sights that entranced Ralegh:

> We saw birds of all colours, some carnation, some crimson, orange-tawny, purple, green, watchet, and of all other sorts both simple and mixed. . . .

> The birds, towards the evening, singing on every tree with a thousand several tunes, cranes & herons of white, crimson and carnation, perching on the river's side.

These brilliant tropical glimpses afford moments of enjoyment to the hard-pressed travelers: "it was unto us a great good passing of the time to behold them." They also provide them with food:

> . . . besides the relief we found by killing some store of them with our fowling pieces, without which, having little or no bread and less drink, but only the thick and troubled water of the river, we had been in a very hard case.

We also see, perched on a high dead branch, a white-headed king vulture, *el rey de samuro.* Vultures are a continuous presence on the journey, but I think of them most in Caracas, circling above the skyscrapers and the brooding Avila Hills, graceful hook-winged creatures in the air but when I see one at rest, on the broken trunk of a streetlight, it looks like a haggard old turkey on the avian equivalent of skid row.

Our first night is spent at a disused *palafito* on the river's edge. This is the typical dwelling of the Warao Indians: an open-sided building of wood and palm-thatch raised up on stilts. (The origin of the word is probably *palo fijo,* i.e., a "fixed stick" dwelling.)

Trevor and Rómulo rig up the hammocks and mosquito nets. Ralegh was a great admirer of the hammock, "those beds which they call *hamacas* or brazil beds, wherein in hot countries all the Spaniards use to lie commonly, and in no other, neither did we ourselves while we were there."

There is suddenly a tremendous crack and splash, and I turn to see Uwe waist-deep in the "thick and troubled water" of the river. A large section of the *palafito* has collapsed. The stove and several plastic barrels are in the water, but the radio teeters safely on the solid part.

We sleep in close ranks, a little island of sighs and grunts and—an inevitable concomitant of sleeping in a hammock—snores. The earlier collapse has more or less halved the usable area of the *palafito,* and we are unsure if the rest of it can support our collective weight. Whenever someone moves there is an ominous creaking.

Twice in the night I wake to the sound of a motorboat heading downriver. They drone by in the darkness, a lingering monotone. They have no lights: contraband boats, perhaps. The sound of the motor has almost faded away by the time the eddy reaches the river's edge and shakes the *palafito.*

At dawn I hear the strange, shifting gargle of howler monkeys.

The next day we have our first argument. Uwe is angry. He told the boatman Rómulo that we wanted to explore some of the little *cañitos;* María told him we wanted to visit a Warao medicine man. Rómulo, caught between two conflicting orders, decided to do what he normally does and head straight down to Tucapita, the main town on the delta, as fast as he can. Uwe feels his control of the boatmen—his job within the expedition as he sees it—has been undermined.

Accordingly we are, at this early stage of our great journey, *turning back.* Rómulo knows of a medicine man at Boca del Tigre, which is now behind us. Already we are losing sight of our destination, sur-rendering to the strange circling flow of the delta.

We do not find the medicine man at Boca del Tigre, only another empty *palafito.* Frank and María remain there while the rest of us go on for ten minutes to replenish the beer supply at a riverside trading-post. They are rewarded by the sight of two freshwater dol-phin sporting in the river.

María teases us, the *gente de filmación:* "It was the right time but you were in the wrong place."

I said, "Perhaps it was the medicine man coming to visit you."

If so, it was appropriate—as events would prove—that she was the one he appeared to.

AFTER SOME days of wandering in the "laborinth" of the creeks and *caños* of the delta, Ralegh's boats came into the broad stream of a "great river," which "because it had no name we called the River of the Red Cross, ourselves being the first Christians that ever came therein." He named it, in other words, after the English flag, the cross of St. George, though, as we shall see, there are other meanings in his mind as well.

They entered this river on May 22. This is the only precise date given by Ralegh in his account of the Orinoco expedition. It was about five days after they had set out from the ships at Trinidad.

It is not easy to identify this "River of the Red Cross." According to Ralegh it led them, after another four days, into a river which he calls "the great Amana." This "ran more directly, without windings and turnings." It was, says Ralegh, "as goodly a river as ever I beheld." This Amana is certainly the Caño Manamo. The name derives from the Warao word for "two," referring to the bifurcation of the river into the two channels now generally called the Manamo and Manamito. Since Ralegh says elsewhere that they entered the delta by the Amana, he seems to understand that they are at this point—about May 26—*rejoining* the river they had been on in the first place. They have been on a long and circuitous detour, lasting in all about nine days.

Francis Sparry adds further confusion. Ralegh clearly says they came from the River of the Red Cross into the Amana, but according to Sparry, the "River of the Red Cross" *was* the Amana: "In the bottom of the Gulf of Guanipa there is the River of Amana . . . which we named the River of the Red Cross." Sparry was writing this seven years after the event, and in this case (though not in others) I think he should be ignored.

The confusion is easy to understand, in this profoundly confusing landscape, and one cannot reconstruct with any certainty these first few days of Ralegh's delta journey. The most likely solution is that the Red Cross is one of the lateral channels running between the Caño Pedernales and the Caño Manamo. The largest of these, marked but unnamed on the TPC, is called by locals Caño Wina or Wina-morena. I suggest that they entered the delta by the eastern mouth of the Manamo; that they wandered off course into the "laborinth" of creeks and *cañitos;* that after four days heading generally southward they came to Caño Wina, which they christened the Red Cross; and that after a further four days rowing westward, they arrived once more on the Manamo, or "great Amana."

By this reckoning, Ralegh and his men had reached the confluence of the Manamo and the Wina by May 26, 1595, about nine days after setting out across the Gulf of Paria. These rivers meet at the place known as Boca del Tigre, the Tiger's Mouth, where we came to look for the witch doctor and found only his empty hut.

[11]

Tivitivas

* * *

I
T WAS on the Red Cross River that Ralegh had his first, unsettling encounter with the natives of the delta.

> We spied a small *canoa* with three Indians, which by the swiftness of
> my barge, rowing with eight oars, I overtook ere they could cross the
> river. The rest of the people on the banks, shadowed under the thick
> wood, gazed on with a doubtful conceit what might befall those three
> which we had taken.

Perceiving that the strangers "offered them no violence," the Indians
"began to show themselves on the bank's side, and offered to traffick
with us for such things as they had." In this tentative moment of
amity, "we came with our barge to the mouth of a little creek, which
came from their town into the great river."

All seemed well until Ralegh's Arawak pilot, Ferdinando, and his
brother decided to go ashore to the village, "to fetch some fruits,
and to drink of their artificial wines, and also to see the place, and
to know the lord of it against another time."

The "lord," or *cacique,* of the tribe ordered his men to "lay hands
on" the two Arawaks. Both managed to escape. The brother made
it back to the creek's mouth, but Ferdinando was trapped in the
woods, where they "hunted him upon the foot with their deer-dogs,
and with so main a cry that all the woods echoed with the shout
they made."

Ralegh's response was to take a hostage from among the villagers.
"We set hands on one of them that was next us, a very old man,

and brought him into the barge." They assured him they would "presently cut off his head" if Ferdinando was harmed.

Eventually Ferdinando escaped, "and swam to the barge half dead with fear."

It was an unsettling experience for the adventurers, very different from the welcome they were accorded by the natives of Trinidad, already under the Spanish yoke and eager to make any alliance against the Spanish. Here they were deemed by the locals a "strange nation" with intent to "spoil and destroy." It was once again as Berrio had forewarned.

But it had one good spin-off. They kept the "old man" of the village they had taken, and it was he who became Ralegh's guide.

> Being natural of those rivers, we assured ourselves he knew the way better than any stranger could, and indeed, but for this chance I think we had never found the way either to Guiana, or back to our ships.

With this new guide they rowed on up the Red Cross River.

RALEGH CALLS the tribe he encountered the Tivitivas: "those people which dwell in these broken islands & drowned lands are generally called Tivitivas; there are of them two sorts, the one called Ciawani, and the other Waraweete." These Tivitivas are undoubtedly the main Indian tribe of the delta, the Warao. Another early visitor, Felipe de Santiago—a protégé of Berrio's—also speaks of the "Tivetives," and a Dutch report of 1637 refers to "Tibetibes" assisting the Dutch attack on the Spanish base at San Thomé. This document distinguishes them from Arawaks and Caribs, who also took part in the assault.

The origin of this name for the Warao is mysterious. According to Dieter Heinen of the Fundación la Salle in Caracas, a leading authority on the tribe, *tivitiva* is a small shore-bird common in the area (perhaps the sandpipers I saw in the bay at Pedernales, which I was told were *tiwing*). However, this is not a Warao word—they call this bird *waharumo*. Another possibility arises from a useful glossary of "the language of Trinidad"—presumably Arawak—compiled by Sir Robert Dudley. In this I find *tibetebe,* meaning "cockles." It is possible that cockleshells were a trading medium in the area, as they were in Virginia, where the Algonquian word *roanoke* also signifies a shell, and gives its name to an island and a tribe.

Either way, this appears to be an outsider's name—Arawak or Carib—for the Warao. It is a name Ralegh hears before he meets them. The two subgroups he identifies are, on the other hand, authentic Warao descriptions. He names one group the Waraweete. This is clearly *warao witu,* which means "true Warao." It is a self-description, a boast even. The other, the Ciawani, is a subgroup of Warao originating around the Caño Siawini, farther east in the delta. (Dudley mentions a region called "Seawano," but places this on the far side of the Essequibo in present-day Guyana. Felipe de Santiago mentions "Chaguanes" as well as "Tivetives," which may be the same as Ralegh's Ciawani, but is more probably a version of Jekuana, a different ethnic group altogether.)

Ralegh later describes their new guide as an "old Ciawan," so it was presumably this "Ciawani" branch of the Warao that they encountered on the Red Cross River.

The name Warao means the people of the boat (*wa,* boat; *arao,* people). All others, outsiders, non-Warao, are lumped together as *hotarao,* people of the land. They have been preserved as a tribe by the difficulties of the delta, and its lack of any precious commodities. Caribs and Arawaks were decimated by the Spanish, and by the end of the eighteenth century were virtually extinct as a coherent tribal group, but the Warao remained intact. According to a Spanish report of 1771, they have good relations with the Dutch, who supply them with "axes, knives and other knicknacks [*bujerías*]," and are difficult to "reduce" to Catholicism. At the end of the eighteenth century their population was estimated by Gumilla as 5,000 to 6,000. It is now about 18,000. In Venezuela, Warao is generally Hispanicized to "Guaraunos" or "Guaraunu"—the same Spanish difficulty with the "w" that turns Walter Ralegh into "Guaterrale" or "Gualtero."

The Warao are acclimatized now in the usual way—T-shirts and petrol motors—but still largely unvisited. They speak Spanish well enough, but with a kind of furtive, floor-gazing reluctance. Their own language is fluid, susurrant. The women seem to speak in sighs and little rapid moans. When a group of them gathers, the decibels rise, until you think they're having a tremendous argument; then you look over and see they're just passing the time in a communal chat.

The basic words in Warao are as defiantly monosyllabic as Chinese: *ho* is water, *ha* is hammock, *wa* is boat. Many words are simple compounds—a house is *hanoko,* "hammock place"; day is *hokonai,* "clear time," and night is *yahanai,* "black time." Other words are made up of echoing repetitious syllables. The ibis is *corocoro,* the little black midges that the Creoles call *la plaga* (the plague) they call *komokomoko.* Best of all we liked their word for stars—*uramokomoko.*

Echoes of Warao language remain in the *Discoverie.* As noted, Ralegh's Amana is actually the Manamo, deriving from the Warao word for "two." The Orinoco itself is from the Warao name, Wirinoko, which means literally "the place of paddling" (*wiri,* to paddle; *noko,* place), a rather nonchalant description of one of the world's greatest rivers. Other delta rivers Ralegh mentions—Waricapana, Waracapari, Wana, etc.—are also of Warao origin.

Ralegh describes them in terms of tremendous admiration. "These Tivitivas," he says, "are a very goodly people and very valiant, and have the most manly speech and most deliberate that ever I heard." He admires their bodies, the product of their tough, simple life.

> Notwithstanding the moistness of the air in which they live, the hardness of their diet, and the great labours they suffer to hunt, fish and fowl for their living, in all my life, either in the Indies or in Europe, did I never behold a more goodly or better favoured people, or a more manly. They were wont to make war upon all nations, and especially on the Cannibals [i.e., Caribs], so as none durst without a good strength trade by those rivers, but of late they are at peace with their neighbours, all holding the Spaniards for a common enemy.

17. Tivitiva tree houses

Against this one sets Ralegh's ironic awareness of himself on this journey, as a man out of shape, grown soft: an "ill footman." The physical superiority of the Indians is something all sensible travelers recognize. I like the comment of Thomas Turner, a traveler in Brazil in the early seventeenth century: "The Indian is a fish in the sea, and a fox in the woods, and without them a Christian is neither for pleasure or profit fit for life."

I have to say that the Warao we met did not match up to Ralegh's description, being smaller and more indolent. There is malnutrition and sickness; they are at that halfway house of "development," where the old self-reliance is diminished without much compensation from new technical amenities.

Ralegh's description of the Warao dwellings is rather curious. In the summer, or dry season, they have normal "houses on the ground," he says, but when the rains come and the land is inundated, "they dwell upon the trees, where they build very artificial towns and villages, as . . . those people do in the lowlands near the Gulf of Uraba." The latter refers to the Cienaga Grande and Lake Maracaibo, where the Indians built their houses on stilts—and still do—so it seems that Ralegh is here describing the Warao's stilted *palafitos.* His phrase is imprecise, however, and sounds like they actually live *in* the trees. Elsewhere he has "the Tivitivas which dwell on trees." He even talks jocularly of having to leave Englishmen here, "to have inhabited like rooks upon trees."

Thus is a minor New World legend born, for in Levinus Hulsius's illustrated edition of the *Discoverie,* the Tivitivas are duly shown living in the tops of trees, which look curiously like European oaks, while the floodwaters lap around the trunks below them.

Sir Robert Schomburgk, who traveled among the Warao in the mid-nineteenth century, was much exercised over this. He saw "not a single instance wherein, as observed by Ralegh, they dwelt on trees." He wonders if this was a hallucination, or at any rate an optical illusion.

> We can well suppose that the numerous fires which were made in each hut, and the reflexion of which was the stronger in consequence of the stream of vapour around the summit of trees in those moist regions, illuminated at night the adjacent trees.

In other words, that Ralegh *thought* he saw fires in the tops of trees and concluded there were actual houses up there. This seems very unlikely. Another nineteenth-century traveler, Hilhouse, described a Warao village in which the platforms were built not on piles, but on the severed trunks of *moriche* palms still standing, with a resulting irregularity of the platform. This is probably what Ralegh saw; they built their houses on the stumps of trees, not in the top of them.

WE ARRIVE at Wakahara at about four in the afternoon. It is a Warao village of about three hundred people straggling along the eastern bank of the Caño Manamo, more or less opposite the mouth of the Morichal Largo. (It would probably be written Guacajara on maps, but I have not found any that mention it. The nearest village marked on the map is Guamal, or Wamal, to which the children of Wakahara go daily to school.)

We first pulled in at a small *criollo* settlement on the opposite bank. We arrive to the unsettling sight of three sandy-colored dogs worrying the slimy corpse of an anaconda. It had killed some chickens, we are told, so the *dueño* killed it with his machete. The anaconda is about ten feet long. At its widest you could only just get two hands round it. It has a shiny, rubbery look, like a wet, black inner tube. The dogs are playing with it, growling and worrying and shaking it, but not making much inroad into its tough, slippery flesh.

There are some boys standing idly around watching. There is something rather atavistic about the whole scene. They call it *culebra de agua,* a water snake.

A man in gum boots greets us: Jovito Cortéz. He is a relaxed, philosophical character of indeterminate age. He *thinks* he has ten children. The family grows cacao, plantains, rice, coconuts, and *ocumo chino;* this is a little pocket of solid, workable land. They have a store and a few boats (one serves as the school boat for Wakahara children).

María asks him about the witch doctor of Wakahara. His name is Eulalio Cabello, we learn. What does he do? "He smokes his pipe, and then you pay him."

Fortified by cold beer, we cross the mainstream to Wakahara. Our reception is friendly enough, and we are offered a *ranchería* to hang our hammocks. We are disappointed at first that the main body of the village is constructed in breeze-block and tin. We wonder if it's "typical" enough. The answer, I suppose, is that it is itself, no more or less typical than the traditional wood and thatch villages.

We are later told that the government has provided the building materials for the houses, and also for the combined school, infirmary, and *casa de convención* that is being built at the northern end of the village.

"Before the elections we are given presents," they say. "After, they do not come."

The *capitán* of Wakahara is Benito, a handsome young man. He is one of three men in the village who build *curiara*. As in Ralegh's time, the Warao are famed as makers of canoes. Various trees are used: cedar, sassafras, laurel. (The latter is not the big-leaved laurel of English shrubberies but a tall evergreen tree more like the Portuguese laurel.) These trees are used because of their high resin content.

He will sell a new *curiara,* he says, for 15,000 bolivars ($200), though the cost of the outboard motor to power it would be many times that.

Watching Benito at work with his hammer and chisel, we see a continuous tradition that goes back across centuries. Schomburgk notes: "The Waraus are to this day the most famous boat-builders, and furnish nearly the whole colony of Demerera with canoes." And Ralegh himself says:

> They that dwell upon the branches of Orenoque called Capuri and Macareo [in the northeast of the delta] are for the most part carpenters of *canoas* . . . and sell them into Guiana for gold and into Trinedado for tobacco, in the excessive taking whereof they exceed all nations.

Here is another aspect of Ralegh's admiration for the Warao: their fondness for tobacco.

At the village jetty women are soaking and beating *moriche.* This is the fiber they extract from the *moriche* palm (*Mauritia flexuosa*). This is soaked, beaten, and then hung to dry. Hanging on the line to dry, a wad of *moriche* looks alarmingly like a giant helping of the breakfast cereal called shredded wheat.

The uses of the *moriche* palm (also called *ita*) are manifold. It is one of those all-purpose tropical plants, like agave. A Pemón Indian called Anita, with whom we later traveled, spoke of *las siete vidas de moriche*—its "seven lives." These are: *techo, ropa, hamaca, curiara, palmitos, gusano, cachire.* The first four are its practical uses: they use the leaves for roof thatch, the fibers for weaving cloth and hammocks, and the wood for boat building. The others are food sources. *Palmitos* are palm hearts, a great delicacy; the stem is carefully shaved with a machete till you get to the white heart, which looks something like a leek and has a crisp bland taste when raw. Ralegh observed this: "They use the tops of *palmitos* for their bread." The *gusano* is a grub that grows in the palm which they fatten for food. We saw some in a little tin in Benito's house: fat yellow maggots the size of a broad bean. These they eat fried, or crushed into a paste or butter, or sometimes just as they come: delta crudités. *Cachire* is liquor, here a palm wine: more often made from fermented manioc.

WE ARE briefly an event in the Wakahara calendar. Last week Ramon's little girl died of cholera; this week a boatload of gringos came in, looking for the medicine man. But soon we are subsumed, and ourselves sink into the slow rhythms of life in a delta village.

Wakahara days: muddy brown river, vultures on the rise, dogs yelping. The fire hisses. The rain drips off plastic sheeting. We lie in our hammocks tormented by *komokomoko*. We are in a gray misty time of lassitude and forgetfulness.

There will be catfish for lunch.

The crop-haired boy who hangs out with us is playing with his collection of CAN-TV phone cards. His dad brings them back from Tucapita.

Pedro has trapped an *acure,* the large wild guinea pig of the region. It squeals like a rabbit in the clutches of a weasel. He kills it inexpertly, first trying to strangle it, then beating its head in with the handle of his machete. As he wrings its neck, its eyes bulge out and its little pink penis appears, like the tip of a carrot.

We lose time here, as perhaps we wish to. I ask the crop-haired boy how old he is. *"No sé."* I don't know. The young men look like teenagers but already have three kids. The old men are wrinkled but their hair does not gray. Pedro has an eight-month-old child, but she has no name yet.

María Teresa, our Indian expert, is charmed by these small, whispering people who smell of woodsmoke. She says, "Among the Warao it is very simple. When a man wants to marry a girl he just goes to her house and puts his hammock up next to hers. If the girl wants him, he becomes a member of her family and works for his father-in-law."

At evening the sky is filled with parrots, always in pairs. *Los inseparables.* We see one who has no mate, invent fantastical tales of separation and loss. The gutted corpse of the *acure* hangs from a string, its body gray in the rain.

[12]

The Medicine Man

* * *

AFTER A few days the medicine man returned. We met him on a Saturday afternoon, sitting outside his breeze-block hut. He is what is known in Warao as a *wasirato* (or *wisiratu*). This is translated into Spanish either as *curandero* or *brujo.* The first describes his status as a healer or medicine man, the second his powers as a shaman or sorcerer. Essentially both are part of his act. It all depends what you hire him for.

As in most tribal cultures, the Warao shaman is seen as a go-between. He is a mediator between the human community and the spirit world. In Warao the spirits are called *hebu;* they are under the command of the *Kanobo Kobenahoro* (the "chief guardian"—this is an interesting mix of Warao and Spanish, *kobenahoro* deriving from Spanish *gobernador,* governor). The shaman is called the *nebu* of the gods—a *nebu* is a younger man who is a servant and errand runner for the elders of the village. Traditionally the village has a sacred stone, used for grinding *moriche.* The shaman is the "guardian" of this stone.

The medicine man of Wakahara is called Eulalio Cabello. He is a small man, not much more than five feet tall, with a skinny, shrunken physique. He is sixty-three years old. He has no teeth left, and his face has an imploded look. It is almost a dwarf's face. His ears are prominent and his eyes have a half-focused sadness. There's a rasp in his lungs and he speaks breathlessly. You always expect something more. You have this image of the medicine man—feathers and potions and jungle weirdness—and instead he looks like a wino.

After due courtesies we ask him to perform a ceremony for us. I burble at him in faulty Spanish, "We have a long journey to make. We are following a journey taken many years ago by an ancient *caballero* from Europe. We hope you will give us good luck, so that we can find what we are seeking." (I was going to mention El Dorado, but María thought it best not to tangle the issue; it gets misunderstood if you come into town talking about gold.)

He nods and grunts, and seems to understand, and it appears that a fee of 2,000 bolivars ($25) is to everyone's satisfaction. The medicine man is always paid for his services, even by members of the village. In some cases a woman who has been cured by him, and cannot pay him, becomes his servant. He, in turn, looks after her welfare and treats her with kindness.

THE CEREMONY begins soon after dark. Eulalio's veranda—a roofed strip of concrete that all these huts have—is lit with makeshift kerosene lamps: a wick tamped into an empty beer can. These throw lurid shadows against the gray walls, the faces of the crowd that has gathered to watch.

We are sitting around on the floor; the cameras are ready. Frank deploys large Maglites for further dramatic lighting. Eulalio appears from a doorway, the priest in his rummage sale clothes. He is carrying a small basket and a breeze-block. He puts the breeze-block down and sits on it. This is significant, a symbol of his status. The block is his *duhu,* or seat. Since Warao houses do not have any chairs as such, only hammocks and boxes, the idea of sitting assumes a significance. When a man is ambitious or disrespectful to the elders, it is said of him, "He wishes to sit." Seated on his breeze-block, Eulalio is in the *duhunoko,* or "sitting place," a position of honor or importance.

He is smoking a long cheroot, rolled in a yellowish leaf. This is the local tobacco, *wina.* I tried some later: It is a smooth smoke, pleasantly flavored. It reminds me of home-cured tobacco I smoked in northern Thailand (*burri*). It has no psychoactive properties that my jaded palate could discern; it is simply a tobacco, a rustic nicotine. Eulalio is what the anthropologists call a "tobacco shaman," a particular part of a general and ancient South American tradition, in which tobacco—smoked, snorted, chewed, or administered rectally—is the drug of transport, equivalent to *coca, datura, yagé,* etc., in other Indian cultures.

The ceremony starts almost without our noticing it. He sits on his brick and takes a few deep tokes of the *wina* cheroot. He takes from his basket a *maraca.* It is made from a large egg-shaped calabash (a type called *tortuma,* he later specified) mounted on a stout club of wood. The gourd is almost exactly the same size as his head. It is carved all over with intricate pictograms—boats, fishes, birds, tapirs, snakes: all the powers of the delta. He made it himself.

He sits in a hunched position, which seems to emphasize his gnarled feet and hands, and make them larger. He shakes the *maraca,* settles to a fast, even rhythm. Soon he starts to chant, a high-pitched droning song, repeated over and over, a note of invitation or exhortation. His eyes are closed. There's a force field of wrinkles around them.

The following day María asked him, at my insistence, what he was doing when he chanted.

He said, "The devil is everywhere. He is in the air, he scatters his bad influence everywhere. So you need to make a ceremony to put him away. When I start to play the *maraca,* the devil comes on the wind. When he comes he smokes the *wina.*"

Hence the sense of effort at this point: He is calling up a "devil" or spirit; he is reeling it in "on the wind"; he is sucking it into his own mouth and letting it smoke the *wina.*

The old man keens and shuffles. In our gringo way—the *gente de filmación*—we are waiting for something to happen. There seems no point to it.

María Teresa is sitting cross-legged to my left. I turn to notice that her head has fallen forward, her thick dark hair hanging down like a curtain. Her eyes are closed. Her wrists rest loosely on her knees, her hands dangle.

Ron turns the camera on her. I ask her if she's okay. She doesn't answer.

Without any warning, the medicine man comes to a halt with a last shuffle of the *maraca.* There is an audible release of tension in the onlookers. I say to him, half jokingly, "What have you done to her, *señor?*" He looks over at María, and there's an odd little smile on his puckered face.

"How do you feel?" I ask her.

"I don't know. Strange. Sleepy. I don't know."

Uwe says, bristling a bit, "I think we should ask this guy what he's doing here."

Ron gets a new angle. Frank's left the clapper board in his hammock so Maggie does a mike tap. I'm just about to start some kind of "interview" when Eulalio starts up all over again. He has slipped off his shirt now, and is standing. Without being able to say how or why, I feel a new kind of intensity in the ceremony. His baby face is lost deep in effort and concentration; his torso is strangely torqued and lined; his shadow dances on the rough gray wall behind him, on which I notice for the first time a little fetish of wood, rope, and cloth.

It seems there is a new focus to his act. Before he was humoring a few gringos with a quick vignette, an Orinoco medicine show, but now he has a real reason for performing, and the reason is María. She is now prone on the floor. She speaks to me drowsily, asks me to take off her shoes. (Seeing it later on the film it has the look of a ridiculous medical cliché, as if I'm about to send someone out for a bowl of hot water.) She also wants her belt taken off. She doesn't want any metal near her.

After this second session—the same wailing, the same monotone of the *maraca,* indistinguishable from the first session except in this sense of his "targeting" now on María—she is confused, speaks first in Spanish, then in English.

He motions her over. She sits cross-legged in front of him. He grips her head and bends toward her. The mood is suddenly sexual; or rather it reveals a murky sort of sexuality that has existed throughout, especially after he took off his shirt. He leans close down into her hair, and for a moment I think he's kissing her, but he is not; he is sucking at her head.

He takes great effortful tokes. I can hear the rasp in his lungs, and then after three or four sucks he blows away and out.

To end with, he reaches into his basket and hands her a little chunk of something that I think is a stone. She smells it and passes it to me. It's a small plug of resin, with a pungent menthol smell. It reminds me of Tiger Balm.

There was talk of stones, or *piedritas*—little stones—but he meant it in another way. As he explained the following day, "The devil puts stones inside people, and I take the stones out." The "little stone," in other words, was what he was sucking out of María Teresa's head. We understood it to mean a tension, an obstruction, some small mass of difficulty in her head, in her life.

THAT NIGHT María was dreamy and slow. She said it was as if she was drunk. She retired early to her hammock. The next day we talked about it. She said she had been carried away by the *maraca:* "There was a moment I could only listen to the *maraca,* and also his voice, even as I was hearing at the same moment all the voices around me, yours and the others."

But there was something else. María is herself partly Indian. Her grandmother (her father's mother) was a Mapuche Indian from southern Chile, one of that defiant tribe who resisted the Spanish invaders long after the other tribes of South America had gone under. I later saw a photograph of her grandmother: a small, dark-skinned woman squinting into the sun. On one side is María's mother, in a cotton-print dress, and on the other side María, aged about thirteen, wearing bell-bottom jeans that are wet because she has been doing the washing.

When the *wasiratu* gripped her head and leaned toward her, she looked in his eyes and thought it was her grandmother. She spoke of what happened that night as an "ancestral meeting." It awoke in her these buried memories of her grandmother, her childhood, her blood.

She had a tape of Violetta Parra, the great Chilean singer who killed herself over an unhappy love affair. She found a song on it. It was one based on the Mapuche rain ceremony, the *guillantun:* a ritual always done by women, a ritual María associated with her grandmother.

"Listen to the rhythm," she said. "It is the same rhythm as the *maraca* of the medicine man."

I found it somewhat ironic. I had come halfway across the world to trace the footsteps of a long-dead Englishman, and instead it was María who had the "ancestral meeting," who was transported, while I remained rooted to the seemingly solid earth of my present life.

IN A historical sense, at least, I now see that we were closer to Ralegh than I thought. The tradition of tobacco shamanism was certainly in place long before Ralegh arrived here. As a smoker and a propagandist for tobacco, he would certainly be interested in it. He may well have seen it among the Tivitivas; he mentions their enthusiasm for tobacco—their "excessive taking" of it—and he mentions talking to tribal "priests and soothsayers." He does not link the two, but it is pretty certain the link was already there in his mind, for tobacco was associated from the beginning with Indian shamanism, and hence (in the mind of King James I and others) with "devil worship."

In his *Brief Report,* Thomas Harriot describes tobacco rituals practiced by the Algonquians of Virginia. They "make hallowed fires and cast some of the powder therein for a sacrifice." They sprinkle tobacco around when setting up a new weir to catch fish, or after "an escape of danger." They perform the ritual with wild gestures—"stamping, sometimes dancing, clapping of hands, holding up of hands, and staring up into the heavens"—and "chattering strange words and noises." John White's marvelous painting of an Algonquian shaman captions him "The Flyer." (In the engraved version by De Bry he is called, more conventionally, "The Conjuror.") He is shown with a small black bird tied to his head—a token of his role as the "Flyer"—and a pouch at his belt, which is elsewhere said to contain tobacco.

In a pseudonymous pamphlet against tobacco published in

1602—*Work for Chimney-Sweepers* by "Philaretes," the first full-scale attack on tobacco printed here, predating King James's famous *Counterblast* by two years—the author says:

> The Indian Priests (who no doubt were instruments of the devil whom they serve) do ever, before they answer to questions propounded of them by their Princes, drink of this Tobacco fume, with the vigour and strength whereof they fall suddenly to the ground, as dead men, remaining so according to the quantity of the smoke that they had taken. And when the herb had done his work, they revive and wake, giving answers according to the visions and illusions which they saw whilst they were wrapt in that order.

In a rebuttal of Philaretes, *A Defence of Tobacco* (1602), Roger Marbeck offered this more lofty interpretation of Indian tobacco rituals:

> In the taking of Tobacco they [the Indian priests] were drawn up and separated from all gross and earthly cogitations, and as it were carried up to a more pure and clear region of fine conceits and actions of the mind, in so much as they were able thereby to see visions.

This kind of view is more eloquently and wittily handled by Francis Beaumont in his paean to the weed, *The Metamorphosis of Tobacco.*

> Thou great god of Indian melody . . .
> By whom the Indian priests inspired be
> When they presage in barbarous poetry:
> Infume my brain, make my soul's powers subtle,
> Give nimble cadence to my harsher style.

In this Beaumont links his own tobacco-inspired poetry to the incantations and presagings of the Indian shamans, those "chattering strange words" heard by Harriot in Virginia.

Tobacco was also championed as a medicine, a panacea, a *curatodo:* "a thing most excellent and divine." Harriot is once again the source close to Ralegh, describing the Indians' daily use of tobacco, or *uppowac* as they called it.

The flyer.

18. "The Flyer" by John White

The leaves thereof being dried and brought into powder, they take the fume or smoke thereof, by sucking it through pipes made of clay, into their stomach and head, whence it purges superfluous phlegm and other gross humours, and opens all the pores and passages of the body, . . . whereby their bodies are notably preserved in health, and know not many grievous diseases, wherewith we in England are oftentimes afflicted. . . .

We ourselves, during the time we were there, used to suck it after their manner, as also since our return, and have found many rare and wonderful experiments thereof.

Harriot stresses it as something special to the Indians: It is "sowed apart by itself"; it is "of so precious estimation among them that they think their gods are marvellously delighted therewith."

For the Elizabethans in both camps tobacco is an intrinsically American experience—as in Henry Buttes's curious periphrasis for smoking: to "breathe Indianly" (*Dyet's Dry Dinner,* 1599). Tobacco was a breath of the tropics, a whiff of the spirit world. As Jeffrey Knapp puts it in his elegant essay "Elizabethan Tobacco":

Virginia can be understood as opening for England not merely economic, but intellectual and poetic vistas, vistas to which tobacco's own heat contributes. . . . Tobacco brings to Englishmen Virginian heat—what Beaumont will call the "Indian sun"—without their having to leave the comforts of home.

In this sense, tobacco came to be the "inhaled New World," a draft of tropical excitement, danger, and good health.

When Keymis returned to Guiana the following year, he found the Indians who had pledged allegiance to Ralegh, and watched them expressing their loyalty to Queen Elizabeth in terms of "tobacco shamanism":

Thus they sit talking, and taking tobacco some two hours, and until their pipes be all spent. No man must interrupt . . . for this is their religion and prayers which they now celebrate, keeping a precise fast one whole day in honour of the great Princess of the North, their Patroness & Defender.

This has a touch of the brochure about it—Keymis's *Relation* is, like Ralegh's *Discoverie,* a work of propaganda—but nonetheless suggests that the ritual use of tobacco among these Indians was already familiar to Ralegh. Keymis is not specifically talking of the Tivitivas, who had made no alliances with Ralegh, but I think that night in Wakahara, listening to those "chattering" sounds in the hot delta night, we touched on an aspect of Indian culture that Ralegh himself would have recognized.

Talking with Eulalio the following day, trying to wheedle some more out of him about the *wina* and what it meant to him, I got the answer I deserved: He smoked his *wina* cheroots because—glancing at the pack of Marlboros at my side—he couldn't get decent cigarettes.

I gave him the pack, of course. Virginia tobacco, with the compliments of Sir Walter Ralegh.

[13]

The Guiana Bend

*   *   *

HAVING JOINED or rejoined the Caño Manamo on about May 26, Ralegh and his crew rowed southward, guided by the old Warao they had seized earlier. They were soon beyond the reach of the tide, and "were enforced either by main strength to row against a violent current, or to return as wise as we went out."

They are properly on their way at last, but that is itself an anticlimax of sorts, and it is now—after the exotic disorientations of the first days in the delta, after the sudden skirmish with the Warao— that the journey settles down into a sweaty, monotonous slog up this wide, dull-watered, curiously featureless river. And so come the first depressions and mutterings: "Our companies began to despair, the weather being extreme hot, the river bordered with very high trees that kept away the air, and the current against us every day stronger." ("Companies" here, as elsewhere, refers in particular to the soldiers: a potentially dangerous unit within the expedition.)

To counter falling morale, Ralegh told the old expeditionary white lie: that the destination was not far. "We had then no shift but to persuade the companies that it was but two or three days work, and therefore desired them to take pains." He also ordered that the "gentlemen" should row alongside the others, and "spell one the other at the hour's end" (i.e., each gentleman rowed for an hour at a time). The hours drag by, the odds grow heavier, exhaustion sets in: "The further we went on, our victual decreasing, and the air breeding great faintness, we grew weaker and weaker when we had most need of strength and ability." They are "brought into despair and discomfort."

When the three days were up, they added another: "We commanded our pilots to promise" that it was "only one day's work more to attain the land where we should be relieved of all we wanted." This too becomes a transparent falsehood, and soon "we were driven to assure them from four reaches of the river to three, and so to two, and so to the next reach."

Thus El Dorado: As in a dream it is forever getting nearer—just another day, just another "reach," just around the corner of the creek—but is never arrived at. I don't mean he literally pretended to his men that El Dorado was just around the corner, but that this elusive place where "we should be relieved of all we wanted" is at this point felt as a metaphor for El Dorado.

THE RELIEF they literally wanted, by now, was food. Their bread was "even to the last." Their fresh water was gone and they had only the "thick and troubled water of the river" to drink. It is at this point that Ralegh mentions using their "fowling pieces" to kill and eat the gorgeous river birds. Ralegh enumerates "pheasants, partridges, quails, rails, cranes, herons" among the edible birds. These would include the pheasantlike *marusi* and the turkeylike *powis* that Schomburgk ate in the delta, as well as the ibis and egrets we saw so plentifully. Schomburgk's favorite fare was wild musk-duck, much superior to the domesticated variety "improperly called Muscovy." He also recommends macaw, which "form an excellent soup, resembling hare-soup in taste."

Without this natural provender, Ralegh says, "we had been in a very hard case." They are living off the land. There is throughout the *Discoverie* a sense of the abundance of the New World. This is partly the conventional propaganda—precious "commodities"—but it is also a sense of gratitude for what kept them alive in this "hard case."

They ate tropical fruits, though they were often "corrupt," or rotten. Of these Ralegh singles out the pineapple, "the princess of fruits that grow under the sun." There were "divers herbs and roots." They had Indians with them—the old Warao guide; Ferdinando the Arawak and his brother—who could identify these: wild manioc, sweet potatoes, *palmitos,* and a hundred others. They laid nets, and "made meals of fresh fish." They harvested turtles and turtle eggs from the sandbanks. And they caught, or more likely shot with their muskets, alligators.

On the journey as a whole they ate various meats as well, but how much the delta yielded I do not know. There is no specific mention of them hunting on land, but one presumes they did, at least around the perimeter of their camps. Ralegh speaks of eating "deer of all sorts." They may have shot or trapped some wild deer in the delta: The Tivitivas had "deer dogs," with which they hunted the hapless pilot, Ferdinando.

They ate other jungle meats, but probably not in the delta. Ralegh mentions "a kind of beast called *cama* or *anta*, as big as an English beef, and in great plenty." This is the tapir, the largest quadruped in tropical America. The Pemón of Venezuela call tapir *danta,* which is probably the same as Ralegh's *anta.* He also mentions "porks" and "hares." The former may be the indigenous jungle pig, the *pakira* or peccary, or it may be European pigs introduced by the Spanish. The "hare" is probably the *acure* or *coboya,* sometimes called *conejillo* ("little rabbit")—the animal we call a guinea pig. This is indigenous to South America. The English name wrongly suggests an African origin. It may possibly be a corruption of "Guiana pig," but the *Oxford English Dictionary* dismisses this and says "Guinea" is applied loosely "as a designation for an unknown distant country." Another American staple, maize, was known at this time as "guinea wheat."

On their return journey, on a lake near the Orinoco, they "saw one of the great fishes as big as a wine-pipe, which they call *manati.*" This is the manatee, or sea cow. He says nothing of eating manatee: The Indians have superstitions against doing so. It was the Spaniards who developed a taste for it—mainly because, being amphibious, it could be eaten on Catholic fast days. Schomburgk also tucked in with gusto ("of good flavour, intermediate between pork and veal"). The manatee is now an endangered species, confined to remote eastern corners of the delta.

They also ate, on the return journey, an armadillo, but this was certainly given to them, not hunted by them.

A sense of American abundance emerges from the *Discoverie* as a whole, but is certainly not the case here in the delta. There were a hundred men here, hungry, tired, fractious. Whatever they scraped from the sandbanks and swamp scrub of the delta, it was precious little to go around.

IT WAS at this worrying stage—"wearied and scorched, and doubtful withal whether we should ever perform it or no"—that they had their second encounter with the Indians of the region.

This was a village of Arawaks. Ralegh was told about it by his Warao guide. It was called Aramiari, and it lay up a river "on the right hand" of the Manamo. From Ralegh's map it is clear he means the western bank of the Manamo, their "right hand" as they traveled upriver. Here, the guide promised, there would be food: bread, fish, hens, and "country wine." At this stage there was no alternative. He decided to halt the expedition and to strike up to Aramiari to replenish supplies. Leaving the galley at anchor in the Manamo, a small detachment set off: Ralegh in his barge with the guide; Captains Gifford and Calfield in the two wherries; and a contingent of sixteen musketeers.

Unfortunately, Ralegh's map does not really identify which of the western tributaries of the Manamo they traveled up. There are lots of them, but the map only shows three. It places Aramiari at the head of the northernmost of them, but one can't be sure which he means. According to the narrative of the *Discoverie* they had at this point been on the Manamo for about four days, after entering it from the "Red Cross." If their point of entry to the Manamo was, as I have suggested, around Boca del Tigre, then the most probable identification of this large western tributary four days upriver is undoubtedly the Morichal Largo, at the mouth of which lies Jovito Cortéz's farm, and opposite which lies the Warao village of Wakahara.

*   *   *

THEY SET off early, in good hope, but the hours passed, and as the afternoon light began to fade, they were still rowing. They had come, Ralegh estimated, "near forty miles." The old Warao kept on assuring them the village was just ahead: "He told us but four reaches more; when we had rowed four and four, we saw no sign." Again this figure of elusiveness: the destination as mirage, always receding.

By nightfall there was still no sign of any village. They were exhausted and scared: "Our poor watermen, even heart-broken and tired, were ready to give up the ghost." There was talk of hanging the old Warao; had they known their way back "he had surely gone."

Ralegh sketches the desperate scene:

> It was dark as pitch, and the river began so to narrow itself, and the trees to hang over from side to side, as we were driven with arming-swords to cut a passage thorough those branches that covered the water. We were very desirous of finding this town, hoping of a feast, because we had made but a short breakfast aboard the galley in the morning, and it was now eight o'clock at night, and our stomachs began to gnaw apace, but whether it was best to return or go on we began to doubt.

This is one of my favorite bits of the *Discoverie.* It is very immediate and intimate. It is being lost, and the sudden loneliness of nightfall, and turning once more to the guide in whom you have no trust, who just keeps saying: "It is but a little further, and but this one turning and that turning."

And then the deliverance: "At last, about one o'clock after midnight, we saw a light, and rowing towards it, we heard the dogs of the village."

They found the village half-empty. The chief was away "upon a journey." He had gone "towards the head of Orenoque, to trade for gold and to buy women of the Cannibals." (They nearly met this missing chief a couple of weeks later: He "unfortunately passed by us, as we rode at an anchor in the port of Morequito in the dark of night; and yet came so near us as his *canoas* grated against our barges.")

Despite the absence of the chief, and despite the inconvenience of several heavily armed gringos arriving in the dead of night, the welcome was cordial. The drooping English were invited into the chief's house, and plied with the promised provender: manioc bread, fish, chicken, and "Indian drink" or *cachire*.

They rested the night, and in the morning went back down to their boats, and there traded "with such of his people as came down." They set off back downriver, with a quantity of food supplies.

Now comes the first view of their surroundings, obscured by darkness on the way up. They find they have passed into a terrain very different from the watery, lugubrious delta:

> We passed the most beautiful country that mine eyes beheld, and whereas all that we had seen before was nothing but woods, prickles, bushes and thorns, here we beheld plains of twenty miles in length, the grass short and green, and in divers parts groves of trees by themselves, as if they had been by all the art and labour in the world so made of purpose. And still as we rowed, the deer came down feeding by the water's side, as if they had been used to a keeper's call. Upon this river there were great store of fowl, and of many sorts. We saw in it divers sorts of strange fishes, & of a marvellous bigness, but for *lagartos* [i.e., alligators] it exceeded, for there were thousands of those ugly serpents.

The description is, as often in this story, both practical and visionary. It makes sense geographically—they have followed this branch river westward, out of the delta system and onto the edge of the Orinoco plains, or *llanos*. If it was the Morichal Largo they followed, they had reached the area around present-day El Rosario, north of Temblador. This is the eastern edge of Venezuela's vast cattle country; it is, as Ralegh says, a very different terrain from that of the delta.

But it is clearly also a kind of heraldic landscape: a wild place endowed with order and regulation. After the hostile profuseness of the delta there is this vista of mown lawns, and artfully placed copses, and picturesque deer, and even an unseen "keeper" leading them down to the riverside to drink. It is an Arcadia, or indeed a Sherborne, with its water gardens and deer parks. And also, one notes, there are the thousands of alligators, decidedly untamed. These "ugly serpents" also inhabit Arcadia: the creature that lurks in the map of El Dorado.

The alligators, in fact, provide the last scene of this highly charged little detour. It happened shortly after their return to the mouth of the river, and their reunion with the hungry "companies." Among the crew was a "very proper" young black. This is the first and last we hear of him, for "leaping out of the galley, to swim in the mouth of this river, [he] was in all our sights taken and devoured with one of those *lagartos.*"

All of this—the magical landscape, the packed rowboats, the black swallowed by an "ugly serpent"—is depicted in a marvelous engraving. I found this pasted into one of the British Museum's copies of De Bry's Latin text of the *Discoverie.* It actually comes from a later edition (1625). A penciled note describes it as "spurious" (not, in other words, by De Bry himself). Spurious it may be, but it captures the dreamlike feel of this stage of the journey. It has never, as far as I know, been reproduced before.

On our own journey, we saw no alligators in the delta, but we did see a *culebra de agua,* or "water snake." We watched Jovito Cor-téz's dogs eating it. We were then by the mouth of the Morichal Largo, which is quite possibly where the unfortunate black was devoured four hundred years earlier.

WE WERE sad to leave Wakahara. Uwe was keen to move on, which was his mode as fixer: keep everyone moving. María Teresa wanted to stay longer, to pursue her Indian feelings.

The last night there was rum, and fires burning around our *ranchería.* One of the villagers shows us his homemade shotgun, which Trevor fires up into the night sky, setting the dogs barking

19. "Devoured by lagartos." *Engraving from the 1625 edition of De Bry's* Guiana

and the cocks crowing and the tethered pet toucans hopping in circles. Around midnight the rum is finished but Uwe is not, and Rómulo the boatman is dispatched to start up the *curiara*. He does not complain, just smiles his Oriental smile.

We speed across the dark Manamo to Jovito's, in search of another bottle. The dogs bark and Uwe hollers, but no one comes. We slither back through the mud to the boat, and across to Wakahara, Uwe's mood on the verge of ugliness, as it tended to be when he was drunk.

The next day we arrived at Tucapita. This is the main town, indeed the only town, in the delta, connected by road to Maturín and Puerto Ordaz. We are back with electricity and daily papers.

We land on a beach under some low, gnarled trees. At the top of some steps is a bar, where we sink some beers. We have a contact: Anthony. He is there to meet us. He has a wolfish smile and an accent you can't place—Palestinian-born, California-educated, smooth-talking, hair swept back. He is one of those well-heeled, well-oiled anthropologists with vague, impressive credentials. He had come into our camp at Wakahara with his leg mashed up: He cut it on some jagged iron below the surface of the water when he was climbing out of his boat. Uwe did his flying doctor bit, patched him up with swabs and bandages and antibiotic powder, and now we are invited to Anthony's apartment.

Tucapita could be just about anywhere in Venezuela: low-built streets, whitewashed houses, a scruffy plaza. The streets are clean. Most of the shops are "general stores."

There's the tawdry evidence of current election fever: graffiti, posters, caps; electioneering land-cruisers with PAs blasting out slogans and music. Badges, flags, and emblems—VOTA MAS NARANJA, CAUSA R.

I think of a graffito I saw once in Bogotá. MI CHICA SE LLAMA ABSTENCIÓN—My girl's name is Abstention.

To a restaurant: ice-cold beers, *churrascos* on wooden platters, dim lights, loud music. The *miniteca* plays "Welcome to the Hotel California." Tucapita is full of the pent-up enjoyments of the frontier town. People come here, as we do, after a spell out in the wilds. People come here for whiskey and women.

Our Indian boatmen sit silent at the other end of the table. We raise our glasses, they respond and grin, then resume their silence. Uwe says this is the first time they have been in a restaurant.

There is a bird hidden in the name of Tucapita. The Venezuelan word for a hummingbird is *tucuso;* there is an owl called *tuco;* and there is of course the *tucán,* or toucan.

That night in Tucapita we argued. There were personal angers and difficulties on this trip. I have no inclination to explain who got angry, and who got difficult, and who got hopelessly entangled and why. I follow Ralegh, my fallible but wise mentor, and omit whatever I choose to.

Nerves get raw on these expeditions, and for us they got raw around Tucapita.

*   *   *

IT WAS not far from Tucapita, a couple of days after their return from the Arawak village, that Ralegh and his crew had another encouraging sign.

The food brought back from the Arawaks had been wolfed down, and they were once more "at the last cast for want of victuals." Captain Gifford had gone up ahead with his boat, looking for a landing place where they could camp and "make fire." There they spotted four canoes. They gave chase; two escaped downriver, and two ran ashore. Turning up a "by-creek," Gifford found the two abandoned canoes, filled with *cassava* bread and "divers baskets of roots, which were excellent meat."

The rest of the party now joined them. (They had apparently missed the two canoes that went on downriver.) They set up a search party for the fugitive canoeists. Ralegh, Gifford, Calfield, and Thynne landed with a dozen musketeers and began to hack through the riverside forest.

Then there comes another of those *moments.* "As I was creeping thorough the bushes, I saw an Indian basket hidden." It was a gold refiner's kit, for "I found in it his quicksilver, salt-petre and divers things for the trial of metals." There was also the dust or tailings of "such ore as he had refined." Like the beautiful vistas he saw earlier, this description seems to be both reportage and something more than reportage—not so much heraldic this time, as folkloric. It describes the event, simply and sharply. (One almost hears the intake of breath as he spots the basket; he has been breathing hard as he struggles through the tangled wood; he is out of condition, an "ill footman.") But it also has the feel of a piece of woodland magic: a "basket hidden," a cache of fairy gold.

The fugitive Indians were rounded up. They were Arawaks, traveling downriver to sell *cassava* bread in Margarita. They said there were three Spaniards with them: a *caballero,* a soldier, and a refiner. They had good quantity of ore and gold with them. They, and the gold, had escaped.

From a Spanish report, written at Margarita at the end of June, we get a corroborative glimpse of this incident. The *caballero* who escaped was, we learn, Felipe de Santiago, an aide of Berrio's (but soon to desert to Berrio's rival, the Governor of Cumaná). "The enemy," says the report, "ascended the River Orinoco above the Guayana Bend" (i.e., beyond the westward turn onto the mainstream of the Orinoco). On the way

> Captain Phelippe de Santiago, a member of Berrio's forces, coming with four canoes, encountered them. He lost two of the canoes, but escaped with the others, and seeing that all was lost he made for the Island of La Margarita, where he now is.

This agrees, in its brief particulars, with Ralegh's account.

The Spaniards and their gold had escaped, but it was a sign, the kind of sign that bedevils the El Dorado searcher—the boat coming downriver, bringing out gold; the great central source of gold farther up that this might betoken. In these two vivid scenarios that Ralegh draws from his journey up the Caño Manamo—the night arrival at Aramiari and the finding of the refiner's basket—there seem to be many such signs. They are real events, as far as we know, but the imagery of legend plays over them, is projected onto them. The events blur into the folklore that has partly caused them in the first place. The succession of "reaches" that reach nowhere is the search for El Dorado; the missing chieftain is the ever-elusive Golden King; the hidden basket is the revelation of gold along the way that draws the searcher on. And the forests of South America are full of enchantment and magic, but full also of "ugly serpents" not unlike the creature that sits so curiously at the center of Ralegh's chart.

WITH THE bread in their stomachs, and a fingertip of gold dust thrust in front of their faces, "now our men cried, let us go on, we care not how far."

A day or two later, they had their first glimpse of the promised land of Guiana.

The 15 day, we discovered afar off the mountains of Guiana, to our great joy; and towards the evening had a slant of a northerly wind that blew very strong, which brought us in sight of the great river of Orenoque.

The highland they could see "afar off" was the Serranía de Imataca, an escarpment that runs for about two hundred miles at the north-eastern edge of the Guiana Shield. These are what Ralegh calls the "mountains of Emeria." It is not a tall range—peaks like Peluca and Paisapa reach about two thousand feet—but it seems so from the lowlands of the delta.

It was the fifteenth day of the *entrada:* about June 1, 1595. They had completed the first stage of the journey. They had come through the "laborinth" of the delta, through the hunger and despair and monotony, through that faint delirium in which the incidents of the journey take on a blurry allegorical life of their own, and were now about to come around the Guiana Bend.

[14]

Dark Eyes

*   *   *

THE STORY that unfolds in Ralegh's *Discoverie* is, besides the physical itinerary we are following, a journey into the habitat and culture of the American Indian. We have already seen his first encounters with the Indians—Caribs in Trinidad, Warao and Arawak in the delta—but these are glancing encounters: a ceremony, a skirmish, a half-deserted village. It is now that he reaches the Orinoco itself, and the tribes he calls the "borderers" of Guiana, that he begins to enter the Indian world.

Ralegh had, of course, met Indians before he actually came to America. American natives had been brought back to Europe ever since Columbus's first voyages. The earliest "Indians" to reach England, it is thought, were three Eskimos brought into Bristol in 1502. It is likely that Ralegh saw the Eskimo brought back by Martin Frobisher from the Labrador voyage of 1577. His demeanor was said to be "sullen and churlish, but sharp withal." His dark sallow skin reminded people of "tawny Moors" and Tartars. He was treated as a wonder—"the like of this strange infidel was never seen, read nor heard of before," wrote one pamphleteer, exaggerating the case somewhat—but he died shortly after his arrival. There is a sketch of him by the Flemish artist Lucas van Heere. On his second voyage (1578) Frobisher brought back a couple. They too died, but not before a son was born to them. He lived for many years, as a kind of mascot, at a London tavern called the Three Swans, and was buried in the churchyard of St. Olave's in Hart Street.

Ralegh had actually come to know two Indians quite well: the Algonquian braves, Manteo and Wanchese. (In present-day Carolina, the latter is pronounced bisyllabically: "Wahn-cheese," the second element rhyming with "geese." Whether this records an original pronunciation I do not know.) They came back with Amadas and Barlowe after the First Virginia Voyage: "We brought home also two of the savages, being lusty men," says Barlowe. They arrived in September 1584 and remained a year in England, as Ralegh's guests, surviving the English winter that often proved fatal to these exotic imports. A German tourist, Leopold von Wedel, noted in his diary:

A certain Captain Rall [i.e., Ralegh] permitted me to see his Indians. They are like white Moors. They usually wear a mantle of rudely tanned skins of wild animals, no shirts, and a pelt before their privy parts. However, on this occasion they were dressed in brown taffeta.

Taffeta was a glossy, silken material; these are Indians dressed up in rather gaudy finery. Von Wedel thinks they "made a most childish and silly figure"—an uncharitable response to their discomfort. They have the appearance of mascots, rather than guests: part of Ralegh's publicity machine as he tried to whip up interest in the full-scale colonization of Virginia.

Communication with them improved during the autumn months of 1584. On October 18 Manteo and Wanchese were said to be unable to make themselves understood in English, but two months later Ralegh was claiming that they had "made known" to him some of the "singular great commodities" of their homeland. The interpreter between Ralegh and the Indians was certainly Thomas Harriot. He may have been on the 1584 voyage; he was surely a member of the colony established at Roanoke the following year, "employed in discovering," as he put it. His extensive research there certainly suggests he was by then fairly fluent in Algonquian.

Thus Manteo and Wanchese play their part in the establishing of English perceptions of America, and of Indian life there. They, as much as his scouts and discovers, are Ralegh's first bridge to America. And now, more than a decade later, Ralegh is crossing that bridge.

*   *   *

IT IS a time of renewed confidence: an upbeat. It is the morning after their first sight, "afar off," of the Guiana Highlands. They were camped "upon a fair sand," close to the confluence of the Macareo (as the upper reach of the Manamo is known) and the Orinoco. They had dined well the night before on turtle eggs. The men were "well filled and highly contented, both with the fare, and the nearness of the land of Guiana, which appeared in sight."

Early that morning, the local chieftain arrived. His name was Toparimaca. Ralegh calls his tribe the Nepoios or Nepoyos. This name seems unknown to modern ethnology. He mentions them earlier, as one of the tribes inhabiting Trinidad, but this does not help to specify them. They are almost certainly a tribe of the Carib family, as are most of these tribes which he calls the "borderers" of Guiana.

Toparimaca arrived, at any rate, in some style: He "came down . . . with some thirty or forty followers, and brought us divers sorts of fruits, and of his wine, bread, fish and flesh." This is altogether grander than anything encountered by the English so far.

Ralegh and Toparimaca "conferred" (his favorite diplomatic term in these circumstances). Ralegh asked "the best ways into Guiana," and received courteous advice. All the while they "feasted" the chief as well as they could. "He drank good Spanish wine (whereof we had a small quantity in bottles), which above all things they love."

Toparimaca then invited them to visit his village. He led the English boats to his "port," or landing, and thence to his "town," a mile and a half inland. The place was called Arowacai. They were at this point west of the Caño Macareo, not far from present-day San Rafael de Barrancas.

Ralegh was struck by the beauty and order of the village. It stood on a small hill, "in an excellent prospect." It had "goodly gardens a mile compass round about it, and two very fair and large ponds of excellent fish adjoining." He sees it as a place of health, and notes the longevity of the Nepoyo people: "We saw very aged people, that we might perceive all their sinews and veins without any flesh."

There were two guests at the village, both *caciques,* one a neighbor and ally of Toparimaca, the other a "stranger that had been up the river to trade." Ralegh sketches the picture:

> They lay each of them in a cotton *hamaca,* which we call brazil-beds, and two women attending them, with six cups and a little ladle to fill them out of an earthen pitcher of wine, and so they drank each of them three of those cups at a time.

He tastes the wine—doubtless *cachire*—and commends it.

> It is very strong, with pepper and the juice of divers herbs, and fruits digested and purged. They keep it in great earthen pots of ten or twelve gallons, very clean and sweet.

A party ensues. Some of the English "garoused" on the *cachire* "till they were reasonable pleasant."

The dominant moment of the visit to Arowacai is not the party itself, but that tableau of lotus-eating indolence—the "lords" in their hammocks—and this is in turn suffused with the beauty of one of the Indian women, the wife of the "stranger" *cacique.* "In all my life," Ralegh says,

> I have seldom seen a better-favored woman. She was of good stature, with black eyes, fat of body, of an excellent countenance, her hair almost as long as herself, tied up in pretty knots. And it seemed she stood not in that awe of her husband as the rest, for she spake and discoursed and drank among the gentlemen and the captains, and was very pleasant, knowing her own comeliness, and taking great pride therein. I have seen a lady in England so like her, as but for the difference of colour I would have sworn might have been the same.

Thus life in Arowacai: fine views, splendid hospitality, strong wine, and beautiful women. No wonder they lived so long.

* * *

*20. Lords in their hammocks
(detail from De Bry)*

I WANT to linger a little over this moment of frisson.

The biographers gallantly claim that Ralegh is alluding to his wife as the English lady whose beauty matches this gorgeous *indígena.* Her spirited character perhaps sounds like Lady Ralegh's—she stood not in awe of her husband, she was a gracious hostess, she was confident of herself and her "comeliness." But the physical description, which is really the point ("a lady so like her"), simply does not tally. Elizabeth Ralegh was a tall, angular woman, auburn or gingerish in coloring. However happily married he was, we cannot make this Indian lady *look* like Ralegh's wife. (Nor, of course, like the Queen, who is also mentioned in this context.)

But if Ralegh does not mean his wife, or the Queen, whom does he mean? And isn't he risking the displeasure of both, by thinking about her, rather than them, at this rhapsodic moment?

Perhaps. He would not be the last writer to regret too late a comment pickled in print. But one solution occurs to me. Ralegh's description of the Indian woman at Arowacai may or may not tally with a particular "lady" in England, but it certainly tallies with a *type* of woman currently admired in England. His description matches exactly certain dark-eyed, Latin-looking ladies—specifically Italian rather than Spanish—who appear in popular fiction at this time, and who presumably mirror current sexual fashions in England. Shakespeare's Rosalind in *Love's Labour's Lost,* sometimes dated to circa 1595, is a "wanton with a velvet brow" and has "two pitchballs stuck in her face for eyes." The Dark Lady of the *Sonnets* (possibly the Italian musician's daughter, Emilia Bassano) has "raven black" eyes and hair like "black wires." And here is the Venetian temptress Diamante, the love interest in Thomas Nashe's picaresque story, *The Unfortunate Traveller,* published in 1594:

A pretty round-faced wench was it, with black eyebrows, a high forehead, a little mouth and a sharp nose, as fat and plum every part of her as a plover, a skin as slick and soft as the back of a swan. It doth me good when I remember her. Like a bird she tripped on the ground, and bare out her belly as majestical as an estrich.

The proud, comely lady of Arowacai—"black eyes, fat of body, of an excellent countenance"—seems close to these feisty dark ladies of the Elizabethan imagination.

Elsewhere Ralegh praises the beauty of the Indian women: "I saw many of them, which but for their tawny colour may be compared to any of Europe." He saw a slave girl, apparently a Carib, who was "as well shaped as ever I saw any in England." In both cases he insists that the native women are as beautiful as the "civilized" women of Europe, and his portrait of the *cacique*'s wife presses this further: She is precisely "sexy" according to the English tastes of the day.

One reading of this is discreetly propagandist. In other words, the region's women are desirable in much the same way as its land is fertile, its climate healthy, its gold abundant, its warlords well disposed, and all the other rose-tinted claims Ralegh makes for Guiana. The *Discoverie* is in part a rather ramshackle brochure for the colony Ralegh hoped to establish there, equivalent to Hakluyt's and Harriot's publications on Virginia, and this praise of Indian women is part of the pitch. So too is the idea that they are very "like" English women.

Another point is how the seductiveness of the natives is so notably *resisted* by Ralegh and the rest of his company. His description of the *cacique*'s wife invites an erotic reaction from the reader, but is itself decorous and restrained (unlike Nashe's lip-smacking portrait of Diamante). This is made much clearer in another passage in the *Discoverie*—indeed, Ralegh goes so far as to swear to it:

I protest before the majesty of the living God, that I neither know nor believe that any of our company, one or other, by violence or otherwise, ever knew any of their women. And yet we saw many hundreds, and

had many in our power, and of those very young and excellently favou-
red, which came among us without deceit, stark naked.

Here again the reader is offered this nubile vision in the text, precisely to learn how remarkably restrained the English had been when
presented with it in the flesh. He goes on to explain the obvious
benefits of this.

> Nothing got us more love among them than this usage, for I suffered
> not any man to take from any of the nations [i.e., tribes] so much as
> a *piña* or a potato-root, without giving them contentment; nor any
> man so much as to offer to touch any of their wives and daughters;
> which course, so contrary to the Spaniards, who tyrannize over them
> in all things, drew them to admire Her Majesty, whose command-
> ment I told them it was.

This is the argument, then. The sexual restraint of the English travelers was a moral victory over the Spanish, whose name was a byword
for rape, and a practical victory in that it won the "love" of the Indians, and their alliance against the Spanish. It also, adroitly relates this
theme of abstinence back to the Queen, "whose commandment I told
them it was." Thus the chaste knight Sir Walter spreads the cult of
the Virgin Queen among the "borderers" of Guiana.

ONE OF of the interesting aspects of this "chaste" colonizing is its
relation to—its apparent inversion of—the conventional sexual imagery associated with American colonization. The famous example
of this motif, as mentioned earlier, is Donne's elegy to his mistress.

> License my roving hands, and let them go
> Before, behind, between, above, below.
> O my America! my new-found-land,
> My kingdom safeliest when with one man mann'd,
> My mine of precious stones, my Emperie,
> How blest am I in discovering thee!

The metaphor is precisely this kind of expedition Ralegh is embarked on. The ardent lover is the adventurer "licensed" to travel, the "roving" explorer, the colonist who "mans" or peoples the region, the prospector who plumbs its "mines." The poem is undated, but is certainly later than the Guiana Voyage, which may be in Donne's mind as he frames this metaphor. (He sailed with Ralegh's fleet to the Azores in 1597, and was himself caught up for a while in the Guiana enthusiasm, as in his epigram "Calez & Guyana.") If it is in his mind, he is using it in an ironic way, as in the last line quoted above, where the "discovering" of America is ironized as the uncovering, or undressing, of his mistress. This turns Ralegh's *Discoverie* into an exercise in voyeurism, a titillation before the main business of colonization.

Donne's poem reunites the American enterprise—and perhaps specifically the Guiana Voyage—with its conventional metaphor of aggressive male sexuality. A parallel poem (probably contemporary, sometimes ascribed to Donne, but not published till the 1650s) adds another item that I have commented on: this exotic darkness that is a common feature of the native woman and the thinking Elizabethan's pinup. It is called "On Black Hair & Eyes."

> So your black hair and eyes do give direction
> To make me think the rest of like complexion:
> The rest where all rest lies that blesseth man:
> That Indian mine, that Strait of Magellan,
> That world-dividing gulf where he that venters
> With swelling sails and ravished senses enters
> To a new world of bliss. . . .

This brings the discovery-as-undressing motif of Donne's elegy to what one can only call a climax. This is the American explorer, or actually his ship, as erect member: a "swelling" vessel, a "ravished" ravisher, venturing into the darkly forested "gulf" of the New World.

Against the background of this kind of macho stuff, one discerns in Ralegh's *entrada* (which word is, of course, fraught with all these meanings) a deliberate undertone of sexual uncertainty. It is a circuitous, faltering entry. The way through the delta is labyrinthine, full of curves, hence detumescent. He fears he is not up to it: an ill swordsman, perhaps.

Or is the motif, rather, one of dalliance, of patient connoisseurship—his lingering progress a kind of foreplay before the firm thrust up the Orinoco; the delta as the dense triangle of vegetation that hides the entrance to Guiana?

It does not really matter, because Ralegh's chief point is that his is a different *kind* of exploration. In his orders to the men, in his own abstinent view of the beautiful Indians, he severs in practical ways that metaphorical link between New World voyaging and sexual possession. He presents himself as a colonist whose methods and intentions are not identifiable as a kind of rape. In this sense his comments on the Indian women are central to his whole attitude to America.

There is an intellectual tradition behind this, a metaphysical idea of the New World, which I will look at later. One aspect of it is a rather cultish idea of Virginia and the Virgin Queen. Richard Hakluyt expresses this in a dedication to Ralegh, written in 1587. In this—prefaced to his new edition of that seminal New World work, Peter Martyr's *De Orbe Novo*—Hakluyt describes Ralegh in terms that mingle, rather as Ralegh himself does in the *Discoverie,* sexuality and purity. He imagines Ralegh as a steadfast "bridegroom" to America.

> You freely swore that no terrors, no personal losses or misfortunes, could or would ever tear you from the sweet embraces of your own Virginia, that fairest of nymphs, though to many insufficiently well known, whom our most generous sovereign has given you to be your bride. If you persevere only a little longer in your constancy, your bride will shortly bring forth new and most abundant offspring.

This represents the potential settlers of America as a wholesome family born of this "marriage" between a great Englishman and a beautiful feminine land, Virginia, with the Queen as the fairy godmother whose handiwork this happy scene is. This is, once again, in contrast to the idea of colonization as a rape.

IT SEEMS apposite to say a word here about those other women of the region, the Amazons, and about Ralegh's attitude to them. He is sometimes taxed with credulousness: unfairly, I think.

The Amazons are a classic "projection" of European fantasies onto the New World. As is well known, the Amazons originally feature in Greek mythology: a tribe of warrior women who swept down from the hills of Scythia to occupy various Hellenic sites, notably the Isle of Lesbos. They shunned men, except once a year for the purposes of procreation; they killed all male offspring; they cut off their right breasts to facilitate the drawing of the bowstring (their name is from the Greek, *a mastos,* "without breast").

These formidable ladies were imported wholesale into America by Columbus. On his first voyage he heard of female warriors inhabiting the island of Matinino (i.e., Martinique). They lived "without men," fought with bow and arrow, and wore "plates of copper" as armor. He describes these women as Amazons, and by implication gives them the attributes of their mythic forebears. Columbus was himself "somewhat obsessed with Amazons," according to D. B. Quinn (he refers to Columbus's gloss on the *Historia Rerum* of Aeneas Sylvius).

At this stage the American Amazons are bodiless: Columbus has not seen them. They are on a par with the "one-eyed people" and the tribe "with dog faces who ate people," of whom he has also heard report. These are also imported images: Both types are found in Pliny and in Mandeville. Then, on a later journey, in 1496, Columbus actually encountered armed Carib women in Guadeloupe. Apart from their readiness to fight, these women shared none of the characteristics of the classical Amazons (they did not live without men, they did not practice automastectomy, etc.) but by then the connection is made. The story circulates and grips the imagination, and when Francisco de Orellana is making his historic transcontinental journey of 1542, and encounters female warriors near the mouth of the Napo River, it is natural that he too should believe they are "Amazons," and equally natural, in this nameless continent, that the river he is traveling down should thereafter be called the Amazon.

Columbus may have been "obsessed" with Amazons, but clearly we are concerned with more than one man's hangup or predilection. At any stage—classical, medieval, New World—the Amazon myth encodes, none too opaquely, an identifiable range of male sexual fears and fantasies. It is these that are projected onto the blankness of the New World; these that become entwined with a sense of the otherness and savagery of America; these that trouble the lonely pioneer, in the night full of noises, with dreams of enslavement to a six-foot dominatrix in a jaguar skin. Like the cannibals, the Amazons come to represent a fear of being swallowed up by America: the fear of disappearance.

In Ralegh's time, the existence of Amazons in South America was accepted lore—Peter Martyr's *De Orbe Novo* and Thevet's *Antartique* were two sources he read on the subject—and while traveling in Guiana, on the northern edges of the Amazon Basin, he was naturally "desirous to understand the truth of those warlike women, because of some it is believed, of others not." He insists that what he has to say is only report, not firsthand: "I will set down what hath been delivered me for truth of those women." This vein of skepticism has to work hard to subdue the fatal attractions of the subject.

He is, of course, aware of the original, classical Amazons.

> The memories of the like women are very ancient, as well in Africa and Asia: in Africa, those that had Medusa for Queen; others in Sci-thia near the rivers of Tanais and Thermadon; we find also that Lampedo and Marthesia were Queens of the Amazons. In many histories they are verified to have been, and in divers ages and provinces.

(This passage throws some light on Ralegh's attitude to mythology. These legends are said to be ancient "memories" of the Amazons, "histories" that "verify" their existence. The legend is seen not as a fiction, but as a kind of prototype. One is reminded of the adage of Saloustios, taken by Roberto Calasso for the epigraph of *The Marriage of Cadmus and Harmony:* "These things never happened and are always true.")

On this basis of Indian report and classical parallel, Ralegh delivers a concise account of the American Amazons. He states their probable location—south of the Amazon River, "in the province of Topago"—and describes their customs as follows:

> They . . . do accompany with men but once a year, and for the time of one month, which I gather by their relation to be in April. At that time all the Kings of the borders assemble, and the Queens of the Amazons, and after the Queens have chosen, the rest cast lots for their Valentines. This one month they feast, dance and drink their wines in abundance, and the moon being done they all depart to their own provinces. If they conceive and be delivered of a son, they return him to the father; if of a daughter they nourish it and retain it, and as many as have daughters send unto the begetters a present, all being desirous to increase their own sex and kind. But that they cut off the right dug of the breast I do not find to be true. It was farther told me that if in the wars they took any prisoners, that they used to accompany with those also, at what time soever, but in the end for certain they put them to death; for they are said to be very cruel and blood-thirsty, especially to such as offer to invade their territories.

This is clearly a sophistication of the usual imagery of the Amazons. The final sentences return to the norm—"blood-thirsty" women carrying men off, using them sexually "at what time soever," and then murdering them—but most of his description has another atmosphere, which is curiously courtly. He depicts the Amazonian coupling as a chivalric, masquelike meeting of kings and queens. There is "dancing and feasting," and—the supremely English touch—the casting of "lots for Valentines." It has the air of one of those elaborate royal picnics he used to attend. It belongs in that landscape he glimpsed on the edge of the delta: that imagined tropical deer-park.

Here again we find Ralegh dramatically modifying a theme of sexual aggression. (The euphemistic "accompany with" is part of this sanitizing.) I would say that Ralegh's Amazons are about as "chaste"

21, 22. Amazons. Hulsius captures both the "bloodthirsty" and the "courtly" images suggested by Ralegh.

as an Amazon could be. They seem a counterpart to these idealistic notions of the "chaste" colonizer.

MUCH OF this is summed up in Ralegh's famous and poignant apostrophe to Guiana, placed in the text as a kind of valedictory synopsis as he prepares to sail back home to England.

> To conclude, Guiana is a country that hath yet her maidenhead, never sacked, turned nor wrought. The face of the earth hath not been torn, nor the virtue and salt of the soil spent by manurance. The graves have not been opened for gold, the mines not broken open with sledges, nor their images pulled down out of their temples. It hath never been entered by any army of strength, and never conquered or possessed by any Christian prince.

In one sense this is a piece of trickery, or casuistry, since it cannot be denied that Ralegh's intentions were, if not to sack the place, then certainly to tear the earth, to break open the mines, and to pull down the heathen images (in other words, to plant, exploit, and convert). Similarly, this conclusion might be seen as summing up the essential failure of his expedition to produce any tangible rewards: No great tracts of land were claimed; no great store of gold was found. Guiana's continued virginity is Ralegh's failure: an impotence.

Against these readings—risking these readings—Ralegh's words appeal to a poetic vision of Guiana as against the pragmatic colonial vision. They champion it as pristine and untouched, and characterize the colonial enterprise as a gross, violent intrusion. The sexual verbs—"entered" and "possessed"—are attributed to "Christian princes," extending this idea of violation to the missionary, Christianizing aspects of colonization: a risky idea at the time, though easy to take aboard now.

Thus Ralegh's discovery of Guiana leads to this awestruck perception of its integrity *as it is:* its intactness as a landscape and a culture. This is prefigured in his comments about the Indian woman in Arowacai. You can, in short, "enter" a country without violating it, and you can admire the comely, defenseless women without raping them, as the Spaniards do.

This whole theme is not to deny the sexual charge of the moment, as he watches and talks and doubtless flirts a little with this black-eyed woman, so exotic that even in strange Arowacai she is herself a "stranger." They had been away from England for nearly four months now. He looks into her dark eyes, feels the powerful allure of these women. Even in his eulogy of Guiana, one notes the familiar Elizabethan pun on "country" (still often spelled "cuntry"). Placed so close to the word "maidenhead" this cannot be unintentional. It seems crude to our ears, but I see it as carrying, indeed accommodating, those real and urgent desires that he felt, that all travelers feel. He wanted desperately to have Guiana, and indeed the *cacique*'s wife, in all the bad old ways.

This moment at Arowacai is full of the poignancy of impossible desire. The *cacica* becomes, like the missing chief a few days before, another of these symbols of elusiveness, another projection of El Dorado.

[15]

Lords of the Borders

*　　*　　*

THERE IS a new sense of momentum, as they leave the profusions and confusions of the delta, and broach the mainstream of the Orinoco. The river is seen as the northern "border" of Guiana. Toparimaca is one of the "lords of the borders." He is the first but not the greatest that Ralegh will meet.

The day after the visit to Arowacai—day seventeen of the expedition—they entered the Orinoco, having "on the left hand a great island which they call Assapana," which he estimates to be twenty-five miles long, and beyond that another island called Iwana, "twice as big as the Isle of Wight." These are the islands now called Isla Matamata and Isla Tortola (the latter is Spanish, Turtledove Island). On the right hand "there opened a river which came from the north, called Europa." This is the Caño Guarguapo: interesting how the English hear and assimilate the native name.

That night, as on later nights, they camped on one of the many small islands that dot the Orinoco here, the riverbanks being too "stony and high" for the purpose.

The following day they entered the territory of a chieftain called Putmaya. They see rocks "of a blue metalline colour, like unto the best steel ore, which I assuredly take it to be." To their right the land opens up: "The country appeared to be champain, and the banks showed very perfect red." A detachment lands to explore: Gifford, Calfield, Thynne; three young relatives, Gilbert, Grenville, and Gorges; and two characters otherwise unknown to me, Captain Eynos and Edward Porter. "They found it all plain level, as far as they went, or could discern from the highest tree they could get upon." Ralegh's new guide tells him that "the same level reached to Cumaná and Caracas." They are of course on the edge of the Orinoco *llanos,* at this time—early June—greening up under the first rains.

They wait for the local *cacique,* Putmaya, but he does not come. (They would meet him on the return journey.) They anchor at another island, close to the "main bank." By the "main" bank he means the southern bank of the Orinoco, which he takes to be the "main," or coast, of Guiana, just as the Caribbean coast is the Spanish Main.

Near this island, on the edge of the shore, stands a "very high mountain called Oecope." This is probably—as Schomburgk suggests—the rocky outcrop now called Cerro Padrastro. (*Padrastro* has two meanings in Spanish: One guesses this is Hangnail Hill rather than Stepfather Hill, but who knows?) This is the site of the two Spanish fortresses known as Los Castillos de Guayana. Ralegh was now about thirty miles downriver from the mouth of the Caroní, which will prove to be his destination. This is not, as is sometimes said, the original site of San Thomé de Guayana, the Spanish garrison founded by Berrio in late 1595, and is not therefore the site of the tragic debacle of Ralegh's Last Voyage of 1617–18. It is clear, from documents first assembled by Harlow in the 1920s, that San Thomé was founded farther upriver, only about three miles from the Caroní. The garrison was not moved to the Cerro Padrastro—its third site— till the later seventeenth century.

The garrison was not there when Ralegh passed, but there may have been a Spanish presence. The lower fortress, down by the river, is called San Francisco de Asís. It was built in the 1670s, but is named after a Franciscan mission that was there earlier. According to some sources, the mission—founded by Domingo de Santa Agueda—was in business as early as 1593. If so, it was there when Ralegh came. The larger, higher fortress, San Diego de Alcalá, was begun in 1734.

They are not contemporary, but they are certainly a potent sight looming up above our boats, an impression of solidity in this shifting landscape: the flagstones, the immaculate walls, and the cannon trained across the brown Orinoco, controlling the narrows west of

Isla Matamata. Below the fortresses is a small village, Guayana Vieja. About 250 live here: fishermen and farmers. In the woods as you walk down there is a bust of Antonio de Berrio: a helmeted figure, a jutting beard, but his features mottled with moss and verdigris, giving him a disregarded air.

After five days on the Orinoco, making slow progress against the ever-rising river, they reached the region that Ralegh calls Arromaia. This was the land formerly ruled by Morequito, a Carib chief whom Berrio had executed the previous year in retaliation for the killing of twelve Spaniards.

They anchored near an island that Ralegh calls Murrecotima. This seems to be Isla Mocua, though this is now smaller than Ralegh's estimate of ten miles by five. It was while they were camped here that the elusive Arawak chief Aramiari, "to whose town we made our long and hungry voyage out of the river of Amana," passed by on his way back home from trading upriver. He came so close that his canoes "grated" Ralegh's barge, but slipped away into the darkness again.

The next day they arrived at the "port of Morequito." This was not, of course, their intended destination—they were still only on the "borders" of Guiana—but it was somewhere they had heard of, and somewhere they were aiming at. It stood on the south bank of the Orinoco. It is convenient to call it Port Morequito, but "port" in this case simply means a landing place, and does not imply that there were dwellings here. According to Spanish documents the port, which was later the site of the garrison of San Thomé, lay about three miles downriver from the mouth of the Caroní. Ralegh states that while he was there he could actually hear the "great roar and fall" of the Caroní. It now lies beneath the newer town of San Félix.

Indian messengers were dispatched to the *cacique* of the region. This was the chief of a tribe called the Orenoqueponi. He lived in a town about fourteen miles inland, called Orocotona. He was the uncle of the late Morequito, and was the most powerful of these "lords of the borders." His name was Topiawari. Ralegh met him the following day, which I estimate to be about June 9, 1595, the twenty-third day of the *entrada*.

*   *   *

RALEGH'S MEETING with "aged Topiawari" is a lavish and heart-
ening scene. The English had received gifts and hospitality, both
from the Arawaks and the Nepoyos. There has been a sense of plenty,
a generosity both of the land and the people. This now reaches a
crescendo, as Topiawari arrives with a whole cavalcade of "followers,"
including women and children. They "came to wonder at our nation," but also they came in the full spate of profligate Indian hospitality, bringing "great plenty" of victuals—"venison, pork, hens,
chickens, fowl, fish, with divers sorts of excellent fruits and roots,
and great abundance of *piñas,* the princess of fruits that grow under
the sun, especially those of Guiana." They also brought gifts of the
forest: birds of all colors and sizes, including "a sort of *paraquitos,*
no bigger than wrens"—hummingbirds, perhaps. And a rare and
exotic treat:

> One of them gave me a beast called by the Spaniards *armadilla,* which
> they [the Indians] call *cassacam,* which seemeth to be all barred over
> with small plates, somewhat like to a *renocero,* with a white horn
> growing in his hinder parts, as big as a great hunting-horn.

He informs us that the Indians use this horny tail "instead of a
trumpet," and adds a learned footnote from Monardus, that "a little
of the powder of that horn put into the ear cureth deafness."
    At his second meeting with Topiawari, a few days later, it is the
same cavalcade.

> With him [came] such a rabble of all sorts of people, and every one
> loden with somewhat, as if it had been a great market or fair in
> England; and our hungry companies clustered thick and threefold
> among their baskets, everyone laying hand on what he liked.

With each meeting with the Indians the scene grows more lavish
and extensive.
    It is this scene of welcome and abundance that De Bry illustrates

23. Ralegh and Topiawari

in his engraving. The Indians in the foreground, bearing their tributes: One has a basket of fruit on his head, another a brace of jungle pheasant. One woman carries maize, another a large round fruit that might be a calabash or a melon or even a large *sapodilla.* The Indians wear skirts or loincloths made of feathers, and brimless, vaguely fezlike caps. The two central figures sit in a tent ("a little tent that I caused to be set up") with an English guard of pikes and muskets at either side. Ralegh wears a natty suit of doublet and breeches, and a tall hat with the brim turned raffishly up. A breastplate and a sword are his only concessions to the exigencies of the situation. And seated on his right, in the place of honor, Topiawari himself, distinguished as chief by his feathered headdress. He extends his right hand, offering the bounty of the region, and—a touch I like very much—he sits with his legs casually crossed. This expresses an easy poise: the Lord of the Borders as genial host offering his guest some refreshment.

In the *Discoverie,* as in De Bry's engraving, it is "aged Topiawari" who steals the scene. He was, Ralegh believed, 110 years old. He described himself as old and weak; he "was every day called for by death" (this was "his own phrase"). Nonetheless, he had walked from his town, Orocotona, to the river—a distance of "fourteen good English miles"—in three hours, and later in the day he walked back again. Ralegh was deeply impressed, not only by his physical toughness, which was axiomatic, but by his dignity and strength of character.

> This Topiawari is held for the proudest and wisest of all the Orenoqueponi, and so he behaved himself towards me in all his answers. . . . I marvelled to find a man of that gravity and judgement, and of so good discourse, that had no help of learning nor breed.

He is a "noble savage," in short: his prowess natural rather than nurtured.

IN HIS meetings with the lords—and indeed the ladies—of the borders, we find tremendous admiration. At its height, here at Port Morequito, Ralegh expresses a highly charged, poetic, utopian view of Indian people and culture. There is honor, beauty, peace, and plenty.

It is at this point, however, that the accounts of Francis Sparry strike a note of discord, and suggest that Ralegh's idealized picture of the "borderers" is achieved by suppressing some of the facts of the matter. In his *memorial* to King Philip of Spain, dictated in a Madrid prison in about 1600, Sparry gives a very different account of Ralegh's dealings with the Orenoqueponi. This is what he says:

> He [Ralegh] entered the Orinoco river to a distance of 130 leagues, and in this place there gathered a large number of Indians in canoes,

to prevent any further ascent of the river. The Indians, seeing what damage the muskets of the English might do to them, promptly turned their backs, and went and hid themselves in various parts of the river and the mountainous land. The English chased after them, and caught five or six, and brought them to Guaterrale.

It is clear that Sparry is speaking of their arrival at Port Morequito. He gives a precise distance: they were 130 leagues (390 miles) up the Orinoco. This compares with Ralegh's own computation that they came 400 miles from the ships. His subsequent comments confirm that he is referring to events at Port Morequito.

According to Sparry, then, their first encounter with the Orenoqueponi was extremely tense—the massed Indian canoes across the river, the flourishing of muskets on the English boats, the frightened scattering of the Indians, the chasing and taking of prisoners. He does not say that the English actually opened fire: The Indians saw what damage the muskets *might* do to them—the verb is quite clearly subjunctive (*hacían*)—and thereupon fled. But the whole episode has a mood of hostility and violence. It is a military encounter.

Not a word of this appears in the *Discoverie*. One cannot be sure Sparry is telling the truth, but I see no reason for him to lie. It has a ring of truth. As the Spaniards knew to their cost, these Indians were tough resisters; this was still the badlands down here. This seems a plausible account of the Indians' reaction to the arrival of a heavily armed party of strangers: more plausible, perhaps, than the tranquil scene described (or anyway implied) by Ralegh.

When these "five or six" captured Indians were brought to Ralegh, Sparry continues,

he embraced them, and made show of much love towards them, and of desiring their friendship. He offered them gifts, giving them some things that were brought from England, such as little mirrors, combs and knives. He gave these as tokens, to let them understand that he did not come to do evil, but to win their friendship, and to give them those things which they needed in that country.

I am guessing about the nuances of sixteenth-century Spanish, but I suspect there is a deliberate cynical overtone when Sparry says Ralegh "made show of much love towards them" (*haciendo demostración de tenerles mucho amor*). It is interesting, also, to hear of the knick-knacks doled out to the Indians: mirrors, combs, knives. This rather degrading type of trade is another thing Ralegh chooses to omit from the *Discoverie*. He speaks haughtily of the Spanish handing out hatchets and knives, but never mentions doing so himself.

Having "soothed" these Indians, Sparry says, Ralegh let them go, and they "brought along others, with whom he dealt in the same way."

> And so the news spread that the English were good friends. Then the king of that region came, with other Indian chiefs, and these in particular Guaterrale embraced, and offered gifts, and made treaties with them, in the name of Her Majesty the Queen of England, by which the English could come there freely to trade.

The "king of that region" is, of course, Topiawari.

It is not that this actually casts a shadow over Ralegh's dealings with Topiawari. It just serves to remind us that the story told in the *Discoverie* is only one version. In this rare instance, we have another. It is a more brusque and cynical version. It is closer to the pragmatic realities of the *entrada,* a language of confrontation, weaponry, negotiation in the context of threat.

We have seen other examples of Ralegh's silence in the *Discoverie*—the taking of prizes in the Atlantic; the raid on San José; the roughing up of Berrio: These are omitted or thoroughly sanitized. The later raid on Cumaná will, likewise, appear only in Spanish documents. The harsher, more military aspects of Ralegh's *entrada* are suppressed in favor of this more idealized exploration: one based on admiration and understanding, respect and restraint—"conferring," in a word, rather than conquering. Sparry is probably right that Ralegh's dealings with the "borderers" of Guiana were, to begin with, rather rougher than he cares to admit.

*   *   *

WHATEVER THE initial hostilities, whatever the more pragmatic aspects of Ralegh's behavior, there is no doubt that his friendship with Topiawari was genuine. We know from later travelers that it was heartily reciprocated, and that Topiawari eagerly awaited Ralegh's return: a promise only partly fulfilled, and long after the aged chief was dead. In Ralegh's *entrada* into the Indian world, this was where he got to.

It was also as close as he got to a firsthand account of El Dorado. In that "little tent," having "dilated" of the Queen's "beauties and virtue," and her "charity to all oppressed nations," he began to "sound the old man as touching Guiana." (A reprise, in a sense, of his session with Berrio a month earlier.)

Topiawari "answered with a great sigh, as a man which had inward feeling of the loss of his country and liberty," and told Ralegh of the occupation of Guiana by a strange and powerful tribe, of the expulsion of his own people and others, of the wars that had been fought, and of the recent death of his son in those wars. The invasion had begun when he was a young man—according to Ralegh's estimate of his age, about eighty or ninety years ago. He said

> that there came down, into that large valley of Guiana, a nation from so far off as the sun slept (for such were his own words), with so great a multitude that they could not be numbered or resisted; and that they wore large coats, and hats of crimson colour, which colour he expressed by showing a piece of red wood wherewith my tent was supported; and . . . that their houses have many rooms, one over the other.

These invaders he called "Oreiones and Epuremei." They were now in complete possession of Guiana.

> They had slain and rooted out so many of the ancient people as there were leaves in the wood upon all the trees, and had now made themselves lords of all, even to that mountain foot called Curaa . . . and

[they] had built a great town called Macureguarai, at the said mountain foot, at the beginning of the great plains of Guiana which have no end.

This town lay four days' journey from Topiawari's settlement at Orocotona. It was the "next and nearest" source of Guiana gold: "All those plates of gold which were scattered among the borderers, and carried to other nations far and near, came from the said Macureguarai." It was also the empire's formidable front line, where "the great King of the Oreiones and Epuremei kept three thousand men to defend the borders."

This appareled, house-building, warlike tribe, migrating into Guiana early in the sixteenth century, is of course the Inca. The word *orejones,* which Topiawari supposedly uses, is the Spanish term for the warrior elite of the Inca, referring to the earplugs they wore. In a later passage Ralegh specifies this, calling the tribe the "subjects of Inga."

So this "King of the Orejónes" is the El Dorado whom Ralegh has sought: an Inca emperor enthroned in the heart of the Guiana Highlands. At last, or so it appears, he is hearing about him at first hand. One has to wonder how much of this information was actually given by Topiawari. The Sparry document shows that Ralegh may have falsified, by omission, his first encounters with the Orenoqueponi. Here too, though we have no alternative source, I suspect some tampering, or anyway wishful thinking. Despite the touches of direct reportage—the colorful quotes, the business about the tent pole—this speech of Topiawari's *confirms* Ralegh's theories to a suspicious degree.

It also, in that very characteristic way, shields the theory from the inconvenience of proving it. Topiawari argued strongly of the dangers of proceeding into Guiana.

He did not perceive that I meant to go onward towards the City of Manoa, for neither the time of the year served, neither could he perceive any sufficient numbers for such an enterprise; and if I did, I was sure, with all my company, to be buried there, for that the Emperor was of that strength as that many times so many men more were too few.

Even as Ralegh learns of the closeness of El Dorado—it is just four or five days to the frontier town of Macureguarai—he learns also of its impregnability. It is there, but it cannot be reached. Even the "border" of it seems to recede. The Orinoco is only an outer border; the empire actually begins at Macureguarai, and Macureguarai is in turn a mere shadow of El Dorado itself. "Plates of gold" are made there, but (said Topiawari) "those of the land within were far finer, and were fashioned after the image of men, beasts, birds and fishes."

So this wonderful meeting with Topiawari is also a disappointment. It produces much that Ralegh will value—the personal friendship, the political alliance, the possibility of a genuine English foothold in South America—but it is also the moment that El Dorado slips from his grasp. It has obsessed him for too long. This is a disappointment, but also perhaps it is a relief.

SO WHO were these people, the Orenoqueponi? It is almost certain that they were Macusi, a tribe of the Carib family still very numerous in the region. The Macusi of Venezuela are generally known as the Pemón.

There is strong etymological evidence, much of it first pointed out by the redoubtable Robert Schomburgk. The name Orenoqueponi is explained by the Macusi preposition *pona,* on: They are "the tribe on the Orinoco." Their town, Orocotona, is formed of Macusi *oroke* (parrot) and *touna* (water): Parrot Water—either a river populous with parrots, or perhaps, in this region of waterfalls and rapids, water that is noisy like a parrot. Another place name mentioned by Ralegh, Wanuretona, would therefore be *wanure touna,* or Heron Water. The mountain called Iconuri is Blue Mountain (*iconuru,* blue). One of the islands in the Orinoco he calls Okaiwita; this is probably a misunderstanding, since *oakai iwotta,* "great river," is actually a

Macusi description of the Orinoco itself. And the town that Topia-wari calls Macureguarai, the border town of El Dorado, probably contains the Macusi word for sword, *macuwari.*

This is an impressive array of linguistic comparisons, and it is likely that "aged Topiawari" and his tribe were a branch of the Macusi family.

This perhaps sheds some light on the mysterious Nepoyos, whom Ralegh met a few days previously. These "border" tribes along the Orinoco are seen as distinct but allied tribes, with Topiawari as their overall "lord." The Nepoyo chief has a similar name, Toparimaca (the *top* element in both probably signifies "chief," though I can find nothing to confirm this in the dictionaries).

The Nepoyos are likely, then, to be a Carib tribe related to the Macusi. One possibility is that they were Waika. This tribe—now small—inhabits the gold-rich Cuyuní and Yuararí rivers, not far to the south of where Ralegh met the Nepoyos. They were formerly found as far east as the Barama River. The twentieth-century Waika, in other words, inhabit the region that Ralegh called Emeria. This was the territory of Carapana, with whom Ralegh links the Nepoyos, as neighbors and allies. The Waika are closely related to the Macusi, and are sometimes considered a subgroup: There is a Macusi village called Waika near the Cotinga River in Guyana. They are perhaps discerned in the name of Toparimaca's town, Arowacai. This shares the *aro* element with Aromaia, the name of Topiawari's province. This element perhaps signifies "place," and Arowacai is "place of the Wacai," i.e., Waika. This is speculative, but the general iden-tification of these "borderers" as Macusi seems pretty certain.

This resilient and engaging people continues to flourish in the region, and we met many Macusi or Pemón in those highlands that Ralegh never reached. We became particular friends with one, Eu-logio Rossi, a Pemón in his early forties who sometimes worked for our fixer Uwe, and who traveled with us on the second half of our journey. He lived in a gold-mining village, San Francisco, in the highlands not far from the Brazilian border. His father had been a gold miner, and had died in a mining accident.

He tells the gringos, especially the women, to call him "I Love You," which is easier for them to say than Eulogio.

Eulogio is a man of great charm and humor: that wonderful Indian mix of propriety and wildness. María Teresa sparred and bantered with him. Of his charming manner, she says, *"Líbrame del agua mansa, que de la brava me libro yo!"* This proverb means, "Save me from the smooth waters: I can manage the rough!" This is a phrase applied to a sweet-talker.

He says to her, *"Ay señorita! Que chúcara."* This is a nice word, used of untamed, frisky ponies.

He has that hunger for partying that Ralegh notes in all the Orinoco Indians: "The borderers . . . are marvellous great drunkards, in which vice I think no nation can compare with them." Uwe grumbled at him when he was too hung over—*enratonado,* "ratted"—to be any use. I remember him one morning in Tumeremo, after a momentous bender, trying to unlock the door of the jeep with his hotel key.

I did not find that Eulogio, or other Pemón I talked to, had any folk memory of El Dorado, or of the history of it that Ralegh gives, allegedly from the mouth of the Macusi chief Topiawari. He is aware of the story, of course, but only as a Hispanic legend. It belongs to the *criollos,* the incomers. It was imposed on the Indians, relentlessly, but made no real impression on Indian consciousness. It is weightless: a projection.

The Pemón do not take us back to the fantasy of El Dorado—they were simply one of the tribes in one of the areas thus named—but to the actuality of those travel-stained Elizabethans drinking cups of "Indian wine" on the banks of the Orinoco.

[16]

Downtown Orinoco

* * *

R ALEGH'S ENCOUNTER with Topiawari was perhaps the high point of his journey, but it was not quite the farthest point. They met on two occasions, and in the period between these meetings, about three days, the English sailed a few miles farther west "to view the famous river of Caroli"—in other words, the Caroní—and to reconnoiter the land about it.

They anchored for the night at an island, which Ralegh calls Caiama, and which is now known as Isla Fajardo, and the following morning they arrived at the mouth of the Caroní. Here they encountered the full power of this river, now nearing spate: "We were not able with a barge of eight oars to row one stone's cast in an hour, and yet the river is as broad as the Thames at Woolwich."

They gave up, and pitched camp on the riverbank. That afternoon Ralegh sent out some of the Orenoqueponi to give news of their arrival to the local *cacique*, Wanuretona. His territory, called Canuria, lay to the west of the Caroní. He arrived the next morning, bringing "all store of provisions to entertain us, as the rest had done," and gave them good information about the tribes upriver.

On this day or the next, three English scouting parties set out to explore the region overland. The largest consisted of Thynne, Grenville, Gilbert, Gorges, and Captain Clarke, plus thirty musketeers. They were dispatched south, following the course of the river. They were to aim for a village called Amnatepoi. (This name clearly contains the Macusi word *tepuy*, mountain, though variants of this word are found in other languages.) If they reached Amnatepoi, they were to hire guides, and go on "towards the mountain foot." There they would come to Capurepana: friendly country in that it was ruled by a nephew of Topiawari. This, in turn, "adjoined to" Macureguarai, the "frontier town" of Guiana. All these towns are marked on Ralegh's chart. This was the toughest of the three assignments; it is given to the young relatives, still full of energy.

Another detachment—Captain Whiddon, the surgeon Nick Mellechapp, and a certain "W. Connock," together with eight shot—was dispatched to look for signs of gold and "mineral stone" in the area.

The third group consisted of the three commanders, Ralegh, Gifford, Calfield, plus Edward Hancock and "some half a dozen shot." These "marched overland to view the strange overfalls" of the River Caroní—not so much a detachment as a small party of tourists.

As listed by Ralegh, these three groups contained altogether fifty-five men—about half of the expedition. The rest remained at camp (some had perhaps remained with the Orenoqueponi at the port of Morequito). The name conspicuously missing from the list, Lawrence Keymis, was probably left in charge at the camp.

RALEGH GIVES a marvelous description of the great falls of the Caroní, now called the Salto La Lovisna (*lovisne* means "spray"). They are still huge, though reduced somewhat by damming farther upriver.

"When we ran to the tops of the first hills," he writes,

we beheld that wonderful breach of waters which ran down Caroni, and might from that mountain see the river how it ran in three parts, above twenty miles off; and there appeared some ten or twelve overfalls in sight, every one as high over the other as a church tower, which fell with that fury that the rebound of waters made it seem as if it had been covered over with a great shower of rain; and in some places we took it at the first for a smoke that had risen over some great town.

This is the farthest point of his journey, and it calls up the finest descriptive passage in the *Discoverie.* I don't want to spoil it by equating it with the schlock ejaculation-imagery found in old-fashioned Hollywood films, but I cannot resist calling this the climax of the journey, and seeing in its furious and foaming "showers" a final release from the tensions and disappointments, and the much-vaunted sexual abstinence, of the expedition. I note also that in the midst of this purely elemental, nonhuman landscape, Ralegh sees or imagines the shimmering spray to be a "smoke" rising "over some great town," and so inserts into this wilderness that mirage of populousness and civility that is so much a feature of the El Dorado legend. Even the falls themselves seem like "church towers."

These observations relate to the language Ralegh uses in this passage, and to the way the psychological motifs of the journey play into it. They do not exclude the simple reading of the scene, which is that Ralegh's journey ends with a sight of the South American landscape at its grandest and most immense. Even through the hard times in the delta, he remained acutely open to the beauty around him. This aesthetic valuing of wilderness was not then a commonplace.

He was content with this view, it seems, and was "well persuaded from thence to have returned." But "the rest were all so desirous to go near the said strange thunder of waters," and so "by little and little" they drew him down into the valley, where they could "better discern" the falls.

It is at this point that he mentions being a "very ill footman." He is, one suddenly sees, exhausted.

But the walk proved its own reward, and the violent crescendo of the falls resolves into a tranquil, Arcadian coda.

I never saw a more beautiful country, nor more lively prospects: hills so raised here and there over the valleys; the river winding into divers branches; the plains adjoining without bush or stubble, all fair green grass; the ground of hard sand, easy to march on either for horse or foot; the deer crossing in every path; the birds, towards the evening, singing on every tree with a thousand several tunes; cranes and herons of white, crimson and carnation perching on the river's side; the air fresh with a gentle easterly wind; and every stone that we stooped to take up promised either gold or silver by his complexion.

The "promise" of gold takes us out into the future, into the possible—which is where El Dorado always is—but the tenor of these passages is that the preciousness is here and now, in front of his eyes. When he draws his famous conclusion about the "maidenhead" of Guiana, it is the natural beauty of its landscape, as much as the cultural integrity of its inhabitants, that he is defending.

WHERE RALEGH stood that day, at the confluence of the Orinoco and the Caroní, there now stands the new Venezuelan metropolis of Ciudad Guayana—half finished, *quarter* finished (the projected population is two million), a sprawl of factories, shopping malls, rush housing, sports stadiums, and cement plants.

A flat scrub landscape surrounds the city: conifer plantations, cattle herds, that red earth that Ralegh noted. The city straddles the mouth of the Caroní. It is really two towns—the old town of San Félix on the east bank, beneath which lies the "port of Morequito" and the garrison of San Thomé; and the new town of Puerto Ordaz on the west.

Port Morequito cannot be far from, may indeed be identical with, the port of San Félix, where the ferry crosses the Orinoco to and from Los Barrancos. It was at Barrancos that we said good-bye to the river, and boarded the ferry, briefly fazed by the size of the vessels in the port, and the bustle of the city.

I taste thick black ship-smoke on my lips. Some Guardia pass the time by giving us hassle. There's a girl selling peanuts on the ferry. She's from Georgetown, Guyana; her black face has the Hindu-Indian touch, like Trevor's. She is twelve years old.

"Don't you go to school?"

"I did when we lived in Guyana."

We land on the other side, twilight falling: *entre dos luces*. A land cruiser parked on the sandy slope above the wharf has its warning

lights on, gives a note of tension as the night falls. The streets
around the landing stage are packed: white strip lights; amplified
sales patter from the Big Ben department store. There is an Avenida
Berrio, and on it a man reading the local newspaper, *El Guyané.*

We have seen much that Ralegh saw, but this is not the place to
contemplate those last paradisal visions of his journey. We are back
in the twentieth century. This is downtown Orinoco.

We cross the bridge to Puerto Ordaz: wide new boulevards where
the land cruisers cruise; sleepy suburbs with TV satellite dishes,
wrought-iron window grilles, padlocks, guard dogs. The notice that
looks like a bed-and-breakfast sign says: MADAME OLGA, CHEIRO-
MANCIA.

In Puerto Ordaz all the lights are shining, all the money is moving. Discos, video shops, *croissanterías.* Gucci, Nike, Canon, Casio.
There are gold and diamond frames in the optician's window, and
ten-foot-tall teddy bears in "Kidtoys," and a gift shop called Cadeau
Guayana, and in each one of these brilliant emporiums stand shop-
girls so lovely they make the breath catch in your throat.

The big cars cruise with their windows down, fight stereo duels
with disco-salsa: *chukka chukka chukka chukka.* The neon flashes above
the Ultima Moda clothes shop: *Stop Stop Stop Stop.* I think of snazzy
Las Mercedes in Caracas, the streets full of smart aggressive revelers:
We queued at the pretentiously French restaurant and ate tough
gigot.

They say that Puerto Ordaz is the richest place per square meter
in Venezuela. The money is made here and spent here: boomtown
economics. The oil city of Maracaibo is not like this. There's money
there, but the big oil-wealth gets dispensed thousands of miles away;
you don't buy and sell oil in situ. Here the deals are cut on the spot:
gold, diamonds, topaz, jasper, bauxite, iron—even water, there
being the usual kickbacks relating to the hydroelectric plants to
which the Caroní is now harnessed. And so the bounty of Guiana is
turned into the products that create the money that buys the goods
that sit in the shiny shopping malls of Puerto Ordaz.

*   *   *

IT TOOK Ralegh nearly four weeks to get from the Golfo de Paria to here; it has taken us half that, but we have not yet finished our journey. He estimates that he had come 400 miles from his ships. The distance is more like 250 miles, though the windings of the delta make it hard to compute, and make it seem much farther.

We check in at the Hotel Rasil, dubbed for the night Hotel Razzle. Cocktails in the low-lit Bar Ejecutivo. One of the bargirls casts a hook: a *mulatta* modeled on Tina Turner circa 1975, getting on for six feet tall, chewing medicated gum to keep her breath sweet.

She calls herself "Sahara." She is twenty-six years old, from the little town of Soledad, farther upriver. "What you want?" she says, in greengo-eenglish. "You want all night? *Servicio full?* That's two hundred U.S."

She fancies Big Frank in his Gap T-shirt. She looks him up and down, chews on her gum, says something he can't understand. She is saying she hopes he isn't an "L." She holds up her hand, forefinger and thumb in the shape of the letter L. "Tall this way but not so big there." She laughs a lot at this, and wipes an imaginary tear from her eye, which looks in the faintly iridescent lighting to be made up in shades of orange and lilac.

She has another trick with her fingers: holds her ring finger out stiff, slips an imaginary ring on it, down it goes. *El casado, no?* The married man.

Indignation from those of us slandered; invitation from her to prove it.

She shimmies off to another group, big-shouldered men leaning inward at a table with a bottle of Chivas Regal and a bucket of ice in the middle. "Hey, *chamo,* tonight's your lucky night."

Ron says something I don't hear. Frank says, "Nah, she'd eat you on toast for breakfast," and I wonder if we've met our first Amazon.

AS RALEGH stood on the banks of the lower Caroní, perhaps at the point now called Parque Punta de Vista, he knew that this was the end of the line for his expedition. These boiling rapids and falls

were in themselves the chief reason. This was an insurmountable
barrier for his boats.

> I thought it time lost to linger any longer in that place, especially
> for that the fury of the Orenoque began daily to threaten us with
> dangers in our return, for no half day passed but the river began to
> rage and overflow very fearfully, and the rains came down in terrible
> showers and gusts, in great abundance, and withal our men began to
> cry out for want of shift.

In the classic manner of expeditions, everything is against them. The
rivers are rising, the rains are imminent, the men are exhausted. The
journey has taken its toll. They had been away from the ships "well
near a month" now. The *entrada* was effectively over.

The "great and golden city" proves to be only the pretext of his
journey: It was what got him here. It is the lower Caroní that turns
out to be his destination, his farthest reach into the interior. He is
here, and El Dorado is up there: farther on, deeper in, where the
map is blank.

"We therefore turned towards the east, and the next day following"—about June 14, 1595—"we left the mouth of the Caroni."

PART THREE

THE
NEW
DORADO

*It was the usual gold-digger's story: true, no doubt,
and yet sounding like a fairy story.*

—B. TRAVEN, *The Treasure of the Sierra Madre*

[17]

Gold Rush

*   *   *

I
T WOULD be conventional to call this the "end of the dream"
but the longer view is that it was only just the beginning, and
that it was not a dream at all. Ralegh and Berrio and all those
other hopeful pioneers were right. There was no "golden city" hidden in the Guiana Highlands, but there was gold in abundance.

The "golden city" is a marvelous euphemism for the actual business of finding gold. It is a place where the gold is sitting there
ready for you: mined, fashioned, portable; plates, ingots, images,
idols. The reality, of course, is the opposite. Gold is usually very
inaccessible. It is found in difficult terrain; is fractionally present in
rocks, gravels, and river mud; has to be wrenched out with back-
breaking toil—hence the old gold diggers' adage, "a ton of sweat
for a grain of gold."

There is a sense of this in Ralegh's text, where the cloudy expec-
tations of fabulous wealth come up against the intractable reality of
the terrain—"whosoever hath seen with what strength of stone the
best gold ore is environed, he will not think it easy to be had out
in heaps." The English break their dagger points and fingernails as
they scrabble frantically at the shiny, auriferous rocks. They did not
have the prospector's tools with them—"We had neither pioners,
bars, sledges nor wedges of iron to break the ground, without the
which there is no working in mines." This lack of equipment seems
curious, but the fact is that most South American explorers were
more interested in plundering gold than digging for it. The last
thing you were going to need when you got to El Dorado was a
spade.

There is gold ore in Guiana, much of it found in a quartz that the miners call *tojo,* and which is probably what Ralegh calls "white spar," and there is also alluvial gold in the gravels and riverbeds. Ralegh learned of this in his discussions with Topiawari:

> I . . . asked the manner how the Epuremei wrought those plates of gold, and how they could melt it out of the stone. He told me that the most of the gold which they made in plates and images was not severed from the stone, but that on the Lake of Manoa, and in a multitude of other rivers, they gathered it in grains of perfect gold, and in pieces as big as small stones.

These "grains" and "pieces"—in other words, gold dust and nuggets—are found by the age-old technique of panning, undoubtedly practiced by the Indians at that time, and still practiced today.

European prospecting probably began in the area shortly after the founding of San Thomé in late 1595. After Berrio's death his son Ferdinando led an expedition for about a hundred miles up the Caroní. Missions were established in the region, always a useful center for prospectors. Toward the end of the eighteenth century there were Mexican miners around Upata, in the foothills of the Guiana Highlands. They were licensed by the *intendente* of Venezuela, Don José Avalo, but seem to have mostly come back with iron pyrites (what Ralegh calls "marcasite," and what is more generally called "fool's gold").

It was not until the 1850s, two and a half centuries after Ralegh reluctantly turned back, that the first major strike was recorded. In 1857, a German prospector, Federico Sommer, found gold nuggets embedded in clay, including one stupendous specimen weighing over fifteen pounds. This was at Tupuquén, north of the Yuarari River, near present-day El Callao. This lies about a hundred miles southeast of the mouth of the Caroní, just about where Ralegh placed the mythic Macureguarai, "the first civil town of Guiana."

The site swiftly grew into a shantytown of eighty houses, with shops and hotels and ironsmiths and carpenters. It was christened Nueva Providencia. Others would follow, with the same rather poignant optimism: villages named Hope and Silence and Persever-

24. Gold working in Guiana (De Bry)

ance, and even one called El Increíble, The Incredible.

By the early 1880s there were over eight thousand settlers in the area. The richest area, the network of mines around El Callao, was producing over fifteen tons of gold a year. (This would be worth about $200 million at today's prices.) For a few years—until the discovery of the Rand goldfields in South Africa in 1886—Venezuela was the biggest gold-producer in the world. It now ranks seventeenth, with an annual production of about twelve tons. Almost all of this comes from the eastern foothills of the Guiana Highlands. This is the reality of Ralegh's El Dorado.

The Venezuelan gold rush of the 1880s attracted many British companies, some of which, like Monarch and Greenwich, still have a stake in the area. It was at this time, and undoubtedly because of the gold discoveries, that the British government renewed a claim to parts of Venezuela adjacent to British Guiana. In the course of its claim, the Venezuelan Boundary Commission combed the Spanish archives, looking for historical precedents of "possession," and there unearthed for the first time many of the documents relating to the early expeditions of Antonio de Berrio and others. Ralegh was one of the keys to the British claim to possession. His own journey did not quite touch on this area, but later expeditions he sponsored and supported—Keymis, Berry, Harcourt, etc.—certainly did.

In 1890, the commission found in Britain's favor, and extended the frontier of British Guiana some way to the west of the Essequibo River. Venezuela does not recognize the boundary, and on a modern Venezuelan map you will see that part of Guyana—about fifty thousand square miles—designated a "Zona en Reclamación." The people inside that zone, officially Guyanese, are considered de facto Venezuelan citizens. Many have migrated to Puerto Ordaz and Ciudad Bolívar, and thus the English you hear spoken in these Orinoco ports—the rich, drawled Guyanese brogue—is a faint echo of those Elizabethan voices first heard here in 1595.

HAVING RESTED in Puerto Ordaz, we now began the second part of our expedition. We had followed Ralegh to the farthest point of his *entrada*. He had turned back, but we were going on, into this region that he believed to contain El Dorado, this region that proved to be so rich in gold, and that continues to draw adventurers in search of that lucky strike which will change their lives: a New Dorado.

You still cannot take a boat up the Caroní at this point, and most of the places we wanted to go are beyond the reach of roads. So we hired a small Cessna, and a pilot called Hannibal, and flew down with a good tailwind to the first of our destinations, the small town of La Paragua. This is on the Paragua River, a tributary west of the upper Caroní.

My interest in the Paragua was twofold. First, it seems to be one of the physical ingredients of the legendary Lake of Manoa. There was no giant inland lake "like unto Mare Caspium" hidden in Guiana, but there were rivers whose annual inundations during the rainy season created a series of lakes. The Paragua is particularly noted for this, indeed the name comes from a Carib word meaning "sea" or "lake." My second interest in the Paragua was that it is rich in gold, and is one of the few places in this part of Venezuela where the *mineros*—independent gold-diggers and prospectors, working up-country in small teams—continue to operate largely undisturbed.

This section of the book is not a "reconstruction," because Ralegh never went to these places. It is a pushing on in the direction of his last, wistful gaze upriver; an excursion into the empty spaces of his map; a chronological and topographical tangent, though one that sometimes seems to double back, in the curious way of these legends, to the main story.

Ralegh, in short, did not have a twin-engine Cessna at his disposal. We did, and it seemed only right to take a look, and—as he would put it—"make trial of" what we found there.

THE FLIGHT takes us over the Guri Reservoir, just south of Ciudad Guayana, where the damming of the Caroní provides electricity for half of Venezuela. South of here the forest begins, fitfully, and after a while we begin to see the effects of heavy gold and diamond mining on the middle reaches of the Caroní.

The land is pitted with what looks from above like a psoriasis: white flaky scabs of exhausted terrain, often merging into a continuous lunar deadness. This degradation is a cumulative result of physical disturbance—clearing, digging, flooding, etc.—and chemical pollution, particularly by mercury, which is used to "fix" particles of gold and separate them from the sludge in which they are found. There is also opportunistic logging in areas opened up by prospectors. We are seeing it from five thousand feet; we would later see it at close hand. This is the dirty reality of the search for gold, the ruined "maidenhead" of Guiana.

I suppose that just by coming here Ralegh is partly responsible for this devastation. I suppose all of us who come to these places take rather more than we give. There is so often in South America

a poignant sense of its generosity as a place, its continued richness
after so much plunder.

We fly over a straggling miners' village called El Paúl or El Pao
(I have seen it written as both). On the edge of town there's a
graveyard, a prospector's Boot Hill. In it are scruffy little shrines
and mausoleums made out of corrugated tin. These seem a palpable
epitaph for the gold searcher.

La Paragua is a small place with the feeling of a frontier town. It
is the point of intersection. You can get here from Puerto Ordaz by
air or by road (five hours, the last section difficult in the wet season),
but beyond there is no transport except the perennial ones: boat,
mule, foot. Like all mining towns in the region it has a high population of immigrants, primarily Guyanese and Brazilian, and also
of prostitutes. The largest indigenous groups here are the Pemón—
the distant cousins of Chief Topiawari—and the Jekwana. Essentially
the interests of the *mineros* and the Indians are at odds; the prospectors are illegally taking and damaging tribal land, with no compensation. In practice, as so often, many of the Indians cut their losses
and join the gravy train.

Night falls on the dirt streets, the air is full of meat smoke from
the *fritanga* stalls. We meet a diamond miner, a rangy Guyanese
called Frank. Finding we already have one Frank with us he says,
"I'm Black Frank." He is just down from a twenty-day stint upriver.
He works for a "Polack" (his word). He will sell his take here, and
go home with the money to his wife and three kids in Ciudad
Bolívar.

I had been told, back in Caracas, that life up the Paragua was
armed and dangerous. I asked him if he carried a gun when he was
up there. Black Frank nods, then breaks out laughing. "Water pistol,
man," he says, meaning the high-pressure hoses they use to sluice
down the mud. "No, it's cool up there. CB [Ciudad Bolívar] now,
that's where I take care."

There's a dance on in the park. Music pounds from a *miniteca*
called Thunder Night, a succession of salsa, meringue, reggae, rap,
etc. I watch Eulogio and María Teresa dancing, moving together in
that seamless Latin mix of formality and sensuousness.

When we leave Eulogio he says he'll stay for one last beer, and the next morning, when we meet him down on the waterfront, he's still on it.

FOUR HOURS upriver from La Paragua, traveling once more by motorized *curiara,* we come to a small trading post called Uraima, which serves the miners and prospectors of the region.

It stands in a clearing on the riverbank: half a dozen wood and tin buildings, and a large *churuata* (the round, open-sided, palm-thatched house of the Pemón) to sling your hammocks. In one of the huts is the shop, called Bodega las Brisas de Uraima. In the Breezes of Uraima stores you can buy cigarettes, liquor, paraffin, candles, rope, canned foods, *arepa* flour—all at upriver prices.

The owner is Javiel Lezama: a moody, faintly bullying *criollo* in his fifties. His white mustache has a military air. He wears one of those wickerwork hats that looks like a topee. It gives him the air of a melancholy colonel in a García Marquez story.

His teeth are full of gold. He flew into Miami once and they asked him if he had anything to declare, "so I very kindly smiled for them."

Also resident, as part of the *bodega's* amenities, is Mariana, an Ecuadorian from Guayaquil, a plump, amiable, slow-witted lady with henna-red hair and a penchant for tight, shiny slacks in Day-Glo colors. She spends the day draped around the place, like some outsize tropical bird, in a turquoise nylon net-hammock. She has a little boudoir in a shack out back, festooned with pictures of Elvis, *el rey de rock-n-roll.*

There are no roads here, of course, but last year they floated an old Toyota truck up on oil drums, to get them across to the other side of the island. This truck is surely the prince of jalopies. It looks a veteran of a hundred stock car races put out to graze. Hold on, they shout, as you're driven off, but there's nothing to hold on to. Javiel's sidekick always drives: a Guajiro Indian a long way from home. You are hunched together in this little cockpit, lurching along the track. He ropes the gearshift to the steering column when we're going downhill.

The truck has a name, handwritten above the windshield—EL CONSENTIDO DE DOS CHICAS, which can be loosely translated as The Two-timer.

There's a trestle table on the shore where they gut and clean the fish. They put out the nets at night. The river is full of big fish— a sign of health: Where there are just a few "independents" working, we are told, the land stays healthy. We cook the fish on an open fire: *payara,* a ferocious looker with a row of needle-sharp teeth; and *coporo,* a browsing fish, which has delicate peach-colored meat not unlike trout.

Javiel has a small mine an hour's walk away, across the high savannah, the silence broken by what sound like larks, the way marked by occasional beer cans stuck on tall poles. The mine is a small scene of devastation: mud and rubble and broken trees, and a deafening noise of generators, diggers, and 1.5-inch high-pressure hoses that they use to clear the mud off.

He has a beautiful pair of scales, Italian made, in a wooden case lined with velvet. He pours out a bit of gold dust: twenty grams. It looks dull; it looks more dust than gold. "There it is," he says. *"La medicina . . ."*

This is the old prospector's joke, that gold is the "medicine" for gold fever. It is Cortés's joke, spoken to the ambassadors of Montezuma, in the summer of 1519: "We suffer from a disease that only gold can cure."

AT URAIMA the gold diggers drift in and out, their boats piled with the tools of the trade: the *suruca* (sieve) and *batea* (pan) tied up with rope; the picks and shovels caked with gray river-mud; the cans of gasoline.

They do not volunteer their names. Often their provenance is their only name. At one time or another we met El Español, an old-timer from Andalucía with a black dog called Bon Ami; and El Maracucho from Maracaibo, with his dandy mustache; and El Caleño, from Cali, in the green Cauca Valley of southern Colombia. He was superstitious. He had red and black seeds for good luck, and recommended *caldo de samuro*—vulture soup—to keep away bad spirits.

They come in to buy provisions, and sit around the fire, and drink. This is the time to soak up the prospector's lore: the mathematics of the lucky strike. I learn that the biggest diamond ever found hereabouts was 154 carats. It was found in 1942 by a prospector named Jaime Hudson, known as Barabas. He sold it to a cutter named Henry Winston for $60,000. Winston cut it three ways: 80 carats, 40 carats, 12 carats. The 40-carat stone alone sold for $185,000.

There's a big, philosophical German called Lobo. His name is Wolfgang, hence *lobo,* wolf. He has prospected all the way down from the McKenzie River. He says, "In Icabarú once I saw two kilos of gold nuggets, piled up on a pool table. You never saw a prettier sight than that heap of gold sitting under the light."

Another time we met Gilbert (pronounced with a soft "G"). Anselmo Gilbert Montez was born in Houston, Texas, of a Mexican father and an Apache mother. He says he's fifty-nine years old, but he looks older; he is very thin and slightly yellow, but still chipper. He reminds me of the Walter Brennan character in *To Have and Have Not.* He has had malaria more times than he can count: both kinds, *especifico* and *vivo.* He's an expert on malaria, he says. His stomach has shrunk; he virtually lives on papaya juice. He came out here in 1976 as a field engineer for a mining company, drifted into independent prospecting. He's gone for diamonds in the Paragua, and gold all over.

Times are hard now for the independents, he says. "The government's closing down all the operations that don't pay them. That's the real problem. You can get better from malaria. Ain't no cure for the government."

Gilbert talks in little aphoristic bursts:

"Some sharpies came down here with metal detectors. They found plenty of iron. Machines can't distinguish, see. . . .

"Where there's nuggets you go easy. You hit a nugget with a hammer, well, you ain't got a nugget anymore. . . .

"The big one's waiting there, all right. You know you didn't plant it, so you don't know where it is, see."

They all know a good luck story, but invariably it's someone else's good luck: "Guy I know bought a diamond off a Brazilian *minero*. He bought it in a bar in Boa Vista for eighty thousand dollars and sold it a month later in Brussels for sixteen million. That's what I call a profit."

The next morning they're off, *curiara* loaded while we're still levering ourselves up out of our hammocks.

Hasta luego. Hope you find what you're looking for. . . .

SOME OF the richest deposits in the Paragua are in the riverbed itself. This is mined from a *balsa*, or raft, with divers going down to hose up the contents of the riverbed. There's a *balsa* not far from Uraima run by a wiry man called Gonzales. He has a big, porous-looking nose, and deep wrinkles and watery blue eyes. He wears a Stetson hat. He's from Guyana, of Portuguese extraction. His name is Godfrey Gonsalves, but here everyone calls him Gonzales. His grandfather came over at the beginning of the century; his father worked as a carpenter.

Gonzales has been prospecting for years in Guyana and Venezuela. He's a professional. He carries a shortwave radio, tunes in to BBC World Service every evening for gold rates and exchange rates. "Then I know just how much I'm worth today."

At his base camp there are hammocks, a generator, chameleons shimmering in the rubbish heap. He has ten men working for him; a team of five does twenty-four hours at the *balsa*, then has the day off at camp. They're playing "rum"—a stripped-down version of rummy—in the shade, slapping the cards down.

There's no money on the table, but they're keeping the score. They are gambling for gold dust. "That's all we got right now." Gold dust is a currency throughout these camps, and when they get down to La Paragua in a couple of weeks' time, they'll buy girls with gold dust, too: "a gram a jump, two grams to stay all night."

Farther upriver is the *balsa* itself. This is a platform sitting in the middle of a deserted sweep of river with thick bush on either bank. It carries heavy-duty suction equipment, powered by a four-cylinder 100-horsepower Ford diesel engine, and a 10-foot sluice box to wash through the mud brought up from the riverbed.

Gonzales says, "You move the sand first, then you get down to the material. That is where your hope lies." This "material" is the alluvial deposits beneath the riverbed: tons of mud and gravel and among it a few grains of gold.

The men dive, in shifts, moving the hose around the riverbed like a truffle-hunting hog. It is dangerous work; the equipment is slap-dash; men get drowned. In Guyana, one of them says, they use hydraulic dredges: the "missile," they call it. This is less dangerous, so consequently it pays less. There's a handsome diver called Charles, whom Maggie asserts to be "very easy on the eyes," and another called Owen, who wears a pink singlet and beach shorts whose dec-orative motif is not palm trees but American Express credit cards.

After the sluice box has shaken down the slurry, the last stage is the same as it has always been. The slow sifting of the fine dust from the water, the mesmeric circling movement of the gold pan, and there it is, glittering in the fine black sediment: the medicine.

Owen picks it up on the tip of his finger, examines it. I see he is holding his breath. He has the obsessive delicacy of a user han-dling cocaine.

The day's yield is unpredictable. As you are told a thousand times, this business is a gamble. On a good day they might get 400 grams of gold dust, another day 60, another day the engine might seize up and nothing get produced at all. The split is fifty-fifty. Gonzales keeps half of everything produced. The other half is shared (four divers, 10 percent each; two boatmen, 5 percent each).

It is an expensive gamble. He enumerates the costs. The engine cost half a million bolivars (over $7,000), and the six 12-foot floats for the raft nearly as much. The hoses cost 50,000 bolivars. The equipment alone represents an investment of about $20,000. Get-ting it up here, welding it together on site, provisioning and fur-nishing the camp; all these add to the costs.

On a middling day, after all this sweat and investment, sixty grams of gold dust are squeezed out of tons of river mud. This represents about $300 for Gonzales, and the same divided up among the divers ($60 each) and the sailors ($30 each).

To be legal, Gonzales must pay 8 percent tax to the government on all he produces. Now the government is tightening the squeeze further, and insisting on concessions only. They are evicting the *mineros,* and leasing the land to big consortiums. Getting a concession, says Gonzales, is a headache. You're supposed to have a working capital of 40 million bolivars (over half a million dollars). It will cost you $10,000 just to do the paperwork. Up here it isn't going to be worth it, he says. They are only selling concessions for land sites, not on the rivers, which are richer.

He's feeling the squeeze. He'll be pulling out soon. "When you're outside, everything seems fine," he says, "but when you're inside you know where the roof is leaking from."

THESE ARE the professionals, but also there are the dilettantes, the adventurers—more like Ralegh himself. One such is an aristocratic German artist I met in Maracay, Heinz Dollacker.

Heinz is in his mid-seventies now, tall, gaunt and suave, potentially sinister if he were not so charming. He has a bullet-scar under his chin, a souvenir of Hitler's Russian campaign. He lives in a scruffy studio on the outskirts of Maracay, a pleasant town a couple of hours west of Caracas. His canvases are intense, dramatic, sometimes surreal: A satyr fondles a naked nymph while behind them waits a yellow Caracas taxi. There is a touch of the Gothic about Heinz: Faust as *brujo*. His eyes are weakening, and he wears clip-on shades most of the time. In a restaurant he snaps them up to admire the *flamenco* girls.

When he first came to Venezuela in the early fifties, he was handsome and penniless, and he decided to become a prospector. "I was playing at it," he says smoothly. "Like you, *ne?*"

He went down to the Aro River to look for diamonds. The Aro is another tributary of the Orinoco; it rises close to the upper Paragua and joins the Orinoco upriver from Ciudad Bolívar; the name means "hoop" in Spanish, referring to its curvacious course. "It was right out in the wildness," Heinz says, and slips into his easy vein of reminiscence.

"We lived in huts by the riverside. There were two settlements; we called them Upriver and Downriver. There was no village; we were far, far away from the last Pepsi-Cola sign. We took with us *cassava;* this is the most important thing because it is always fresh. And we fished, and we hunted, and we ate the fruits, because there is no agriculture there. There is nothing. It's wonderful. You are so lost.

"People were finding diamonds. At Upriver there was already a company, with machines. I think it was a French company. We hated them because they worked so much easier. They dig with the machines, the suction pumps on the *balsa.* We had to do it with our hands. You are moving these enormous stones. The water's almost dried up, then the rains come up, and the river rises and you get more stones.

"On the banks of the river there are thousands of *cakes.* Cakes are what is left after you make your last *suruca,* the last sieving, the finest one, where is supposed to be the diamond. The first one you make fast, like a pancake—boh!—and you turn it onto the sand. In the middle it is always dark, and then you go very carefully with a little stick and try if there is maybe a diamond. If there is nothing, then you leave it, and so there are thousands of these cakes.

"Sometimes you found these stones that were a kind of crystal, and had a shine, but they were not yet diamonds. They were worth, well, next to nothing. These stones we called *casi-casi* [nearly-nearly]. Just another couple of million years and you would have a diamond."

He pauses, turns to the dark girl in the chair whose name is Matilda. "Honey," he says. "How many times have we said this in our lives? *Casi . . .*"

The story breaks off because some people arrive, but later he said to me, "You know, it was the most wonderful time of my life. It is hard work, okay, but I would do it right now again."

He was trying to sum it up. "It was . . . I *did* things. I don't believe in theory. I had a lot of theory, I studied a long time. But I don't believe it until I do it."

I thought Ralegh would appreciate that: the adventurer as skeptic—"I don't believe it until I do it."

[18]

Jimmy Angel

*   *   *

I SAID AT the start of this book that I wanted to find the "reality" that lay behind the legendary quest for El Dorado. In a sense the gold mining we saw on the Paragua is just that: It is the dirty, sweaty, ecologically ruinous reality of the search for gold in South America. There is no Golden King, no palace full of massy idols, just a series of jagged holes in the jungle. But those prospectors we met at Uraima seem also to *belong* to the legend. They speak the archetypal language of the gold searcher. They are looking for the "big one"; they are craving the "medicine"; they would "quit tomorrow" if they knew how. They have the etched, obsessive, leathery faces that those early searchers for El Dorado must have had, as they paddled upriver in their overfreighted little boats.

One goes to somewhere like Uraima to see the reality, the New Dorado of the 1990s, and it seems not to displace the legend so much as continue it. This is a genuine impression, based on real people I met at Uraima and elsewhere, but I am aware also that it is my construction of what I saw. This is how I wished to see it. This idea of the continuity, or recurrence, of legend was already in my mind. It was there right from the start.

I now turn to that "other story" that I mentioned at the beginning of the book, which was the chief motive of this tangential excursion into the Guiana Highlands: the story of Jimmy Angel.

THE GOLD rush towns of the 1880s were foothill settlements. The heart of the Guiana Highlands remained unbroached. There were expeditions up the rivers, by Schomburgk and others—Arthur

Conan Doyle's *The Lost World,* published in 1912, was based on Everard im Thurn's accounts of Mount Roraima—but it was the advent of the light aircraft that finally opened up the heartlands of Ralegh's El Dorado. This was the 1920s, the first great era of the "bush pilots," flying over the forest on a wing and a prayer, filling out those last empty spaces in the South American map. One of the first of the bush pilots, and by most reckonings the greatest, was Jimmy Angel.

I have tacked together a patchy account of his early life: a few scraps from people who knew him, but most of it from archive material in Caracas and in Missouri, where he was born.

James Crawford Angel was born in 1899, in the small mining town of Springfield in the Ozark Mountains of Missouri. His brother, Clifford, gives the following account, in a letter written to the *Springfield News Leader* in June 1949:

Jimmie was born in the suburbs of Springfield, out towards Rogersville. He is the son of G. D. Angel, who lived there from 1898 to 1918. We lived in West Plains in 1919. There are five of us: Clyde, Parker, Edward, Jimmie and myself.

All five brothers became "aviators," Clifford continues, and at one time had a flying circus. (This was the Angel Brothers' Flying Circus, which toured the southwestern United States in 1926; there was also the Angel-Burns Flying Circus, whose moniker can be seen on Jimmy Angel's biplane in an old photograph.)

Another account of his childhood was given by his friend, the Venezuelan explorer Carlos Freeman, in the *Caracas Daily Journal* (1972). He gives Angel's birth date as August 1, 1899. He says his father had served in the Philippines during the Spanish-American War, and lived thereafter a "rootless" life as a farmer, copper miner, and logger. "During Jimmie's childhood, the family moved at least eight times," and lived in various towns in Missouri, North Carolina, Tennessee, Arkansas, and Oregon. They were in Lead Hill, Arkansas, in 1908, and in Eugene, Oregon, in 1912. It was at Eugene that

Jimmy fell in love with flying, at the age of thirteen, when he saw the stunt pilot Weldon B. Cooke performing at a fair there.

This seems to contradict Clifford Angel's statement that the family lived in Springfield for twenty years, 1898–1918. One would trust Clifford, except that there seems to be no documentation of the family in Springfield or its environs. I trawled through the county censuses for 1900 and 1910, looking for G. D. Angel and his sons. There is a George Angel in both, but he has no children living with him, and he lives way out in Randolph County. There are five possible Jimmy Angels. Four of these—James Angel, James Anglen, James Angelo, and James Ancell—are too old. The fifth, James Angle, is exactly the right age, born in August 1899; and lives in the right district, Greene County (which includes the town of Springfield). But his father is called Francis, and his brothers are George and Frank, none of which tallies with Clifford's account of the family. Also, they had been in the area since at least 1884, whereas Clifford says his family moved there in 1898. Any of these might be related to Jimmy Angel the air ace, but none of them is he.

Another item that catches my eye is a brief death-notice in the *Springfield Republican*. On December 12, 1905, a certain Lucien Angel died in Washington State. He was born in Houston County, Texas; he was a veteran of the Spanish-American War; he had presumably lived in Springfield, hence the notice of his death here. Carlos Freeman states that Angel's father served in that war, and also that the family lived for a while at or near Eugene, Oregon, which is just a few miles from the Washington state line. It is hard to reconcile Lucien with G. D. Angel, but it is just possible they are the same.

The census is a demographic snapshot: It records people's whereabouts on a certain date. Jimmy Angel's family, one concludes, was not present in the Springfield area when the censuses of 1900 and 1910 were taken. They perhaps lived there off and on during that twenty-year period mentioned by Clifford Angel, but they were also on the move, as Freeman says. According to Clifford, Jimmy was proud of his Missouri origins: "He still says he is from the Show-Me State."

We also have no clue to Angel's ethnic origins. The census suggests the name could be Germanic (as in Engel or Anglen) or Hispanic (Angelo). Early photographs show a swarthy, low-browed young man with black, center-parted hair: a Mexican look, perhaps. Latin America became his patch, and later his home, first in Mexico, then in Panama.

If Jimmy Angel wasn't born with wings, he acquired them as soon as possible. The legend—largely self-generated—has it that he first flew in a homemade glider fashioned from his mother's window blinds; that the famous Angel Ride at Coney Island was based on a machine he invented at the age of nine; that he made his first proper flight at the age of fourteen when he took off "by mistake" in a plane he was repairing; and that he once demonstrated his skill at low-level flying by slicing off, with his wingtip, the top of a hard-boiled egg held up by his brother.

These apocrypha shade into documented feats of aerobatic prowess. During the Great War—in which he served, under age, in the Royal Canadian Flying Corps—he broke records for the highest flight (26,900 feet, in a Le Pierre fighter plane); highest landing (14,112 feet, on Pikes Peak, Colorado); and most loops (310, in a Moran Parasol). After the war he had various adventurous jobs—running the mails through Mexico; training pilots in Shanghai for the warlord Sun Yat-sen; herding reindeer in Canada for the Hudson Bay Company. He knew Charles Lindbergh and the boxer Jack Dempsey, and the photographer William Berry. He was even in the movies, stunt-flying in Howard Hughes's *Hell's Angels.* He made and spent big money. He purchased two mines—a lead and zinc mine in Oklahoma, the Kicking Mule; and a silver mine at Copaletis in Mexico—but they both went broke.

All of this is the prelude to the Amazing True Story of his discovery of the waterfall now known as Angel Falls.

THE STORY begins in Panama in the year 1921. There, in the Metropole Hotel in Panama City, Jimmy Angel met a certain J. R.

McCracken, who intrigued him with prospector's talk about a "river of gold" in the Guiana Highlands. Angel's own brusque, corner-of-the-mouth account of the meeting is recorded by another acquaintance, L. R. Dennison. "I was in Panama," Angel says, "broke as usual, and wondered just what I was going to do next. While I was sitting in the hotel lobby an old fellow came up to me, and asked if I would fly him to Venezuela." Angel describes McCracken as an "engineer."

They flew out of Panama on May 12, in a Bristol fighter plane (Angel had been selling surplus warplanes in Lima). They hopped from Cartagena to Maracaibo to Caracas to San Fernando de Apure in the *llanos*. From there they flew south up the Caroní, then eastward along the course of a tributary river, the Carrao. They had no instruments and no map: McCracken was guiding with hand signals. Eventually they came to the promised river. It was (judging from Angel's later efforts to relocate it) somewhere on or near the table mountain called Auyán Tepuy, which overlooks the Carrao. This is one of a number of towering, granite-and-sandstone mesas—known in Pemón as *tepuy*—which rise up out of the forest in this extraordinary "Lost World" landscape. It was, said Angel, "a hell of a place to land a plane."

In three days they panned out a huge quantity of paydirt—forty pounds of pure gold is the generally repeated figure, but according to Dennison, Angel himself said seventy-five pounds. "We could have taken more but I was afraid to put too much extra weight in the plane."

For years afterward Angel flew around the area, trying to relocate that "river of gold" in the still unmapped regions of the upper Caroní. On August 2, 1933, he flew out of Brownsville, Texas, with Dick Curry, an old partner from his days at the Kicking Mule mine. They arrived in Venezuela at the end of September. Using Ciudad Bolívar as their base, they flew around the area for months, but rains and administrative problems—at one point Angel was ordered out of the country by President Gómez himself—combined to frustrate them.

The following year Curry returned, and tried to reach the *tepuy* from the east, via British Guiana. He was drowned, together with three natives, when their canoe turned over in rapids.

Early in 1935, Angel made another expedition, this time with backing from a New York company, Case, Pomeroy and Company. He flew with his chief investor, F. I. "Shorty" Martin, and a pair of prospectors, Durant Hall and L. R. Dennison. On March 25, 1935, a clear day, he piloted his single-engine Cessna up a narrow canyon close to Auyán Tepuy, and there saw the stupendous waterfall that now bears his name.

Back in Caracas his accounts were dismissed as exaggeration, but he found the place again two years later. He succeeded in landing his plane, a Flamingo called *El Río Caroní,* on the summit of Auyán Tepuy, but it "nosied up" and the entire party—which included his wife, Marie—had to walk for twelve days through the forest, eventually arriving at the mission station at Kamarata. Two years later he was back in the area, with Marie, piloting for a scientific expedition. It was on this expedition that Carlos Freeman first met him. He had a knack for friendship with the local Indians—Pemón of the Kamerakoto clan—and adopted a teenage boy, whom he taught to service his plane. The boy was baptized in Ciudad Bolívar, under the name of José Manuel Angel.

It was not until 1949 that an overland expedition, led by the American journalist Ruth Robertson, reached the base of the falls. They were able to establish scientifically what Angel had claimed all along—that he had discovered the longest waterfall in the world, 3,212 feet from summit to foaming base.

This story is the stuff of South American exploration-legend. Angel is up there with Colonel Fawcett and Hiram Bingham, the discoverer of Machu Picchu, but the man himself seems to step out of the hard-bitten pages of a B. Traven novel like *The Treasure of the Sierra Madre.* Photographs of him at this time show a thickset, jowly man in a battered porkpie hat. Freeman remembers him as a "stocky, pock-marked man with a wheezing, bull-frog voice." (The pock-marks were actually burns, from a plane crash in the Chilean Andes in the 1930s.)

Terry Leon, a journalist with the Caracas daily *El Nacional,* who scooped one of the last interviews with Angel when he spotted him having his shoes shined in the Plaza Bolívar, told me, "He was a gold prospector, not a heroic type. He was fat. He smoked too much, drank too much whiskey."

In his later years, Angel could be found lurking at the American Club in Caracas, an exclusive haunt in the diplomatic quarter, surrounded by a grove of tropical trees. "He would surreptitiously pull out one or several nuggets from his pockets," and regale people with stories about the riches still hidden down in the Guiana Highlands.

In June 1956, back in Panama, he crashed a plane. It was the umpteenth time, but it proved fatal. He suffered a stroke a few days later, and fell into a coma. He died at a hospital in Balboa, in the Panama Canal Zone, on December 8, 1956. He was fifty-seven years old. *The New York Times* ran a small obituary, describing him as "a flier who specialized in traversing otherwise impenetrable South American jungles."

IT WAS really Jimmy Angel, as much as Ralegh himself, who drew me into this journey, and this book.

I first heard some of the details of his story in 1986, when I met the journalist Terry Leon on a visit to Caracas. I had heard of Angel Falls before, but had assumed the name was merely poetic. I was intrigued. I did a bit of desultory research, took the tourist flight over the falls, spent the lazy weekend at the jungle resort of Canaima. I learned there was an old friend of Jimmy Angel's still living, up the Carrao River, not far from the falls. He had later guided the Ruth Robertson expedition that established an accurate measurement of the falls, but now he lived as a hermit.

I wrote in my notebook: "Laime the Hermit."

I left Venezuela soon after that, and more or less forgot about Angel and Laime. Until, that is, the day I unrolled Ralegh's chart at the British Museum, and made a few calculations, and discovered that Sir Walter Ralegh's "golden city" and Jimmy Angel's "river of gold" were in one and the same place.

I realized, of course, that the location of Lake Manoa on Ralegh's chart is purely notional. Jimmy Angel's "river of gold" is pretty notional as well—he seems never to have found it again, and he was a noted yarn-spinner. Nonetheless, the coincidence is strange, or seemed so that night. According to Ralegh's chart, Manoa lay 150 miles due south of the mouth of the Caroní River, the farthest point of his *entrada*. According to the real map, what actually lies at that point is the table mountain called Auyán Tepuy, which is the site of Angel Falls, and thus the approximate site of Jimmy Angel's "river of gold."

I felt at that moment a sense of rather spooky continuity: that two quite distinct stories, separated by three and a half centuries, were in a way the same story. I am not discounting the possibility of a strictly practical link. In other words, Jimmy Angel may have *known* that Ralegh's, or indeed Berrio's, hopes of El Dorado were focused on this general region of the upper Caroní, and this is what brought him down here in the first place.

In the story as we have it, it would be J. R. McCracken—Angel's first guide—who had this prior knowledge of El Dorado. This McCracken is a very shadowy figure. At least one person I talked to, "Jungle Rudy" Truffino, stated his firm belief that McCracken never existed. "I never heard of anyone who met him," he said. Carlos Freeman certainly thought he was real, however, and gives the only biographical information about him that I know of. This says that McCracken was about sixty years old when he met Jimmy Angel; that he had a sidekick called Al Williams who died of a snakebite in Ciudad Bolívar; that Angel bumped into him again, about ten years after their first flight, on a train bound for Denver; and that he died in Colorado Springs in about 1932 or 1933. This sounds fleshy enough, though Freeman did not know Angel till a few years later, and could be reiterating an Angel hoax or fantasy.

Let us take McCracken as real. Is it possible that his discovery of the "river of gold," some time prior to 1921, was inspired by some knowledge or rumor concerning the old El Dorado claims of Ralegh and Berrio? Ralegh's text was available. Berrio's papers were excavated by the Venezuelan Boundary Commission in the late nineteenth century, and may have percolated into prospecting circles (some of them were published in English in 1898). It is possible, though nothing is anywhere mentioned.

There is also the matter of Ralegh's "Mountain of Crystal," and its waterfall, which seems to have a bearing on the case. On his return journey down the Orinoco, Ralegh took a brief detour, and continued down the Orinoco some way east of the point where they had joined it before. There, on a branch river he calls Winicapora, he was "informed" of this "Mountain of Crystal." They were not able to reach it—it was too far and the weather was "evil"—but he does claim to have seen it.

> We saw it afar off, and it appeared like a white church tower of an exceeding height. There falleth over it a mighty river which toucheth no part of the side of the mountain, but rusheth over the top of it, and falleth to the ground with a terrible noise and clamour, as if 1000 great bells were knocked one against another. I think there is not in the world so strange an overfall, nor so wonderful to behold. Berrio told me that it hath diamonds and other precious stones on it, and that they shined very far off; but what it hath I know not.

This mountain sounds remarkably like a *tepuy,* with its sheer sides and the unbroken fall of the water over its edge. But Ralegh and his men were by now once more on the edge of the delta; they were somewhere around present-day Santa Catalina. They were certainly not near enough to any *tepuy* to see it, let alone to hear the sound of the waterfall like "1000 great bells." If there were any mountains in view, they were only the foothills of the Serranía de Imataca, or as Ralegh calls it Emeria.

I am certain that Ralegh is fudging this. He has heard of this "Mountain of Crystal" from Berrio, and now he hears of it again. He puts in a made-up description, which appears to be a firsthand viewing of it "from afar," but which is really only a refraction of what he has heard, first from Berrio, who had not himself seen it either, and now from the Indians of Emeria, some of whom doubtless had. His description echoes that earlier, climactic passage about the

Caroní waterfalls, the memory of which is here added in. It *is* a *tepuy,* in short, but Ralegh himself never saw it. It could be Roraima, which is indeed in parts crystalline; it could be Auyán Tepuy, whose "overfall" is indeed the strangest in the world; it is, most likely, a generic description. The place where he was "informed" of it has an Arawak name, Winicapora (*wuin* rain; *cabara,* a small river). It seems, therefore, that Ralegh's crystal mountain is, in essence, an Arawak account of the extraordinary table mountains of the Gran Sabana.

None of this explains the apparently exact agreement between McCracken and Ralegh. Ralegh's "crystal mountain" *may* contain a rumor of Auyán Tepuy, but is certainly not a location for it, and anyway it is seen as a source of diamonds, not gold. And to say that Ralegh's El Dorado was "somewhere" around the upper Caroní, which is all that could be deduced from the written evidence, is not the same as pointing to a particular mountain on a particular tributary of the Caroní. This more precise location—one part of what is still today a huge tract of wilderness—can only be deduced from Ralegh's chart.

There seem to be two possible explanations for the proximity of Auyán Tepuy and Lake Manoa. One is that Angel's interest in this area actually was based on Ralegh's chart, which had been acquired by the British Museum in 1849, and was therefore available for scrutiny. (I have a pleasant image of old "J. R." himself poring over it, but this is not obligatory.)

The other explanation, by far the more plausible, is that the whole thing is complete coincidence. Jimmy Angel had struck gold somewhere around the Carrao River; he happened to find Angel Falls when searching the area later; this happens to be where El Dorado is placed on Ralegh's map. (It is also coincidence that Angel's sidekick Dick Curry made the same westward approach to the mountain in 1934 that Keymis had tried to make on his return to Guiana in 1596.)

Out of such coincidences are journeys—and indeed legends—made. The Jimmy Angel story seems to reiterate, in bush pilot guise, the old folk-story of El Dorado. There is the half-apocryphal source, "McCracken," not unlike the figure of "Juan Martínez" who gives such impetus to Ralegh's search. There is the "river of gold," which sounds much like the alluring motifs of the El Dorado chronicles, especially that recurrent lake. There is the suspicious richness of the strike. They took out forty or sixty or seventy-five *pounds* of gold? In a few *days*? And there is the mislaying of the place, its receding into the reservoir of rumor. As far as I can gather, no one found that river again: There are major gold-producing rivers not far from the falls—the lower Chicanán, for instance—but these were already known about before the 1920s. Was it all just another tall story, as he fished a handful of nuggets out of his capacious pockets?

The maps agree in a way that seems measurable but is probably an overheated coincidence arising in my mind. The true coincidence is in this realm of folklore or legend. It only happened sixty years ago, but already the Jimmy Angel story has *become* a legend, has been blurred and molded into a shape it may never have had. (I have told the story of it, but none of the narrative is firsthand; it was all constructed and communicated long after the event.)

Thus Ralegh's and Angel's expeditions seem like different versions of a single, ongoing South American folk tale. It begins with a search for a lost river or lake filled with gold; it ends with the breathtaking vision of a waterfall. It is, curiously, the water that is discovered, and not the gold. It sounds like a neat little fable, but one has to remember these are *actual* journeys. My measurements on the map are at least a reminder of that: an eerie exactitude when you most expected vagueness, romance, illusion.

In this way Ralegh's chart led me to my old file of notes on Jimmy Angel, and there I read the name: "Laime the Hermit." I wondered if he was still there. He was, and after a short Cessna hop from La Paragua, we were now touching down at Canaima to pay him a visit.

[19]

Canaima

* * *

THERE IS a plaque on a wall at Canaima that reads:

JAMES "JIMMIE" ANGEL
1899–1956
Jungle Pilot—Explorer—Aeronaut
Discoverer
of
ANGEL FALLS.
FOREVER WITH THE WINDS
THE SPIRIT OF THE ANGEL FLY
THE LAND HE LOVED—THE WATERFALL
HIS MEMORY WILL NEVER DIE
"The Jungle Pilots" 1969

No one seemed quite sure who had put it there, or indeed, who wrote it.

It was not actually Jimmy Angel who discovered Canaima, but another legendary bush pilot, Charlie Baughan. It is another waterfall place: not record breaking, but stunningly beautiful. Baughan is long dead, but the old painter Heinz had known him well, and recalled many rackety trips they took down to Canaima. "I always had some lice in my pants," said Heinz, "because this thing was really flying. You could feel the tops of the trees just under you!"

In those days, Heinz's Russian mother-in-law, Nusha, had a little *pensión,* near the Plaza Venezuela in Caracas. It was here that he first met Baughan. He describes him with relish. "He had always a cigar, this size." He makes the fisherman's gesture. "He was a fat man, very strong, a big guy. He had a little potato as a nose, you know.

He was just typical American: square-faced, strong, red, and always, always smoking his big, big cigar. Big cigar and a lot of whiskey; this is more or less what he lived on."

This was the early fifties. Baughan was trying to commercialize Canaima. He had a card printed: CANAIMA TOURS. He formed a company: Empresas Gran Sabana S.A., capital assets 300,000 bolivars, President Captain Chas. C. Baughan. He hit on the idea of flying Heinz to Canaima, to paint the scenes of tropical beauty for a promotion.

In his cluttered studio, with a rainstorm beating on the roof and cans of beer on the table, and his young friends Chico and Matilda who like to listen to him talk, Heinz lights an Astor Rojo and recalls his first flight down to Canaima with Charlie.

They were in an old military plane. As they cruised across the jungle, Baughan shouted to Heinz to take the joystick, and started rummaging around in a mess of wires in the cockpit. "There was no button, there was nothing left, just cables. The only thing I could hear from him, 'Damn it, it's not that one!' He kept on trying, and I was the pilot. Finally it made this noise: *Krrrrr!* We all thought, that's it, it's over for us. But I could see out along the wing. It was the flap. It was so rusty it wouldn't move. *Krrrrr! Krrrrr!* At last the flaps were down, and then he was very happy.

"Later I was looking for the landing strip. All I could see was water and trees and bush. I said, 'Charlie, where are we landing?' And he said, 'Well, just about here I guess.' And then we landed, just past the lake, on the savanna."

Heinz did his drawings and paintings, and put on an exhibition of them, in Caracas, in 1954. He showed me the brochure: *"Canaima, Un Pedacito de Cielo en la Tierra"*—a little piece of heaven on earth.

When they got back to Ciudad Bolívar a few days later, the police were waiting. "The plane was arrested. He hadn't paid for the gas. He had no money, he never had money. He was flying on credit."

Flying on credit was probably his undoing. Fat Charlie Baughan died around the same time as Jimmy Angel, in a plane crash—how else?—on the *litoral* not far from Caracas. "He went right into a mountain," said Heinz. "People say it was because the tower didn't give him permission to land. He had to go further on. He probably ran out of gas, because he always flew with the last drop. This must be the reason; he was too, too good a pilot to crash."

CANAIMA MUST have been a "piece of heaven," and even today—when the Avensa 747s disgorge tourists twice a day for a spell of jungle leisure—it is hard to resist. There is the wide, dark-watered, palm-fringed lagoon. At one end is the tourist complex in wood and thatch, with a small Pemón village annexed, like servants quarters; at the other, suitably viewed from the lagoon-side bar, the Hacha Falls.

In a secluded corner of the lagoon is a small island, Isla Anatoly. It is named after Anatoly the Russian: another adventurer. Heinz had told me about him. He was a gold searcher, had a gang of Italians with him: pretty rough characters. In later years he settled on this island in the Canaima lagoon. He learned the secret herbal medicines of the Pemón, became a *brujo*.

It's a five-minute boat ride to the island. There we saw Anatoly's grave: four white pillars supporting a corrugated tin roof; a cheap reproduction icon; a vase of plastic flowers; and the legend

ANATOLIY FODOROVICH POCHEPZOV
BORN IN RUSSIA 12.7.1926
DIED AT CANAIMA, *LA TIERRA QUE MÁS AMO*, 31.8.1986

His house is still there. It is built—with the profligacy that seems natural down here—out of jasper, a semiprecious stone. The stones are an ordinary sandy brown on the outside, but where they are cut they show a green, cool, glassy surface.

Anatoly's hideaway island is now inhabited by another émigré, Tomás Bernal. Tomás is a Peruvian, from the town of Ayacucho. He bought the whole island from Anatoly for $1,000. The tour companies wanted it, and Tomás found his boats disabled by mysterious helpings of sugar in the gas tanks, but he "sorted things out." Tangling with Tomás is not, on the face of it, a good idea. He is a short, broad, muscular, almost toothless man with polished skin. He has a small black mustache but otherwise looks semiferal.

"I'm the ugliest man in Canaima," he says cheerfully, "but everyone comes looking for me."

After the relative austerity of the delta and Uraima, we have prescribed ourselves a dose of leisure before heading on upriver in search of Laime. And for kicking back there are few finer places in the world than Isla Anatoly. We crack open a bottle of Pampero, and watch the sunset hit the falls, which Tomás calls his TV. The sand is full of kaolinite, which gives it a pinkish bloom, and at certain times it sighs beneath your feet, as if in pleasure.

Tomás is another hermit. He's a very sociable hermit, and earns his living off passing gringos like us, but when he first came here he was a real hermit. He lived, for nearly ten years, in a cave next to Sapo Falls. The only way to get to it was up a path he cleared behind the curtain of the falls. He takes us there; it is predictably stupendous. Walking up Tomás's thunderous garden path we are as close as we can get to the waterfalls that have become a motif of this story.

The cave has a natural chimney and an overhang for a roof, and the clutter of his *objets trouvés:* rocks and driftwood in a menagerie of shapes. He makes a fire, brews up some coffee he's brought.

He was cut off here for three days once. The falls were too full to get out. He had spaghetti and sugar and nothing else for three days. Wasn't it lonely living in a cave? Not on this occasion, he says. He had these three Swiss girls with him.

Not far from Canaima lives a Dutchman named Rudy Truffino, known to the world as Jungle Rudy. He's another of this old-time Canaima set. We saw him one day, heading in to the lagoon in a fast low *curiara,* a gaunt, imperious figure in a wide-brimmed leather hat, with an extremely pretty Pemón girl beside him (his "secretary," as we later learned). Later we paid him a visit, at the neat expensive lodge he runs just outside Canaima. He came down here, like they all did, in search of gold and diamonds. "I kind of got stuck," he said in his clipped, sardonic way. "It's a nice place to get stuck in. I guess being a little bit of a nut helped."

THE INDIANS of the region, the Pemón, are understandably skeptical about these daring "discoveries" of places they had known about all along.

Angel Falls was known to the Pemón as Churún Meru. I have read in a guidebook that the name literally means "the sound of the jaguar roaring." This is picturesque nonsense; it simply means the falls (*meru*) at or near the Churún River. The Pemón did not settle around the falls area, mainly for practical reasons, but also because of superstition. The waterfall was inhabited by an evil spirit, a *mamacatón*. This is also reflected in the name of Auyán Tepuy, which translates as Devil Mountain.

This sort of superstition is also, I learn, behind the name Canaima. I was told about this by the local Pemón headman, Jorge Calcaño. (The Calcaños are the most important clan of the Kamerakoto Pemón: Jorge's grandfather, Alejo Calcaño, is frequently mentioned by Ruth Robertson in her account of the 1949 expedition to Angel Falls.) Jorge says the name was originally given to the falls at the end of the lagoon. These (now the Hacha Falls) were called Canaima Meru. A *canaima,* or more properly *canaimo,* is a bad spirit—not, perhaps, an evil one, more a trickster. Other Pemón chip in here: The *canaimo* is "the bad boy" (*el chico malo*), the boaster or bully (*el matón*). "According to our tradition," Jorge continues, "these are spirits who come at night. They grab people [*agarran a uno*]. In the old days, the people believed they should not go too close to the falls because the spirits would jump out on them, like water dogs."

It is often said, by Rudy and others, that there was no one here when Charlie Baughan discovered Canaima. This is also untrue. There was a Pemón village near the lagoon; it was not where the present village stands, but on the stretch of savanna that lies east of the lagoon. It was removed to make way for the airfield.

Jorge spoke of the Pemón's resentment at this rewriting of local history. He said:

"There were always the *indígenas* here. When the whites came, the *criollos,* they had already been here a long time. Well, these people came: Captain Baughan was the first who landed here, then Rudy and others. They came as visitors. This was before Avensa, who began in 1958, I think. And now they are saying there were no people here before them. It is a lie. It is a lie of Rudy's and others, to make it seem to people that they were the discoverers of Canaima. When Rudy came here he had no work. He stayed here with us, with the *indígenas*. He ate like us. He ate *picantes* and he drank *cachire*. He even ate *gusanos del moriche* [palm grubs] and the butter we make of them. He lived with us, among us. But when the tourists came, when the Avensa DC-3 came, he worked with them, and guided them, and he told them, 'I am from here; I am a native here.' And so he made this propaganda that he was the discoverer of Canaima, and the people from outside believed this was true."

THIS IS a useful corrective, but I am still full of admiration for these pioneering "whites" who came to Canaima. What brought them here—invariably—was gold, but what made them return, and stay, was the place itself. It was the lake, the falls, the forest: all the poetry and drama of the South American landscape. They came here—Charlie, Heinz, Anatoly, Tomás, Rudy—and what they saw took their breath away, just as it took away Ralegh's on the lower Caroní and Jimmy Angel's as he flew his Cessna up Devil's Canyon. It is tempting, if corny, to say they found their El Dorado at Canaima, this miniature Lake Manoa in the highlands, filled with tranquillity if not with gold.

And none of them went deeper, or stayed longer, than Alexander Laime, whom it was now time to visit. I asked Rudy about Laime. They have known each other for nearly forty years, but now, well, "we don't see each other much." He rubs his chin, shakes his head. "Jungle got that guy a long time ago," he says, and looks genuinely regretful about it.

[20]

Meeting Laime

* * *

"**T**HERE'S LAIME," says the boatman, and steers in toward the riverbank.

We are two and a half hours upriver from Canaima. I am with Uwe, who has met Laime before, and a Pemón boatman, Nazario Rossi. There is a small cove. I see a stocky, stooped figure in a tattered red shirt. He watches us come in. It seems for a moment he is expecting us, but he cannot be. We come unannounced, like all his visitors. As I climb out of the *curiara* and walk toward him, he turns away and starts fiddling with a fishing line.

He has already summed me up, correctly enough: another gringo in search of the picturesque; another visitor with a pile of questions to ask, when all Laime wants—and time is running out—is an *answer*.

Alexander Laime (pronounced "limey") was born in Latvia in about 1910, left Europe at the onset of World War II, and arrived in Venezuela, via Canada and the United States, in 1940. He was another prospector who got bitten by the Canaima bug. He has lived here for the last forty years: to begin with as a guide, a trailfinder, a character; then latterly as a hermit, living in a little hut on an island in the shadow of Auyán Tepuy. But even here, this far up the line, it's hard to be a hermit. Laime has become a legend of his own, and so he gets these visitors.

He has a slow, precise, almost pedantic manner. He speaks fluent Spanish and English, both with a mid-European twang. He looks up and away as he talks, like a professor outlining a tricky theorem. "It is unusual," he says, "to see an Englishman here, because it costs them a lot of money to come here, you see, and they don't like to spend money."

Uwe has brought him provisions: canned food, oats, batteries. He looks at them and nods, but does not take them. He does not recognize Uwe. "It was last year," says Uwe, and Laime looks away as if he's trying to remember what a year is.

He has rheumy eyes, and smells of river water. He wears an EDELCA baseball cap (Electrificación del Caroní: They have a substation near Canaima). When he takes the cap off, I see his hair is still sandy, like an old street dog's: remarkable enough for a man of eighty-three who subsists on a diet of rice, macaroni, sugar, and lemon-grass tea, but everything about Laime is remarkable in this way. His life seems a feat of endurance; a triumph of eccentric individualism; a long, close dance with futility.

His hut is a five-minute walk from the riverside, through tall trees resonating with baroque bird trills. He walks easily and in silence. The hut is a simple affair: wattle walls, tin roof. An acre of gently sloping ground surrounds it, with plots of maize, manioc, beans, cucumber, etc. The place is shaded with tall mango trees. I ask if he planted them himself. "Who else?" he replies, and with a touch of formality gestures us to enter.

Inside, the brilliant afternoon light squeezes through the chinked wooden walls, illuminates the charred firewood, the tins of Quaker Oats, the log chairs, the grubby old hammock like a moored boat at the back of the hut. There are shelves of yellowing books, some with the covers facing out from the shelves, as in a bookshop. He once had three thousand books, he says, but gave most of them away. There is Sartre's *Situations,* and a couple of Arthur C. Clarkes, and some Spanish books with pop-science titles like *El Cerebro y Sus Incógnitas* and *Nuevas Fronteras de la Genética.* But the book he reaches down is one I have always admired: Steinbeck's *Log from the Sea of Cortés.* He praises its toughness and clarity. "In Spanish they take so many words to say something, but this—each word, just right, just so."

I am surprised to see, pinned on the wall, four lines of poetry that

take me straight back to my childhood, and to the precise fusty odor
of a certain *Child's Treasury of Verse:*

> Up the airy mountain
> Down the rushy glen
> We daren't go a-hunting
> For fear of little men.

Beneath it are the words "Weik Tepuy." (Weik Tepuy, a smaller
neighbor of Auyán Tepuy, is the subject of one of Laime's wilder
"theories.") I ask him why he has these words on the wall. He sucks
on his silver-capped teeth, makes those little pouts with his mouth
that look like a prelude to some dry witticism, and probably once
were. "Well," he says slowly, "there are many strange things on the
mountain." I wait for more, but that's it.

I want to talk to Laime about his days as a friend of Jimmy Angel;
about the arduous trails he carved to the base of the falls in advance
of the Ruth Robertson expedition; about his discovery on the summit of Auyán Tepuy of the plane Angel crashed in 1937, left there
with the words ALL OK written on the wings in strips of cloth torn
from his wife Marie's skirt. I want dusty legends and hard-bitten
Traven-style romance.

He is reluctant; he is sick of all this. He says, "Jimmy Angel
didn't do anything; Jimmy Angel didn't discover anything, so why
do people . . . ?" The question tails off, not worth the trouble. He
withdraws from the conversation, as often, and sits with his head
cocked, like an old parrot on a perch. He pronounces the name the
Hispanic way, "Ahn-ghel."

Eventually, however, as a kind of weary ritual, he takes down an
old suitcase full of clippings and photos. Here he is on the Robertson
expedition: bearded, bare-chested, skilled at jungle tasks. (She said
of him, "He was a human dynamo. His energy never seemed to let
up, and at the end of the day he was still fresh.") And here he is in
his early sixties, on a visit to Caracas: cropped hair, black glasses,
the truculent look of an American professor whose views have not
gained acceptance.

And here, among the yellowed papers, is the message left in the cockpit of Jimmy Angel's plane after he landed on the summit of Auyán Tepuy in 1937, written in Angel's angular, right-sloping American script. The message reads:

> By Jimmie Angel. This Flamingo Airplane was landed here Saturday Oct 9 1937 at 11.45 a.m. The landing was intentional. Switch was cut, also gas. We were on the ground 750 feet before we hit soft spot. Plane nosied up. And tore entering edge on left wing tip. And pulled one hose connection loose on oil radiator. No more visible damage done. Passengers Mrs Angel, Gustavo Heny, Miguel Delgado. Today is eleventh of October. We are walking out in good health for Camarata Camp.

This scrap of paper, the bush pilot's version of the "black box," was retrieved from the cockpit by Laime when he found the wreckage nearly twenty years later.

BUT ALL this trailblazing stuff is no longer on Laime's agenda. He has talked too much about "all this nonsense." He is reaching down another box of papers now, from the smoke-darkened shelving.

Whatever your reason for visiting Laime you will sooner or later have to listen to his "theories." They will be illustrated by diagrams drawn in the dirt with his stick; by piles of jottings in his large rounded script; by tatty cardboard models too small to convey the meanings he intends. You will be given a peep of trailing equations and long-division sums, which he will hurriedly turn over because he cannot yet trust you. You will hear of the "solar year" of 28,000 years, and the 6½-degree tilt of the earth's axis which has occurred in this time; and of a certain "Stairway," and a "Stone Table," and other Narnian-sounding places he has found on, or as he puts it, *in* the mountain.

As he warms to his theme, Laime seems like one of those scholarly hermits of the old esoteric tradition, wandering in this maze of numerology and occult correspondence, his brow furrowed as he struggles to find the pattern, the system, the *answer*. More than once he interjects, suddenly desperate for me to understand, "It all *fits*, you see!"

His chief theory concerns the shape and significance of the *tepuys*, in particular the beautiful, anvil-shaped outline of Weik Tepuy. He believes that its peculiar indentations are evidence of a prehistoric solar observatory. This belongs, he believes, to the previous "solar year." The earth has tilted 6½ degrees since then; the *tepuys* now stand at 6½ degrees north of the equator. Thus, one "solar year" ago, the *tepuys* stood—as did Ralegh's El Dorado—on the "equinoctial line," perfectly placed for their role as astronomical computers. *Quod erat demonstrandum.*

"So do you believe that the *tepuys* were put here, like Stonehenge?"

"I cannot explain it in any other way."

There is a messianic tone in it, too, which I find grating. These theories are a "message" he is getting. We *need* this message, but people are stupid, greedy, uncomprehending. "The world is falling into chaos, you see. It is a very dangerous time. It is very important to understand these things, because they will save us." I never heard him commend anyone. Jimmy Angel was a tale spinner who "didn't do anything." Jungle Rudy was a parasite who came in after Laime and claimed Laime's trails as his own. That's what it's like here in paradise: Your nearest neighbor lives two hours downriver and you aren't on speaking terms anyway.

AND THEN there are his "creatures."

He saw a pair of them. This was in about 1955, on one of his first expeditions onto the *tepuy.* He saw them "sunbathing" by the side of a small pool near the summit. They slithered off, "very fast, like this"—a snaking movement—before he could photograph them.

He fishes out a drawing he made, in crayon, grubby thumbprints in the corner where he has often held it. It shows a smooth-skinned creature, seal-like but also reptilian, with a thin head and four finlike limbs. He says the ones he saw were about three meters long.

He has told this story before: I was expecting it. It has been suggested that Laime's creatures (if they existed at all) were a species of long-necked otter, found elsewhere in Venezuela. Laime dismisses this with contempt. There are no fish in the bogs and streams of the high *tepuy*. These were prehistoric creatures, he says. "They looked"—reaching down a book—"something like plesiosaurs." Plesiosaurs were aquatic mammals of the Jurassic period. They are generally thought to have gone extinct between 60 and 100 million years ago.

There is some scientific ground at the bottom of this. The *tepuys* are biological islands, sandstone pedestals that separated from the surrounding terrain nearly 2 billion years ago. On their wild, boggy, stalagmitic summits are found unique species of plants—orchids, bromeliads, and at least five new types of *heliamphora,* the carniverous sun-pitcher. The botanist Richard Schomburgk (brother of Sir Robert) called Roraima a "botanical El Dorado." There are fauna too: two new subspecies of flycatcher, for instance. There is even a prehistoric reptile of sorts, *Oreophrynella quelchii,* discovered on Roraima in 1894. This is a species of toad so rudimentary that it can neither hop nor swim. It is barely an inch long, however, and is not Laime's plesiosaur.

But the scientific ground is also a fertile legend, and it is hard not to see Conan Doyle's *Lost World* as the prototype of Laime's *tepuy* beasties. Doyle's book was based on lectures he heard by Everard im Thurn, the first explorer to the summit of Roraima. The isolation of the summit is elaborated into a "lost" world of screeching pterodactyls and stompy iguanodons: the throwback or time-warp fantasy of a hundred horror movies, most recently Spielberg's *Jurassic Park.*

This is probably the sensible answer to the plesiosaurs of Auyán Tepuy: a hallucination by Laime, a projection from a mind full of bizarre images and patterns. But I felt the oddity of it, sitting there in the hermit's hut. I had seen that "creature" lurking in the map all those months ago, and now here I was, at the place where the map said I should be, staring at it once again: a sketch of it in childlike pencil and crayon, a *sighting* of it, for God's sake.

But, as Rudy would have said, it was just the jungle getting at me.

ON THE floor next to his desk, in permanent readiness, sits his old canvas backpack, with ropes and sleeping bag and boots. All is prepared for what he impassively calls his "last expedition."

"When the time comes I will go. Up there." He gestures out of the window, toward the brooding *tepuy*. He means it. For a spell in the fifties he virtually lived up there, in a house of wood and tar paper that was dropped in stages by friendly pilots.

"Then you won't see me anymore. Laime will be gone. I will disappear."

It will not be long, one fears. In a sense, he already has "disappeared": an old man marooned upriver, his eyes fixed on the strange and suggestive shapes of the *tepuys,* his mind tuned to inaudible signals.

As we prepare to leave he is fitting the batteries we brought into his radio cassette. He puts on a tape. A hiss, an aged orchestral opening, a violin. It is Paganini. The sound follows us as we walk down through the woods to the *curiara.*

[AUTHOR'S NOTE: Shortly before this edition went to press I learned, with regret, of the deaths of both Alexander Laime and Rudy Truffino.]

[21]

Welcome to El Dorado

* * *

W
E RETURNED a few days later to film at Laime's hut. He said he had been awake all night; he didn't think he could go through with it. He was quavery and confused. I felt like a heel. We filmed an interview anyway, desultory and often incoherent. We gave him our gifts, which he accepted impassively, like old Mr. Brown in *Squirrel Nutkin*. We shook his hand, and left him in his doorway, in his silence, and headed on up the river.

We were now on the last leg of our jaunt through the New Dorado, and from here on it was going to be rather less of a jaunt. We had two *curiara* and a team of seven Pemón—three boatmen, three *chinos* or lads, and an interpreter, Anita. (María Teresa had returned to Caracas.) We were going on upriver to the top of the Carrao. We would cross the watershed on foot—an escarpment called the Sierra La Lema, at the northeastern edge of the Guiana Shield—and from there descend into the Cuyuní River system.

Our final destination was a small mining town on the Cuyuní, close to the disputed border with Guyana. It was one of those settlements that sprang up during the gold rush of the nineteenth century.

It was nothing special, except for its name, which was El Dorado.

FIRST, WE had one last detour to make. We couldn't miss Angel Falls.

An hour upriver from Laime's we turned southward and headed up the fast, dark rapids of the Churún, which runs through Devil's

Canyon, and from which, rounding a certain bend, you get your first view of the falls: a distant precipice and a thin silver tail of water.

These rivers are dark from the tannin that leaches off the forest trees. The light changes the color of the water: iodine-yellow, blood-red, tea-brown. From above, the rapids of the Churún look like boiling molasses.

We spend the night at Rat Island, the base camp for the falls. We play a few hands of "rum" with the boatmen. The mood is good. Their leader is Melquiades Calcaño, another of that clan: a quiet, droll man. The joker of the crew is plump Poli. He has already been in trouble—we had to bail him out at Canaima, having run up 3,000 bolivars on the slate for drinks. The other *lanchero* is Franco, who looks like a Chinese bandit. The younger lads are the *ayudantes,* assistants: really apprentices. They spend two years learning the skills of the river.

They all seem glad to be traveling. This is a good time. It is safer when the river is high, but it must not be too high. Melquiades said he liked working for tourists, but that many Pemón were suspicious. "They do not like this contact with people [i.e., from outside]. They want to be separate. They want to eat their traditional foods and follow their customs."

The following morning we made the gentle uphill hike that leads, after an hour, to a plateau near the base of the falls, which is where Ruth Robertson came forty years ago, and which is known as Mirador Laime, or Laime's Viewpoint. I will not bother to relate the falls' stupendousness. The details are in the adventure brochures. It is tremendous and dramatic and, yes, tall. It does make the sound of a roaring animal, even if the Pemón do not allude to this in the name Churún Meru, and it does thunder at the bottom like a thousand bells, even if Ralegh never heard it do so himself.

The following day we are whisked back down the Churún, and funneled into the Carrao once more. The falls are the outer edge of Canaima tourism (two days up, one day down, back in time for a sundowner at the Lagoon Bar). We are now moving into an unvisited corner of the highlands. I asked Franco if he had been to the Sierra

La Lema before. He shook his head. *"Un turista más,"* he said. He'll be a tourist as well.

Two hours upriver, at the Kwai rapids, is a small camp. Here we meet the second contingent of Pemón. There are the two Calcaños: their leader Jorge, a slight man in his early forties, and his brother Ladislaus, in a blue and white cowboy hat. With them are half a dozen strong young *chinos,* our porters for the overland hike. Head of the *chinos* is Enrique. He alone, it transpires, knows the trail that will lead us across the Sierra. He is eighteen, very handsome. He wears a necklace with a turquoise. *Un regalo,* he says: a gift.

There is a smoldering fire in the damp air, a couple of shelters to string our hammocks, a rocky inlet with the *curiara* docked at angles. Jorge gives me some meat; it has a venisonlike taste. It is salted tapir. Jorge called it *danta;* Ralegh called it *anta,* and described it as a "kind of beast as big as an English beef."

The men are cleaning their guns. There's a hunting trip on. Two parties: one along the river, the other into the forest. The guns are old rifles and shotguns (*escopítas*). Enrique has a 16-bore shotgun, United States manufacture, bought in Kamarata for 18,000 bolivars (about $250).

We take Jorge's well-appointed *curiara.* He finds a quiet creek, cuts the engine. Dusk falls with its celebrated abruptness. Enrique in the bow makes birdcalls, which are sometimes answered, but distantly and timidly. Nothing breaks up from the dark vegetation on the banks. The guns rest easy between their knees. We sit and smoke and talk in low voices, and from time to time paddle to a new spot, and wait some more.

The moon is up as we head back, and clouds riding over Weik Tepuy.

We play a rowdy card game called *mariquito.* The name is a diminutive of *maricón,* a slang word for a homosexual. There are no winners, only a loser, who is the *mariquito* of the round. We play with the old Spanish pack that has the tarot suits; this came over with the first *conquistadores.* The Pemón jokingly call the sword suit *machetes.*

Cups and coins, sticks and machetes. We play late into the night, perched on plastic barrels, with the hurricane lamp swaying and the river roaring behind us.

We turn in one by one. Uwe addresses the dozing boatmen in one of his angry monologues.

AT MIDDAY we pass the mouth of the Akanán, which comes down from Kamarata, and soon arrive at a small settlement on the left bank: Campo Carrao.

This is the last spot marked on our TPC: our last coordinate before we head off into the Sierra. We are at 5°58' north, 62°15' west, at an altitude above sea level of 5,055 feet. Canaima is about sixty miles behind us and 300 feet lower. To the east, the direction we're going, the map goes into white-out: Relief Data Incompatible.

For Anita, our new interpreter, it is something quite different: her birthplace. Anita's mother lived in a village inland from here, Huaytay (a Pemón word meaning a mud flat or bog). She is only half Pemón. Her father was Lebanese, a gold trader, António Salon; one glimpses another adventurer. He died in 1965, when Anita was less than a year old. She was brought up at Huaytay by her mother and her Pemón stepfather.

Campo Carrao was then a little riverside settlement of gold diggers. It is now quite deserted except for an EDELCA radio station and a couple of Pemón huts. Anita remembers coming here with her stepfather, on the way to the *conucos,* the village fields. *Conucos* are worked in rotation, and are sometimes quite distant from the village. The soil down here is sandy, she says. For planting you must go higher up, where the earth is red. They would also gather here on Saturdays and Sundays, to "dance the Halleluja." She calls this an "indigenous religious dance," but there is obviously an admixture of Seventh Day Adventism, which has migrated into the area from British Guiana, and is probably stronger among the Pemón than Catholicism.

She left Huaytay in 1974, to go to school in Kamarata, and did not return till the early eighties. She found the place quite changed. Gold mining became illegal here when the area was declared a national reserve (Parque Nacional de Canaima). Now there are only a few houses in the village. The people have gone to Kamarata or Canaima, and the *mineros* have gone to Paúl, Dorado, Kilometro 33, San Antonio, and elsewhere.

The place is still rich in gold and diamonds, she says, and the Pemón carry on small-scale mining. They work, as she puts it, in the old "rustic" way.

Out on the savanna stands the corroded hulk of an abandoned DC-3. It was here before she can remember. She thinks it got stuck in the mud and couldn't take off. She remembers playing here with her little brother. The seats were still in it then. The insects buzz around it. Shrubbery pokes out of the empty sockets of the cockpit: a skeleton in a field, a memorial to the bush pilots.

TWO HOURS up from Campo Carrao is a Pemón village, Sara Uraipa. Half a mile from the north bank, up a narrow path between forest and tall maize, the round, palm-thatched houses—*churuata*—squat like beehives around a clearing.

The headman, Mario Gonzales, is thin and lethargic, and seems unwell. The village has 130 people, a schoolhouse with lessons in Pemón, a thatched Catholic church, and a little cemetery. The graves are humps of dust, marked with wooden crosses, oil cans, Carabobo biscuit tins. A chief's grave is a bigger hump, and a little mausoleum of wood, wire, and corrugated tin. It also has a wonderful football field, in the wide valley, with the immense, somber, purple-gray face of the *tepuy* looking down. The waterfalls that run down the *tepuy* are called Los Testigos, The Witnesses.

The center of the village is a clearing of stamped earth. We are invited to camp here. There are some mango trees for shade, but not enough for our hammocks. We must pitch tents, and the boatmen must build one of their marvelous instant benders out of whippy branches and sheets of polyethylene.

We are now at an altitude where it is either raining or about to rain. Uwe hacks small trenches around the tents. "Come on, we must dig graves," he shouts.

Foxy dogs patrol the perimeter of the camp. The village is quiet. Most of the men are up at the *conucos.* Woodsmoke seeps out of doorways where the women whisper and rustle. Among the chickens runs a mangy runt reminiscent of the monstrous birth in the movie *Alien.* What I stupidly take for a totem pole is—the patient Anita explains—a kind of mangle for squeezing juice out of the manioc root. It is used in conjunction with the woven sausage-shaped basket called a *sebucan.*

Uwe is spinning the dials of the radio. "Sierra La Lema calling Neptune Central," then the deadpan voice of Jim's radio girl Lorna at the other end, in Tumeremo: our lifeline. Jim is an American prospector who owns a *balsa* and a small concession on the Cuyuní River. He is hiring a boatman to come up and fetch us when we get to the other side of the Sierra.

"Okay, listen, Jim. We gonna need chicken, some cans, batteries, oil, two hundred Astor Rojo, and plenty of rum and beer. We gonna have a party, over."

They talk of Puerto Chicanán as the rendezvous, which sounds reassuring, but then there's discussion at this end with Enrique, and Uwe amends: "Jim, we mean the *puerto arriba.* This guy needs to get right up to the top of the river." Jim says there's problems with gasoline. There's gas rationing in El Dorado: an expedient means of suppressing the *mineros,* for whom it is as necessary as water.

The next day, drama in the village. A woman, Eusabia, is sick. She was pregnant; now the baby is dead inside her. There is talk of a *curandero,* or witch doctor, and certain leaves she had eaten four, maybe five, days ago.

Uwe summons a helicopter from Canaima, courtesy of Channel 4. It arrives after two hours. All the village is out as it approaches through the valley: a Bell Ranger. In the cockpit can be seen two white shirts, two mustaches, two pairs of aviator shades. The blades whip up the tall grass, and hats fly off in the wind, and Eusabia is carried aboard by her husband, wrapped in a cheap blanket, looking thin and terribly young.

IN SARA Uraipa, just when we needed it, we began to run out of steam. It rained a lot. The tents were small and leaky. The helicopter drama meant a day's delay.

We had been on or by a river for nearly four weeks now. Apart from a couple of nights at the Hotel Razzle in Puerto Ordaz, we had spent the whole time in hammocks, boats, and bumpy little airplanes. Reaching Laime had seemed a kind of ironic climax to the trip, and the rest was just, well, a name.

I suppose in a way we were now closer to Ralegh's experience than we had been on the Orinoco. This was, for better or worse, an expedition. There were about twenty of us in all, moving through difficult terrain, carrying a lot of equipment. It would take us six days to get from Sara Uraipa to El Dorado, a crow's flight distance of just sixty miles.

We set off early from Sara Uraipa. It was barely midday when Uwe announced we should make camp. It was already too late to start our walk up the Sierra, he said, and according to Enrique this was the only place to camp. There was an argument. I wanted to press on. Uwe shrugged; the boatmen looked disgruntled. We moved off. The rain started: an instant deluge. I gave in. We turned back and made camp. If I had had a tent to go to, I would have gone and sulked in it—the indecisive leader—but instead spent a pleasant day fishing with Jorge.

That night we huddled under tarps in our steep encampment, spooning "sardines"—the meager tiddlers we had caught—out of a thin broth. It was Saturday night.

Enrique spoke of the trail starting at Puerto La Lema, but when we got there the next morning we found it was just a hole in the trees, probably much the same as Port Morequito was when Ralegh met Chief Topiawari. The walk was steep, muddy, and beautiful. We came down into lusher, warmer forest: peppery smells, scattered tree tomatoes, monkey debris.

It took less than six hours to cross the Sierra, about half what we'd expected. I remembered Heinz: "I don't believe it until I do it." He said you must learn your *facts* by doing them, which is the meaning of the word: something done, not something told to you.

Puerto Chicanán is another hole in the trees, resounding with birdsong, most notably one that sounds like a slow jazzy riff on an electric glockenspiel. This bird has a long yellow tail, and a conical hive-shaped nest. The Pemón call it *kinotori,* so we nicknamed it the keynote bird.

There was no boatman waiting for us that afternoon. Nor all the next day. The food dwindled, the last cigarette was smoked, the damp firewood spat. Radio static; Donald Duck voices: Neptune Central says the boatman had left, as arranged, and where he was now they didn't know.

"*Coño,* Jim, but this guy is an asshole, over."

The river was high; there could be trees across it. It was suddenly possible that the boatman couldn't reach us. Melquiades said there was a trail to El Pistón.

How long?

They conferred. "About five days."

The Pemón spent the time lounging, whittling, fishing, tinkering, gun cleaning. There was no problem as far as they were concerned.

We dined that night on wild turkey. As the light faded Enrique went off hunting. We heard the shots. He came back with a brace of fat, black-feathered birds that they called *bauhee.* They pluck them immediately. The feathers come out with a faint creaking sound. The heads and feet are scorched in the fire, to get the small feathers out, then chopped off to go into a broth. Oiled and salted by Anita, the birds are roasted on a wooden griddle. The meat is dense, brownish, nearer goose than turkey.

At around nine o'clock the next morning, forty hours later than planned, we heard the thin whine of an outboard, and hurried down to the landing in time to see Jim's *curiara* nosing tentatively through the foliage with two young *criollos* aboard.

*   *   *

FOUR HOURS down the Chicanán we came to El Pistón, a gold
digger's squatter camp, typical of many in the region: a makeshift
street built of tin and wood, tapering quickly off into the wilderness.
Some of the shacks have a homely look: little kitchens, and clothes-
lines, and backyards shaded with papaya and guava trees. Others
serve as bars, stores, workshops, stables. And here is the village flop-
house, its walls painted blue, a dirt floor to dance on, and a row of
short-time cubicles out back.

The only thing missing is the people. The place is quite empty:
a ghost village. In this too, increasingly, El Pistón is typical.

One day last September the National Guard came in helicopters.
They gave the people of El Pistón twenty-four hours to clear out.
"There were four hundred people living here," says Victor, a handsome young man from Maracaibo who once worked here. "There
were families with children. The Guardia threw everything out into
the street. There were fires burning. The people didn't want to go,
but they had no choice." El Pistón, and several thousand hectares
around it, is now part of a concession leased by the Venezuelan
government to a consortium from Japan.

The demise of El Pistón was one incident in the government's
tough new stance against the independent (and officially illegal) gold
diggers. The government describes the policy as a "rationalization."
The miners call it *el desalojo:* the eviction.

Twenty minutes downriver, at Chivao, the story is much the same.
Two years ago this rambling shanty town housed five thousand people; now there are about twenty families. Right next door is a new
camp: a neat grid of wooden huts, radio antennae, aluminum speed-
boats. This is Camp Guayana 6: an "exploration concession" along
about five miles of the Chicanán, operated as a joint venture between
Goldfields of South Africa and the Cisneros group, a powerful local
dynasty that owns TV channels, supermarkets, and the national fran-
chise for Pepsi-Cola.

The chief engineer, a bearded Brit from Hampshire, Peter Brown, is impassive. "We do not forcibly evict the *mineros*," he says, "but the longer we stay, the harder it is for them to work here."

No one should romanticize the life of the *mineros*, he says, nor minimize the damage they cause. Their camps are "havens of vice," where prostitutes sell their bodies for a gram of gold dust (worth about $10). Malaria is endemic, cholera and AIDS growing (the latter largely blamed on immigrants from Brazil). The indiscriminate use of mercury poisons the rivers, and indeed the people, for miles around.

AND SO, finally, to El Dorado. At the edge of town stands a sign, sponsored by Consul cigarettes, that says: BIENVENIDOS A EL DORADO.

There's nothing much to the place. It's the kind of sleepy, low-built little South American town you can see anywhere. Its lifeblood is being throttled by the new mining policies. It used to be a trading center for the *mineros*, but now the line of gold stores stands empty. The gold is helicoptered straight out nowadays; it never touches El Dorado.

I eventually manage to buy a gold nugget, down at Las Claritas. In shape it resembles a piece of used chewing gum.

The moon is up, the low roofs fall away toward the brown Cuyuní. Across the river is a jumble of gray-walled buildings: the remains of the notorious prison that once held the famous French jailbreaker Henri Charrière, better known as Papillon. I drink beers in the little town-square with Eulogio. Our journey is over. Tomorrow we will drive to Puerto Ordaz in time for the evening flight to Caracas. It has taken us five weeks to get to El Dorado, and it will take us a little more than twelve hours to get back.

I say, with beery solemnity, "Plenty of water under the bridge."

Eulogio weighs this. "Yes," he says. "The river is full in December."

In the empty streets of El Dorado, as in the ghost towns of the Chicanán, and inevitably soon on the Paragua, one sees that the gold rush is over. The *independientes,* the old-style adventurers and prospectors, will soon be as extinct as Laime's plesiosaur. It is a dirty, generally unrewarding life, but it still has a charisma. I felt the same in the old hermit's hut on the Carrao—that we had come in at the tail end of the adventure; that after four centuries this really was the last episode of that extraordinary soap opera called El Dorado.

PART FOUR

THE
RETURN

———

It is no dream which I have reported of Guiana.

—RALEGH TO SIR ROBERT CECIL,
November 13, 1595

[22]

Downriver

*   *   *

O N ABOUT June 14, 1595, with a last look upriver in the direction of El Dorado, in the direction of these future events, Ralegh manned his boats and rowed back down the Orinoco to Port Morequito. "We had now been well near a month, every day passing to the westward farther and farther from our ships. We therefore turned towards the east." His journey toward the sunset was over.

The following day he had his second meeting with "aged Topiawari," cementing the friendship of the first encounter, and formalizing the political alliance between Queen Elizabeth and the "lords of the borders" of Guiana.

The final exchange between them is human. As a "pledge," Topiawari gave Ralegh his son, Caywaraco, to take to England. The old chief had "but a short time to live," and hoped that "by our means his son should be established after his death." (Ralegh says it was his only son, which seems unlikely: Sparry says, more plausibly, "one of his sons.")

In return, Ralegh left with the Indians "two of ours."

I left with him one Francis Sparrow, a servant of Captain Gifford, who was desirous to stay, and could describe a country with his pen; and a boy of mine called Hugh Goodwin, to learn the language.

Topiawari initially asked for fifty English soldiers to be left. There was no shortage of volunteers. Captain Calfield offered to remain as captain of a garrison. So, in turn, did Ralegh's young relatives, Grenville and Gilbert. But Ralegh rejected this idea. He told Topiawari that he could not spare the "companies he desired," that

> I had no provision to leave them, of powder, shot, apparel or aught else, and that without those things necessary for their defence they should be in danger of the Spaniards . . . [and] must needs have perished. For Berrio expected daily a supply out of Spain, and looked also hourly for his son to come down from Nuevo Reyno de Granada with many horse and foot.

His fears proved accurate: Just four months later Berrio arrived at Port Morequito, and in December his son Ferdinando's men arrived from New Granada (though only thirty of them), and there they founded the Spanish garrison of San Thomé de Guayana.

Ralegh urged patience, and they agreed to "forbear the enterprise against the Epuremei till the next year," and when the company departed the following day there were just the two Englishmen left on the riverside, watching the boats move downriver and disappear around a bend.

RALEGH SAYS Sparry was "desirous to stay": the plucky volunteer. He could also "describe a country with his pen." It is possible this penmanship refers to mapmaking—there is in fact a later record of a map drawn by Sparry—but it probably means what it appears to mean, which is that Sparry was observant and literate, and could verbally "discover" those parts of Guiana not included in Ralegh's own *Discoverie*. Specifically, Ralegh says he instructed Sparry "to travel to Macureguarai with such merchandizes as I left with him, thereby to learn the place, and if it were possible to go on to the great city of Manoa."

Sparry has his own account of all this, as delivered to the Spanish authorities early the following year, and summed up in a report by his interrogator, Pedro Liaño:

Guaterral promised to return the following March with a thousand men, to settle there, and as a proof that he should do so he left two Englishmen under his [Topiawari's] charge. One was twenty-five years old, and the other sixteen. They were to learn the language, and acquaint themselves with the region, so that they could act as interpreters on his return. The *cacique* gave Guaterral one of his sons, who was eighteen or twenty years old, and three other Indians, whom he took away with him. They then took leave, and the two Englishmen remained among the Indians. The *cacique* and all the other Indians treated them most kindly, and gave them presents, and respected them.

This adds one or two specifics not mentioned by Ralegh—the promised date and strength of his return; the three other Orenoqueponi who went with the chief's son—and ends on a touching note of gratitude for the kind treatment the castaways received from the Indians. Sparry is not given to sentiment, and this comment does much to confirm Ralegh's vaunted claims of amity with the Orenoqueponi.

The chief's son, Sparry tells us, is about twenty. (By Ralegh's reckoning, Topiawari sired him at the age of ninety.) It is just possible we glimpse him again, many years later. Sir Robert Harcourt, setting out for Guiana in 1609, carried with him from England an Indian interpreter, Anthony Canebre. He "was a Christian," says Harcourt, "and had lived in England fourteen years." He had come to England, therefore, in 1595; it is very likely he was brought back by Ralegh's expedition. While in Guiana, Harcourt met at "Wiapoco" (i.e., Oyapak) an Indian called John, who "sometime had been in England, and served Sir John Gilbert many years." He spoke good English and was recognized by some of Harcourt's company. He proved "firm and faithful" to them, but died while they were there. Sir John Gilbert is Ralegh's nephew, who as plain John Gilbert was here on the Orinoco in 1595.

These Indians have a connection back to the Guiana Voyage, and it is possible that both Anthony Canebre and Indian John were among the four Orenoqueponi who left Port Morequito with the

English, in exchange for Sparry and Godwin. One or other of them may be Topiawari's son. We know of two other Guiana Indians, Leonard and Harry, who attended on Ralegh in the Tower, but there is nothing to connect them with this first voyage.

Francis Sparry did not see England for another seven years, though much of that was spent in a Spanish jail. After his return in 1602 he penned a brief account of his adventures, or rather a topographical account of the region with a few lush details thrown in. This was later printed in Samuel Purchas's *Pilgrims*. Some of it is based on Ralegh's text, which he had clearly read with interest and was careful not to contradict. But much is vividly firsthand, and derives from Sparry's explorations westward along the upper Orinoco. He was almost certainly the first Englishman to reach that far inland. He was in part following Ralegh's instructions, looking (as he puts it) for "a perfect and ready way to go to Peru"—the route, in other words, that would confirm Ralegh's cherished theory of the Inca migration to Guiana.

He traveled as far as Quesada's old domain, the Rio Papamene, or Caqueta. He claims it is over five leagues (fifteen miles) wide. In this region, far from anyone but his Indian guides, in a place "not inhabited by any," he came upon a "most sweet, pleasant and temperate island" in the river. The natives call the region Athul. (Athul is perhaps Ature, the huge rapids on the upper Orinoco, close to the mouths of the Meta and Caqueta.) In this region, he enthuses,

> there are great store of freshwater rivers, and no want neither of fish, tortoises (which the Indians name *catsepames*), fowls, nor other good things. It hath wood great store, fruits all the year in abundance, many good places to make a town if you will, cotton and balsamum, brazil, *lignum vitae,* cypresses and many other sweet trees. The earth of this island doth promise of the eye to be good: it is very sad [i.e., dark] and much like to ore, which is found in divers places.

The place is appraised with an eye to survival, but he is struck too by its beauty, and says rather wistfully: "If I had had company to my liking, I could have found in mine heart to have stayed there, and spent my life."

Another time he visits a native slave-market, at Camalaha, south of the Orinoco.

Camalaha is a place where they sell women at certain times, in the manner of a fair. And there you shall buy colours such as the salvages paint themselves with. In this fair . . . I bought eight young women, the eldest whereof I think never saw eighteen years, for one red-hafted knife which in England cost me one halfpenny. I gave these women away to certain salvages which were my friends, at the request of Warituc, the king's daughter of Morequito.

He is not an expert in gemstones—"my knowledge in them is nothing"—but diligently collects specimens from the gullies and riverbeds. At Curaa are "mines of white stone." At Tulaha he finds freshwater pearls, though "they were nothing round, orient, nor very great." He tried to trade them with some Spaniards. They told him "they were no pearls but topazes."

He writes in the brusque, produce-oriented manner of the Elizabethan traveler—the tone familiar throughout the great collections by Hakluyt and Purchas—but the peculiar iridescence of the tropics pierces through: the sweet trees, the fast-flowing rivers, the pearls, the birds, the face paints, the hint of a certain fondness for Princess Warituc.

Thus Sparry accomplished much that Ralegh charged him with: to explore, to "learn," to "describe with his pen." The journeys he describes took place over a period of about six months in late 1595. The English left him with Topiawari in the middle of June, and by the end of December he was in captivity, having been taken by a squad of Spanish jungle soldiers under Berrio's former protégé, Felipe de Santiago. He was captured "in the Province of Morequito," while "sailing one day down the river." He was perhaps present, as a prisoner, at the founding of San Thomé on December 21. In February he was brought to Margarita Island, where his "declaration" was taken by the *licenciado* of the island, Pedro de Liaño.

Lawrence Keymis, back in Guiana in early 1596, heard the news of his capture. He writes: "Santiago passed up into Topiawari's country, and there took Francis Sparrowe, Sir George Gifford his man, prisoner, who with plenty of gold ransomed his life, and is now abiding in Cumana." It may or may not be true that Sparry was by then in Cumaná. The next we hear of him is in 1597, by which time he is languishing in a little cell, a *calabozo,* at the town prison in Madrid.

AND WHAT of Sparry's companion, young Hugh Goodwin or Godwin? Ralegh does not say whether or not he was also "desirous to stay." He simply says Godwin was left "to learn the language." According to Liaño's report, much of it based on Sparry's "declaration," Godwin was killed within a few days or weeks: "In June 1595, the younger of the two Englishmen, going out into the country in English dress, was attacked by four tigers who tore him to pieces." Leaving aside the non sequitur—as if the tigers had noticed what clothes he was wearing—this seems an unequivocal epitaph. It is repeated in another report, written at Cumaná in April 1596: "Captain Felipe de Santiago . . . took from the Indians one Englishman only of the two who had been left there, whose name was Francisco Espari, and found that the other had been eaten by a tiger."

Keymis heard the same story, from a former servant of Berrio's:

> that Topiawari, soon after our departure from the river, fled into the mountains, carrying Hugh Godwyn with him, and leaving a substitute in his country, as aforesaid; and that the next news they heard of him was that he was dead, and the English boy eaten by a tiger.

However, the same informant added that "the Spaniards believe neither one nor the other"—neither, in other words, that Topiawari was dead, nor that Godwin had been killed by a tiger. (In all these reports "tiger" means panther or jaguar; there are no tigers in South America.)

There is this shred of hope for Hugh Godwin, that the reports of his death are false, but it is not enough to support the mini-legend that has sprung up about him. It is invariably stated in modern biographies of Ralegh that Godwin survived; that Ralegh met him at Caliana, or Cayenne, on his return to South America in 1617; and that Godwin had all but forgotten how to speak English. This is not so much a legend as plain error. I am not sure when the mistake first occurred. (It is not, for instance, in Oldys's biography of 1736, where it is said that "the English boy Ralegh left was devoured by a tiger.") The usual source for the story is the monumental Victorian *Life* by Edward Edwards, published in 1868. Citing Ralegh's logbook of the 1617 voyage, Edwards writes: "Goodwin remained amongst the Indians and had his desire [i.e., to learn their language]. Sir Walter found him at Caliana, 'having almost forgotten his English,' in November 1617." What is missed by those who repeat this story is Edwards's own correction of it. In a note inserted in the index (s.v. Goodwin) he says that this is an error, "arising out of a misconception of the passage in Ralegh's MS journal there referred to."

The misconception is, in fact, a simple misreading. The entry in question reads: "After I had stayed in Caliana a day or two, my servant Harry came to me, who had almost forgotten his English." This refers not to Hugh Godwin but to a Guiana Indian named Harry, who had been in Ralegh's service in England. This is made clear by preceding entries, referring both to him and to another former servant, "Leonard the Indian" (Leonard Regapo).

There is no evidence of Godwin's survival, and not much reason to doubt the contemporary reports that he had died in the summer of 1595, at the age of sixteen.

THE JOURNEY back downriver was swift and furious, and for anyone who has seen the uglier moods of the Orinoco, pretty heroic. "Our hearts were cold to behold the great rage and increase of Orenoque." Ralegh twice states that on the return leg, with the river in spate, they "went no less than 100 miles a day." As he believed that the distance back to his ships was four hundred miles, I infer that the return journey took them four or probably—given certain brief detours and forays—five days.

There were important events in these last few days, though all of it is suffused with the anticlimactic qualities of returning the way you came. They met Chief Putmaya, whom they had missed as they went upriver, and were shown a certain gold-rich hill by him. This particular site was one of the goals, or pretexts, of Ralegh's last voyage of 1617. (Another was a gold mine they had visited on the Caroní: These two sites tend to blur into one in Ralegh's statements of intent, and neither was located by the 1617 expedition.) There were other *caciques,* and other interesting side trips. On one, they saw a manatee; on another they heard of, but certainly did not see, that "Mountain of Crystal" that sounds so like a *tepuy.* They tried to make contact with the powerful *cacique* Curapana, the lord of Emeria, but "the old fox" was absent—deliberately so, Ralegh thought, so he could remain uncommitted and play off the new invaders against the old Spanish enemy.

Having explored as well as they could the forests and savannas on the southern banks of the Orinoco—the outer "borders" of Guiana—they reentered the swamps of the delta. They paid a last visit to Toparimaca, the Nepoyo chief who had treated them so hospitably before, but departed the same evening, "with very foul weather and showers." They were unable to return by the Caño Manamo, or Amana, by which they had ascended, "both the breeze and the current of the sea were so forcible." Instead they struck off down a more easterly river, which he calls the Capuri but which is more probably the Caño Macareo.

Bobbing along down the turbid brown waters of the Macareo, the five boats arrived once more on the coast, debouching about forty miles east of the Boca Bagre, by which they had entered the delta over a month previously.

A storm was raging in the bay. They were almost back—the fleet was waiting off Trinidad, just around the beaklike promontory of Icacos Point—but it seemed they might be dashed at this last moment of the *entrada.* "When we were arrived at the seaside, then grew our greatest doubt, and the bitterest of all our journey forepassed." The small boats huddled "close under the land," but the heroic old galley was in trouble: "She had as much ado to live as could be, and there wanted little of her sinking, and all those in her."

Night was falling. There is a moment of fraught indecision: he is "very doubtful which way to take." Should they risk the open sea crossing, or wait for the storm to blow over? "The longer we tarried, the worse it was." A decision is made. They would leave the "pestered galley" at anchor in the bay, while Ralegh's barge made the crossing alone.

Around midnight the storm seemed to ease a bit, and Ralegh, Gifford, Calfield, and Grenville, together with eight rowers, set off: "We put ourselves to God's keeping, and thrust out into the sea."

> And so, being all very sober and melancholy, one faintly cheering another to show courage, it pleased God that the next day, about nine of the clock, we descried the Island of Trinedado, and steering for the nearest part of it, we kept the shore till we came to Curiapan [i.e., Icacos Point].

There they found the ships at anchor, "than which there was never to us a more joyful sight."

THIS IS really the end of the narrative element of Ralegh's *Discoverie*. From here he moves, with a typically elegant sentence, into a last few pages of summary.

> Now that it hath pleased God to send us safe to our ships, it is time to leave Guiana to the sun, whom they worship, and steer away towards the North; I will therefore in a few words finish the discovery thereof.

He does so with a detailed résumé of the peoples, rivers, mountains, species, and products of the region, "which myself have seen," together with a resonant affirmation of the richness of Manoa, which he had not seen.

But here, once again, we find Ralegh glossing over those parts of the expedition that do not quite fit the *type* of journey he is trying to express. There is one more episode to follow: the raid on Cumaná. It is omitted by Ralegh because it was such a disaster for him, and is amply documented in the Spanish sources for much the same reason. The best account is the report by Simon Bolívar, *contador* of Margarita, dated July 8, 1595. This, together with Spanish eyewitness accounts from Cumaná, can be pieced together into the following narrative.

On about June 21, lookouts at Margarita saw a fleet of "four vessels with some launches," bearing down on the island. This was Ralegh's fleet. They must have set off almost immediately after the *gallego*'s safe arrival at Trinidad.

> Being seen and suspected of being those of Trinidad [i.e., Ralegh's fleet], the Governor despatched to the port fifty mounted arquebusiers, who proceeded to defend the place. Seeing so many people there, the enemy passed on, and anchored at Punta de Mosquitos . . . Here they put ashore Captain Alvaro Jorge, Juan Lopez and two others whom they held prisoner along with Captain Antonio de Berrio.

Berrio was not released at this stage. The English wanted a ransom for him and Jorge: 1,400 ducats. Jorge brought ashore the ransom demand. The money was found, and delivered to Jorge, but at this stage Governor Salazar intervened: "He would on no account consent to the arrangement, as he considered the conditions had not been fulfilled." The English had "broken their word." It is not clear what this quibble is, but all this is a firsthand account by Bolívar—"I was present when the ransom was demanded"—and seems authentic.

The next day, they left Margarita, taking Berrio with them, and proceeded to Cumaná, a small port on the mainland. This is about sixty miles' sailing from Punta Mosquito where the ransom attempt was made. It is a charming town today; its old quarter dates almost back to this time. It was a trading point for gold, tobacco, and pearls, and was well known to English traffickers. Its governor, Francisco de Vides, had designs on Guiana, and was a rival of Berrio's in this respect. It was, it appears, rather better defended than Ralegh expected.

Here the Spanish authorities in Cumaná take up the story. On the afternoon of Thursday, June 22,

> there arrived at the port of this town an English pirate, with three great war-vessels, and one pinnace or galliot with oars, and four launches. It is believed that the commander of this fleet is an Englishman named Milo Guaterral. The following day he embarked a large number of Englishmen in the said pinnace and the four launches, as is stated by Governor Antonio de Berrio, who was prisoner on the flag-ship with them. There were 210 fighting men, musketeers and pikemen, who landed to burn, pillage and devastate the city.

The English had with them a local Indian, Juan Caraca. He "knew what he had to do, and led them by a crafty [*diablosa*] route." They landed and took possession of the waterfront, attacking "with the fury of demons." The Spanish defense force numbered only seventy, and had to retire. The English swiftly took over the high ground called Guayana Quintera, and had musketeers on the roofs of the houses. They had lost six men in the assault, and had some wounded.

By now, however, the Spanish were regrouping at a fort above the town. Reinforcements arrived from a garrison across the river. Governor Vides "went about putting heart into all the soldiers." Pinning the English down with "strong musket fire," he led a counterattack.

Among the first to die was the commander of the landing force, Captain Robert Calfield—"Carofal" or "Carofilde" in the Spanish reports. It is not quite clear who else was left dead in the streets of Cumaná. Vides names three, "a nephew of the General's named Juanes Gilbarte; a Captain named Glenfilo; and another, the captain of the little galliot, named Thechen." The first is obviously meant to be John Gilbert, but in this he is mistaken, since Gilbert was alive for many years after this. "Glenfilo" is presumably Ralegh's young cousin, John Grenville. The third, "Thechen," is mysterious. Lawrence Keymis was captain of the "galliot"—on the outward voyage, anyway—but was not killed at Cumaná. It has been suggested that the name is a Spanish garbling of Thynne, but as we have seen, Henry Thynne—the most plausible candidate for the Captain Thynne of Guiana—was undoubtedly living after this, and later married John Gilbert's widowed aunt. Another account names the important dead as Calfield and Gilbert, plus three other captains, a sergeant major, and "a Portuguese who was esteemed a brave soldier."

Leaving the dead and wounded, the English began to retreat back down to the shore. Now the casualties start to mount. Governor Vides tells it with grim satisfaction.

> [The English] became so exhausted that they were compelled to abandon the height, and began to flee, whereof I was witness. As they were retiring, I rallied all our men there at the fort, and all who could followed up the victory to the sea-shore. . . . [Our men] continued to fire their muskets, and the Indians their arrows, and down near the harbour the enemy was completely broken. They ran into the sea trying to regain their boats, while our men and the Indians shot them down at pleasure. As a result they abandoned all their weapons, including muskets, and the rest of their belongings. We took much spoil from them.

The spoil is specified in another report: "great store of muskets and corselets, a quantity of money, as well as the war-chest."

According to Vides, the English left forty-eight men dead at Cumaná on June 23. Many more were seriously wounded, some of them with poisoned arrows. Five days after the attack, compiling his report, he says that twenty-seven English have since died of their injuries aboard the ships. (He has this information from Berrio.) "We therefore know," he concludes, "that the number of English killed amounts to seventy-five." Another report says seventy-two.

Berrio was released, probably on June 28. He had been in captivity, aboard the flagship, for about eleven weeks. No ransom was demanded, Vides says, because the English assumed some of their men were alive, in Spanish hands, and wished to exchange them. In fact, there was only one, "a drummer who had his leg broken by a bullet." At Berrio's request he was released, and rowed back out to the ships. This was a final twist of the knife: Berrio's rich ransom lost in exchange for a single English drummer boy.

Of Ralegh's feelings we can guess. If the Spanish arithmetic is right, he had lost more than a quarter of his men. Among the dead were Calfield and Grenville, and many others who had shared with him the rigors of the Orinoco. These are personal losses. Another death that touched him was that of his faithful scout Jacob Whiddon, "a man most honest and valiant, whom to my great sorrow I left buried in the sands of that island [i.e., Trinidad]." It is not said, but it is likely that Whiddon died of injuries received at Cumaná.

Nothing is said. This episode is completely blotted out of Ralegh's account. As to his feelings, we must content ourselves with Governor Vides's remarks, which have the witness of Berrio behind them.

> The English losses, I am told, have caused great sorrow to the General of the fleet, and such are the lamentations of the sick because of their wounds, that he betakes himself by day to the Flemish merchantmen, returning to his own ship at night.

It is a last image of Ralegh in South America. It indicates his distress, perhaps even a kind of breakdown. The commander of the fleet is absent from his ships: retired from view. He is across the bay where he cannot hear the screams of the wounded. He converses all day with some Dutch traders, a people he has never much liked. He comes back in at night, slipping across the dark water like some secretive *cacique.*

This comes from Berrio. A measure of bitter satisfaction is in it, but it is also something shared. Berrio has been there. He sees that sudden access of exhaustion, that slumping, and he knows it. These are the despairs of the *entrada,* the defeats that attend the search for El Dorado. He knows the essence, if not the actual words, of that old Venezuelan boat song recorded by Schomburgk in the 1830s—

> *Quien se va al Orinoco*
> *O se muere o vuelve loco*

—which may be loosely translated: "Those who go up the Orinoco wind up dead or come back loco."

ON JUNE 30, 1595, the English fleet left Cumaná. Governor Vides added a postscript to his report: "Today the Englishman has sailed away in the direction of Macanao. It is said he goes to England, and he does not go away as pleased as he could wish."

For a while they roamed around the Caribbean. We have no knowledge of this period. All we know is that two weeks later they were off Cuba. (There are confused Spanish reports of a skirmish at Margarita. A careful reading of these shows that this was an earlier movement of Ralegh's fleet, around the end of May, while Ralegh and his "troupe" were still in the delta.)

The last event on the voyage that can be pinpointed with certainty is his meeting, off Cuba, with the fleet of Preston and Somers, for which he had waited at the beginning of the voyage. The meeting was on July 13, and is described by Robert Davie, one of Preston's crew.

> The 13 day in the morning we were under this cape [Cape San Antonio, Cuba] and the same day we met with the honourable knight Sir Walter Ralegh, returning from his painful and happy discovery of Guiana, and his surprise of the Isle of Trinidad. So with glad hearts we kept him and his fleet of three ships company till the 20th day at night, what time we lost them.

This is exact as to date but ambiguous as to Ralegh's fleet. It sounds as if there are only three ships now (though "him and his fleet of three" might make four). Perhaps the old *gallego* has been finally scuppered.

Ralegh had spoken of visiting Virginia, but says that "contrary winds" prevented him from going there. They were last seen by Preston's ships on July 20. Shortly after this, probably, they hoisted sail and set off home.

[23]

Home

*   *   *

ON AUGUST 12, from Compton Castle in Devon, Sir John Gilbert—Ralegh's half brother, John Gilbert's uncle—writes to Sir Robert Cecil, and says in passing that he "trusts" Ralegh "will now shortly return." There may be advance news that he is on his way back, or it may just be that Sir John was assuming a voyage of about six months, and this period was now up.

The exact date of Ralegh's return is not recorded, but I think it can be estimated quite precisely. The key document is undated. This is the letter written by Lady Ralegh to Cecil, from Sherborne, containing the first news of Ralegh's landing. It is endorsed "September 1595" by one of Cecil's secretaries. The endorsement refers to the receipt of the letter rather than the sending of it. It was sent, therefore, some time in September or at the very end of August.

Bess Ralegh's letter, in her inimitable spelling, reads as follows:

Sur hit tes trew i thonke the leving God Sur Walter is safly londed at Plumworthe with as gret honnor as ever man can, but littel riches. I have not yet hard from him selfe. Kepe thies I besech you to your selfe yet; only to me lord ammerall. In haste this Sunday.

Your pour frind E. Raleg

Mani of his mene slane; him selfe will now. Pardon my rewed wryteng with the goodnes of the newes.

This is marvelous. It is like those dramatic moments of TV news, when a story is suddenly breaking and has not yet the gloss of

263

interpretation or even narrative. This is the first breathless bulletin as it arrives at Sherborne. It is news of Ralegh but not news from Ralegh—she has not yet "heard from himself." We learn it as she did. Her husband is alive; his ship is at Plymouth; the voyage has been a success ("great honour") yet also a failure ("little riches"); men have been killed.

Everything about her letter suggests immediacy: the fact that Ralegh himself has not got word to her; the fact that she assumes her news is so current that Cecil himself will not yet know it. Only he and the Lord Admiral—Ralegh's two sponsors—should know about it, she says. She wrote the letter on a Sunday. It is pretty certain she received the news of his return that day.

From Plymouth to Sherborne is a journey of some seventy miles, though the country was rough. I have found another dispatch that passed from Plymouth to Sherborne in September 1595; by good fortune it has a precise account of its progress written on the back of it. This letter was delivered to the postmaster in Plymouth at nine-thirty in the morning. It was at Ashburton by one o'clock, at Exeter by four-thirty, at Honiton by six-forty, at Crewkerne some time shortly after ten, and was "received at Sherborne after 12 of the clock in the night." In this case the message, carried by a relay of post-horses, took about fifteen hours to travel from Plymouth to Sherborne. I doubt this time could be much bettered. Thus Bess Ralegh's letter, written "this Sunday," suggests that Ralegh had landed on the Saturday (or, at the latest, in the early hours of Sunday morning).

The earliest dated allusion to Ralegh's return, as far as I can find, is in a letter written by Sir Thomas Heneage on September 9. This was also addressed to Sir Robert Cecil. Heneage thanks him for a recent letter, and is "not a little beholden" for certain "advertisements" it contained. Among these, apparently, was news of Ralegh's return, for Heneage writes that he is "much pleased that Sir Walter Ralegh is come home well and rich," and is glad to learn that Cecil will "have no hurt by it"—in other words, will not be out of pocket.

Some time shortly before September 9, then, Cecil has written to

Heneage that Ralegh is back. Heneage is a high-ranking Elizabethan politician and an old ally of the Cecils. If this is news to him, it is pretty fresh news, though it has already undergone a bit of trimming, since Cecil tells him that Ralegh has come back "rich." In an earlier letter, to which Heneage replied on September 2, there was no mention of Ralegh.

On the evidence of these two letters to Cecil, from Heneage and Lady Ralegh, I would say that the date of Ralegh's safe landing at Plymouth was Saturday, September 5. Lady Ralegh received the news on Sunday the sixth, and immediately—"this Sunday"—sent word to Cecil. Her letter would have reached Cecil the following day, Monday the seventh. He was probably at his house at Staines; according to that other dispatch, which also passed on from Sherborne to Staines, this was a seventeen-hour journey. He may have had news of Ralegh's return from his own sources, but they cannot have got it to him much sooner than Lady Ralegh did. On that day or the following, the eighth, Cecil relays the news up to Heneage, at Copthall in Hertfordshire. On Wednesday, the ninth, Heneage writes back, thanking him for this "advertisement."

If this dating is correct, then Ralegh and his men arrived at Plymouth exactly seven months after their departure. Preston's fleet returned a few days after them, on September 10.

ONE FUSSES around a few fragments of evidence to provide a date, which is just about the least significant aspect of the scene as it happened.

Of the tearful reunion at Plymouth; of how he looked and felt after this long strange trip; of the changes he saw in his little boy, Wat, now nearly two; of the tinged September light after the glare of the tropics; of the personal griefs felt by those whose husbands and sons had not returned; of the stale cabin air and bilge stench that clung to those who had—of these no record remains.

For a brief period all the familiar things seem strange; then there is a kind of awakening, as if the journey had all been a dream.

Something of it disappears at that moment, floats away from your grasp, and despite all the souvenirs, and the meticulously kept diaries, can never quite be recovered.

Let us call this the *salida*, the exit: as dangerous in its way as the *entrada*, and never as well prepared.

So you're back.

I think so.

And already the courtly wits and wags were putting it around that he hadn't really been to Guiana at all. He had bought some gold ore for show, on the Barbary coast of Africa, and had spent the rest of the time skulking in an obscure Cornish cove.

"I have undergone many constructions," he complains. "I was neither hidden in Cornwall or elsewhere, as was supposed. They have grossly belied me."

OTHER EARLY rumors about the voyage and its achievements are found in some letters written by Rowland Whyte, servant and chief gossip to Sir Robert Sidney:

> Sir Walter Rawley is returned with an assured loss of his bravest men, as Gifford, Whiddon, Cawfill, Greenson, Vincent, Thynne and others. As for his wealth, in my Lord Treasurer's opinion, 'tis made little; in Sir Robert Cecil's very great. [September 25]

> Sir Walter Rawley's friends do tell Her Majesty what great service he hath done unto her by his late voyage, in discovering the way to bring home the wealth of India, and in making known to that nation her virtues, her justice. He hath brought hither a supposed prince, and left hostages in his place. The Queen gives good ear unto them. I am promised, for you, his own discourse to the Queen of his journey. [September 27]

Whyte is wrong about Gifford being dead, and I think also wrong about Thynne; otherwise (assuming that by "Greenson" he means John Grenville) his death list conforms with the Spanish account. He notes that Cecil's hyping of the voyage is not endorsed by the ever-wary Lord Burghley, Cecil's father. The Queen is guardedly interested, but only through the offices of friends at court: Ralegh has not himself been summoned. And we hear of Ralegh's "discourse of his journey," which Whyte is keen to get hold of: an early notice, it would seem, of the *Discoverie,* already written three weeks after his return, or at any rate being talked of.

Our first actual glimpse of Ralegh is in October. He is up in London, at his town residence on the Strand, Durham House. Here, on October 9, he dines with Dr. Dee. This is mentioned in Dee's diary. He does not say what passed between them, but the mere fact of the meeting is interesting. It introduces into the aftermath of Ralegh's journey that philosophical, idealized notion of America and American colonization that I have touched on earlier, and of which Dee (though now largely disgraced and neglected) was the leading advocate.

Shortly after this, in another gossipy letter from Rowland Whyte to his master, written in London, there is a further snippet: "Sir Walter Rawley is here, and goes daily to hear sermons, because he hath seen the wonders of the Lord in the deep: 'tis much commended and spoken of." The date of this letter is October 15.

I don't know if Ralegh was literally attending sermons daily. It is possible: The will and providence of God feature strongly in the *Discoverie.* The main impression Whyte's comment gives is of a man profoundly altered by his experience. Ralegh's behavior is implicitly contrasted with his former reputation for atheism—a false reputation, an overreaction to the skeptical, "scientific" tone of Ralegh's circle, but this is surely Whyte's point, and the reason why it was "much spoken of." The biblical allusion is to Psalm 107: "They that go down to the sea in ships, that do business in great waters, these shall see the works of the Lord and His wonders in the deep." It comes out rather pat in Whyte's letter, and one suspects that it might be a portable sort of quip applied to people who come back from long voyages behaving strangely. I am reminded of John Aubrey's comment about the navigator Roger North, who accompanied Ralegh on the last voyage of 1617: "Captain North . . . was a learned and sober gentleman, and good mathematician, but if you happened to speak of Guiana he would be strangely passionate, and say 'twas the blessedest country under the sun, etc."

These are our first impressions of Ralegh back from South America—a conversation with Dr. Dee, an uncharacteristic display of religiosity, a mind touched with some lingering fever.

On November 10, back in Sherborne, he writes to Cecil. His mood is gloomy: "From this desolate place I have little matter, from myself less hope, and therefore I think the shorter the discourse the better welcome." He is "thankless busied in things" that do not interest him. He is beset by financial worries but these at least obliterate other thoughts: "We that have much ado to get bread to eat have the less to care for."

He, and his Guiana Voyage, are in this kind of limbo.

> What becomes of Guiana I much desire to hear, whether it pass for a history or a fable. I hear Mr Dudley and others are sending thither. If it be so, then farewell all good from thence, for although myself like a cockscomb did rather prefer the future in respect of others, and rather sought to win the kings to Her Majesty's service than to sack them, I know what others will do when those kings shall come simply into their hands. If it may please you to acquaint my Lord Admiral therewith, let it then succeed as it will.

He has also learned, from a ship recently arrived at Lyme, that the Spanish are preparing something big—"a fleet either gone or going, of sixty sail." It is said they are bound for Ireland, but he fears that "there is somewhat more," that they too are bound for Guiana.

There is a sense of helplessness, both for himself and for his precious Guiana. He knows "what others will do" to those simple Indian "kings" or chiefs. "Farewell all good from thence"—ostensibly a loss of opportunity, a strategic waste, but carrying also that idea of violation, an extinction of innocence and goodness, a sacking rather than his own pacific winning.

And over it all hangs this question, as yet unresolved. Is it—Guiana, El Dorado, the whole adventure—"a history or a fable"?

He means in the minds of others, but one senses that he needs to hear the answer because he is not quite sure in his own mind.

THREE DAYS later Ralegh received a letter from Cecil. In it—as we gather from Ralegh's reply—was a copy or digest of certain Spanish papers that had been seized by an English privateer, Captain George Popham, who had recently arrived home. Popham had been involved with Sir Robert Dudley's expedition, which did not endear him to Ralegh, but the reports he brought in were full of exciting tidbits about El Dorado, and were immediately considered by Ralegh as prime propaganda for his cause. An abstract of them was appended to the first edition of the *Discoverie.*

One of these reports of the "late discovery called Nuevo Dorado" described the arrival in Cartagena in 1593 of "a frigate from the said Dorado, bringing in it the portraiture of a giant all of gold, of weight 47 quintals, which the Indians there held for their idol." Ralegh immediately seizes on this, and writing back to Cecil, "an hour after the receipt of your letter"—no time to waste—he says:

> You may perceive by this relation that it is no dream which I have reported of Guiana, and if one image have been brought from thence weighing 47 quintals, which cannot be so little worth as 100 thousand pounds, I know that in Manoa there are store of those.

He is back on the offensive. It is "no dream" after all. As so often in the El Dorado story, as in the world of the prospectors and *mineros* today, the actual find is only a sign of what might be found. A statuette worth a hundred grand? Go to Manoa and you'll find a whole "store" of them stacked up waiting. He *knows* they are there.

He returns once again to the urgency of the matter: "I know it will be presently followed both by the Spanish and French, and if it be foreslowed by us I conclude that we are cursed of God." The Queen must be moved, by Cecil, to support his "enterprise," so that "those kings of the borders which are by my labour, peril and charge won to Her Majesty's love and obedience, be not by other pilferers lost again."

It is now nearly six weeks since his return. He speaks of the follow-up voyage he is planning: "I am sending away a bark to the country [i.e., Guiana] to comfort and assure the people, that they despair not." This is Lawrence Keymis's expedition, the Second Guiana Voyage, mentioned here for the first time. It is already in preparation. It would set out from Plymouth in mid-January 1596.

And then there is the map. This—with the help of Thomas Harriot, and perhaps of Dr. Dee—is also ready.

> I know the plot is by this time finished, which if you please to, command from Harriot that Her Majesty may see it. If it be thought of less importance than it deserveth, Her Majesty will shortly bewail her negligence therein, and the enemy, by the addition of so much wealth, wear us out of all. Sir, I pray esteem it as the affair requireth.

This is just three days after his previous, "desolate" missive. The mood has swung. Suddenly he sounds like Sir Walter Ralegh again.

He signs off: "As God will, so shall it be, who governs the hearts of kings. I rest your assured to be commanded, poor or rich."

[24]

Ordinary Prizes

*　　*　　*

WE HAVE these glimpses of Ralegh's moody demeanor in the autumn of 1595, as he gingerly picks up the pieces of his previous life, and begins to gear up his campaign for the continuance of the "enterprise." But what, other than his beliefs and opinions of the place, had he actually brought back from Guiana?

Not a lot, it appears. It is a constant theme of the *Discoverie* that his interest lay in a future English settlement there, and not just a short-term "pillage of ordinary prizes."

He presents himself as having actually resisted the chance of personal enrichment. "I am returned a beggar, and withered," he says. "I might have bettered my poor estate . . . if I had not only respected Her Majesty's future honour and riches." This is one of many excuses why he had returned with so little. It has a ring of self-justification, of papering over a failure, and must certainly have seemed so to those who had invested in the voyage. To his chief sponsors, Cecil and Lord Howard—he says with an airy tone that may just have irritated them—he has "returned only promises."

He did bring back some gold, but not in the quantity that the magic name El Dorado had led people to expect. There were also rumors that the gold was poor quality. He contests this in the *Discoverie*. It is the fault of his men, he says, who grabbed any stone that glittered. Much of this was "marcasite," or white pyrites—that glittery sulphide of iron generally known as fool's gold—and these worthless specimens have cast a shadow over the genuine material they found.

They brought back both gold dust and some samples of gold ore.

The gold dust was probably from the mine that Topiawari showed them. According to Francis Sparry, this was one league inland from Port Morequito. The English "carried away three or four tons of earth from a mountain," he says, "and put it on board to carry to England as a specimen."

The gold ore was "environed" in a "hard stone which we call the white spar." This is the auriferous quartz, or *tojo,* that is still mined around El Callao and Payapal. Ralegh describes collecting some:

> Near unto one of the rivers I found of the said white spar or flint a very great ledge or bank, which I endeavoured to break by all the means I could, because there appeared on the outside some small grains of gold . . . I found a clift in the same, from whence with daggers and the head of an axe, we got out some small quantity thereof.

(Lack of mining equipment is another excuse he advances for their slim pickings.) On his return he had this auriferous "spar" assayed, first by a gold refiner named Westwood, living on Wood Street, and later by Messrs. Palmer and Dimoke, respectively the controller and assay-master of the Royal Mint. The best of this ore held nearly 27 pounds in the ton, in other words gold was present in a proportion of just over 1 percent. This compares very favorably with the fractions considered viable nowadays.

He also brought back gold "plates" and "images." Plates need not be round so much as flat (French *plat*), and are simply ingots or bars (Sparry says Ralegh was given three or four "ingots" by Topiawari). Images may either be statues or decorated ornaments. He sends some samples to Cecil and Howard, "such as I could by chance recover, more to show the manner of them than for the value." One such "image" was analyzed, and found to be an alloy of two parts copper to one part gold.

Among his meager belongings in the Tower, at his death in 1618, was an "idol of Guiana," but whether this was a memento of the First Voyage or not is unknown.

Like many Elizabethans, Ralegh was a connoisseur of gemstones.

They had found a kind of crystal near the Caroní, "but whether it be crystal of the mountain, Bristol diamond or sapphire, I do not yet know." (It was almost certainly the first, i.e., rock crystal.) They also brought back "spleen stones" (perhaps green jasper), pearls, and—most seductive of all—diamonds. "I assure myself," he wrote to Cecil, "that there are not more diamonds in the East Indies than are to be found in Guiana." He has two large diamonds, and plans to "have them cut by Pepler, who is skillful, and dwells here [Sherborne] with A. Gilbert." (This is his youngest half-brother, Adrian Gilbert, alchemist and American enthusiast, a shadowy but important figure in Ralegh's circle.) Another stone—also cut by the skillful Pepler and later sent to Sir Robert Cecil—was an amethyst with "a strange blush of carnation."

These he has, but as always, "these stones bear witness of better," which he does not yet have.

MINERAL WEALTH was only part of Guiana's richness in natural "commodities," or as we would say, resources. There are "great quantities of brazil wood" (a generic term for various tropical hardwoods). There is "abundance of cotton, of silk, of balsamum, of all sorts of gums, of Indian pepper." There are "berries that dye a most perfect crimson and carnation" (i.e., *arnatto*). He may well have brought back samples of these, and seeds, as the Virginia expedition certainly did.

This abundance of "commodities" is part of his propaganda for Guiana, a computation of future profits, but it is also a part of Ralegh's more philosophical sense of the New World. In tropical America he finds a place of almost unimaginable variety and novelty. Time and again he speaks of the impossibility of describing and classifying it all.

On the banks of these rivers were divers sorts of fruits good to eat, flowers and trees of that variety as were sufficient to make ten volumes of herbals. . . .

> To make mention of the several beasts, birds, fishes, fruits, flowers, gums, sweet woods, and of their several religions and customs, would for the first require as many volumes as those of Gesnerus [i.e., Konrad von Gesner, author of the encyclopedic *Historia Animalium*], and for the rest another bundle of *Decades* [i.e., the *De Novo Orbe* of Peter Martyr]. . . .

> Guiana [has] divers sorts of beasts, either for chase or food. . . . To speak of the several sorts of every kind I fear would be troublesome to the reader, and therefore I will omit them.

This sense of a baffling profuseness, an *embarras de richesse,* is part of the mystery of America. The continent is unembraceable and therefore unknowable. You cannot get your head around it: the effort becomes "troublesome." You would have to write ten volumes of herbals, or emulate the dreadful prolixity of Professor Gesner (who published seventy-two books and had another eighteen in progress when he died). It is almost too much, too various, to cope with: the Linnaean dementia.

And this is just what he saw: "What else the countries may afford within the land we know not, neither had we time to abide the trial and search." Just as each speck of gold dust betokens the vast wealth of the interior, so each new variety suggests a boundless hinterland of new species. This is as true of the region's people as of its creatures. The perceived novelty of the Indians—their physical and cultural difference—shades off into imagined forms, fantastical "nations": cannibals and Amazons and that other New World staple, the "people whose heads appear not above their shoulders." Ralegh calls them the Ewaipanoma and places them on tributaries west of the Caroní (just beyond the limit of his personal knowledge, of course: "For my own part I saw them not"). They have "their eyes in their shoulders and their mouths in the middle of their breasts." He hears of them from the Orenoqueponi, to whom they are merely commonplace: "It was no wonder among them." These grotesques caught the imagination of the engraver Hulsius, and indeed of Shakespeare, who doubtless had Guiana in mind when he writes in *Othello* of

25. *"Men whose heads do grow beneath their shoulders"*

> . . . the cannibals that each other eat,
> The Anthropophagi, and men whose heads
> Do grow beneath their shoulders.

Ralegh is still on the margins of true knowledge of the continent. Its commodities are unplumbed and unknown; they are part of the innocence of Guiana, the hiddenness of the "land within."

ON THE evidence available it appears that the messenger had it just about right when he arrived at Sherborne with the news that Ralegh was back with "little riches." What we hear of are scrapings of wealth—gold, gems, statuettes—but little substance.

But as so often, my curiosity is piqued by something he does not mention, which one feels he ought to have. He says almost nothing, on the entire trip, about the one commodity everyone associated with him, and indeed with America—tobacco.

That it was there is in no doubt. Robert Dudley, exploring the mainland coast just a few weeks before Ralegh's arrival, notes "good store of cane tobacco" growing in the Paria Peninsula. Ralegh himself describes the fondness of the Warao for tobacco, "in the immoderate taking whereof they do exceed all nations." Had he returned to the Caroní a year later, as he intended, he would have found the Spanish garrison of San Thomé established there, and the area around it full of new tobacco plantations.

26. Elizabethan smoker. This woodcut from Anthony Chute's Tobacco *(1596) is perhaps intended to be Ralegh.*

So there was tobacco there, and of high quality. The Virginia tobacco that Harriot praised was not such good quality; it had a "biting taste." Most of the tobacco smoked (or as they still put it, "drunk") by the English in the 1590s was from South America. "Tobacco" was considered a Spanish word, and the trade a Spanish monopoly. It is said that the Spaniards "say tauntingly to us, when they see all our goods landed, *Que todo eso se pagará con humo:* that all will be paid in smoke."

It was highly prized merchandise, monopolized by the enemy, and it seems plausible that Ralegh brought some back. The idea that Ralegh *introduced* tobacco to England is wrong—it is first mentioned in 1565, and Harrison records it as growing in England in 1577—but he undoubtedly did much to popularize its use among the Elizabethan smart set.

Writing at the end of the century, Henry Buttes says of tobacco: "Our English Ulysses, renowned Sir Walter Ralegh, . . . hath both far fetcht it, and dear bought it." Taken literally, this might refer to the Guiana Voyage, the only occasion that Ralegh was a "Ulysses"—a voyager himself, rather than the stay-at-home sponsor—and the only occasion he could have "fetcht it" himself. This is not conclusive; it may only refer to the general idea of Ralegh's expeditions bringing back tobacco.

I also note Lawrence Keymis's involvement in tobacco transactions. In 1610, a London grocer named Axtell owed £53 to Keymis. This was "for tobacco bought by your said subject Henry Axtell of Sir Walter Ralegh." This is a considerable sum, about £20,000 in modern terms. It seems that Keymis is not so much a moneylender here, as Ralegh's agent for the sale of tobacco.

There is also the reported boast of Ralegh's, in 1617, as he set out for the Orinoco a second time, "that he knew a town in those parts upon which he could make a saving voyage in tobacco, though there were no other spoil." It may well be the case that he did so on the First Guiana Voyage, which was also rather short on "spoil."

These are at least pointers toward the possibility that Ralegh recouped a portion of his losses by the sale of high-quality cane tobacco from Guiana and Trinidad.

[25]

Balsam of Guiana

*   *   *

SOME GOLD, some gems, some seeds, and perhaps some to-bacco—the chapter on Ralegh's Guiana cargo is a short one. But there is one other item he may have brought back: a medicine. The evidence is hard to assess, but leads me down an interesting and neglected byway to consider that famous elixir which is generally called his "Great Cordial," but which in its earliest appearance on the record is called "Balsam of Guiana."

Ralegh had a considerable reputation as a "chymist." (At this time, "chymist" suggested someone involved in the more practical, experimental end of the business, and particularly in the preparation of medicines, as distinct from the more esoteric concerns of the "al-chymist," but the two often merge.) The earliest biographers ranked his chemical skills alongside all the others. "Authors are perplexed under that topic to place him," wrote John Shirley in 1679, "whether of statesman, seaman, soldier, chymist or chronologer [i.e., historian], for in all these he did excel." John Aubrey confirms:

> Sir Walter Ralegh was a great chymist, and amongst some MSS re-ceipts [i.e., recipes] I have seen some secrets from him. He studied most in his sea voyages, where he carried always a trunk of books along with him, and had nothing to divert him. He made an excellent Cordial, good in fevers, etc. Mr Robert Boyle has the recipe.

This is an interesting conjunction—the sea voyage, the study of chemical books, and the famous cordial that is also known as Guiana Balsam.

Ralegh's cordial is associated with his years in the Tower, but his interest in the subject goes back much earlier. In the early 1580s, the distiller John Hester dedicated a book of medical recipes, *114 Experiments and Cures,* to him. This was published before 1585, since Hester addresses him as "Walter Ralegh, Esquire." The book is claimed to be the work of Paracelsus, the occultist German healer whose teachings were fashionable in Elizabethan England. Hester was an enthusiastic Paracelsian, a promoter of the new "chymicall physick." This was still highly controversial, and Paracelsians were denounced and fined by the Royal College of Physicians. Hester's dedication is in part for protection: He ventures into print "under the comfortable shield of your favour." It seems to have been accepted—it appears unchanged in the 1596 edition—and is evidence of Ralegh's interest in medicinal "chymistry" in the early 1580s.

His half brother Adrian Gilbert may well be an influence here. A noted chemist himself, he was later employed as the Countess of Pembroke's "laborator" at Wilton House. He was closely associated with Ralegh, as a cofounder of the Institute for Navigation in 1584, and was later a member of Ralegh's circle at Sherborne, where he kept that skillful diamond-cutter Pepler.

Another member of Ralegh's circle—and one closely associated with the Guiana Voyage—is known to have been a chemist. This is his faithful captain Keymis, whose skills are praised by Dr. Gabriel Harvey. In the British Museum is an old fly-sheet advertising the wares of the distiller Hester: a marvelous list of arcane Paracelsian potions. In 1588 this was in Harvey's hands. He covered it with his usual obsessive marginalia, and then added at the bottom: "Now M. [i.e., Master] Keymis, the great Alchymist of London." Though he uses the word "alchymist," the context suggests Harvey is thinking in terms of Paracelsian chemistry. In this year Keymis was still nominally a fellow at Balliol College, Oxford, but the following year he resigned his fellowship at Balliol, and joined his friend Thomas Harriot in Ralegh's service at Durham House. His chemical skills must be one of his credentials. Thomas Harriot was also fascinated by alchemy. His diaries record some lengthy experiments, but there is no evidence of a particular medical aspect to them.

Ralegh's library (judging from his own manuscript catalog of about 1606) contained various books on the subject. Among those listed are Bairo's *Secreti Medicinali* (1585); Wecker's *De Secretis* (the 1586 edition: Ralegh's copy of this, with marginalia, is still extant); another work by Wecker on antidotes; and a book he describes as "Besson distillations," which is probably Besson's *Art et Moyen Parfait de Tirer Huyles et Eaux* (1573). He also owned a copy of *De Ortu Metallorum* (1576), by the French Paracelsian Josephe du Chesne, known as Quercetanus. This book was translated by John Hester (*The Original and Causes of Metals*, 1591). The book listed by Ralegh as *Philosophia Chimica* may be another Paracelsian work, Gerhard Dorn's *Clavis Philosophiae Chymistiae,* part of which was also translated by Hester (*The Key of Philosophie,* 1596). In Walter Oakeshott's classification of Ralegh's library there are seventeen works on medicine and chemistry.

In the Tower, Ralegh devoted a considerable part of his enforced leisure time to chemical and medicinal work. In August 1605 his keeper, Sir William Waad, writes: "In the garden he hath converted a little hen-house to a still-house, where he doth spend his time all the day in his distillations." His chemical notebook, now in the British Museum, probably dates from these years. A compact, vellum-bound book, filled with his small neat handwriting, it describes various processes and experiments—"to fix antimony," "calcining Saturn [i.e., lead]," "to give a golden tincture to copper," etc. He employed an assistant, a young man named Sampson, who was still alive in 1661, "very old," when the diarist John Ward met him. He told Ward he had been "operator" to Ralegh for twelve years, "while he was in the Tower."

Ralegh's friend Henry Percy, ninth Earl of Northumberland— popularly known as "the Wizard Earl"—joined him in the Tower in 1605, suspected of complicity in the Gunpowder Plot. He also had a "still-house" built there. The costs of equipping it are recorded in his "kitchen accounts": 18s. 6d. for furnace bricks, 15s. 10d. for two lead cisterns, 8s. 6d. for two stills, etc. The Earl's distiller, Roger Cook, was set to work. He requires "glasses for strong waters" (i.e., *aqua fortis,* usually nitric acid). He purchases musk and ambergris, and distills them with "spirit of wine." This is "to make a medicine

27. *The distiller (from a chemical handbook of 1599)*

for my Lord's teeth." He also brews up exotic liqueurs for the Earl's table. One batch required eighteen gallons of the sweet wine called "sack," four pounds of "sugar candy," and some spirit of roses. The end product of this was a "distillation called *Spiritus dulcis.*"

These happen to remain on record. It is likely that the occultist Earl's pursuits ranged wider and deeper than the preparation of luxury mouthwashes and liqueurs called "Sweet Spirit." The mood of

Ralegh and Northumberland in the Tower was one of a "little Academe," attended by their scholarly followers. There were Harriot and Keymis, and Walter Warner, whose studies of the circulation of blood predated the more famous William Harvey's. There was Ralegh's physician, Dr. Peter Turner, whose man brought them a "sceleton" one day, and a surgeon called "Doctor John." Sir Francis Bacon, jotting a memorandum about his planned *Instauratio Magna*—a kind of scientific think tank—proposes "the setting on work my Lord of Northumberland and Ralegh, and therefore Harriot, themselves being already inclined to experiments."

IT IS in this year 1605, when he is immured in his converted henhouse, spending "all the day in his distillations," that we first hear of his balsam or cordial. The wife of the French ambassador, Mme. de Beaumont, visited the Tower one summer day, to see the lions in the Royal Zoo, and perhaps also to see that other grizzled occupant, Ralegh. At any rate, she spotted Ralegh in the Tower garden, and sent a message to him, asking for "some of his Balsam of Guiana." Ralegh sent her some by the messenger, a certain Captain Whitelock.

The new Queen—King James's Danish wife, Anne—was also a devotee of Ralegh's tincture. It is said to have cured her of a dangerous fever. In 1612 she requested some for the dying Prince Henry. The official physicians fussed and prevaricated, and it was not administered for several days. It failed to save him, though it gave him for a while the power of speech. The gossip John Chamberlain says that Ralegh's cordial was also administered to the Duchess of Rutland. In this case too it failed; indeed Chamberlain suggests it actually poisoned her!

Whatever its efficacy, Ralegh's balsam enjoyed a long and illustrious afterlife. In 1652 his son Carew sent to Lord Conway "a parcel of papers, old, rotten and dirty, such as a person less intelligent would hardly understand: all receipts, most in my father's hand." Perhaps these papers contained Ralegh's own instructions for compounding the cordial, or they may have passed down by other routes. There is also an abbreviated list of ingredients in Ralegh's notebook, headed "Our Great Cordial"; the page immediately following (folio 64) is mysteriously missing from the book. At any rate, Sir Kenelm Digby—whose family now owned Ralegh's house at Sherborne—knew the ingredients, and added certain exotic items of his own, like vipers' hearts. Robert Boyle, the author of *The Sceptical Chymist* (1661), also had the recipe, according to Aubrey. So too did Sir Robert Killigrew. A manuscript dated March 29, 1659, gives a list of his ingredients, and has some interesting remarks on the dosage.

> The quantity of a great pease is a dose for sucking children. The quantity of a kernel of a filbert [i.e., hazelnut] is the ordinary dose for men and women, but if in a fit of extremity you may give double or treble as much . . . You may take it on a knife's point, or else dissolve it in a spoonful of liquor hot or cold.

It is said to be "good for women after delivery, & old people who have fainting fits by the decay of nature." It will also "drive all venom from the heart if taken in time after poison."

The fullest account of the cordial's ingredients is given by Nicolas Le Fèvre, who held the grand title of Royal Professor in Chymistry and Apothecary in Ordinary to His Majesty's Household. He brewed up a sample of it in October 1662. The event is recorded by the diarist John Evelyn, who "accompanied King Charles II to Monsieur Febure, his chymist, to see his accurate preparation of Sir Walter Ralegh's Cordial." Two years later, by order of the King, Le Fèvre published his *Discourse upon Sir Walter Rawleigh's Great Cordial*. The imprimatur is dated April 23, 1664. (This is a translation by one Peter Belon, "student in chymistry"; the original French text was published the following year.) Le Fèvre seems to have had access to Ralegh's own papers, or at least to a copy of Ralegh's original recipe, since he mentions ingredients added by Kenelm Digby and Sir Alexander Fraiser, "though the first prescription does not mention them."

The ingredients are an exotic broth that includes decoctions of hart's horn, bezoar stone, musk, pearl, ambergris, "oriental bole" [ie., bole of Armenia, a pale reddish earth] and "*unicornu minerale,* otherwise called white lodestone"; together with a gardenful of herbs, roots and fruits, including angelica, birthwort, white dittany, betony, marjoram, borage, bugloss, mace, rosemary, saffron, marigold, elder, juniper berries, cloves, cardamom, and nutmeg.

All these are steeped in a potent, syrupy suspension of sugar and "spirit of wine." This spirit of wine is, of course, the colorless liquor nowadays variously called *eau de vie*, aquavit, etc.

A CYNIC might suggest it was the shot of acquavit that got Prince Henry talking on his deathbed, rather than any curative virtues entailed in the other ingredients. However, it is not the efficacy of Ralegh's cordial that interests me, but the possibility that it contained some special ingredient brought back from Guiana.

There are certainly New World products among the ingredients— sassafras bark and aloes, for instance—but these were known about before Ralegh's *entrada,* and have no particular association with Guiana. Sassafras is mentioned in Monardus's *Joyful News of the New World* (1579) and in Harriot's *Brief and True Report of Virginia.*

> Sassafras, called by the inhabitants *winauk,* [is] a kind of wood of pleasant and sweet smell, and of most rare virtues in physic for the cure of many diseases. It is found by experience to be far better, and of more uses, than the wood which is called *guaiacum.*

(The latter is guaiac wood, also called *lignum vitae,* which was popular as a treatment for syphilis.)

Perhaps the most intriguing ingredient is one of the roots, described as "the serpentary of Virginia." Le Fèvre, who gives a little gloss on each of the ingredients, appears at a loss here. "We cannot well specify the virtue of the serpentary of Virginia," he says solemnly, "because it has not as yet been written." We must depend on "those that have learned it *viva voce* from the inhabitants of the American islands, amongst whom it is in great request against poisons and fevers."

This certainly sounds like a secret ingredient: its "virtues" as yet unwritten. What is it? The serpentary is a native American plant,

Aristolochia serpentaria. The root contains a volatile oil used as an antidote to poison, specifically (as the name suggests) to snakebite. It is also called "viper's grass" and "Virginia snakeroot." It was still in use, as an all-purpose tonic, in Victorian England. The *London Pharmacopoia* of 1837 recommends an infusion of serpentary as "diaphoretic, diuretic, stimulant."

The association with Virginia does not seem to be specific. Harriot mentions various medicinal plants in his *Brief and True Report,* but says nothing of serpentary or snakeroot. Nor, it seems, do later Virginia colonists. The earliest reference in the *OED* is from Phillips's *Dictionary* of 1658, just a few years before Le Fèvre's slightly puzzled reference to it here. The plant is actually found elsewhere in America: "Virginia" is simply shorthand for its American provenance and native usage.

Is it possible, I wonder, that this "serpentary" was originally an ingredient brought back from Guiana—either *Aristolochia serpentaria* itself, or some other indigenous antidote to "poisons and fevers"?

Turning to the *Discoverie,* we find several instances of Ralegh's interest in native medicine, and particularly in the antidotes they used against poison. This was of practical interest, given the dire effect of the Indians' poisoned arrows. He describes the "insufferable torment" caused by these: The victim

> abideth a most ugly and lamentable death, sometimes dying stark mad, sometimes their bowels breaking out of their bellies, and are presently discoloured as black as pitch, and so unsavoury as no man can endure to cure or to attend them.

He does not actually say he saw this himself, but of course he did: those lingering deaths aboard his ship after the raid on Cumaná.

There was "nothing whereof I was more curious," he says, "than to find out the true remedies of these poisoned arrows." This was a closely guarded secret, known only to the Indian "soothsayers or priests." They "conceal it, and only teach it but from the father to the son." The Spanish could not get the "true knowledge of the cure" from them, either by "gift or torment." Ralegh was luckier, or a better inquirer, and claims to have learned these secrets. In this, he states, he was especially "beholding to the Guianians," who "taught me the best way of healing all poisons."

He mentions two types of antidote. The sovereign remedy, the one that cures the most powerful venoms, he does not identify. (This refusal is open to the interpretation that he didn't actually learn what it was.) The other, which is used as an antidote to "the ordinary poison," is the juice of a root that the Indians call *tapara*. This also "quencheth marvellously the heat of burning fevers, and healeth inward wounds and broken veins within the body."

In his account of the Second Voyage, a year later, Keymis lists four "herbs good against poison" to be found in Guiana. These are *turara, cutarapama, wapo,* and *macatto.* The first may be the same as Ralegh's *tapara*. One of the others may be the yet more powerful remedy that Ralegh does not name.

There is some ethnological basis for this. Ralegh says he learned of these remedies from the "Guianians," in other words the "borderers" along the Orinoco, as distinct from the Tivitivas of the delta. His most extensive contact was with Topiawari's tribe, the Orenoqueponi. As we have seen, the linguistic evidence suggests that the Orenoqueponi were Macusi, and the Macusi are particularly associated with the most notorious of South American poisons, *curare*. This word is a corruption of Macusi *wourari:* the initial "*c*" is an orthographized vocal click. Lawrence Keymis's list of Guiana produce includes *ourari* among the "poisoned herbs" of the region.

The Macusi were past masters in preparing this poison. Caribs did not have the skill, and purchased it from them. (The Carib word, *wourali,* is also a version of the Macusi word.) For a long time the active principle was thought to be derived from venomous fauna—ants, snakes, etc.—but in the nineteenth century was established as an alkaloid extracted as a resin from the plant *Strychnos toxifera.* Schomburgk describes it as a "ligneous twiner or bushrope," in other words a *liana,* and says it was now rare, found only "in three or four situations in Guiana." He gives a detailed account of its preparation by the Macusi (*Annals of Natural History,* Vol. 7, p. 407) and himself prepared it "by concentrating merely the infusion from the bark of the plant."

So when Ralegh conversed with Orenoqueponi priests and "soothsayers" in June 1595, he was talking to the acknowledged experts on the preparation of the deadly poison, *wourari* or *curare*. Given the atmosphere of amity among them, they may well have shared some of the secrets of curing it, as he claims they did.

This series of plausible but unprovable connections runs as follows. The root called *tapara* is a Macusi remedy. It counteracts the effects of poison and "quencheth marvellously" the fevers of the tropics. Ralegh learned of it in Guiana, probably at Port Morequito, and brought a quantity back home. It formed the vital ingredient of his famous medicine, which he (or anyway his earliest known customer) called "Balsam of Guiana." It is this ingredient that Le Fèvre calls "serpentary of Virginia." This term, unrecorded before 1658, is his approximation. Its description—an American plant, whose root is used by the natives as an antidote to "poisons and fevers"—corresponds to an ingredient in the original recipe that he cannot otherwise identify. That ingredient is *tapara*.

I do not know what *tapara* is, or was. The word was unknown to Pemón I asked. Many medicinal species have been lost to deforestation, and the secret of Ralegh's Guiana balsam may have vanished with them.

[26]

A Golden World

*   *   *

NOT LONG after Ralegh's return to England, the poet George Chapman penned a stirring "epic song," *De Guiana*. The poem champions Ralegh's pioneering voyage, and urges the Queen to back him in further exploration. It was possibly commissioned by Ralegh himself, or perhaps by Thomas Harriot, whom Chapman elsewhere calls his "admired and soul-loved friend." It was apparently written before Keymis set out on the Second Guiana Voyage of 1596, since Chapman urges the Queen to

> . . . be a prosperous forewind to a fleet
> That, seconding your last, may go before it
> In all success of profit and renown.

De Guiana was therefore composed some time between Ralegh's return in early September 1595 and the departure of Keymis's "seconding" expedition on January 26, 1596. It was printed later in 1596, as a preface to Keymis's account of his expedition, *A Relation of the Second Voyage to Guiana*. Its inclusion suggests that Ralegh liked and accepted the poem as a contribution to the ongoing Guiana propaganda.

That he should accept it is hardly surprising, given Chapman's depiction of him as one of a type of intrepid, patriotic knights-errant.

> You patrician spirits that refine
> Your flesh to fire, and issue like a flame,
> In brave endeavours . . .

288

> You that herein renounce the course of earth,
> And lift your eyes for guidance to the stars;
> That live not for yourselves, but to possess
> Your honoured country of a general store.

These are men not content "to hold a threadbare beaten way"; men "that in things hardest are most confident." This casts Ralegh's journey in agreeably heroic mold.

Chapman's poem is a kind of counterpart to the *Discoverie*. It is composed at much the same time, and printed shortly after it. It presents in poetic form certain ideas found in the *Discoverie:* the idea, for instance, that Ralegh made the journey not "for himself" but for the future good of England. Above all Chapman is interested (as always) in the philosophical aspects. His apostrophe to Guiana evokes that cultish imagery of American colonization that had been a feature of the Virginia enterprise.

> Guiana, whose rich feet are mines of gold,
> Whose forehead knocks against the roof of stars,
> Stands on her tiptoes at fair England looking,
> Kissing her hand, bowing her mighty breast,
> And every sign of submission making,
> To be her sister and the daughter, both,
> Of our most sacred maid, whose barrenness
> Is the true fruit of virtue, that may get,
> Bear and bring forth anew in all perfection,
> What heretofore savage corruption held
> In barbarous chaos.

Here too are ideas that appear, obliquely, in the *Discoverie*. I discussed them earlier with reference to that dark-eyed lady of Arowacai, and to the "maidenhead" of Guiana. It is an image of colonization as a kind of platonic embrace between cultures, rather than as an aggressive sexual penetration. In Chapman's trope, Guiana and England are both feminine. Guiana appears as a beautiful giantess: submissive and lovelorn. England is represented in the figure of the Virgin Queen, "our most sacred maid."

Thus Chapman depicts the Guiana Voyage as a kind of mystical English quest, and draws on this imagery of a "virgin" union. Out of their chaste but productive liaison ("barrenness" and "fruit") will come a new "perfection," which is a purification of what was before corrupt and chaotic.

His poetic and idealized view of the Guiana enterprise is summed up in his exhortation to the Queen, urging her to support Ralegh's continued efforts.

> Then, most admired Sovereign, let your breath
> Go forth upon the waters, and create
> A golden world in this our iron age.

It is only a metaphor, formed in the mind of a poet who tends toward the fustily metaphysical, but it seems to me an important one. It is part, by its presence in Keymis's book, of Ralegh's Guiana propaganda. It is a synopsis of certain philosophical notions about the Guiana Voyage: about what it was, and what it represented. Ralegh's search for El Dorado is seen as an attempt to create, or anyway to find, a "golden world in this our iron age."

In this chapter I want to look at this idea of America as a "golden world." It is evoked here by Chapman *after* the Guiana Voyage, as a kind of rhapsodic gloss on it, but it is an idea that was certainly around before. The more I look at it, the more it seems to me that it is an idea intrinsic to Ralegh's voyage; that it is a preconception that to some extent defines the voyage; and that it is encoded all along in the goal of the voyage, namely El Dorado.

So at the end of the book I return to a theme I mentioned at the beginning: the idea of projection, by which I mean the idea that this image of El Dorado, which drew Ralegh and so many others into the wilds of South America, has a stratum of meanings quite distinct from the overt meanings of wealth and possession.

We know what Ralegh didn't find, what he didn't bring back. The failures of the expedition are plain to see: "little riches." Perhaps, by pursuing this image of the "golden world," we might get an idea of something that he *did* find.

*　　*　　*

I HAVE said that Ralegh's *entrada* into South America is most meaningfully an "entrance" into the culture and habitat of the American Indians. Like all travelers, and particularly those entering the unknown, he carried with him certain preconceptions about what he would find there.

From the very earliest European contact, there was a radically divided reaction to the "savages" of the New World. The instinctive, populist reaction was precisely that—the savagery, the near animality, of the Indians and their culture: nakedness, face paint, animal pelts. In the popular imagination they were imbued with the imagery of the Wild Man. The illustration of a Brazilian Indian in Vespucci's *De Novo Mundo* (1505) is based on conventional images of the Wild Man—he is naked, profusely bearded (which the actual Indians were not), and waves his bow and arrows like the Wild Man waving his club. The Wild Man, or "wodewose," was a familiar figure in medieval paintings and pageantry. He features in Elizabethan entertainments such as the Queen's Progresses: a symbol of the greenwood, of Nature without Art, of something irreducible and dangerous.

The word "savage" in itself shows this reaction. It is derived from Latin *silva* (forest). The frequent Elizabethan spelling, "salvage," maintains the link (as does modern Spanish *salvaje*). In this original sense "savage" is definitive—a forest dweller—rather than pejorative, but by the sixteenth century it carries these other connotations of savagery. In the cast list of Shakespeare's *The Tempest,* Caliban is described as a "salvage and deformed slave," and the portrayal of him draws on this popular linking of the medieval Wild Man and the New World Indian.

Out in America itself, this "savage" aspect of the Indians is worked up into the idea of the cannibal. (Caliban is himself, by simple anagram, a cannibal.) Like the Amazons, this is an importation of a preexistent idea. Man-eaters and *anthropophagi* were a staple of the early travel-writers on which Columbus and others were reared: principally Pliny, Marco Polo, and the Mandeville corpus (i.e., the collection of travel tales fathered onto the shadowy medieval globe-trotter, Sir John Mandeville).

The etymology of "cannibal" is a hodgepodge dense with colonial misapprehensions. The earliest written appearance of the word is Columbus's "*canibales*," in his journal (November 23, 1492). It is essentially a variant of "Carib." Other early European forms are *Caniba, Calibi,* and *Camballi.* Columbus's first reaction was that *canibales* were "*el gente de Grand Can*" (the people of the Great Khan). In other words he perceived the word within the context of his belief that he was on the outskirts of Asia. Similarly, when he was told of a region named Cibao—which means in Arawak, "stony mountain"— he fancied it to refer to Cipango, i.e., Japan. There is also an admixture of the "dog-faced men," another tribe Columbus supposedly heard of on his first voyage. Thus the cannibals are also canine. (According to the *OED,* this connection was "a later delusion entertained by Geraldini, Bishop of San Domingo," which "tickled the etymological fancy of the 16th Century.")

Out of this jumbled etymology emerged a simple and expedient equation: that all aggressive Indians of the region are Caribs, and that all Caribs are cannibals. By royal decree, issued by Queen Isabella in 1504, the Caribs were deemed "undeserving of Christian commiseration," and were legally condemned to slavery and extermination.

In her Reith Lectures (1994), Marina Warner discusses the "deep-seated racial myth of cannibalism" in relation to the Spanish conquest of America.

The fantasy [of cannibalism] lay on the surface of the minds of the explorers from Europe, from centuries of myth-making, an expression of deep desires and terrors, when they reached those places called the Indies. That imagery of forbidden ingestion masked other powerful longings and fears—about mingling and hybridity, about losing definition, about swallowing and being swallowed—fears about a future loss of identity, about the changes that history itself brings. Cannibalism helps to justify the presence of the invader, the settler, the

trader bringing civilization . . . [It] marks its practitioners as throw-
backs, barbarians, stone-age men, yet the conqueror's imagery can
betray that he is himself the devourer.

She takes this as an instance of "how deeply fantasy has shaped the
story and the chronicles of conquest," a perception that might also
be applied to El Dorado.

THIS IS one side of the European reaction to the natives of the New
World: a fearful reaction, an idea of evolutionary backwardness, of
monstrousness. The legend of the Amazons expresses a similar fear,
and is also imported wholesale: part of the cultural and psychological
luggage with which the first voyagers arrived.

There was, however, another type of reaction entirely: one that
saw in the Native Americans something pristine, pure, indeed utopian. It is well known that Sir Thomas More's *Utopia* (1516) was
partly inspired by descriptions of life among the Brazilian Indians,
by Vespucci and others. In the same year appeared the *De Orbe Novo*
by Peter Martyr, which waxes lyrical about the natural harmonies of
Indian life, where the land was held to be "as common as sun and
water," and where the natives knew no difference between "mine
and thine." This work was widely read in England, in the translation
by Richard Eden. In it can be found that phrase used by Chapman:
a "golden world."

In France, far more than England, there was a surge of interest
in the Indians. The poet Ronsard championed America as a "Western Arcadia," free from the numbing artificiality of French court life.
At Rouen, a troupe of Brazilian Indians performed a masque before
Charles IX. In a "mimic forest" by the Seine, they did war dances
and performed a mock battle. Among those who met and conversed
with them after the show was the philosopher Michel de Montaigne.
His famous essay *Des Canibales* recalls the meeting.

In this essay, published in 1580, Montaigne sums up this utopian
view of native Indian society.

These people are wild in the same way as we say that fruits are wild, when Nature has produced them by herself. . . . [They] are still very close to their original simplicity. They are still governed by natural laws, and very little corrupted by our own. . . . What we have seen of these people with our own eyes surpasses not only the pictures with which poets have illustrated the Golden Age, and all their attempts to draw mankind in the state of happiness, but the ideas and the very aspirations of philosophers as well. They could not imagine an innocence as pure and simple as we have actually seen.

As with the "Wild Man," the Indians correspond to something already present in the European imagination—the lost "Golden Age."

Montaigne ends this passage with a tag from Virgil: *"Hos natura modos primum dedit"* (These are the customs that Nature first gave). This, from the *Georgics,* suggests another interesting link, between this idealistic notion of Indian society and the literary idea of the pastoral, the Arcadian. This feeds into Elizabethan intellectual pastoralism—Spenser's *Faerie Queene* is an obvious example, in particular the "Bower of Bliss" episode, which has been interpreted as an allegory of America. The idea of Arcadia, so popular in late Elizabethan poetry and prose, is entwined with this utopian view of America, and its "sun-burnt Indians, that know no other wealth but peace and pleasure." Shakespeare's pastoral comedy, *As You Like It* (c.1599), depicts a courtly society flourishing in the wilderness: a kind of colony. In the Forest of Arden, as in the forests of Montaigne's idealized America, "they fleet the time carelessly, as they did in the golden world."

Shakespeare returns to the theme more intensely in his last play, *The Tempest,* with the Caribbean overtones of its magic isle and its anagrammatic cannibal Caliban. Montaigne is certainly in Shakespeare's mind in the passage where Gonzalo outlines his perfect "commonwealth."

> . . . No kind of traffic
> Would I admit; no name of magistrate;
> Letters should not be known; riches, poverty

> And use of service none; contract, succession,
> Bourn, bound of land, tilth, vineyard, none;
> No use of metal, corn, or wine, or oil;
> No occupation; all men idle, all,
> And women too, but innocent and pure.

This is drawn closely from Montaigne's essay, via the English translation by John Florio, published in 1603.

> It is a nation . . . that hath no kind of traffic, no knowledge of letters, no intelligence of numbers; no name of magistrate nor of politic superiority; no use of service, of riches or of poverty; no contracts, no successions, no partitions; no occupation, but idle; no respect of kindred, but common; no apparel, but natural; no manuring of lands, no use of wine, corn or metal.

SOME OF these literary references are later than Ralegh's voyage, but this is the intellectual context in which the voyage is made. There is this dual attitude to the Indians—that they are bestial creatures given to unbridled lust and cannibalism; that they are pristine inhabitors of a pastoral "golden world" untouched by greed and falsehood. Spenser's *Faerie Queene,* dedicated to Ralegh in 1590 and full of New World themes, features two "salvage men." The one who carries off Amoret (Book 4, Canto 7) belongs in the first category: "He lived all on ravin and rape." The one who treats Serena so gently (Book 6, Canto 5) is full of a naive tenderness. These precisely reflect the two versions of the American Indian in Elizabethan thinking.

It is undoubtedly true to say that the first view of the Indians as subhuman—or "human beasts," as they are described in the Council of Virginia's *True Declaration* of 1610—is more convenient to the colonizer than the second. Yet from the outset, Ralegh's interest in America tends toward that other, more poetic, utopian view. It is interesting to note, in this context, that his half brother Humphrey Gilbert's last words aboard the sinking *Squirrel* in 1583—"We are as near to heaven by sea as by land"—are probably a quotation. It is said he was reading a book as the ship went down, and that book was almost certainly More's *Utopia,* in which is found the line: "The way to heaven out of all places is of like length and distance."

Ralegh read widely on America, and probably knew Montaigne's essay prior to the English translation of 1603, but it was his own Virginia enterprise that fixed the image of America in his mind. Perhaps most piquant of all to him was that first account brought back in 1584 by his scout Arthur Barlowe. Barlowe's Virginia is a vision of Arcadia. They "smelt so sweet and strong a smell as if we had been in the midst of some delicate garden." They looked out over "replenished" valleys. They found "incredible abundance" and "plenty" and fertility everywhere. And then there was the hospitality: Barlowe's report ends with an almost comically copious display of generosity from an Indian *cacica,* the sister-in-law of Chief Wingina. When the English visited her, at Roanoke, they were carried by porters from the shore to her house, and set down in her outer room by a "great fire." There, "some of the women plucked off our stockings, and washed them. Some washed our feet in warm water. She herself took great pains to see all things ordered in the best manner." They were then treated to a feast of venison, fish, "frumenty" (gruel), manioc, and melons, washed down with a sea-grape wine spiced with cinnamon and sassafras. They ate off "platters of sweet timber." They were "entertained with all love and kindness." Barlowe concludes: "We found the people most gentle, loving and faithful, void of all guile and treason, and such as live after the manner of the Golden Age." Here the idea of the Golden Age arises out of a narrative of Indians giving, which in itself seems a function of the plenty and abundance of the region. This is again a preexistent connection, part of the classical idea of the Golden Age, where the land is so plentiful that work is unnecessary: "The earth itself, without compulsion, untouched by hoe or ploughshare, of herself gave all things needful" (Ovid, *Metamorphoses,* 1:100). This too is a feature of Gonzalo's imagined "commonwealth" in *The Tempest.*

> All things in common Nature should produce
> Without sweat or endeavour . . .

> Nature should bring forth,
> Of its own kind, all foison, all abundance,
> To feed my innocent people.

The following year the first colony was established at Roanoke. From this came John White's graceful watercolors depicting Virginian, or Algonquian, life; and Harriot's *Brief and True Report,* a more scientific and systematic study, but also suffused with this mood of pastoral simplicity.

> This people, therefore, void of all covetousness, live cheerfully and at their heart's ease. . . . To confess a truth, I cannot remember that ever I saw a better or quieter people than they.

Beauty, plenty, simplicity, harmony: a people living "at their heart's ease." This is the utopian image of America that Ralegh was immersed in—it is, of course, part of his propaganda for the Virginia venture, but I think it is also something that fascinated and touched him.

It is precisely these qualities that we find in Ralegh's depiction of the Indians of Guiana, those "lords of the borders" whose simple lives, beautiful surroundings, abundant harvests, and profound generosity he records in the *Discoverie.* He does not *say* that Guiana is an Arcadia, because he is not writing that type of text. It is left to the poet Chapman to express this idea in appropriate poetic terms, as he imagines the triumphant return of Ralegh's colonizers to "Guianian Orenoque."

> And now a wind as forward as their spirits
> Sets their glad feet on smooth Guiana's breast,
> Where, as if each man were an Orpheus,
> A world of savages fall tame before them,
> Storing their theft-free treasuries with gold.
> And there doth plenty crown their wealthy fields.

Here is Guiana as Arcadia, the colonizers as Orphic enchanters whose music moves the savages to "tame" obedience. Here is "theft-free" gold, and plenty in the meadows.

> There Learning eats no more his thriftless books,
> Nor Valour, estridge-like, his iron arms;
> There Beauty is no strumpet for her wants,
> Nor Gallic humours putrefy her blood;
> But all our youth take Hymen's lights in hand
> And fill each roof with honoured progeny;
> There makes society adamantine chains,
> and joins their hearts with wealth whom wealth disjoin'd;
> There healthful recreations strow their meads,
> And make their mansions dance with neighbourhood,
> That here were drown'd in churlish avarice;
> And there do palaces and temples rise
> Out of the earth, and kiss the enamour'd skies,
> Where new Britannia humbly kneels to heaven.

A vision of purity, togetherness, devotion: Guiana as a purified Britannia.

I believe this idea of Guiana as Arcadia is also expressed in De Bry's engraving of Ralegh's meeting with Topiawari. Among the crowd of tribute-bearing Orenoqueponi is one figure who looks quite different. She faces toward the viewer, and she looks not Indian at all. She is a classical figure. She carries in her hand some shocks of maize. She looks to me like Ceres, the goddess of fertility and plenty so often associated with the classical Arcadia. Topiawari gestures to Ralegh to receive the bounty of his land, and Ralegh's eyes seem to fix on this symbolic figure among the Indians. In his hand Ralegh holds a baton or rod of wood: This is a symbol of possession (a reference to the ritual of "rod and turf"). In these details, I think, De Bry depicts Ralegh as taking possession of Arcadia. This too, like Chapman's poem, is an imagery sanctioned by Ralegh, though not explicitly voiced in the *Discoverie.*

*   *   *

THESE ARE the antecedents of Ralegh's conception of the American Indian. It has a literary pedigree that includes More's *Utopia,* Montaigne's *Des Canibales,* Spenser's *Faerie Queene,* and the Virginian accounts of Barlowe and Harriot. These express the idea of America as an Arcadia, a "bower of bliss," a "golden world." He carries this idea with him to the Orinoco. It suffuses the actuality of his encounters with those "lords of the borders," in particular with Topiawari. (It would be unfair to say it falsifies those encounters, but one

28. Ceres amid the Orenoqueponi (detail from De Bry)

remembers that Francis Sparry has a less idyllic view of Ralegh's dealings with Topiawari.) It also suffuses his experience of the South American wilderness, especially in those passages where the landscape takes on a heraldic kind of orderliness: those "deer park" visions.

For the traveler to the New World, the view of the Indians as bestial and violent is embodied in the American legend of the cannibal, the man-eater. Is there some equivalent legend or fantasy that embodies this other view of the Indians, as the naturally noble inhabitants of an untouched "golden world"?

My answer is, of course, that there was. It was the legend of El Dorado.

As frequently mentioned, El Dorado was not originally a place at all, but a person: *el dorado,* the golden man. He featured in a ritual of the Muisca or Chibcha, who lived in the Andean highlands of what is now Colombia. In this ritual, often described loosely as an annual "sacrifice," the *zipa* or chief of the tribe was anointed with gold dust and set adrift on a lake. He was then immersed, washing off the gold dust into the lake. Other precious offerings were also thrown in. This took place at certain sacred lakes: Guasca, Siecha,

Teusaca, Ubaque and—the most important—Guatavita. It is fairly certain that this was an actual rite, rather than a legend, though its significance within the spectrum of Chibcha ceremony may now be exaggerated. At its root are two practices—body painting and lake worship—known to be used by the Chibcha. There is archaeological evidence of it in the quantities of gold and emeralds found in or near Guatavita and the other lakes. Though real, it is fairly certain that it had died out before the first European arrival: It was already a memory. No Spaniard ever *saw* this gilded priest or chief at Guatavita, though some may have heard of him from Chibcha eyewitnesses.

The Chibcha were conquered, by Berrio's mentor Quesada, in the mid-1530s. By 1541 this shadowy figure, the gilded *zipa* of Guatavita, has been mingled with other rumors to become El Dorado. The earliest written account of him is by that excellent New World reporter Fernandez de Oviedo y Valdes, then living in Santo Domingo on the island of Hispaniola. It is news brought by Spaniards from Quito, news from the mountains. Everyone is talking, he says, of a great Indian prince. They call him the "Golden Chief or King."

> They tell me that what they have learned from the Indians is that this great lord or prince goes about continually covered in gold dust as fine as ground salt. . . . He anoints himself every morning with a certain gum or resin that sticks very well; the powdered gold adheres to that unction. His entire body is covered from the soles of his feet to his head. He looks as resplendent as a gold object worked by the hand of a great artist. . . . He washes away at night what he puts on each morning, so that it is discarded and lost, and he does this every day of the year. . . . I would rather have the sweepings of the chamber of this Prince than the great meltings of gold there have been in Peru.

Already the story has grown layers. This gilding ceremony is now performed daily; it is a royal *toilette*. The reference to the king's "chamber," with its floor carelessly dusted with gold and a broom to get up the "sweepings," reinforces the courtly imagery of Oviedo's version. We are no longer on the shores of a wild Andean lake, but in an implied palace of some sort. We see here the first lineaments of that "golden city" which becomes the dominant image of El Dorado.

This is the first documentation of El Dorado as it comes to be understood: a Golden King in a palace—and by implication a city and a kingdom—of untold wealth. The lake has temporarily slipped from view, but it is soon reinstated in the versions that follow. Fifty years later, Ralegh's El Dorado—as described in the *Discoverie*—is recognizably based on the original image that crystallized around the Guatavita ritual. It is a "golden city" high in the mountains, on the shores of a lake. Its people perform this same gilding ritual.

> When the Emperor carouseth with his captains, tributaries and governors, the manner is thus. All those that pledge him are first stripped naked, and their bodies anointed all over with a kind of white *balsamum* . . . When they are anointed all over, certain servants of the Emperor, having prepared gold made into a fine powder, blow it through hollow canes upon their naked bodies, until they be all shining from the foot to the head.

In De Bry's Latin edition of the *Discoverie,* published in 1599, this is accompanied by an elegant engraving of the gilded "emperor" of El Dorado, thus further fixing the image in the European imagination. Another Englishman exploring the area at the time reports the same rumors—a "rich nation that sprinkled their bodies with the poulder of gold, and seemed to be gilt." These are refractions of that primary lacustrine ritual.

Perhaps the single most important aspect of this image of the Golden King, aside from his wealth, is one of courtliness and civilization in the midst of nature, precisely that Arcadian idea of natural nobility. It is one of the first accretions, as seen in Oviedo's account of 1541. The Golden King, with his palace or city in the wilderness, embodies this utopian view of the American natives, just as the cannibal embodies that other, "savage" view of them.

The image of El Dorado plays over Ralegh's imagination, contains

29. The Golden King

all those yearning ideas of America. That first "relation" of it by Sarmiento comes in 1586, at the height of the Virginia enthusiasm. Indeed, Harriot and White returned from Virginia while Sarmiento was actually there, as Ralegh's guest, in September 1586. The vision evoked by Sarmiento entwines with these first accounts of the Virginian Indians who live "after the manner of the Golden Age." And ten years later, when so much in his life has changed, he sets off in search of this "golden world" in which a man might "bring forth anew"—as Chapman puts it—those things that are now all corruption and chaos.

[27]

On Red Cross River

*   *   *

THIS IDEA of native America as a "golden world," and hence a relic of the fabled innocence of the Golden Age, has certain spin-offs that to the orthodox mind of the mid-1590s were questionable and possibly heretical. It becomes entwined with an idea of the antiquity of Indian culture and religion, and this in turn leads to problems with conventional biblical chronology. It was among the "damnable opinions" of Christopher Marlowe, as reported by the spy Baines in 1593, that "the Indians and many authors of antiquity have assuredly written above 16 thousand years agone, whereas Adam is proved to have lived within 6 thousand years." Marlowe was a close friend of Thomas Harriot, who is also mentioned in Baines's report ("one Heriots, being Sir W. Ralegh's man"). Another associate of Marlowe's, the pamphleteer Thomas Nashe, also has the story:

> I hear say there be mathematicians abroad that will prove men before Adam; and they are harboured in high places who will maintain it to the death that there are no devils. [*Pierce Penniless,* 1592]

> There are atheists who impudently assert . . . that the late discovered Indians are able to show antiquities thousands before Adam. [*Christ's Tears,* 1593]

This undoubtedly glances at Marlowe and Harriot—the "discoverer" of those "late discovered Indians"—and through them at Ralegh, who "harbours" them in high places.

It is not just a matter of the arithmetic of Creation. This predating of Adam is purely speculative. There is nothing that Harriot or anyone else could have learned from the Indians that would enable that spurious, Laime-esque computation of "16,000 years agone" which Baines attributes to Marlowe. What is at stake here, rather, is the primacy of the Christian religion, and so this vein of speculation about Indian "antiquities" becomes entwined with the current Elizabethan interest in what was called the *prisca theologia,* or "first theology."

This was essentially the religious underpinning of Renaissance occultism. It was based on various mystical tracts and fragments recovered by Marsilio Ficino and others in the late fifteenth century. These writings—gnostic, hermetic, Neoplatonic, cabalistic—were mistakenly held to be pre-Christian, and even pre-Mosaic (though almost all were actually from the early centuries A.D.) and were seen as part of an original, magico-mystical religion having its origins in Egypt.

We know, from the *History of the World,* Ralegh's deep interest in the *Corpus Hermeticum* (the "Polymander" in his library list is probably Ficino's *Pymander*). We know the Earl of Northumberland's admiration of the Italian occultist Giordano Bruno, an outspoken advocate of this "magical religion" who disputed in England in the 1580s. We know the poet Peele's description of the intellectual ambiance of the Ralegh-Northumberland circle:

> Leaving our schoolmen's vulgar trodden paths,
> And following the ancient reverend steps
> Of Trismegistus and Pythagoras.

(In other words, studying Hermes Trismegistus, the apocryphal high priest of Egyptian magic; and Pythagoras, the supposed founder of occult numerology or "mathesis.")

All this, to the orthodox, spelled "atheism," and so the rumors fly: of "Sir Walter Rawley's school of atheism," and of "the conjuror that is Master thereof" (i.e., Harriot), and of "the diligence used to get young gentlemen to this school," and of the "atheist lecture" read there by Christopher Marlowe. The questioning of Ralegh, Harriot, and others by a special commission in 1594, and perhaps the stabbing of Marlowe the previous year, show how seriously these allegations were taken. (This inquiry into Ralegh's beliefs was chaired by Lord Howard of Bindon, a cousin of Ralegh's Guiana sponsor, Lord Admiral Howard.)

And so—as Baines and Nashe show above—Ralegh's American interests become implicated in this broad current of atheistic rumor. There is dangerous talk of the Indians as men before Adam, and indeed of a living, breathing Golden Age, and this links in people's minds with occultist notions of the *prisca theologia*—two forms of paganism rolled into one.

THE WORD "atheist" need not detain us: It is part of the language of the Elizabethan police state. That Ralegh was a devoted believer in God is abundantly plain; that he had also an inquiring, voracious, tolerant, subtle, and highly skeptical turn of mind is enough to earn him this label. But the truth of these trifling charges is also interesting. These speculations *did* go on, behind the closed doors of Durham House and Sherborne; and Ralegh's idea of America *was* invested with certain occultist notions.

There are two key figures here: Dr. Dee, the grand old man of Elizabethan occultism; and Edmund Spenser, the rarefied pastoralist of the *Faerie Queene.*

John Dee straddles these worlds of magic and exploration—worlds that are at the time inextricably linked anyway, via the central importance to each of mathematics. Dee was, like Harriot and Keymis, a mathematician and navigational expert: See his *Mathematicall Preface* (1570) and his *General and Rare Memorials of Navigation* (1577). He was closely associated with Sir Humphrey Gilbert, and at one point held a "patent" on all American lands above 50° north. But for Dee, the mathematician was a magician who could "mount above the clouds and the stars," and the voyage to America was part of an elaborate, mystical, Arthurian conception of a New Britannia, a purified continent, a New Age.

There is no space to go into this in detail, and I do not think the Guiana Voyage needs a detailed correspondence with Dee's arcane imperial theories. But I would say that the motifs that emerge from the *Discoverie,* and Chapman's *De Guiana*—the idea of the "golden world," the idea of "chaste" colonizing, the idea of "virgin" territory as related to the Virgin Queen cult—spring in general from Dee's occultist musings on the new British Empire (as he was the first to call it). Chapman's previous work, especially *The Shadow of Night*— published in 1594 and addressed to, among others, the Earl of Northumberland—shows he was deeply imbued in Dee's occult philosophy.

Ralegh is associated with Dr. Dee through thick and thin (in fact, Dee thought that *he,* rather than Harriot, was the "conjuror" referred to in the "school of atheism" smear). And there is that tantalizing meeting in October 1595, a month after Ralegh's return from Guiana. Their conversation is unrecorded, and it is merely evidential chance that makes this his first known meeting after the voyage, but clearly he had matters to discuss with Dr. Dee.

Edmund Spenser is, like Dee, a longtime associate of Ralegh's (they met in Ireland in 1581), and his twelve-book Arcadian epic, *The Faerie Queene,* was dedicated to Ralegh in 1590. Scholars have shown that this work, which Spenser describes as a "continued allegory or dark conceit," is filled with occultist and Neoplatonic themes, and that much of its "ancient British" allegory chimes in with Dee's "British" imperial themes.

Dee's influence on Ralegh's Guiana Voyage is felt as a general irradiation of occultist notions of America, these joining that other pedigree of literary sources discussed in the previous chapter, and imbuing the idea of the American "golden world," and indeed of El Dorado, with a certain tinge of late Renaissance magic. Spenser's influence, by contrast, steps startlingly to light at a precise and verified moment among the mangrove swamps of the Orinoco Delta.

They were "entering into a river," says Ralegh, "which because it had no name we called the River of the Red Cross, ourselves being the first Christians that ever came therein."

30. *Dee's mystic imperialism. Emblematic title page of the* General and Rare
Memorials *(1577)*

*   *   *

THE IMMEDIATE interpretation of "Red Cross River" is that it refers to the patron saint of England, Saint George, whose emblem is the Red Cross. The naming of the river is thus a straightforward act of English possession.

Almost as immediate, to anyone with half an eye on the literature of the day, was the undoubted allusion to the "Red Cross Knight," the chivalric hero of the first book of *The Faerie Queene*. These are, of course, linked. Spenser's Red Cross Knight is himself a version of Saint George, particularly as a defender of the Anglican Church. He is the "knight of holiness," and is led by his companion Una (glossed by Spenser as "the one true religion") into the House of Holiness, and finally weds her after killing the dragon. Spenser's poem is no mere jingoistic allegory about the triumph of Protestantism, however. The Red Cross Knight draws also on more mystical notions about England—or that pseudohistorical Arthurian "Britain" of Dr. Dee's—and the "one true religion" shades toward that magical *prisca theologia* currently associated with utopian views of America. As mentioned earlier, *The Faerie Queene* also contains numerous New World allusions (the "salvage men," the "bower of bliss," etc.).

So, in this act of naming, Ralegh is being patriotic in a rather particular and, to some extent, controversial way. This obscure South American *caño* is claimed less as an English possession, more as a Spenserian "British" possession: part of this "brave new world," this purified Britannia. (The quote from *The Tempest* is specific: Prospero is a Dee-like figure and his "magic island" partly a comment on Dee's colonial aspirations.)

More telling still is the strong suggestion that Ralegh's name for this river is also a name for himself as its discoverer, and that he is here equating his own voyage into Guiana with the allegorical knight-errant quest of Spenser's hero. (Keymis would later call the Orinoco "Ralleana," but this did not catch on.) I do not want to sound like a cinema poster, but I feel strongly that at this point of his American journey, Sir Walter Ralegh *is* the Red Cross Knight.

This moment on the Red Cross River, on about May 21, 1595, is an incongruous piece of intellectual chivalry, a display of this highly refined Elizabethan symbolism in circumstances of heat, mud, and desolation. Francis Sparry seems to confirm that the river was named there and then, rather than retrospectively, by Ralegh. There is some little ceremony, some possession rite with rod and turf. Words are spoken. There is that note of gimcrack theatricality that attends Elizabethan pageants. The words float off into the air, only dimly understood by the muttering, hungry "companies."

Whether this rite was witnessed by local Indians is not clear: The possession formula had ways of getting around this inconvenient requirement. Their first encounter with the Warao seems to be the following day, so it is quite possible that the only audience for this surreal *pièce de théâtre* were the monkeys, toucans, and turtles of the delta.

THE INFLUENCE of Dee and Spenser is found in another, rather shadowy area: the early Rosicrucians. (This sounds oddball, but I am using the term in a strictly historical sense.) It can certainly be argued that Ralegh's particular phrasing—they named the river "Red Cross" because they were "the first Christians" there—contains a highly suggestive echo or pun on the name of Christian Rosy Cross (or Rosencreutz), the legendary founder of the Rosicrucians.

The Rosicrucians, or Brotherhood of the Rosy Cross, are hard to pin down. They emerge as a definable movement, in Germany, in the early seventeenth century (a movement but not, perhaps, the cohesive sect or "fraternity" they pretend). The earliest surviving manifesto, the *Fama Fraternitatis,* was printed at Cassel in 1614. It proclaims a "general and universal reformation," has inflammatory political and millenarian aspects, and invokes the occultist trinity of "Magia, Alchymia, Cabala." It is certain, however, that there were earlier stirrings of the movement, in such figures as Johann Valentin Andreae, who wrote a lost early version of *The Chemical Wedding of Christian Rosencreutz* in about 1603; and Johann Thölde, who "edited" and probably wrote a series of alchemical texts attributed to Basil Valentine, the earliest of which—the *Zwolff Schlussel,* or Twelve Keys—appeared in 1599.

It is also certain that Dee was a major early influence on the movement. His occult symbol, the *monas hieroglyphica,* appears in Rosicrucian manifestos. The seeds of Rosicrucianism, it is argued, were broadcast during Dee's obscure mission to central Europe (1583–89). His diaries record a rather lurid series of "angelic conferences" or séances, alchemical transmutations, and even a spirit-ordained session of wife swapping with his sinister associate Edward Kelley, but also meetings with key figures in oc-

31. Maier's Atalanta

cultist circles in Poland and Bohemia. The influence of Spenser is evident in the name of Christian Rosy Cross, or Rosencreutz, the invented knight-errant founder of Rosicrucianism, who reflects the mystical, reformist overtones of Spenser's "Red Cross Knight."

The Rosicrucians have no documented identity as early as 1595, so one cannot say that Ralegh intends a pun on the name Christian Rosy Cross. What one can say is that in 1595 he was intimately close, through Dee and Spenser, to occultist themes that will shortly be called Rosicrucian, and that the echo is not fortuitous, or rather is not an echo at all but a foretaste.

An interesting sidelight on that idea is that one of the leading printers of Rosicrucian literature in Germany was none other than Johann de Bry, the son of Theodore de Bry, whose lavish edition of Ralegh's *Discoverie* provides the nearest we get to a visual account of the Guiana Voyage. I mentioned that beautiful classical face that stands out among the Orenoqueponi in Theodore de Bry's engraving of the conference with Topiawari. You see that face again and again in his son's engravings in works such as *Atalanta Fugiens,* by the Rosicrucian theorist, Michael Maier. I have interpreted her as an Arcadian Ceres, with her shocks of American maize, but there is room also for her to be some more esoteric manifestation along the lines of Maier's fleeing Atalanta.

This foretaste of Rosicrucian ideas in the naming of the Red Cross River leads me back to the idea of the Golden Age, which began this excursion. References to the return of the Golden Age are a staple of the stirring reformist imagery of the Rosicrucians. In Michael Maier's *Themis Aurea* (1618), which sets out the "laws of the Rosicrucian fraternity" (*de legibus Fraternitatis R.C.*), we learn that the Rosicrucians

> wish and are ambitious of the Age of Solomon, wherein there was so great plenty [of gold] at Jerusalem as tiles on the houses; silver as common as stones in the street; so in the Golden Age its use was not known.

This introduces an irony in this equation between El Dorado and the "golden world." This city of shimmering plenty—roof tiles of gold and paving stones of silver—sounds very like that fantasy of the "golden city," El Dorado, yet the point of it is the idea that the plenty of the Golden Age was a *freeing* of man from the search and scrabble for wealth. The discovery of the golden city, the recovery of the Golden Age, is a removal of the power of gold, and indeed Maier's Rosicrucians say of gold: "This dust of the earth is of no value with them, because those things are low in their eyes which others much adore. They had rather find out a mystery in Nature than a mine." They sound rather like Ralegh in South America: all mystery and no mining. And their vision of the Golden Age, which is also the rosy Rosicrucian future, sounds much like that utopian "commonwealth" that Montaigne and others saw as actually existing in native American society.

> Men were contented with what Nature freely afforded them, living friendly under the government of the father of the family, without

broils, luxury, pride, much less war. . . . If every man duly receives whatever belongs to him, he hath no cause of commencing a suit with any, or to complain, much less to engage in a war; but on the contrary, all (as in the Golden Age) shall enjoy peace and prosperity.

In these ramifications of Ralegh's "Red Cross River" we find some curious undertones to his journey into South America. It becomes— in a part of his mind, at least—a kind of highly charged chivalric quest. The tone of the journey is tinged with exotic symbolism of the kind found in Spenser's *Faerie Queene,* in Dee's esoteric British imperialism, and in the utopian manifestos of the Brotherhood of the Rosy Cross. Something of this is expressed in his comments on the rigors of the journey in the *Discoverie.*

Of that little remain I had, I have wasted in effect all herein. I have undergone many constructions, I have been accompanied with many sorrows, with labour, hunger, heat, sickness and peril. . . . [They] were much mistaken who would have persuaded that I was too easeful and sensual to undertake a journey of so great travail. But if what I have done receive the gracious construction of a painful pilgrimage, and purchase the least remission, I shall think all too little.

This is Ralegh as Red Cross Knight, renouncing wealth and ease to make this "painful pilgrimage" in search of the Golden King: an image that belongs more to romance or mysticism than to the highly factual travel book that follows. But as always in the El Dorado story we find this blurring between the symbolic and the physical, this mud-stained enactment of empty metaphors and impossible desires.

[28]

The Shut Palace

*   *   *

I HAVE TRACED Ralegh's physical journey along the rivers of Venezuela, and I have tried to trace some of the symbolic meanings the journey might have had for him: an excursion into the landscapes of Arcadia, into the innocence of the Golden Age, into all those highly charged ideas and ideals of noble savagery that the name of America conjured up in certain intellectual circles of the late sixteenth century, and which the pristine image of El Dorado came to represent to Ralegh. I like that moment of naming on the Orinoco Delta because it belongs to both types of journey: He is a middle-aged Englishman with river water in his boots and mosquitoes around his head, and he is the Red Cross Knight on an allegorical pilgrimage into the New World.

He is, as he would say, "making trial" of these ideas. He is there, traveling or travailing through them (these words were not distinguished at the time), and seeing what he finds. It is an experiment, an *essai*.

THERE IS one final key to the symbolism of Ralegh's El Dorado journey: a kind of language that unites these various themes I have outlined. It is not a language that is normally associated with the literature of travel, but you could just about call the following passage of verse a piece of "travel writing," so it will serve as an introduction.

It appears to be a description of a sea voyage, perhaps even one bound for the New World. The words are spoken by "two poor men," who say:

We are now ready to the sea, pressed,
Where we must abide three months at the least,
All which time to land we shall not pass,
No, although our ship be made of glass.
But all tempest of the air we must abide
And in dangerous roads many times to ride.
Bread we shall have none, nor yet other food,
But only fair water descending from a cloud;
The moon shall burn us so, in process of time,
That we shall be as black as men of Ind.
Shortly we shall pass into another climate,
Where we shall receive a more purer estate;
For this our sins we make our purgatory,
For the which we shall receive a spiritual body.

This ramshackle but very vivid narrative is part of a long poem called "The Breviary of Natural Philosophy." It was written, in the 1550s, by a Somerset man named Thomas Charnock. One notes that this voyage has certain curiosities: the glass ship, the burning moon, the transforming qualities of this "other climate" they arrive at. This is because Thomas Charnock was not really a voyager at all, nor indeed a poet. He was an alchemist, and the entire passage is an allegory expressing ingredients and processes of the alchemical *opus*.

Another alchemical journey is found in the writings of the medieval adept Sir George Ripley. It has something of the same imagery of Charnock's purgatorial sea voyage, as the alchemist ventures resolutely "under the moisture of the Moon, and under the temperate heat of the Sun" to win the final "Mastery."

It is also described as a chivalric quest in search of the entrance to the "Philosopher's Castle." The twelve chemical stages of the *opus* are represented as the twelve "gates" into this castle.

Proceed wisely that thou may win
In at more gates of that castle,
Which castle is round as any bell.

(This round castle, like Charnock's "glass ship," is an image of the alchemical vessel; it is also a repository of secrets—"the strong Castle of our wisdom"—and is, in a sense, matter itself, into which the alchemist must penetrate.) It is an arduous journey full of despairs: Sometimes "thy spirits shall so be a-down." Each gate is a "conquest," and with it much relief: "That sight will greatly comfort thee." On this chemical journey men stumble, exhausted "with odours and smokes and waking up by nights." Their clothes are "bawdy and worn threadbare," their eyes are "bleared," and "thus for had-I-wist they suffer loss and woe." They sound like the despairing searchers of El Dorado, exhaustedly following their "had-I-wist" illusions.

In these the alchemical process is dramatized, is given a topography—a sea journey, a search for a castle—and draws on a sense of arduousness and danger associated with voyaging or questing: a "painful pilgrimage," as Ralegh puts it. Another tract—*De Lapide Philosophico,* ascribed to a shadowy medieval figure called Lambspringk, but first published in 1599 in an edition by the French alchemist Nicolas Barnaud—has a topography that sounds rather like Ralegh's Guiana. It begins on a "vast sea," but most of the action takes place in a "forest," wherein various allegorical creatures are concealed. This forest is also called a "dark and rugged valley." At one point it is actually specified as American: "In India there is a most pleasant wood." ("India" is, of course, a synonym for the "Indies," meaning America.) This work was published, in Prague, in the same year as De Bry's edition of the *Discoverie,* and features engravings similar in style (though inferior) to De Bry's. It is probable that "Lambspringk," like Thölde's "Basil Valentine," is actually the creation of the book's editor, Nicolas Barnaud. This New World touch, this allegorized Indian forest, thus links to those early Rosicrucian stirrings discussed in the previous chapter.

And in that hard-to-plumb "castle" or "forest," I need hardly add, dwells a Golden King, this being the conventional alchemical symbol for gold: "There are seven bodies, of which gold is the first, the most perfect, the King of them, and their head" (*Tractatus Aureus,* 1625). This king is sometimes sick, in which case he is common gold (*aurum vulgi*), and sometimes triumphant and resplendent, as the "philosophical gold," or philosophers' stone, which is the end product of the *opus*.

Although the King of the Philosophers seems dead, yet he lives, and cries out from the deep: "He who shall deliver me from the waters, and bring me back to dry land, him will I bless with riches ever-lasting."

[Michael Maier, *Symbola Aureae Mensae*, 1617]

Methought he was a prince of honour,
For he was all in golden armour.

[Thomas Charnock, *Aenigma ad Alchimiam*, 1572]

For there is harvest, that is to say an end
Of all this Work unto thine own desire;
There shineth the Sun up in his own sphere,
And after the eclipse is in redness with glory
As King to reign upon all metals and Mercury.

[George Ripley, *Compound of Alchymy*, 1591]

This connection between the Golden King of the El Dorado legend and the Golden King of the alchemists seems to me quite irrefutable, especially when one compares them visually in the engravings of De Bry. Again the connection seems particularly strong in that book of "Lambspringk" (or Barnaud), whose "Indian" touches have already been noticed. Lambspringk's alchemical king is called the "noble Lord of the Forests"—almost, one might say, a *cacique*—and says:

I am a great and glorious King in the earth. . . .
I give power and lasting health,
Also gold, silver, gems and precious stones,
And the panacea for great and small diseases.
Yet at first I was of ignoble birth,

Till I was set in a high place,
To reach . . . the state of royal sovereignty.
Therefore Hermes has called me the Lord of the Forests.

This is redolent of El Dorado: the "ignobly born" savage who becomes a royal king; his forest kingdom as a repository of gold and
gems and medicinal secrets. This is a close conjunction of metaphors,
and is underpinned by the closeness of Lambspringk's text, in time
and milieu, to De Bry's edition of the *Discoverie.*

There is also the conventional alchemical linking of gold with the
sun, or Sol—

> The chymists give it [gold] the name of the Sun, because that they
> believe it hath some correspondency and harmonical relation not only
> with the celestial sun of the great world, but also by reason that it
> has a sympathetical affinity with the sun of the little world, which
> is the heart of man.

32. Maier's King Sol

—which would tie in with the sun wor-
shiping of Ralegh's "Inga" emperor, and
other Guianians. He leaves Guiana "to
the sun, whom they worship."

Having perceived this connection, it
seemed to me impossible that Ralegh
did *not* have an alchemical understanding of El Dorado, and of his "pilgrimage" in search of it, as at least a kind of
alchemical field-trip, if not a full-blown,
purgatorial, *opus*-like quest. (Jason's
search for the Golden Fleece was glossed
as an allegory of the *opus*, by Maier and
others; this is satirized in Jonson's *Alchemist.*) We know that Ralegh was immersed in the subject: an expert in
distillation, in the preparation of bal-
sams and cordials and other "chymical"

products, but also a student of the more esoteric concepts of alchemy. In his chemical notebook are found such formulations as "our Aquila unwinged" and the "Mercury of Jupiter," etc. In the *History of the World,* alchemy defines his concept of lawful "Magick," which is superior to the "brabblings of the Aristotelians." It is a "whole Philosophy of Nature," which

> bringeth to light the inmost virtues, and draweth them out of Nature's hidden bosom to human use: *virtutes in centro centri latentes:* virtues hidden in the centre of the centre, according to the Chymists.

The search for these "inmost virtues" leads the "chymist" into the "centre" of matter: This seems to equate with a journey into the center of South America, which is precisely where El Dorado is placed—at the expense of geography, and no doubt to the irritation of Thomas Harriot—in Ralegh's chart.

There is an old alchemical riddle that reads: *"Visita Interiora Terrae Rectificando Invenies Occultum Lapidem."* This means: "Visit the interior of the earth and by purifying you will find the hidden stone." (It is a riddle insofar as it also spells, acrostically, "Vitriol.") Some tag of this kind may have hovered in Ralegh's mind as he set out on his own visit into the "interior" of America.

And not just in Ralegh's mind, either. We know that just about everyone involved in the El Dorado voyage at a theoretical level—Dee, Harriot, Adrian Gilbert, Keymis—was an enthusiastic experimenter in esoteric alchemy. Even George Gifford, I find, was said to have ruined himself chasing the chimera of the Philosophers' Stone. He did not much improve his fortunes chasing this other chimera across South America.

THUS RALEGH'S *entrada* becomes what the alchemist Philalethes calls an "entrance into the shut palace of the King."

For Carl Jung the alchemical process was symbolic of a struggle toward inner "wholeness." (I realize this term is vague, but it indicates the kind of terrain into which these alchemical perceptions lead.) Commenting on the dour warnings of the alchemists—"*Nonulli perierunt in opere nostro*" (not a few have perished in the course of our work)—he says:

> The right way to wholeness is made up, unfortunately, of fateful detours and wrong turnings. It is a *longissima via,* not straight but snake-like, a path that unites the opposites in the manner of the guiding *caduceus* [of Mercurius], a path whose labyrinthine twists and turns are not lacking in terrors.

This sounds like the circuitous, mazy entrance into the delta, and accords with an idea of Ralegh's journey as being in part symbolic of an inner journey along the "way to wholeness."

I have talked of El Dorado as a projection: an image thrown out from the mind, an idea that played over the emptiness of *terra incognita,* and then over the faces and landscapes that he actually found there, imbuing them with hidden meanings as well as conscious ones. Alchemy offers a parallel imagery—one in which Ralegh was well versed—and Jung's interpretations offer a key to its hidden meanings. The "Golden King" that Ralegh sought is seen as a coded image of psychic wholeness. This is how Jung interprets the figure in its alchemical guise. In *Mysterium Coniunctionis* (1956), a study of "the separation and conjunction of psychic opposites in alchemy," he writes:

> The apotheosis of the King, the renewed rising of the sun, means, in our hypothesis, that a new dominant of consciousness has been produced. . . . Consciousness is no longer under the dominion of the unconscious, in which state the dominant is hidden in the darkness, but has now glimpsed and recognized a supreme goal. The apotheosis of the King depicts this change and the resultant feeling of renewal. . . . The renewed King corresponds to a renewed consciousness.

To Jung, the redeeming or rescuing of the "King" represents a process of internal transformation or growth in the alchemist himself. We find this expressed in Lambspringk: the alchemist who rescues the "unicorn" and "deer" (glossed as spirit and soul) from the forest "may justly be called a Master, for we rightly judge that he has attained the golden flesh, and may triumph everywhere." This reminds me of Ralegh's Golden King, who is "all shining from the foot to the head."

In this sense the search for El Dorado proves to be an *entrada* into the difficult interior of the self—"the land within," to use Ralegh's own phrase—in search of "wholeness" and "renewal." I do not claim to know exactly how these ideas might be applied to Ralegh's psychological circumstances in 1594–95, but I think it is plausible that they do apply. He departs on a note of despair, of breakdown even. The fruits of his life had "fallen from the tree"; only the "dead stock" remained. "I did therefore even in the winter of my life undertake these travels." Against this imagery of winter and barrenness one places the perception of America that emerges from the *Discoverie*— a sense of fecundity, of luxuriance, of an Arcadian lavishness in the people and landscape—and sees in it a corresponding imagery of spring and renewal.

Something of this is felt in Ralegh's own comments on the Golden Age, in the *History of the World*.

Our younger years are our Golden Age, which being eaten up with time, we praise those seasons which our youth accompanied; and indeed the grievous alternations in ourselves, and the pains and diseases which never part from us but at the grave, make the times seem so differing and displeasing.

This arrives at a similar idea of loss and renewal: the Golden Age as a primal state lost not in the mists of antiquity but in one's own childhood, a state of innocence and happiness anterior to the "grievous alternations" of adulthood. Is this what Ralegh was seeking in the virgin world of Guiana, a "country that hath yet her maiden-head"?

FOR THE alchemists, this redeeming or rescuing of the "King" entailed a conquest of the corrupt and divided nature of matter: the "raw stuff" on which they worked, breaking down the solidity of the four material elements to release the hidden, spiritual "fifth element," the *quinta essentia,* or quintessence. The "privy quintessence," says the Elizabethan alchemist William Bloomfield, must be "forced out of chaos dark," where it resides "as in a prison."

   This corrupt, chaotic, unredeemed aspect of Nature is represented in alchemical symbolism as a monster: typically a snake or a toad or a dragon, its reptilian greenness representing the "raw" or "crude" state that must be worked on by the alchemist.

   Ripley speaks of killing a "serpent within a well"—

> Thus ye shall go to putrefaction,
> And bring the Serpent to reduction

—and of a toad in a "secret den" whose "poisoned bulk" must be "brast" (burst) with corrosive juices. It is called a toad, Philalethes explains,

> because it is an earthly body, but most especially for the black stink-ing venomosity which this operation comes to in the first days of its preparation. . . . This operation is by ingenious Artists called extrac-tion of natures, and separation, for the Tincture begins now to be separated from the body.

Most commonly, the raw stuff is depicted as a dragon. This is the "old Dragon, which hath a long time had his habitation among stones, and creepeth out of the caves," as described by the Rosicru-cian Johann Thölde (a.k.a. Basil Valentine); and the "poison-dipping dragon" of the anonymous *Aurelia Occulta* (also attributed to "one of

33. "A black beast in the forest." Engraving from Lambspringk's De Lapide
Philosophico

the Rosy Brothers"), which addresses the alchemist with these
alarming words: "If you do not have exact knowledge of me, you
will destroy your five senses with my fire. From my snout there
comes a spreading poison that hath brought death to many." In
Lambspringk's *De Lapide,* the dragon is the first of the creatures
encountered in that symbolic forest: "You straightway behold a
black beast in the forest." The alchemist must slice off its head:

"When the beast's black hue has vanished in a black smoke, the sages rejoice." In the engraving of the "Lord of the Forests," the dragon is shown beneath his feet. He says: "I have trodden the venomous dragon underfoot."

I have suggested that Ralegh's journey into America might be seen—seen by him, that is—as a kind of alchemical quest, and I have shown how the image of the Golden King is a compelling common denominator between the alchemist's *opus* and the search for El Dorado. I am struck now by the possibility that these alchemical creepy-crawlies might also be part of the story—that they might indeed solve the puzzle of that ugly, wriggling "creature" that one discerns at the center of Ralegh's chart.

According to Jung, these alchemical creatures are part of an archetypal imagery that presents the unconscious as something hidden, ugly, and bestial, a lurker in the den. The "slaying" of them symbolizes a confrontation with these dark and disturbing aspects of the self. This confrontation is dangerous—*"nonulli perierunt,"* not a few have perished—but is essential to psychological growth and renewal, that inner process of transformation that he sees as the true business of alchemy.

I have puzzled over the creature in the map because it seems so inappropriate: the way it sits there, grotesque and faintly comic, at the symbolic heart of the quest; the way it seems to represent the actual goal of the quest. We can now see how this might make sense. If Ralegh's "discovery" of Guiana is—as one often feels it to be—a journey of self-discovery, then the creature in the map really does represent the goal of his quest: that part of himself that is hidden and unknown.

It is doubtless a cliché to say that the true gold of El Dorado is self-knowledge, but that is what one arrives at. It is either the point or the pointlessness of the search: to look at last into the waters of Lake Manoa, in search of its treasures, and to see only your own face staring back at you.

I am not saying that Ralegh, or whoever drew the map for him, actually intended such a meaning. The imagery of alchemy is a dream language, a disclosing of unconscious contents. This creature hovers over the physical surface of the map, somewhat in the way that the legend of El Dorado plays over these journeys upriver. It is a projection, a figment, a kind of haunting. Like El Dorado itself, it is not really there at all. There is just an old drawing of a lake, the ink now faded to the color of ash.

Epilogue

*   *   *

A S AN actual destination, little is heard of the "golden city" of El Dorado after the end of the sixteenth century. A few sporadic revivals apart, belief in its existence faded in the light of so many arduous disproofs. The intertwined stories of Berrio and Ralegh constitute the last chapter of that strangely actualized myth. The search for gold continued, of course—not least at Lake Guatavita, the original source of the legend. The latest attempt to plumb the lake's treasures was made in 1965, by American diver Kip Wagner of the Real Eight Corporation salvage company, but the search was no longer wrapped in this imagery of golden kings and lost cities.

The name, often compressed into a single word, "Eldorado," lives on as a kind of folk memory, conveying an idea of riches, of quests, of exotic obsessions, as in the phrase "it became his Eldorado." A glance at the back of *The Times Atlas of the World* shows its popularity as a place name, usually in connection with a gold strike. It is found not just in Venezuela, but also in the United States (eight sites), Mexico (two), Canada, Argentina, Brazil, Zimbabwe, and the Philippines. It has also been the name of a famous gold diggers' saloon in San Francisco; of a Danish nudist magazine of the 1950s; of a brand of ice cream; of a model of Cadillac, as in the Jonathan Richman song "Pablo Picasso"—

> The girls go the colour of an avocado
> When he drives down the street in his Eldorado

—and of a TV soap opera set among the expatriate English of the Costa del Sol, which became a byword for awfulness and was pulled by the BBC in the summer of 1993.

In Ralegh himself there was a separation—one has perceived its emergence during the journey itself—between his belief in El Dorado and his fascination with the reality of South America. After his return we hear nothing more of that "great and golden city," but a good deal more about Guiana per se: as a potential English settlement, as a region rich in gold and other "commodities," as a vivid particularization of the New World. The thrill of it never quite dimmed. For a while it was an enthusiasm shared by many, in the restless, expansive mood of the late 1590s. John Donne's epigram, "Calez & Guayana," written shortly after the Cádiz ("Calez") expedition of 1596—

> . . . From spoil of th' old world's farthest end
> To the New World your kindled valours bend

—sums up the mood, though there was also much skepticism about this "long-spoken-of Guiana voyage and other such-like India piracies."

Scarcely a year went by during his life without some kind of effort or scheme or enterprise toward Guiana. In January 1596, Lawrence Keymis was dispatched with the pinnace *Darling* and a couple of other small vessels. According to Rowland Whyte, this expedition had the backing of Lord Treasurer Burghley, who ventured £500; of Sir Robert Cecil, who contributed "a new ship bravely furnished"; and of Sir George Carey and Lord Thomas Howard. Keymis reconnoitered the rivers east of the Orinoco, and posited a yet more easterly location for Manoa, among the headwaters of the Essequibo and Rupununi in present-day Guyana.

In December 1596, a third expedition went out, under Captain Leonard Berry. There were probably others undocumented. In 1598, for instance, a Dutch ship met a galley owned by Ralegh off St. Lucia. There was also talk of John Gilbert returning to the area. According to a Catholic newsletter, written in November 1598, he was "preparing with all speed to make a voyage to Guiana" with a fleet of thirteen vessels, intending "to inhabit it with English people." This is probably a false rumor; at any rate, nothing came of it. Around this time, some Dutchmen arriving on the Guiana coast were welcomed by natives who ran toward them crying, "Anglee! Anglee!"—testimony, as they themselves observed, of the esteem Ralegh still enjoyed out there.

Ralegh's detention in 1603—on trumped-up charges arising from the Catholic conspiracies against King James known as the Main Plot and the Bye Plot (or, as we would say, subplot)—did not diminish his interest in the region. Both Harriot and Keymis were in frequent contact with him during his imprisonment. In 1607 he wrote to Cecil (now Lord Salisbury), offering to return to Guiana to locate a certain "mountain of gold" he had seen twelve years previously. He estimated the cost of the voyage as £5,000, of which he could muster a third. Further letters followed—to James's favorite, Lord Haddington; to Secretary of State Sir Ralph Winwood; and to the King himself—outlining once more the potentials of Guianian wealth. Anticipating that his claims would be interpreted as an excuse to get out of the Tower, he said: "I am more in love with death than with falsehood."

The idea rumbled on for a while, and finally, in 1616, after nearly thirteen years in the Tower, Ralegh received royal permission for the voyage. There were two stipulations: that there should be no clashes with the Spanish, which would threaten James's policy of peace; and that there should be tangible rewards in the form of Guianian gold. In the event, neither of these conditions was met. The expedition was a fiasco, and Ralegh returned from his second visit to South America a broken man, facing almost certain execution. He had traveled "under peril of law," and the failures of his expedition—together with rumors of his intended desertion to a foreign power—gave James ample pretext to renew the death sentence that had been passed on him, then reluctantly commuted, back in 1603.

The fleet sailed in June 1617: some twenty ships, led by Ralegh's newly built flagship, the 440-ton *Destiny*. Among his captains was

NEVVES
Of Sr. VValter Rauleigh.

WITH
The true Defcription of GVIANA:

As alfo a Relation of the excellent Gouernment, and much hope of the profperity of the Voyage.

Sent from a Gentleman of his Fleet, to a moft efpeciall Friend of his in London.

From the Riuer of Caliana, *on the Coaft of* Guiana, *Nouemb.* 17. 1617.

LONDON,
Printed for *H. G.* and are to be fold by *I. Wright,* at the figne of the Bible without New-gate. 1618.

34. A last image of Ralegh in South America

his elder son, Walter junior, invariably known as Wat, an impulsive young man aged twenty-three; and the veteran scholar-explorer Lawrence Keymis. The outward journey was a nightmare: storms and fever-deaths and discontent among a crew that he called a "scum of men." Ralegh himself, weak from his years of confinement, contracted a "violent calenture," and for three weeks "never received any sustenance but now and then a stewed prune, but drank every hour day and night, and sweat so strongly as I changed my shirts thrice every day and thrice every night."

By November they were coasting off South America. One of the captains, Peter Alley, suffering an "infirmity of his head," was sent home aboard a Dutch ship. He carried with him a newsletter, dated November 17, written by a "gentleman of his fleet" (identified only as "R.M."). Arriving at Portsmouth three months later, Alley promptly sold this to a publisher. It was printed up as a pamphlet, *Newes of Sir Walter Rauleigh,* the title-page woodcut dwelling on his sunken-eyed, careworn features.

Anchored off Cayenne, too sick to venture onshore, he was struck once more by the warmth and hospitality of the natives. He was coaxed back to health. He tasted once again armadillo meat and pineapple. He wrote to his wife: "To tell you I might be here King of the Indians were a vanity, but my name hath still lived among them." This strikes the last poignant note of Ralegh in South America, before the full tragedy of the voyage overtakes him.

The fleet moved on to Trinidad. An expedition set off inland: two hundred and fifty men, under the command of Keymis, following the old delta route up to the Caroní. There, on January 2, 1618—in circumstances still not wholly explained—Keymis's men did what had explicitly been forbidden: They attacked and overran the Spanish settlement of San Thomé. In the course of the assault, Wat Ralegh was killed. According to an eyewitness he was shot through the throat by a Spanish musketeer. He had advanced with "unadvised daringness" and "was unfortunately welcomed with a bullet, which gave him no time to call for mercy to Our Heavenly Father for his sinful life."

Meanwhile, aboard the *Destiny,* Ralegh waited for news. His log-book of the journey (brief and factual, in no way comparable to the *Discoverie*) ends abruptly on February 13. That night or the next day, probably, he received the fateful dispatch from Keymis.

"God knows," he wrote to his wife, "I never knew what sorrow meant till now."

Keymis and his party were back with the fleet by March 2. He found Ralegh in grim mood. What followed can be reconstructed from Ralegh's own accounts. "I told him," Ralegh writes, "that he had undone me." Keymis had already penned an apologia for his actions, but Ralegh refused to endorse it. "I will not favour or colour in any sort your former folly," he said.

"Is that your resolution?"

"It is."

"I know then, Sir, what course to take."

Keymis retired to his cabin on a higher deck. A few moments later there was the sound of a pistol shot. Ralegh sent someone to investigate. Keymis was lying on his bed, apparently unhurt. He said he had shot the pistol out of his cabin window, "to cleanse it." Half an hour later, however,

> his boy going into his cabin found him dead, having a long knife thrust under his left pap, through his heart, and the pistol lying by him, with which it appeared he had shot himself, but the bullet, lighting upon a rib, had but broken the rib and went no further.

Thus the story of Ralegh and El Dorado ends with the death of his son and the suicide of his loyal captain Keymis. It was as it had been foretold by the ferocious Aguirre half a century earlier: "There is nothing on this river but despair."

Ralegh returned to England: "a broken mind, a sick body." The process of law—the formalizing of James's long-held desire to be rid of him—was swift. He was beheaded in the Palace Yard at West-minster on Thursday, October 29, 1618. The date chosen was the Lord Mayor's Day, in the hope that the pageants might draw away the people from his execution. The ruse did not succeed; the yard was packed, and accounts of the scene, and of his speech from the scaffold, are many. When he first placed his head on the block, he was facing west. Tradition demanded that the condemned man faced east, toward redemption. "So the heart be right," he said, "it is no great matter which way the head lieth."

His severed head was placed in a red velvet bag, and kept by his widow until her death in 1647. It is said that it now lies, together with the body of his younger son Carew and some of his grandchildren, beneath the floor of St. Mary's Church in West Horsley, Surrey, close to the manor house where Carew lived. If you visit the church today you will find nothing to commemorate this curious relic. The side chapel that is supposed to contain the Ralegh vault is filled with lumber; the floor was partly concreted over in the 1940s to accommodate a new church organ; and so the trails of history and folklore wind up in this junk room in a church in Surrey.

Of the others who traveled with him to South America in 1595 there is little further news. His second-in-command George Gifford prospered briefly, and was in action at Cádiz in 1596 under Lord Admiral Howard. He was knighted there, as was his colleague from the Guiana adventure, John Gilbert. The following year Gifford was wounded in a brawl, incurring royal disfavor. In 1601 he was associated with the Earl of Essex's faction, and was thought of as a "man of resolution" who might help to spring Essex from prison. His last years were a story of debt and decline: He mortgaged his manor houses, suffered a £2,000 fine for customs evasion, and was, in his own words, "as deep in disgrace as years." He died in 1613, at the age of sixty. It was sourly remarked that "his loss would have been less, both for himself and his posterity, if he had gone thirty years ago."

John Gilbert, knighted at Cádiz in June 1596, became a landowner in September, inheriting Compton Castle in Devon on the death of his uncle, the elder Sir John. It was probably some time after this that he married. His wife was Alice Molyneux, daughter of a rich Lancashire landowner, and a relative of the globe maker

Emery Molyneux. Thereafter he settled into the Gilbert mold: maritime ventures, land deals, law suits, quarrels. He captained the *Antelope* in the Atlantic in 1597, and owned a privateer called (somehow characteristically) the *Refusal*. He was a forceful businessman, and profligate with the profits. "Use your fortune wisely," his uncle cautioned. "I hear you spend vainly and use carousing: it is time to be wise and look to your estates." His hot blood continued to make him enemies. Rowland Whyte reports a squabble with one of Essex's cronies, Sir Christopher St. Lawrence, in 1599. He had taunted Lawrence to stab him "because he did not pledge my Lord of Essex." He behaved, said Whyte, with "great unadvisedness." In 1606 he visited Ralegh in the Tower: their last recorded meeting. This is roughly the time of his portrait, with its rather chilly, reclusive feel, its hint of disappointment. Two years later he contracted smallpox. He died in London on July 5, 1608, and was buried in Devon a fortnight later. He was still only in his mid-thirties—an eventful, blustery, fast-burning Elizabethan life.

Antonio de Berrio died at San Thomé in about 1597; Captain John Clarke is heard of in Admiralty Court documents for a few years; Nicholas Mellechapp the surgeon was living in Shropshire in 1618; Thomas Harriot died of cancer in 1621.

Francis Sparry finally won his release from prison in Madrid—part of an exchange deal with Spanish prisoners—and made it back to England in late 1602 or early 1603, some eight years after he had set out from Plymouth aboard the *Lion's Whelp*. He penned a brief account of his adventures, later published by Samuel Purchas. While in Madrid he had married a local woman, and in about 1600 had a son by her. Whether they traveled to England with him is not known. Thereafter he fades from view. A "Frances Sparry" was living at Northfield, Worcestershire—close to the family seat at King's Norton—and had a son, John, who was baptized there in January 1614. This could be Francis, or it could equally be his female cousin Frances.

"Old Francis Sparry" was buried in the little Midlands town of Dudley on May 21, 1648. If this is the Sparry of Guiana he was then seventy-nine years old. He had lived through three reigns, and the turmoil of the Civil War, lost in provincial obscurity, his adventures all but forgotten. The sound of a storm outside his window would sometimes remind him of those nights on the Orinoco, when the roaring of the river woke him in his hammock.

APPENDIX 1:

THE SPARRY PAPERS

There are two accounts of Ralegh's *entrada* given by Francis Sparry. Both are preserved at the Archivo General de Indias (AGI) in Seville.

The first was his "declaration," made at Margarita Island on or shortly after February 25, 1596. This was incorporated into a longer report sent to Spain by Pedro de Liaño, *licenciado* of Margarita. Much of the report is based on other witnesses, but the details of Ralegh's expedition come solely from Sparry, as Liaño acknowledges.

The second and longer account appears in Sparry's "petition" (*memorial*) to the King of Spain, dictated at the town prison in Madrid. It is undated, but from external evidence can be assigned to late 1600 or 1601. It was discovered by P. Beyle in the AGI miscellany, the *Indiferente General,* and published in 1943 (*Revista de Indias,* No. 11). It is given here for the first time in English.

In the same bundle is an "interrogation" of Sparry by Licenciado Benavides, somewhat later than the above (c.1602). This has nothing further on the expedition itself, but adds some autobiographical remarks, and some interesting comments about the Orinoco Indians.

A. Extract from Licenciado Pedro de Liaño's report, c. April 1596 (AGI, Santo Domingo: Cartas de la Isla de Margarita, 1537–1610, Estante 54/4, Legajo 6. English translation in Venezuela Boundary Commission papers, BM, Additional MS 36317, f.61 et seq.).

After being three days in the port [Port of Spain, Trinidad], Guaterral set sail and went to Punto del Gallo in that island, where he anchored with the ships. He built a fort there on the shore and landed a piece of artillery, all the Indians of the island assisting him by bringing provisions and other goods from the country. After he had been there fifteen days, he equipped five barges and sailed with them and some of his soldiers up the Orinoco, [the estuary of] which is situated on the mainland at a distance of two and a half or three leagues from the island. He sailed up the river with the barges as far as the settlements of a *cacique* called Moriquito, which stand at a distance of more than eighty leagues from the mouth of the Orinoco. He spent thirty days in this voyage, because they sailed by day only. When he arrived at that settlement, he sent an Indian (whom he had brought with him from England) and another, whom he took in the Island of Trinidad, to the *cacique* Moriquito [i.e., Topiawari] to inform him how matters stood there. The *cacique* arrived at the end of four days accompanied by three or four hundred Indians, bringing him many articles of food, and offering him his friendship, and declaring to him that there was a large quantity of gold to be found in the country, that he should land, that the mine was a league inland, and that he would go with him to show it to him. He went there and they carried away three or four tons of earth from a mountain and put it on board to carry it to England as a specimen.

The *cacique* gave Guaterral three or four ingots of gold, telling him that all that country was his and that they would be happy if he would come and settle there, and he would surrender it to him. Guaterral gave the *cacique* and Indians some curious things which he had brought from England, and they remained in fast friendship and shook hands; the *cacique* promising to give up that country to him, and that all should serve him. Guaterral promised to return in the month of March of the following year with a thousand men, to settle there, and as a proof that he should do so he left two Englishmen under his charge. One was twenty-five years old, and the other sixteen. They were to learn the language, and acquaint themselves with the region, so that they could act as interpreters on his return. The *cacique* gave Guaterral one of his sons who was eighteen or twenty years old, and three other Indians, whom he took away with him. They then took leave, and the two Englishmen remained among the Indians. The *cacique* and all the other Indians treated them most kindly, and gave them presents and respected them. In the month of June of the year 1595, the younger of the two Englishmen [Hugh Godwin], going out into the country in English dress, was attacked by four tigers who tore him to pieces. The other Englishman, when sailing one day down the river, was seized by four Spaniards, who brought him to the Island of Margarita on the 25th of February of this year, where his declaration was taken. He related most of what has been narrated.

B. Extract from Francis Sparry's Petition to King Philip II of Spain, c. 1600 (AGI, Indiferente General, Legajo 747).

Petition of service presented to Your Majesty by Captain Francisco Sparri, Englishman, detained at the town-prison of Madrid, concerning eight hundred thousand ducats and the discovery of the kingdoms bordering on the Orinoco River in the Indies; all of which he has offered to Your Majesty by the hand of Licentiate Miguel de Heredia, priest of the General Hospital of this town of Madrid. It states as follows.

In the year of ninety two[1] Count Guatre Rale, Englishman, Captain of the Guard of the Queen of England, set sail with four ships, of 200, 100, 80 and 60 tons respectively, and in them went in search of the Orinoco River and the kingdoms of El Dorado. Having discovered the entrance to the river, he left the four ships anchored at its mouth,[2] and embarked his men in boats [*lanchas*] which he brought on purpose from England to ascend the said river, which has many shoals and in some parts cannot be navigated with ships.

Thus he entered the river to a distance of 130 leagues,[3] and in this place there gathered a large number of Indians in canoes, to prevent any further ascent of the river. The Indians, seeing what damage the muskets of the English might do to them, promptly turned their

1. The date is a deliberate error by Sparry, and need not throw doubt on other statements. He is exaggerating the length of time he spent in Guiana, and therefore his fitness for the "service" he offers the King. His later statement that he was with the Indians "three years and seven months" is precisely parallel. In his "interrogation" he repeats the falsehood, and adjusts his own age at the time accordingly.

2. This is loose. One of the four ships, the *gallego,* was converted in Trinidad for the expedition upriver. Sparry omits any mention of Ralegh's being at Trinidad, not wishing to stir up memories of the English attack on San José.

3. *"Entro el rio adentro 130 leguas."* I give the most obvious translation, but it is possible Sparry means he "entered the river which is 130 leagues within," i.e., the Caroní. Cf. his later description of the gold mountain as *"una sierra del rio adentro."*

backs, and went and hid themselves in various parts of the river and the mountainous land. The English chased after them, and caught five or six, and brought them to Guaterrale. He embraced them, and made show of much love towards them, and of desiring their friendship. And he offered them gifts, giving them some things that were brought from England, such as little mirrors, combs and knives. He gave these as tokens, to let them understand that he did not come to do evil, but to win their friendship, and to give them those things which they needed in that country.

These Indians, thus soothed, brought along others, with whom he dealt in the same way, and so the news spread that the English were good friends. Then the king of that region [i.e., Topiawari] came, with other Indian chiefs, and these in particular Guaterrale embraced, and offered gifts, and made treaties with them, in the name of Her Majesty the Queen of England, by which the English could come there freely to trade. And he found out from them where there was gold, and learning that there were gold-bearing stones in a mountain near the river, he led his boats there. Seeing these stones to contain gold metal, and all in a mountain adjacent to the river, he had the boats loaded with them, and determined to return with them to England to assay them. And because of this he dealt cautiously[4] with the Indians, saying that to be sure of the peace they had struck between them, they should leave hostages with one another; that he would leave two principal Englishmen with them, and they should give him two sons. They were content with this agreement. They gave him two royal sons, which he took to England, and he left with them Captain Francisco Esparri, being a man skilled in languages,[5] and instructed him to take care to learn the language, and to find out the secrets of the region, during the year that would elapse before his return. And so Esparri remained, with another man as his companion or servant,[6] who was later eaten by tigers.

---

4. *"De cautela,"* "with caution," carries also an overtone of cunning or deceit.

5. *"Por hombre plático."* The adjective, no longer current, derives from *platicar,* to talk or converse. This word can be used for formal addresses, lectures, etc., or simply just for chatting. I am not sure whether Sparry is describing himself as a linguist or just a good conversationalist. Cf. Ralegh's estimation of him: He "could describe a country with his pen."

6. Hugh Godwin or Goodwin.

Guaterrale returned to England, where he assayed the stones, and found that they contained much gold. This is affirmed by Doña Maria Carillo, wife of Don Sancho de Arce, because she witnessed it during the time of her captivity in England, and saw with her own eyes the Indians brought as hostages, and the house where the assay took place. Then Count Sicilia, the Queen's most intimate adviser, who was assisting Guaterrale to return to the kingdoms of El Dorado, prevented him from doing so, because of the passion and envy he felt when he saw that he [Ralegh] had come back so rich.[7] This was why the English did not return to those kingdoms, and for this reason Francisco Esparri was with the Indians three years and seven months,[8] always occupied in the tasks Guaterrale had left him to perform, and entered into the interior of the region, pretending that he wished to make the same accords with other Kings, of which he says there are many in the region. The Indians were pleased by this, and gave favourable reports of him to others, and with this strategy he travelled in many parts of those kingdoms, and was very well treated by the chief Indians, and received many gifts from them in return for some little mirrors, knives and combs which he traded. The gifts he received were bars of gold, and precious stones of various types and colours, and balsam. This was in eight hundred and eight calabashes, altogether a million ducats' worth.[9] This gold which they gave him came down from other, much richer mines, further into the interior than he travelled. And all this million and treasure Francisco Esparri

7. "Count Sicilia" is clearly Sir Robert Cecil. Sparry's idea that Cecil felt "envy" (*envidia*) at Ralegh's success is not backed up by the evidence, and makes little sense anyway as a reason for Ralegh's failing to return to the Orinoco. This is partly expedient—Sparry needs to explain to his captors why the English did not come back—but may also in an exculpation of Ralegh in Sparry's mind.

8. See above, note 1.

9. A *calabasa,* or calabash, is a gourd, i.e., a pumpkin or squash hollowed for use as a container. It appears here to indicate a specific quantity or value of treasure, viz.,1,000 ducats. The title of Sparry's petition refers to him offering the King 800,000 ducats. This sum is not mentioned in the text, and must be a computation from the 808 calabashes mentioned here. I have therefore interpreted Sparry's *"junto un millón"* to mean "altogether a million ducats' worth," a rounding upward of the value, but Sparry may just mean that there was an awful lot of it. Cf. *"este millón y thesoro,"* "this million and treasure," in the next sentence. In the plural, *millones* meant imported goods, especially precious metals from the New World. The Spanish excise board was the *sala de millones.*

buried, in a certain place which cannot be mistaken on the bank of
the said river. And no longer trusting in the return of the English,
seeing so much time had passed without them coming, and sick of
living among those savages, he went downriver to see if there were
any English ships coasting around the mouth, or Spaniards, thinking
it preferable to be their prisoner than to remain among the Indians.

And there it happened that he encountered the soldiers of Antonio
Berrio, Governor of Trinidad. They took from him sixty thousand
ducats, in precious commodities which he and some Indians were
carrying, and sent him as a prisoner to Spain.

(This concludes the narrative portion of Sparry's petition. The rest
is a restatement of his offers to the King, together with assertions
of his newfound loyalty to Spain and Catholicism.)

C. Extract from Interrogation of Francis Sparry by Licenciado Benavides de Benavides, c, 1602 [AGI, Indiferente General, Legajo
747].

Asked where he was born, he said he was from the city of London in
England.

Asked of what people he was, he said that his forebears were gentlemen and that he was a kinsman [*deudo*] of Guaterrale, Captain of
the Guard of the Queen.[10]

Asked what people Guaterrale had brought into those kingdoms
[of El Dorado], he said there were two hundred and fifty people[11] in
canoes, because the rest of the people remained to guard the four
ships in which they had come to the mouth of the river.

Asked if he had learned the language [of the Indians] during his

10. Unless there is some unknown connection, this appears to be an exaggeration of a
tenuous link via his uncle, Richard Sparry of Totnes, whose first wife's niece married
Ralegh's cousin Charles Champernowne.
11. A confusion in the telling, perhaps, rather than a deliberate falsehood. We know from
Ralegh that only 100 men went up the Orinoco. The figure of 250 is, as I have conjectured,
the number of the whole expedition.

time there, he said he had not learned it perfectly, but enough to understand it well.

Asked how many leagues he entered into the interior of the country, he said more than 120 leagues, and that there was much peopled land in the interior which he could not know or reach.

Asked if the natives of those regions went clothed, he said that they did not go fully clothed, because they went all in skins, and the chiefs were distinguished by holding their right arm raised and held in that hand a flintstone.

Asked if they lived gathered together in settlements, he said yes, and that some of the settlements are very large, and not very distant from one another, as two or three leagues or less, and that the houses are of cane-wattle [*chamiza*], resembling shepherds' huts in Spain, and each one occupies much land, for as well as containing their dwelling they have their patch of land where they sow maize.

Asked if they had horses or cattle or asses, he said no, but they had much wild game, both large and small, and poultry both of the Spanish kind and of the Indian kind.

Asked if they had weapons or tools, he said that the only weapons they have are bows and arrows, and that they have no sort of tools, but make do with flintstones and certain shells from the river, and with these they cut little things, and for big things they have no recourse but to set fire to them.

Asked if they had gold and silver, he said that he was not aware of any silver, but that of gold they had plenty, in many places, and especially in certain mines in the interior, of which he took much notice, and that the Indians only use gold for ornamentation [*galantería*] such as half moons used as nose-plugs and ear-rings.

Asked how they purified this gold, and if they extracted it with fire, he said that they only whittled the rock with their flintstones, and having thus separated the grains of gold from the rock they beat them with flintstones and made a paste, and from that they made either ingots of gold like a dice, or those half-moons which they wear, and that working this way they lost more than two parts of the gold, and that they then smelted it with fire.

Appendix 2:
RALEGH'S CHART

The chart in the British Museum (Add. MS 17940A) is drawn in ink on a sheet of vellum measuring approximately 27 inches long and 30 inches wide. The place names are almost certainly in Ralegh's own hand: the neat, small, semi-italic script found in his chemical notebooks, in the manuscript fragment of the "Ocean's Love for Cynthia," and so on. (Like most Elizabethans he used a variety of scripts.)

Its date can be fairly closely established. In the *Discoverie,* he refers to a map still in preparation: "Your Lordship [i.e., Lord Howard] shall receive a large chart or map, which I have not yet finished, which I shall most humbly pray your Lordship to secrete, and not to suffer it to pass your own hands." It will show, he says, information based on his own exploration of the Orinoco and its tributaries, and on what he has gleaned about the earlier Spanish expeditions of Quesada and Berrio.

> How all these rivers cross and encounter; how the country lieth and is bordered; the passage of Cemenes [i.e., Jiménez de Quesada] and of Berreo; mine own discovery, and the way that I entered; with all the rest of the nations and rivers.

This intention seems borne out by the chart as we have it. Ralegh must have been writing this some time before November 13, 1595, on which date he writes to Sir Robert Cecil:

> I know the plot [i.e., map] is by this time finished, which, if you please to, command from Harriot, that Her Majesty may see it. If it be thought of less importance than it deserveth, Her Majesty will

344

shortly bewail her negligence therein, & the enemy, by the addition
of so much wealth, wear us out of all.

I am not sure that these are one and the same map. Ralegh is
writing from Sherborne; Harriot is in or near London (perhaps at
the Earl of Northumberland's house, Syon Park, at Isleworth, where
he frequently resided). Given that the script of the extant map is
Ralegh's, and that the writing of place names is necessarily later
than the actual drawing of the map, I cannot see how it is being
"finished" a hundred miles away from Ralegh. It seems likely that
the "plot" that Ralegh writes of in November is actually a *copy* of
his own chart, being made for Sir Robert Cecil by (or under the
supervision of) Harriot.

Either way, the extant chart must have been completed some time
before the writing of this letter in mid-November 1595.

A later reference to it occurs in a letter from Harriot to Cecil,
dated July 11, 1596, shortly after the return of Lawrence Keymis's
second voyage to Guiana.

I have been framing of a chart out of some such of Sir Walter's notes
and writings which he hath left behind him [in London], his principal
chart being carried with him [to Sherborne?]. If it may please you, I
do think most fit that the discovery of Captain Kemish be added, in
his due place, before I finish it. It is of importance, & all charts which
had that coast before be very imperfect, as in many things else. And
that of Sir Walter's, although it were better in that part than any
other, yet it was done but by intelligence from the Indians, and this
voyage [i.e., Keymis's] was specially for the discovery of the same.

Here again we have two quite separate maps of Guiana—the earlier
map, completed by November 1595, and now described by Harriot
as Ralegh's "principal chart"; and a later map that Harriot was
"framing" in July 1596, based on Ralegh's notes from the voyage,
and into which he intended to incorporate Keymis's further "discovery" of the region.

It has been suggested (Skelton, p. 140) that the map in the British

Museum is the second, but this is unlikely since the handwriting is Ralegh's, and anyway the discoveries of Keymis are not noticeably incorporated in it. The map shows the Essequibo and other rivers explored by Keymis, but they are not given with any topographical detail, and are probably, as Harriot says, based on Indian information rather than reconnaissance.

The map was unknown to Sir Robert Schomburgk when he was preparing his edition of Ralegh's *Discoverie,* published by the Hakluyt Society in 1848. Just a year later, it was purchased by the British Museum. It was one half of a lot described as "two vellum rolls." (The other is a map of Patagonia drawn by William Hack in 1687.) At the time of the purchase, curiously, the map was not recognized as Ralegh's. In the British Museum's *Catalogue of Additions, 1848–53,* it is described erroneously as "a map of Guiana *circa* 1650." This catalog was published in 1868. Some time later a handwritten note was added to the copy now in the Manuscripts Reading Room. This deletes *"circa* 1650" and adds: "by Sir Walter Raleigh, post 1596. Holograph." (Still not quite accurate, the true date being 1595.) A yet later hand adds a question mark to "Holograph": wrongly, I think.

There is at least one other copy extant. It was formerly owned by Ralegh's philosophical friend Henry Percy, Earl of Northumberland. It remained in the family library until March 1927, when it was sold at Sotheby's. I do not know its whereabouts now, nor whether it is an actual copy of, or merely similar to, the British Museum map. If the former, it is perhaps the copy I have inferred from Ralegh's letter of November 13 1595; if the latter, it would be the map of mid-1596, incorporating Keymis's discoveries. Either way, it comes into the Northumberland collection from Harriot, who was closely connected with the Earl at this time.

MY COMPUTATION of the scale of the map, in the areas that Ralegh visited, is based on the following observations.

    1. **The Orinoco estuary.** In the *Discoverie* Ralegh describes the mouth of the Orinoco River: "from the first branch of the north to

the last of the south it is at least 100 leagues, so as the river's mouth is no less than 300 miles wide at his entrance into the sea." On the map, which marks the outflows of the Orinoco very clearly, I find the distance from the northernmost channel ("Amana") to the southernmost ("Wiini") to be slightly more than six inches. (I am measuring two sides of a notional triangle that has the Macareo headland as its apex.) This suggests that the Orinoco estuary is represented at a scale of roughly 1 inch to 50 miles.

2. **Trinidad.** Ralegh does not give any verbal statement of Trinidad's length, though he spent some time exploring the coastline, and intended a "discourse" on the island (which he mentions in the *Discoverie,* but which has not apparently survived), so he must have had a pretty good idea. In fact, Trinidad has an unusually uniform length (an average of 48 miles north to south; at its longest point 50 miles). On Ralegh's chart Trinidad is almost exactly one inch, so once again a scale is suggested of 1 inch to 50 miles.

3. **The Gulf of Paria.** Ralegh says: "We had as much sea to cross as betwixt Dover and Calais." This distance is axiomatically 20 miles. On the map the distance between Icacos Point, where the ships were anchored, and the easternmost outlet of the Amana or Manamo is just under half an inch.

4. **Assapana Island.** Ralegh correctly describes Assapana (i.e., Matamata Island, at the Macareo fork off the Orinoco) as "some five and twenty miles in length." It is half an inch long on the map.

5. **The *entrada.*** Ralegh twice states that at their farthest point, on the Caroní, they were 400 miles from their ships. This is seconded by Francis Sparry, who says they entered 130 leagues up the Orinoco (390 miles). This is an exaggeration—the actual length of the journey is little more than 200 miles—but that is the estimate they give. It is very hard to measure distances in the delta because the rivers are so circuitous. However, one can say that on Ralegh's chart the straight-line distance from Point Curiapan (i.e., Icacos) to the mainstream of the Orinoco is about four inches, and the distance from there to the mouth of the Caroní is also four inches. Thus what Ralegh believed to be a 400-mile journey is represented as eight map inches, which is once again the same scale.

I am not pretending that this is exact or scientific. There are other measurements that do not fit in—for instance, he estimates the distance from Cumaná to the Orinoco as 120 leagues (360 miles), but it is shown as only five inches on the map. Nor is it possible to establish a scale from the latitudinal lines on the map, since Ralegh's computations of latitude are rendered haywire by his insistence that the Guiana Highlands lie "under the equinoctial line" (i.e., on the equator), whereas in fact the relevant area is around 5 to 6° north. As noted elsewhere, this causes all sorts of geographical fudging in the *Discoverie,* for example, giving the latitude of southern Trinidad as 8° north (actually 10°), and so on.

These caveats aside, I believe that in the areas actually traveled by Ralegh, the map accurately represents his measurements of the distances involved, and that it does so at a scale of 1 inch to 50 miles.

APPENDIX 3:

THE FLEET

The sparse information provided by Ralegh about the ships of the Guiana Voyage can be summarized as follows. The admiral of the fleet, or flagship, was an unnamed vessel that he describes as "mine own ship"; its captain was Jacob Whiddon, its master John Douglas. The vice-admiral was the *Lion's Whelp,* owned by Ralegh's backer, Lord Howard, and captained by George Gifford. With them were two other ships: one described as "a small bark of Captain Cross's"; the other as an "old Spanish *gallego,*" under the command of Keymis.

To this can now be added the information provided by Francis Sparry's *memorial* (Appendix 1), in which he states that Ralegh "set out with four ships, of 200, 100, 80 and 60 tons."

This gives us, for the first time, the tonnages of Ralegh's fleet. Are they accurate? Tonnages are always approximate (the ton here is a unit of capacity, hence of size rather than weight—it measured, in theory at least, the ship's capacity to carry "tuns" or "hogsheads" of wine). So Sparry's figures are round, but are expected to be. He has no reason for lying about the size of the fleet, and every reason, since he had sailed with it himself, to be well informed about it.

In one case it is possible to test his estimate: The vice-admiral of the fleet, the *Lion's Whelp,* was variously rated at 120 tons and 90 tons, so Sparry is accurate enough in describing her as a 100-ton vessel.

Can we build upon this, perhaps, to identify the flagship that carried Ralegh to South America?

RALEGH TELLS us just one thing for certain: that she was one of his own ships. Sparry now adds that she was a ship of about 200 tons' capacity. We are disposed to believe him, but once again we need to test his estimate.

A 200-tonner is a large ship. It is bigger than the *Golden Hind* in which Drake "circuited the whole earth," bigger than the flagship

of the Virginia fleet of 1585. These were both around 160 tons. A
survey of English merchant shipping in the early 1580s (Friel, p.
30) shows that out of a total fleet of 1,630 vessels, only 19 had a
capacity of over 200 tons.

The report of the Portuguese fisherman, Juan Gonzaliques, confirms that she was a large vessel. He was briefly aboard the flagship,
as a prisoner, off the Canaries. He states that she was carrying a
"pinnace in two halves" on her deck. His interrogators at Plymouth
took this to be a "particular token" of the ship—in other words,
this detail confirmed in their minds the general truth of the fisherman's story. A pinnace is a variable term, but is something larger
than a normal ship's boat: typically twenty tons or so. This argues
that the flagship was a vessel with considerable deck capacity.

She must also have been carrying a large number of men at the
outset of the voyage. In the attack on San José in Trinidad, Ralegh
advanced with a fighting force of 100 men. At this point he had
only two ships, his own and the "small bark." The other two ships
had not yet arrived at Trinidad. Those hundred fighting men may
also include a few crew, but in general they are distinct from crew.
They are mainly soldiers—the "companies" referred to when Ralegh
stops at the Canaries "to relieve our companies with some fresh
meat"—with a few gentlemen in command. Judging from other
similar expeditions, the ship's crew—the "mariners"—is generally
about the same size as the expeditionary force per se. The situation
at Trinidad certainly supposes a workable crew being left aboard the
two ships while the 100 men advanced into unknown territory. One
can thus say, broadly, that the flagship and the bark were carrying
between them about 200 men.

How would this tally with Francis Sparry's estimate, which gives
the flagship and the bark a combined tonnage of 280 tons?

The Admiralty rule of thumb for costing out victuals was three
rations for every 5 tons of ship's weight. In other words, their norm
was that a ship of 100 tons had 60 men on board. Ralegh's 100-
ton *Falcon* in 1578 was a little more crowded: It carried 70 mariners,
soldiers, and gentlemen. In 1594 Sir Robert Dudley's 190-ton *Bear*
and a small pinnace carried between them 140 men; the pinnace

sank, and the whole lot had to travel in the *Bear,* and were very
cramped and "pestered." This is again slightly more than the Admiralty standard of 3:5. So too is Robert Harcourt's 80-ton *Rose,*
which carried 5 officers, 31 "land men" (i.e., settlers), 23 mariners,
and 2 Indians to Guiana in 1609.

These are American expeditions broadly similar to Ralegh's. They
suggest that the Admiralty norm is useful, but a bit low, for this
kind of expedition. These were crowded ships, and we know that
Ralegh expected seamen to put up with overcrowding. "Man may
not expect the ease of many cabins," he wrote in his *Observations
Concerning the Royal Navy.* "Two decks and a half is sufficient to yield
shelter and lodging for men and mariners." This was to avoid the
top-heavy, "high-charged" design, which had tiers of cabins.

By this reading, the Admiralty victuallers would expect a 200-
ton ship and an 80-ton ship to carry between them about 170 men,
but that ships on an American adventure of this sort would be carrying somewhat more—some 200, perhaps, which was the approximate figure arrived at from the evidence of the action at Trinidad.
There are many approximations in this argument, but it shows that
Francis Sparry's estimate of the flagship as a 200-ton vessel is confirmed by the meager scrapings of evidence from elsewhere.

To summarize, we are looking for a ship owned by Ralegh in
1595. It is described by Sparry as a 200-ton ship, and the fact that
it was large enough to accommodate a small pinnace on its main
deck, and a sizeable contingent of troops belowdecks, as well as its
regular crew, makes his estimate plausible. There are only two of
Ralegh's ships big enough to fit these criteria: the *Bark Ralegh* and
the *Roebuck.*

The *Bark Ralegh* was Ralegh's first ship: a purpose-built privateering vessel built to his specifications in 1582. Lacey describes the
ship as "sizeable, fast and heavily armed." She was a "private war-
ship," a "sea-raider." Her capacity was reckoned as 200–250 tons.
Ralegh sent her out for America as part of Sir Humphrey Gilbert's
expedition—Gilbert's last, of 1583—but the ship returned to port
after a few days (the reports vary as to why; either an "infection"
aboard or a summons from the Queen). The ship's master on that

occasion was Robert Davis, who is later connected with the Guiana Voyage as part of Preston's company. The *Bark Ralegh* may also have been the unnamed flagship, under Captain Amadas, of the First Virginia Voyage of 1584. In 1591 she was part of the squadron that raided the Azores, when Sir Richard Grenville died on the *Revenge* (the latter ship owned by Robert Davies of Lyme, probably the Robert Davis above). The *Galleon Ralegh* under Captain Middleton in 1592, described as an "armed merchantman" of 250 tons, is probably the same ship.

The *Bark Ralegh* fits the bill for the Guiana flagship: a seasoned oceangoer of about the right size and disposition. When Ralegh refers to the flagship as "mine own ship," does he perhaps mean, specifically, "the ship that bears my own name"? His failure to identify the flagship is certainly puzzling, and perhaps the answer is that this phrase *does* identify it, to the immediate understanding of the reader of 1596, as the *Bark Ralegh.* His assumption of his status as a household name would be typical enough.

But the *Roebuck* also has a claim to lie behind this casual notation: "mine own ship." It was the largest of his ships, the pride of his fleet. According to the privateering expert Kenneth Andrews, it was the best ship of its kind in the country, "probably superior to any merchantman in design and armament." The name of the ship is also Ralegh's own. The roebuck was Ralegh's heraldic beast, his crest; he *was* the Roebuck, just as Leicester was always the Bear (and his son set sail for America in the *Bear's Whelp). The Roebuck's* power and maneuverability were shown, under the captaincy of Sir John Burgh, in the famous capture of the *Madre de Dios* treasure carrack in 1592. (This *Roebuck* is clearly different from the ship of that name that was part of the Virginia voyage of 1585, which was a 140-ton flyboat, probably owned by Thomas Cavendish.)

Finally, as we have seen, the *Roebuck* served as the flagship of Burgh's expedition to Margarita in 1593, a voyage that I suggest is the first of the El Dorado reconnaissances. On that occasion, too, there was a large contingent of soldiers aboard (four hundred in three ships, according to the Spanish).

In general terms of suitability both ships could fit. The key witness is therefore Francis Sparry, and his estimate of the flagship's tonnage. His description fits the *Bark Ralegh* precisely, while the *Roebuck* is almost always rated at 300 or 350 tons. The latter is Ralegh's own reckoning, in 1592.

I conclude that the flagship of the First Guiana Voyage was probably the *Bark Ralegh*. This ship is not to be confused with the *Ark Ralegh,* built in 1588, purchased by the Queen and renamed *Ark Royal,* the first of that illustrious line.

THE *LION'S Whelp,* the only ship actually named in Ralegh's account of the journey, can be traced before and after the voyage.

On February 1, 1592, John Froude of Newport, Isle of Wight, deposed that he had previously served on five "viadges with reprisalls"—or privateering ventures—including one on "the *Lion's Whelp* of the Lord Admiral's," captained by Thomas Roche. This is probably the same as the *Lion's Whelp* that appears in a list of the Queen's ships drawn up on May 23, 1591. However, this states that the ship had been "lost in the storm of May 17." Either she turned up safe after all, or the subsequent history of the *Whelp* concerns a different ship, built or purchased by the Lord Admiral after 1591.

Lord Howard also owned a "man o' war" called the *White Lion,* 150 tons. She sailed with Drake's West Indian fleet in 1585, and was later in action against the Armada and at Cádiz. It is possible these two ships of the Lord Admiral's are twinned, that the *Lion's Whelp* is the smaller partner (or "cub") of the *White Lion.*

In 1592, the *Lion's Whelp* is listed, along with the *Roebuck,* in Ralegh's privateering fleet, but does not seem to have sailed on the *Madre de Dios* foray. She is rated at 120 tons, though a much later computation gives 90 tons. In 1593, she was sent by Lord Cobham to the Low Countries; she is described as the Lord Admiral's "bark." She is elsewhere described as a large pinnace, and in 1605 as a "frigate."

Having ventured to South America as Ralegh's vice-admiral in 1595, the *Whelp* was sent on another West Indies voyage in 1596–97. The captain on that expedition was Henry Reynolds, described as a servant of the Admiral's brother, Lord Thomas Howard. The *Whelp* also saw action against the Spanish at Cádiz in 1596. There the ship had forty-five men aboard, and a single commander who combined the role of captain and master. This was quite possibly George Gifford, who was certainly there at Cádiz, and was knighted for his services.

In 1601, Lord Admiral Howard sold the *Whelp* to the state. She was later refurbished at Chatham by the famous shipwright Phineas Pett, and was still serviceable in 1625, when the dying James I gave her to his favorite, Buckingham, himself now Lord Admiral. Her last intended voyage was in an expedition under William Hawkridge in search of the Northwest Passage to Asia—the dream that had fired Sir Humphrey Gilbert half a century before. However, James died, and Buckingham found that the gift of the *Whelp* had not been "ratified," so he had to start a whole legal process with the new King. He perhaps considered the vessel no longer worth it; nothing more is heard of her.

She lives an afterlife, however, for Buckingham instituted a class of warships named the Lion's Whelps. He may have liked the allusion to his coat of arms, a rampant lion, or he may have considered the original *Whelp* a lucky ship that had served an eminent former admiral. The Whelps are described as a "class of light men o' war of the fifth rate." There were ten of them—named *First Lion's Whelp* and so on—built during the late 1620s. They were built at the Duke's expense, though masted and armed from the Royal Stores. He spent about £7,000 on them. After his murder in 1628 they were taken into the Royal Navy. The appraisers drove a hard bargain, and the Buckingham estate received only £4,500 for them.

These Whelps flit in and out of view, a minor but sparky class. The *First* and *Second* were converted to chain ships for the Chatham "Barricado" in 1641. The *Fourth* went down off Jersey. The *Fifth* was also lost, with seventeen men drowned; there were complaints about the "mean sappy wood" used in her construction. The *Seventh* was blown sky-high off the coast of Suffolk, due to "negligence in the powder-store." One of the few survivors was her captain, Dawtry Cooper. It is said his reason was affected by the blast, in which he lost his son and nephew. He later captained the *Ninth,* where his eccentric behavior caused near mutiny.

The last of the Whelps, the *Tenth,* was built by Robert Tranckmore of Shoreham. In a naval list of 1651 she is described as 180 tons, and carrying eighteen guns and sixty men. She was active in the Civil War, coming over to the Royalists after the fall of Bristol in 1643, and recaptured by Parliament in 1645. In 1650, she was fitted out as a fire ship in the fleet that pursued Prince Rupert to Lisbon.

The *Tenth Whelp* ended her days as a convoy ship and dispatch boat to the Low Countries, and was "sold by the candle" for the sum of £410 on October 19, 1654.

THE TWO smaller ships have no precise identity. The "small bark" is presumably the eighty-ton vessel itemized by Sparry. Technically a bark (or barque) was a three-master, usually with the fore and main masts square-rigged and the mizzen rigged fore and aft, but in Elizabethan usage the term is too vague, the type too common, to make any useful comment about this vessel.

Ralegh describes the ship as a bark "of Captain Cross's." The biographers loosely assume this to mean he was the captain of the ship. He was a highly experienced seaman, and had traveled on Drake's West Indies voyage. However, he is nowhere else mentioned in the *Discoverie,* and when the "small bark' is next heard of, reconnoitering the Guiana coastline, she is under the command of Captain Calfield.

In the summer of 1595, Cross is listed as being "on the high seas" in the Queen's ship *Swiftsure,* and in October he is back in Plymouth, writing to Cecil from on board the *Swiftsure.* I have considered the possibilities—that he went with Ralegh's fleet but later joined up with another; that the *Swiftsure* was itself the "small bark" of the Guiana Voyage—but they do not quite jell, and there is nothing in his letter to Cecil to suggest he had been with Ralegh at all.

The evidence, such as it is, points to Captain Robert Cross as the owner, rather than the captain, of the "small bark." This may make it possible to identify her, but I have not so far been able to do so.

The smallest of the ships, sixty tons according to Sparry, is the one described by Ralegh as a "*gallego.*" It was probably a Spanish vessel captured during one of Ralegh's privateering voyages. Ralegh variously describes it as "small," "old," "bad," and "cast." The term *gallego* appears to be a loose usage. It is obviously a galley of some sort—i.e., a low-built ship designed for rowing as well as sailing—though the Spanish word for a galley is *galera.* Ralegh also calls it a "bad *galiota*," which suggests it was a galliot, defined in the *OED* as "a small galley used for swift navigation."

In Drake's ship list for his 1585 voyage there is a "galley or galliot," the *Duck.* She was a vessel of twenty tons. This was undoubtedly intended for reconnaissance work along the American coastline, and one assumes Ralegh's larger *gallego* was brought along for the same purpose, which indeed it served, pluckily, after being modified by the carpenters at the Icacos Point base camp.

NOTES

INTRODUCTION

1   **Ralegh**: Biographies of him are legion: 213 books and articles are listed by Armitage. The Victorian *Life* by Edwards is still the major documentary source. The early biographers (Naunton, Fuller, Aubrey) are a rich but often unverifiable source. Recent portrayals by Lacey, Winton, and Coote have contributed to the background of this book, though none of them examines this journey in any detail.

2   **"Spake broad Devonshire"**: Aubrey, p. 255.

2   **Variant spellings**: Willard Wallace, *Sir Walter Raleigh* (Princeton, N.J.: Princeton University Press, 1959), pp. 319–20.

CHAPTER 1: MAPPING EL DORADO

9   **Site near Boa Vista**: Chilean ethnologist Roland Stevenson, excavating burial grounds at Ilha de Maracá in northeast Brazil, has found petroglyph art, evidence of gold working, and shell fossils that suggest the former presence of a lake (*Folha de São Paulo*, May 27, 1993).

10   **Origins of El Dorado**: On the evolution of the legend from Chibcha lake-rites, see note to p.299 below.

10   **The Omagua**: Hemming, pp. 134–42. This advanced, gold working, Tupi-speaking tribe was contacted by Orellana and Von Hutten in the early 1540s, and became a focus for El Dorado expeditions in upper Amazonia.

10   **Manoa**: The origin of this name is variously interpreted. Schomburgk (p. 18) links it to the Mahanaos, a tribe formerly found around the upper Rupununi in Guyana; Ojer to the "river called Maroa" mentioned by Von Hutten in the 1540s (Ojer [1966], p. 472). The Manau Indians of the Río Negro, whose name is the origin of the Amazon port of Manaus, are often mentioned. More convincing is the observation first made by the Jesuit historian José Gumilla (*Historia Natural del Río Orinoco*, Vol. 1 [1791], p. 356), that *manoa* is simply the word for "lake" in the language

of the Achagua, whom Antonio de Berrio encountered near the Meta River in 1585. The name is Berrio's coinage, based on Achagua rumors about the Guiana Highlands. See Hemming, p. 153; Gregorio Hernández de Alba, "The Achagua," *Handbook of South American Indians*, Vol. 4 (1948), p. 412.

10   **Printed information**: The reference to Manoa in Juan Castellanos, *Elegías de Varónes Ilustres de Indias* (Part 3, Canto 2) dates from the mid-1580s, but the third part of the *Elegías* remained unpublished during Ralegh's lifetime. It is anyway a dismissal of the claims for Manoa as El Dorado.

10   **"Concerning the Eldorado"**: Harriot to Cecil, July 11, 1596 (HMC Cecil 6, p. 276).

11   **Domingo de Vera**: A captured report of his expedition to the lower Orinoco, and his possession of the "provinces of Guiana and Dorado" on behalf of Berrio, is appended to the *Discoverie* (pp. 105–10). It was "taken at sea" by Captain George Popham in 1594.

13   **Ralegh's chart**: See Appendix 2.

16   **Eleven days' march**: Report by Berrio, c. 1593: "Eleven days journey from where the Spaniards arrived, they [the Indians] say there is a very large lake, which is called the land of Manoa" (Harlow [see Sources/2], Appendix A/6).

CHAPTER 2: RALEGH'S AMERICA

20   **Forty years old**: A birth date of c. 1552–54 is still sometimes given, based on conflicting portrait inscriptions. He was actually born some time between June and November 1554. See Agnes Latham, "A Birth-date for Sir Walter Ralegh" (*Études Anglaises*, Vol. 9, 1956).

20   **"He had a most"**: Aubrey, p. 255.

20   **"He can toil"**: Cecil to Sir Thomas Heneage, September 21, 1592 (Edwards, Vol. 1, p. 154).

22   **"I have long been"**: Transcript of Ralegh's scaffold speech by Archbishop Richard Bancroft (Bodleian, Tanner MS; Lacey, p. 425).

22   **"Whom do you know"**: BM Harley MS 6849, ff. 183–90.

23   **"I marvel not"**: Preface to *Divers Voyages* (1582); Hakluyt, *Original Writing*, Vol. 1, p. 175.

24   **Virginia patent**: Hakluyt, *Principal Navigations,* Vol. 3, pp. 297–301. On the naming of Virginia, see Porter, pp. 223f.; Quinn, *Raleigh*, p. 63.

26   **English activities**: Lorimer, *English and Irish Settlement*, p. 9.

26   **"All that part"**: Hakluyt, *Original Writing*, Vol. 2, p. 255. On Mercator's

map (1587), Cape St. Augustine corresponds to modern Punto de Calcanhar, southeast of the mouth of the Amazon.

27 **"I spake with a captain"**: *Discoverie*, p. 22. Ralegh dates this conversation to the "year that my ships came first from Virginia," i.e., 1584. The passage from Hakluyt's *Discourse*, cited above, was taken verbatim from notes "gathered by an excellent French captain," possibly the same.

27 **Aguirre**: See study by Minta; contemporary Spanish accounts gathered in Elena Mampel González and Neus Escandell Tur, eds., *Lope de Aguirre: Crónicas* (Barcelona, 1981); doomy verse epic by Robert Southey, *Expedition of Orsua and Crimes of Aguirre* (1821); and portrayal by Klaus Kinski in the Werner Herzog film, *Aguirre: Wrath of God* (1972).

28 **Printed sources**: E.g., Cieza León, *Crónica del Peru* (1553). Ralegh also uses an unpublished Portuguese account of Aguirre from a "discourse of the West Indies" by Lopez Vaz, who was captured by the Earl of Cumberland's ships in 1587. See Lorimer, *English and Irish Settlement*, p. 12.

28 **"I remember it"**: *Discoverie*, p. 18.

29 **Antonio de Berrio**: See biography by Ojer; Hemming, pp. 151–77; Naipaul, pp. 10–62. Berrio's letters and reports are quoted from Harlow (see Sources/2), Appendix A.

CHAPTER 3: A GENTLEMAN OF SPAIN

32 **Pedro Sarmiento**: See biography by Clissold; Markham's introduction to the *Voyages*. His dealings with Ralegh can be followed in CSP Spanish (1580–86) and CSP Foreign (1586–88).

32 **Capture of Sarmiento**: Account by John Evesham in Hakluyt, *Principal Navigations*, Vol. 6, pp. 435–37.

34 **"Many years since"**: *Discoverie*, Epistle, sig. A3v.

35 **The "pretty jest"**: Ralegh, Book 2, Chapter 23, Section 4.

36 **Inca origin of Manoa**: *Discoverie*, pp. 9–12, 62–64. On the evolution of the Paititi legend, see Levillier; Gott, pp. 287–93.

38 **Cortés as precedent**: Hakluyt, *Original Writing*, Vol. 2, pp. 368–69; cf. Ramos Perez, "Walter Ralegh."

38 **"I cannot forbear"**: Ralegh, Book 5, Chapter 1, Section 8.

39 **"By land and sea"**: Clissold, p. 200. This petition is probably c. 1591. Sarmiento sailed for America in April 1592, commanding an escort of galleons; this is the last definite information about him.

39 **Retud's expedition**: Lorimer, "Ralegh's First Reconnaissance"; BM Add. MSS 36314–6, 36353.

Chapter 4: Love and Exile

41   **"O my America"**: Elegy 19, "Going to Bed" (Donne, Vol. 1, p. 119).

43   **Elizabeth Throckmorton**: The best account of her and the circumstances of the marriage is by Rowse. He draws on the diary of her brother Arthur, rediscovered in the 1950s. See also Pierre Lefranc, "La Date du Mariage de Sir Walter Ralegh" (*Études Anglaises*, Vol. 9, 1956). On Francis Throckmorton, see Conyers Read, *Mr. Secretary Walsingham*, Vol. 2 (Oxford: Clarendon Press, 1925), pp. 381–86.

44   **"S.W.R"**: Frequently quoted by the biographers, despite a dubious provenance. It was first printed by J. P. Collier in 1852 (*Archaeologia* Vol. 34, p. 161). Many, but not all, of his *trouvés* are now known to be forgeries.

44   **"I mean not"**: Letter to Cecil, March 10, 1592 (Edwards, Vol. 2, p. 46).

45   **Sherborne Castle**: See March; Lacey, pp. 199–202; Aubrey, p. 254. I am grateful to the archivist, Ann Smith, for information. The original of Simon Basil's "plott" of Sherborne, c. 1600, is at Hatfield House.

46   **The gardens**: On Harrington: Winton, p. 134. Gilbert claimed to have spent £700 of his own money in "making and planting of his [Ralegh's] walks and gardens" (*Acta Cancellariae*, ed. Montroe [1847], p. 206; Lacey, p. 201).

Chapter 5: Preparations

49   **Burgh's expedition**: PRO HCA 25/3, No. 9; 24/61, no. 51; Andrews, pp. 225–35; Ralegh, Book 4, Chapter 2, Section 16.

51   **Whiddon's expedition**: *Discoverie*, sig. A3v, pp. 4–8.

53   *Edward Bonaventure*: Barker's narrative in Hakluyt, *Principal Navigations*, Vol. 2, pp. 108–10; Andrews, pp. 287–91. This was her last voyage; she sank near Santo Domingo in November 1593. Ralegh's references to Whiddon's voyage as "the year before" (i.e., 1594) are presumably sloppy, a failure to revise in 1595 what he had first written in 1594. According to the "Old Style" year, which ran from March 25, and was still widely used, Ralegh landed at Trinidad in the last days of 1594 (March 22). He could at that point have described Whiddon's expedition as "the year before."

54   **Harriot's rutter**: BM Sloane MS 2292.

54   **Captain Marlowe**: He also supplied Harriot with a copy of his MS treatise, "Ars Naupegica, or the art of ship-building" (BM Add. MS 6788, f.39; Shirley, *Thomas Harriot*, p. 99).

54   **Captain Parker**: *Discoverie*, sig. A3v–A4; Andrews, pp. 214–19, 308–25.

56   **"For aught I hear"**: Letter to Lord Howard, June 21, 1594 (HMC Cecil 4, pp. 551–52).

57 **William Sanderson**: On his financing activities and the later lawsuit (PRO C24/372, Bundles 125–26; STAC 8/260, Bundle 4), see Shirley, "Sir Walter Raleigh's Guiana Finances."

58 **"I hope for my sake"**: HMC Cecil 4, p. 485.

59 **"This unfortunate year"**: Undated letter to Cecil, assigned to c. September 1594 (Edwards, Vol. 2, p. 101).

59 *Lion's Whelp*: Troughton to Cecil, June 24, 1594, HMC Cecil 4, p. 552.

60 **"Where by my last"**: Edwards, Vol. 2, p. 105. The reference to "places least infected" may indicate it was written during the summer of 1594, when the plague was, in Ralegh's words elsewhere, "very hot."

60 **"It is more"**: Letter to Cecil, endorsed "December 1594," HMC Cecil 5, p. 52.

60 **Robert Dudley**: See A. G. Lee, *Son of Leicester* (London: William Heinemann, 1964). Warner's edition gives accounts of the voyage by Dudley and by two of his crew, Captain Wyatt and Abraham Kendall. None of them actually went on the foray up the Orinoco, led by Captain Thomas Jobson, in February 1595. Jobson's sixteen-day *entrada* predated Ralegh's presence on the Orinoco by three months, but did not venture as far upriver.

61 **Dudley and Popham**: Warner, p. 105. Dudley states that Jobson entered the Orinoco using Popham's "discoverie" [i.e., rutter] of the coast; yet also that Popham's ship joined the fleet, off Trinidad, some days after Jobson had set out. One infers that Dudley had the rutter in his possession when he left England. Popham had captured Spanish papers about El Dorado in 1594 (*Discoverie*, p. 102) and perhaps the rutter was among them.

61 **The Guiana patent**: PRO SP12/250, No. 46.

62 **Harriot's lectures**: BM Add. MS 6788; Taylor; Shirley, *Thomas Harriot*, pp. 86–99.

64 **Letters from Sherborne**: HMC Cecil 5, pp. 42, 49, 77.

64 **Preston's fleet**: Andrews, pp. 377–98. The four ships were the *Ascension*, the *Gift*, the *Angel*, and the *Darling*. The latter was owned by Ralegh, and crossed again under Keymis in 1596. An account of Preston's voyage, by Robert Davie or Davis, is in Hakluyt, *Principal Navigations*, 1600 ed., Vol. 3, pp. 578–83.

64 **Ralegh's fleet**: See Appendix 3.

CHAPTER 6: THE CREW

67 **The list**: BM Add. MS 3272.

69 **Nicholas Mellechapp**: The Shropshire Mellechapps or Millichaps were

probably connected with Millichope, near Ludlow, though by the early seventeenth century the house was owned by the Moore family (information from Mrs. Sarah Bury, Millichope Park).

69 **Vincent**: Rowland Whyte to Sir Robert Sidney, September 25, 1595 (HMC Sidney 2, p. 163). Whyte names him as one of Ralegh's "bravest men."

70 **Captain Eynos**: Conceivably John Enneas or Annias, found on the fringes of political conspiracy in the Netherlands, and questioned about a plot to "fire" the Tower in 1594 (PRO SP12/247, No. 33).

70 **George Gifford**: See Hasler (s.v.); J. H. Pollen, "Politics of the English Catholics During the Reign of Queen Elizabeth," Part 5, and "Dr William Gifford in 1586," (*The Month*, June 1902, March–April 1904); T. P. Knox, ed., *Letters of Cardinal Allen* (1882), pp. 388, 412–14; interrogations of John Savage, CSP Scots 9. On Nix: PRO SP12/160, No. 29. Going to Constantinople: SP78/30, No. 78.

75 **Lawrence Keymis**: See *Dictionary of National Biography* (s.v.); Eccles, pp. 78–79; Harlow, *Ralegh's Last Voyage*. On Hester's broadsheet (British Library, shelf mark C.60.o.6), see my *Chemical Theatre* (London: Routledge and Kegan Paul, 1980), pp. 66–67. His signature is on Ralegh's 1597 will (Sherborne Estate Office), and an autograph letter to Silvanus Scorie, November 18, 1617, is at Cambridge University Library (MS EE/5-2, f.3). It is probable Keymis wrote the rather tedious brochure, "Of the Voyage to Guiana" (BM Sloane MS 1133, f.45), prior to his voyage in 1596.

76 **Robert Calfield**: Depositions of "Capt. Cawefield of the *Roebuck*," September 28, 1592, and of Thomas Favell, September 29, 1592 (HMC Cecil 4, pp. 230, 233).

77 **Robert Cross**: Cross to his brother John, September 20, 1592; and to Cecil, October 1, 1595 (HMC Cecil 4, p. 226; 5, p. 397). Ralegh to Cecil, September 21, 1592 (Edwards, Vol. 2, p. 71). References to the *Swiftsure*, August–September 1595: HMC Cecil 5, pp. 307, 387. He was an alderman in Southampton in 1591, and was still associated with Ralegh in 1603.

77 **Jacob Whiddon**: *Dictionary of National Biography* (s.v.).

77 **John Clarke**: Andrews, p. 167; Quinn, *Roanoke Voyages*, Vol. 2, pp. 85–86; PRO HCA 13/30.

78 **John Douglas**: Andrews, p. 57; PRO HCA 24/57, No. 27; BM Sloane MS 2292.

78 **Edward Hancock**: Ralegh to Cecil, August 15, 1593 and November 26, 1595 (HMC Cecil 4, p. 356; 5, p. 472); Sir John Gilbert to Cecil, April 10, 1594 (HMC Cecil 4, p. 507).

78 **John Gilbert**: See Roberts; *Dictionary of National Biography*, s.v. Burgh; and contemporary copies of the letters between Burgh and Gilbert, March

1594, PRO SP12/248, No. 54. Ralegh's letter to Gilbert (BM Add. MS 4231, f. 85) is dated c. 1597 by Edwards and c. 1601 by Roberts.

82 **Henry Thynne**: On the family, see Hasler (s.v. Thynne, Sir John); Hoare, *Modern Wiltshire* (s.v. Heytesbury). On Henry: Ralegh's letter, February 25, 1594 (Edwards, Vol. 2, pp. 86–87); Roberts, pp. 207–8. He had, like Gilbert, served under Sir John Norris. He was a "coronet" (i.e., cornet, a cavalry officer carrying the colors) in Norris's troop in 1588.

83 **Francis Sparry**: His adventures in America: see Appendix 1, and his "Description of Guiana" in Purchas, Part 2, Book 6, Chapter 11. Information on his family from Stella Sparry. On Richard Sparry, see Hasler (s.v.).

85 **The *Geomancie***: British Library, shelf mark 1609/784; Arber, Vol. 2, p. 265. On Wolfe, see Harry Hoppe, "John Wolfe, Printer and Publisher," *The Library*, 4th series, Vol. 14 (1933). On Eliot, Chute, etc., see my *Cup of News* (London: Routledge and Kegan Paul, 1984), pp. 175–79.

86 **Poets at sea**: Lodge's preface to *Rosalynde* (1590); Eccles, p. 81; Bodleian Library, Bodley MS 617; R.C. Bald, *John Donne: A Life* (New York: Oxford University Press, 1970), pp. 86–92.

87 **Reading *Orlando Furioso***: "Relation of the Port Ricco Voyage" (1596) by Dr. Layfield, chaplain to the earl of Cumberland, in Purchas, Part 2, Book 6, Chapter 3.

CHAPTER 7: ATLANTIC CROSSING

90 **Captured Portuguese**: PRO SP12/256, No. 100. "Bonitoes" refer to *bonitos*, tuna; "purgose" to *pargos*, red snapper.

91 **Captain White**: Letter to Lady Ralegh, PRO SP12/252, No. 18.

92 **Taint of privateering**: He says as much in the *Discoverie* (sig. A3v): "It became not the former fortune in which I once lived to go journeys of picorie, and to . . . run from Cape to Cape & from place to place for the pillage of ordinary prizes." ("Picorie," from Spanish *pícaro*, rogue, has the sense here of piracy.)

CHAPTER 8: TRINIDAD

93 **"This Terra"**: From Ralegh's log of the Last Voyage (BM Cotton MS Titus B8, f. 153), December 31, 1617; cf. *Discoverie*, pp. 2–3.

93 **"Well adapted"**: Schomburgk, pp. 2–3.

94 **At Trinidad**: Ralegh narrates his actions in Trinidad in *Discoverie*, pp. 1–8.

95 **Spanish reports**: Pedro de Salazar, c. June 1595; Pedro de Liaño, c. April

1596 (AGI, Santo Domingo: Cartas de la Isla de Margarita, Estante 54/4, legajos 2 and 6; Harlow [see Sources/2], Appendix B/1 and 2).

100 **The remnant of those tribes**: Schomburgk, p. 4.

101 **Gilbert in Newfoundland**: Account by Edward Hayes, in A. L. Rowse, ed., *The First Colonists* (London: Folio Society, 1986), p. 26.

102 **"The Captains"**: Account of Domingo de Vera's Guiana expedition of 1593, in *Discoverie*, p. 106.

103 **Ralegh and Berrio**: *Discoverie*, pp. 8–36: Ojer, pp. 116f.

103 **Juan Martínez**: *Discoverie*, pp. 13–16; Ramos Perez, *El Mito del Dorado*, pp. 534–43. According to Ralegh, he was marooned on the Orinoco by Diego de Ordaz, captured by Indians, and led blindfold to the "palace of Inga" (i.e., the Inca) at Manoa. He returned after a few months, "loden with gold," and told his story on his deathbed at Puerto Rico. He appears to be a fevered conflation, by Berrio, of two figures: the actual castaway of the Ordaz *entrada* (1531), whose name was not Martínez but Gonsalez; and a later traveler, Juan Martín de Albujar, who turned up in Margarita in the early 1580s after seven years among the Guiana Indians. Castellanos, however, says Martín brought no news of Manoa (see note to p. 10 above).

CHAPTER 9: THE GULF OF SADNESS

110 **May 17, 1595**: I estimate this date as follows: (1) The *entrada* lasted altogether about thirty-four days. The journey upriver took "well near a month" (Ralegh) or "thirty days" (Sparry: see Appendix 1/A). The return journey, traveling downstream with the river in spate, took about four days: Ralegh says they traveled "above a hundred miles a day" and he estimated the distance as four hundred miles. (2) The latest date for their return to Trinidad is June 20, for on the following day they were sighted by Spanish lookouts off Margarita. Thus the latest date for setting off is May 17. (3) Their first encounter with the natives of the Orinoco Delta was on May 22 (the only actual date furnished by Ralegh). They had "wandered," lost, for some days before this. The earlier they set out, the longer their initial wandering; it is *at least* five days, according to the above computation, and it seems implausible to stretch it out longer.

110 **"Prisons and corners"**: Hakluyt, *Original Writing*, Vol. 2, p. 233.

111 **Over the past weeks**: Reconnaissance, preparation, and embarkation are described in *Discoverie*, pp. 36–39.

111 **Bay of Guanipa**: The river flowing into the western side of the bay is still called Guanipa. It rises near Maturín, and is not part of the Orinoco system. The bay now takes its name from Caño Bagre, the westernmost branch of the Orinoco.

112   **Caño Manamo**: Felipe de Santiago (see Chapter 13) reported in 1596: "There is another mouth of the Delta called Manavo, by which it is known that the Englishman Guaterrale entered last year" (Heinen, p. 598). This "Manavo," like Ralegh's "Amana," is the Manamo, but does not identify which of the Manamo's mouths they entered by.

113   **Channel 4**: *The City of Gold and How to Get There*, directed by Ron Orders, was shown in Channel 4's *Travellers' Tales* series, London, July 19, 1993.

117   **"Being all driven"**: *Discoverie*, pp. 8–9.

Chapter 10: The Delta

121   **Cholera**: A 1984 health-study shows gastroenteritis as the chief threat to the Warao (470 deaths between 1950 and 1980) followed by pneumonia, TB, cancer, and tetanus (Werner Wilbert, "Infectious Diseases and Health Services in Delta Amacuro," *Acta Ethnologica et Linguistica*, Vol. 58, Vienna, 1984). The cholera epidemic of the late 1980s has now spread into the region. In 1992, I was told, new cases of cholera were appearing at the rate of fifteen a week.

123   **"For I know"**: *Discoverie*, p. 39.

124   **"We saw birds"**: *Discoverie*, pp. 46, 67.

124   **"Those beds"**: *Discoverie*, p. 34. Warao hammocks, woven by the women from *moriche* palm fiber, are still highly prized. A "matrimonial" hammock could be bought in Wakahara for 4,000 bolivars (about £30).

126   **"In the bottom"**: Sparry's "Description of Guiana" (Purchas, Part 2, Book 6, Chapter 11).

Chapter 11: Tivitivas

129   **Tivitivas**: *Discoverie*, pp. 39–43; on the origin of the name see Heinen, p. 595. Dudley refers to both Tivitivas and "Veriotaus," the latter perhaps corresponding with Ralegh's "Waraweete."

130   **Warao in eighteenth century**: Report of Colonel Centurion, 1771 (Heinen, p. 603); José Gumilla, *El Orinoco Ilustrado*, Vol. 3 (1791), pp. 133–34.

132   **"The Indian is a fish"**: "Relations of Master Thomas Turner" (1610), in Purchas, Part 2, Book 6, Chapter 8.

132   **Tree houses**: *Discoverie*, p. 42; Schomburgk, p. 51; Kirchhoff, p. 872, citing the account by Hilhouse (1830s).

135   **"The Waraus are"**: Schomburgk, p. 49.

135   *Siete vidas*: Anita Castro, Campo Carrao, December 3, 1992.

Chapter 12: The Medicine Man

138   *Wasirato*: My comments on Warao shamanism are based on conversations with Eulalio Cabello at Wakahara, November 14–15, 1992; Heinen, pp. 663–69; Kirchhoff, pp. 880–81. See also María Matilde Suarez, "Los Warao: sus creencias magico-religiosas sobre la enfermedad," *Boletín Indigenista Venezolano*, Vol. 9, 1967.

139   **Tobacco shaman**: See Wilbert, *Tobacco Shamanism*, and Wilbert, "Tobacco and Shamanistic Ecstasy."

143   **Algonquian tobacco rites**: Harriot, p. 16.

144   **"The Indian priests"**: "Philaretes," *Work for Chimney Sweepers*, sig. f. 4v; Knapp, p. 277.

144   **"In the taking"**: Roger Marbeck, *Defence of Tobacco* (1602), p. 58; Knapp, pp. 289–90.

144   **"Thou great God"**: Francis Beaumont, *Metamorphosis of Tobacco* (1602), in *Poems*, ed. Alexander Grosart (1869), p. 276.

146   **"Virginia can be"**: Knapp, p. 290.

146   **"Thus they sit"**: Keymis, sig. C3.

Chapter 13: The Guiana Bend

149   *Marusi* and *powis*: Schomburgk, p. 54–55. The latter is perhaps the same as the *bauhee* shot by Enrique at Puerto Chicanán (see Chapter 21).

151   **Their second meeting**: *Discoverie*, pp. 46–48.

157   **Another encouraging sign**: *Discoverie*, pp. 48–53.

157   **Spanish report**: Pedro de Salazar, c. June 1595 (see note to p. 95 above).

Chapter 14: Dark Eyes

160   **Frobisher's Eskimos**: Lee, pp. 337–38.

160   **Manteo and Wanchese**: Shirley, pp. 105–13; Porter, pp. 229f.; Von Wedel, in W. B. Rye, *England as Seen by Foreigners* (1865), p. 323.

162   **Nepoios**: Ralegh's sojourn at Arowacai is in *Discoverie*, pp. 54–56. On possible identity of the Nepoios, see Chapter 15.

164   **Dark Ladies**: *Love's Labour's Lost*, III.i.177–78; Sonnets 127, 130; Nashe, Vol. 2, p. 261.

165   **"I protest before"**: *Discoverie*, pp. 51–52. Their restraint toward the Indians was probably enforced, as in the Virginia colonies, where rape was

punishable by death, and striking or "misusing" an Indian earned twenty
blows of the cudgel.

166 **"License my roving"**: See above, note to p. 41. On the sexual "discourse"
of colonization, see Montrose.

167 **"So your black hair"**: BM Add. MS 11811; Donne, Vol. 1, pp. 460–61.
It was first printed in *Parnassus Biceps* (1656).

168 **"You freely swore"**: Hakluyt, *Original Writing,* Vol. 1, p. 367.

169 **Amazons**: *Discoverie,* pp. 23–24. On the transmission of the myth into
the New World, see A. Wettan Kleinbaum, *The War Against the Amazons*
(New York: McGraw-Hill, 1983), pp. 71f. On Columbus's "obsession,"
see Quinn, *Explorers and Colonies,* pp. 73–74. Ralegh returns to the subject
extensively in *History of the World,* Book 4, Chapter 2, Section 15.

173 **"To conclude, Guiana"**: *Discoverie,* p. 96.

174 **Country/cuntry**: The *locus classicus* of the pun is *Hamlet,* III.ii.120: "Do
you think I meant country matters?" See Eric Partridge, *Shakespeare's
Bawdy* (London: Routledge and Kegan Paul, 1968), pp.87–88, for other
examples.

CHAPTER 15: LORDS OF THE BORDERS

175 **The mainstream**: Their passage up the Orinoco (*Discoverie,* pp. 56–61)
was painfully slow. It took them six days to reach the "port of Morequito,"
a distance of about forty miles.

175 **Steel ore**: Ralegh's surmise was undoubtedly correct. Cerro Bolívar, to the
south, contains some of the largest iron deposits in the hemisphere, up to
1,000 feet deep, with an estimated capacity of 400 million tons of ore.

176 **Los Castillos**: Harlow, *Ralegh's Last Voyage,* pp. 357–68. Cf. *Discoverie,* pp.
96–97: "[Guiana is] so defensible, that if two forts be builded in one of
the provinces which I have seen, the flood setteth in so near the bank,
where the channel also lieth, that no ship can pass up but within a pike's
length of the artillery'." This sounds like a prescient allusion to the site
at El Padrasto.

178 **Meetings with Topiawari**: *Discoverie,* pp. 61–64, 74–81.

180 **Sparry's account**: See Appendix 1/B.

185 **Macusi**: See Schomburgk, p. 78; Gillin, pp. 808–9. The Brazilian Makusi
are today in conflict with gold diggers in areas of northeast Brazil not far
from the putative Lake Manoa (Survival International, Urgent Action Bul-
letins, 1993).

186 **Waika**: Gillin, p. 812. They "show close linguistic resemblance" to the
Macusi.

Chapter 16: Downtown Orinoco

188   **Isla Fajardo**: Named after the Portuguese trader and traveler Lucas de Fajardo, then based at Cumaná. He is perhaps the friendly "man of great travel" with whom Ralegh conversed, off Cumaná, in late June 1595. See *Discoverie,* pp. 70–71; Harlow (see Sources/2), pp. lxxvi–lxxxi.

188   *Tepuy*: The word is used in Venezuela to designate the flat-topped *mesas* of the Guiana Highlands. Humboldt relates it to Carib *tebou,* Tamanac *tepu* and Mexican *tepetl* (as in Popocatépetl, Smoking Mountain); and, more ambitiously, to an Asiatic root, Tartar *tep,* "stone."

189   **"When we ran"**: *Discoverie,* p. 67.

Chapter 17: Gold Rush

198   **European prospecting**: My sketch of the Venezuelan gold rush is based on conversations with Giles Fitzherbert, Paul Henley, Lobo Loffler, and Uwe Neumann; and on contemporary records assembled by Adolf Ernst, a Silesian who lived for nearly forty years in Venezuela. His "Statistical Annotations on the State of Guayana" (1876) and "Gold in Venezuela" (1883) are published by the Venezuelan National Library Institute (see *Caracas Daily Journal,* December 6, 1992).

199   **Annual production**: Figures for 1992, from the Venezuela Desk at the U.K. Department of Trade. Total capacity is said to be 250 tons per year.

200   **Boundary Commission**: The Venezuelan Boundary Arbitration papers (Spanish documents recovered by the Foreign Office from AGI, and assembled in 1897) are in BM Add. MSS. A selection was published as *British Guiana Boundary Documents,* 12 vols. (London: HMSO, 1898).

201   *Mineros*: In 1988, it was estimated, there were 40,000 independent *mineros* in Venezuela, producing about 25 tons of gold (an average of 12 grams per week each), as against the 2 tons extracted by the state mining company, Minerven.

202   **Conflict with Indians**: Marcus Colchester (World Rainforest Movement, 1992) reports mining and logging incursions into the Imataca Forest Reserve on the Venezuela-Guyana border. Confrontation is more serious in Brazil, where up to eighty Yanomami were massacred by gold miners in mid-1993 (Survival International; Isabel Hilton, "After the Gold Rush," *Independent Magazine,* November 13, 1993).

203   **Uraima**: The rest of the chapter is based on conversations at Uraima, November 21–24, 1992, and elsewhere (with Gilbert Montez, Ciudad Bolívar, October 28–29; with Heinz Dollacker, Maracay, October 22). No names or details have been changed. We spent altogether about two weeks

among the *mineros* of Venezuela, and were met throughout with courtesy and good humor.

204   **"We suffer from a disease"**: Cortés to Teuhtile, Vera Cruz, April 23, 1519, as reported by his chaplain, Father Bartolemé de Olmeda. See W. H. Prescott, *Conquest of Mexico* (1901 ed.), Vol. 1, pp. 187–89.

CHAPTER 18: JIMMY ANGEL

211   **Jimmy Angel**: Parts of this chapter first appeared in my article "Yellow Fever," *Independent Magazine,* July 17, 1993. Information from: censuses for Greene County, Missouri (microfilm at Springfield Main Library); *Springfield News Leader,* June 26, 1949; *New York Times,* December 9, 1956; *Caracas Daily Journal,* November 12, 1972 and December 3, 1989; account by L. R. Dennison, quoted in Uwe George, "Venezuela's Islands in Time," *National Geographic,* May 1989; conversation with Terry Leon, Caracas, December 1986; interview with Rudy Truffino, Canaima, November 29, 1992.

216   **Bears his name**: In 1949, a retired Venezuelan naval officer, Ernesto Sanchez La Cruz, claimed that he had seen the falls back in 1903, while on a rubber-hunting expedition out of La Paragua, and that they should therefore be known as Sanchez Falls (*Caracas Daily Journal,* May 23, 1949).

216   **Ruth Robertson**: See her account of the expedition, "Jungle Journey to the World's Highest Waterfall," *National Geographic,* November 1949.

219   **"Mountain of Crystal"**: *Discoverie,* pp. 84–85.

CHAPTER 19: CANAIMA

222   **Charlie Baughan**: Interview with Heinz Dollacker, Maracay, October 22, 1992. There is an account of him (as Charlie "Vaughan") by the Italian adventurer, Sadio Garavini de Turno, in *Lolomai* (Rome, 1962).

226   **The name Canaima**: Interview with Jorge Calcano et al., Puerto Chicanán, December 6, 1992.

CHAPTER 20: MEETING LAIME

228   **Laime**: Interviews with Alexander Laime, Carrao River, November 1 and 30, 1992.

228   **These visitors**: Among them North American journalist Tim Cahill, on

assignment for *Geo* magazine. His entertaining account ("The Lost World") is in *Jaguars Ripped My Flesh* (New York: Bantam, 1987).

233 **Biological islands**: See Uwe George, "Venezuela's Islands in Time," *National Geographic,* May 1989.

CHAPTER 21: WELCOME TO EL DORADO

235 **The last leg**: This chapter is drawn entirely from notes, tapes, and film of our journey from the upper Carrao to El Dorado, November 30–December 10, 1992.

244 **El Dorado prison**: See Henri Charrière, *Papillon*, trans. Patrick O'Brian (New York: Morrow, 1970), pp. 537f. At that time (early 1940s) it was a hard-labor camp with four hundred prisoners under the brutal regime of a *mestizo* commandant nicknamed El Negro Blanco.

CHAPTER 22: DOWNRIVER

249 **Second meeting**: *Discoverie,* pp. 74–81.

249 **His son**: Named as Caywaraco in the "Advertisement" prefacing the captured Spanish papers (*Discoverie,* p. 103).

250 **Sparry's account**: Appendix 1; Purchas (see note to p. 83 above).

251 **Anthony Canebre**: Harcourt, pp. 70–79 (also on "Indian John"). Ralegh gives a rather sour account of Harcourt's dealings with the natives (logbook of the Last Voyage, November 11, 1617).

254 **Hugh Godwin**: Liaño's report (extract in Appendix 1/A); Keymis, sig. D2; Edwards, Vol. 1, p. 192, Vol. 2, p. 511; Ralegh's logbook, November 11–20, 1617.

255 **Back downriver**: *Discoverie,* pp. 81–90.

258 **Raid on Cumaná**: Accounts in AGI by Simon de Bolívar (July, 8 1595), Francisco de Vides (June 28), Francisco López Urquilla (July 6), and Don Roque de Montes Colmenares (October 15); Harlow (see Sources/2), Appendix B/4–7.

259 **Thechen/Thynne**: The garbling (either oral or scribal) is plausible, in which case the report is an error. It is also possible that "Thechen" is a genuine crew member, unmentioned elsewhere.

261 **"*Quien se va*"**: Schomburgk, p. 46.

262 **"The 13 day"**: Hakluyt, *Principal Navigations,* 1600 ed., Vol. 3, p. 582. Robert Davie is probably the Robert Davis who was master of the *Bark Ralegh* in Gilbert's 1583 voyage (Andrews, p. 377).

CHAPTER 23: HOME

263   **Ralegh's return**: All these letters are in HMC Cecil 5: Gilbert, p. 315; Lady Ralegh, p. 396; the dispatch from Plymouth to Sherborne (September 23, 1595), p. 387; Heneage, pp. 368–69.

265   **Come back "rich"**: Another of Cecil's circle, Hugh Beeston, writes of his joy at Ralegh's "rich return" (September 26, 1595, HMC Cecil 5, p. 391). This was clearly the approved line.

266   **Rowland Whyte**: HMC Sidney 2, pp. 163–64, 166.

267   **Ralegh's "discourse"**: It is not unlikely that the *Discoverie* was completed by September 27, as Whyte's letter implies. In the "Advertisement" appended to Ralegh's text (p. 102), it is said that Captain Popham returned to England two months after Ralegh, "as also so long after the writing of the former discourse." This suggests that the *Discoverie* was substantially complete when Ralegh returned in early September, i.e., that he wrote it during the homeward voyage (about six weeks). After an interval of private circulation, it was licensed for publication in March 1596, and was probably on sale soon after.

267   **Dines with Dee**: John Dee, *Diary 1595–1601,* ed. Bailey (1880), p. 23.

267   **"Sir Walter Rawley is here"**: Letter to Sir Robert Sidney, HMC Sidney 2, p. 173.

267   **Captain North**: Aubrey, p. 258. He returned to Guiana in the late 1620s. His "collections and remarques of his voyages" were destroyed in the Great Fire, 1666.

268   **Letters from Sherborne**: HMC Cecil 5, pp. 444–45 (November 10), pp. 457–58 (November 13).

269   **"You may perceive"**: The "relation" Ralegh refers to here is sometimes misinterpreted as the text of the *Discoverie,* which is therefore said to have been finished in mid-November. See note to p. 267 above.

CHAPTER 24: ORDINARY PRIZES

272   **"Near unto one"**: *Discoverie,* p. 54. This apparently refers also to Topiawari's mine on the lower Caroní. Ralegh is deliberately vague, and in his later statements (prior to the 1617 voyage) very confused, about the location of these "mines." I do not think it possible to pinpoint them, given the range of possible sites in the region.

272   **The assaying**: *Discoverie,* sig. B2v. *Dictionary of National Biography* claims Ralegh's unit is the "assay pound" of 12 grains, but this makes the ore in his samples very meager: about 0.1 percent.

273   **Spleen stones**: The Spanish called them *piedras hígados* ("liver stones") for

their supposed efficacy against liver disease. In the nineteenth century they were called "Amazon stones," "ophites," and (in Demerara) "calicot stones." Schomburgk (p. 29) describes them as green, cylindrical, usually about two inches long.

273   **"I assure myself"**: HMC Cecil 5, p. 457.

273   **"On the banks"**: *Discoverie,* pp. 45, 82.

274   **Ewaipanoma**: *Discoverie,* pp. 69–71.

276   **Cane tobacco**: Warner, p. 48; cf. John Harington, *Epigrams* (1612): "tobacco . . . of Trinidad, in cane, in leaf, in ball." On early English tobacco tastes, see Joan Thirsk's essay, "New Crops and Their Diffusion: Tobaccogrowing in 17th Century England," *Rural Economy of England* (London: Hambledon, 1984), p. 259f.

276   **"*Que todo eso*"**: Edward Bennett, *Inconveniences of the Importation of Tobacco* (c. 1620); Knapp, p. 304.

276   **"Our English Ulysses"**: Henry Buttes, *Dyet's Dry Dinner* (1599), sigs. P5v-P6.

277   **Axtell and Keymis**: Eccles, p. 79.

277   **Reported boast**: According to the *Declaration of the Demeanour and Carriage of Sir Walter Ralegh* (1618); Harlow, *Ralegh's Last Voyage,*, p. 342.

CHAPTER 25: BALSAM OF GUIANA

278   **Ralegh as "chymist"**: See Shirley, "Scientific Experiments"; Rattansi; and my *Chemical Theatre* (London: Routledge and Kegan Paul, 1980), pp. 15–17.

278   **"Authors are perplexed"**: John Shirley, *Life of the Valiant and Learned Sir Walter Rawleigh* (1677); Rattansi, p. 122.

279   **John Hester**: The earliest extant edition of *114 Experiments* is 1596, three years after his death. In *Chemical Theatre,* pp. 75–80, I trace a connection between Hester's posthumous editor, James Forester, and Shakespeare's *Merry Wives of Windsor* (c. 1597), which has satire on Paracelsism (and which also contains a topical Shakespearean allusion to Guiana: "She [Mistress Page] is a region in Guiana, all gold and bounty." I.iii.64–65).

279   **Adrian Gilbert**: There is no biography of this interesting character. Aubrey (p. 139) says he "was a great chymist in those days, and a man of excellent natural parts, but very sarcastic."

279   **Harriot's alchemy**: Shirley, *Thomas Harriot,*, pp. 268–87.

279   **Ralegh's library**: Oakeshott, pp. 308–9.

280   **Distilling in the Tower**: Waad's report, BM Add. MS 6178, f. 14v; John Ward, *Diary,* ed. Severn (1839), p. 169. Ralegh's chemical notebook is BM Sloane MS 359.

280 **Northumberland's experiments:** Shirley, "Scientific Experiments," pp. 60–63.

282 *Instauratio Magna:* Bacon, *Works,* Vol. 11, ed. Spedding (1868), p. 63.

282 **His Balsam:** See Knott; Le Fèvre; Winton, p. 275. Killigrew's recipe: BM Sloane MS 203, ff. 124–25. Le Fèvre's preparation: John Evelyn, *Diary and Correspondence,* Vol. 1, ed. Bray (1850), pp. 368–69.

283 **Ingredients:** Le Fèvre (pp. 6–62) includes all those mentioned in Ralegh's chemical notebook and in Killigrew's recipe, plus several others found in neither. On serpentary, see *OED* (s.v.).

285 **Native medicine:** *Discoverie,* pp. 59–60. Cf. Ralegh, Book 1, Chapter 7: "A skilful and learned chymist can . . . draw helpful medicines out of poison, as poison out of the most helpful herbs."

286 **Curare:** Schomburgk, pp. 71–72. Charles Waterton, *Wanderings in South America* (1825), pp. 53–71, gives an entertaining account of Macusi use of *wourari.*

CHAPTER 26: A GOLDEN WORLD

288 *De Guiana:* In Chapman's *Works,* ed. Swinburne (1875), pp. 50–52.

290 **Golden world:** I have drawn throughout this chapter on Levin; Porter, Chapter 1; and Frank Kermode's introduction to the Arden edition of Shakespeare's *The Tempest* (London: Methuen, 1954).

292 **Marina Warner:** "Managing Monsters" (Reith Lectures, BBC Radio 4, February 23, 1994).

294 **"These people are wild":** Montaigne, *Essays,* trans. Cohen (New York and Harmondsworth, England: Penguin, 1958), pp. 109–10.

294 **"*Hos natura modos*":** Virgil, *Georgics,* II.20.

294 **"Bower of Bliss":** See Stephen Greenblatt, *Renaissance Self-Fashioning* (Chicago: University of Chicago Press, 1979), pp. 103–5.

294 **Shakespeare:** *As You Like It,* I.i.188–89; *Tempest,* II.iv.144–51; Montaigne, *Essays,* Vol. 1, trans. Florio (1603), Chapter 30.

295 **Spenser's "salvage men":** Kermode, introduction to Arden *Tempest,* p. xliii.

295 **Gilbert's last words:** Quoted in Edward Hayes's account (Hakluyt, *Principal Navigations* [1600 ed.], Vol. 3, pp. 143–62), and related to *Utopia* by Samuel Eliot Morison, *The Growth of the American Republic,* Vol. 1 (New York: Oxford University Press, 1930), p. 35.

296 **Barlowe's account:** Quinn, *Roanoke Voyages,* pp. 91–116. There is a suspicion of editorial tweaking, in these rose-tinted passages, either by Hakluyt (who published it in 1589) or Harriot (whose presence on the 1584 voyage is inferred but not recorded), or possibly by Ralegh himself.

296   "**All things**": *Tempest,* II.i.155–60.

299   **Golden man:** The evolution of El Dorado from Chibcha religious rites is
       exhaustively studied in Ramos Perez, *El Mito del Dorado.* See also Hem-
       ming, pp. 97–109; A. L. Kroeber, "The Chibcha," *Handbook of South Amer-
       ican Indians,* Vol. 2 (1947), pp. 905–9. I describe a visit to Lago de
       Guatavita in *The Fruit Palace* (London: Heinemann, 1985), pp. 105–7. The
       name El Dorado is first heard (as *"el indio dorado"*) in a report by Luis
       Daza, a lieutenant of Benalcazar's, in 1534, but he refers not to the Chib-
       cha but to a more southerly Andean tribe, probably Sinu or Quimbaya
       (Ramos Perez, *El Mito del Dorado,* pp. 216–17, 470). The imagery and the
       name are initially disparate, but have merged by the beginning of the
       1540s.

300   "**They tell me**": Fernandez de Oviedo, *Historia General de las Indias* (Seville,
       1535–47), Book 49; Hemming, pp. 97–99.

301   **Versions that follow:** The new focus on the Guiana Highlands in the
       late 1560s, by Quesada and others, reinstates the mountain lake imagery.
       See, e.g., report of Juan Salas, governor of Margarita, c. 1571 (Hemming,
       p. 153): "Beyond the *sierra* [is] a very mighty lake. . . . It is a very rich
       land: lords who possess riches order that when they die all their treasures
       should be thrown into the lake."

301   "**When the Emperor**": *Discoverie,* pp. 16–17.

301   "**A rich nation**": See Abraham Kendall's synopsis of Dudley's 1595 *en-
       trada,* in Warner, p. 182.

CHAPTER 27: ON RED CROSS RIVER

304   "**Damnable opinions**": Richard Baines, report on Christopher "Marly,"
       May 1593, BM Harley MS 6848, f. 185; Nashe, Vol. 1, p. 172, Vol. 2,
       p. 114.

305   **Northumberland and Bruno:** See Hilary Gatti, "Giordano Bruno: The
       Texts in the Library of the Earl of Northumberland," *Journal of the Warburg
       Institute,* Vol. 46, 1983.

305   "**Leaving our schoolmen**": George Peele, *Honour of the Garter* (1593).
       Northumberland paid him a £3 "liberality" for the poem in June 1593.
       It contains the earliest printed allusion to the killing of Christopher Mar-
       lowe.

305   "**Atheism**": School of atheism: "Andreas Philopater," *An Advertisement*
       (Antwerp, 1592), p. 18. Atheist lecture: statements of Richard Cholmeley,
       c. May 1593, BM Harley MS 6848, f. 190.

306   **Dee's imperialism:** See Frances Yates, *Astraea: The Imperial Theme in the
       16th Century* (London: Routledge and Kegan Paul, 1975); Peter French,

John Dee (London: Routledge and Kegan Paul, 1977); Ian Seymour, "The Political Magic of John Dee," *History Today,* January 1989; Margery Corbett and Ronald Lightbown, *The Comely Frontispiece* (London: Routledge and Kegan Paul, 1979), pp. 49–56.

307 **Spenser**: On Dee and Spenser, see Frances Yates, *Occult Philosophy in the Elizabethan Age* (London: Routledge and Kegan Paul, 1979), Chapter 9. On Ralegh and Spenser, see Greenblatt, *Sir Walter Raleigh,* pp. 109–10.

307 **Red Cross River**: *Discoverie,* p. 39.

310 **Early Rosicrucians**: See Frances Yates, *Rosicrucian Enlightenment* (London: Routledge and Kegan Paul, 1972), and the documents and manifestos gathered in A. E. Waite, *Real History of the Rosicrucians* (1887). On Basil Valentine, see my *Chemical Theatre,* pp. 81–93.

312 **Rosicrucian Golden Age**: Maier, *Laws of the Rosy Cross,* p. 44. Mebane (p. 83) sums up these connections: "The rhetoric of universal reform that was developed by Ralegh, Dee, Spenser and others as an idealistic rationale for the British Empire, was influenced in part by the emphasis on the purification of humanity which lies at the heart of the occult tradition."

313 **"Of that little"**: *Discoverie,* sig. A3. The phrase "painful pilgrimage" is used by Spenser, describing the journey to "New Jerusalem" (*Faerie Queene,* I.x.61).

CHAPTER 28: THE SHUT PALACE

315 **"We are now ready"**: Ashmole, pp. 291–92. On Charnock, see F. Sherwood Taylor, "Thomas Charnock," *Ambix,* Vol. 2, 1946.

315 **Sir George Ripley**: His *Compound of Alchymy* (Ashmole, pp. 107–93) was written c. 1471, and first published in 1591, with a preface by Dee.

316 *De Lapide Philosophico*: Waite, Vol. 1, pp. 271–306.

316 **"There are seven"**: "Hermes," *Tractatus Aureus,* in Israel Regardie, *The Philosophers' Stone* (St. Paul, Minn.: Llewellyn, 1970), p. 40.

318 **"The chymists give"**: Le Fèvre, pp. 58–59.

319 **Lawful "magick"**: Ralegh, Book 1, Chapter 11, Section 2; Rattansi, p. 127.

319 *"Visita Interiora"*: See Salamon Trismosin, *Toyson d'Or* (1613), Daniel Stolcius, *Viridiarum Chymicum* (1624), etc.

319 **Gifford's alchemy**: On his arrest in 1586, he was described as pursuing the "discovery of the Philosophers' Stone" (PRO SP12/192, No. 42; HMC Cecil 3, p. 209).

319 **"Shut palace"**: *Introitus Apertus ad Occlusum Regis Palatium* ("The Open Entrance into the Shut Palace of the King") is an alchemical classic (1678) by "Eirenaeus Philalethes," whose identity is still debated.

320   *"Nonulli perierunt"*: Anon., *Rosarium Philosophorum* ("The Rose Garden of the Philosophers"), mid-sixteenth century.

320   **"The right way"**: Jung, *Psychology and Alchemy*, p. 6.

320   **"The apotheosis"**: Jung, *Mysterium Coniunctionis*, p. 355.

321   **"Our younger years"**: Ralegh, Book 1, Chapter 9, Section 3; Levin, p. 148.

322   **"Privy quintessence"**: Ashmole, p. 313.

322   **Alchemical monsters**: Ripley's *Scrowle* (Ashmole, p. 378); Philalethes, *Ripley Revived* (1677); Valentine, *Twelve Keys* (trans. 1670), p. 238; *Aurelia Occulta*, in Zetzner, ed. *Theatrum Chemicum*, Vol. 4 (1613), p. 501.

EPILOGUE

327   **Lake Guatavita**: On the subsequent history of the lake, see Hemming, pp. 195–98; *Gold of Eldorado* (Royal Academy catalog, 1981). Since 1965 it has been a protected site.

328   **"Calez and Guyana"**: Donne, Vol. 1, p. 76.

328   **"Long spoken-of"**: Unsigned letter to the earl of Essex, November 16, 1597, PRO SP12/264, No. 60.

328   **Rowland Whyte**: Letters to Sir Robert Sidney, December 13, 1595 and March 4, 1597 (HMC Sidney 2, pp. 198, 244).

328   **Captain Berry**: An account of his expedition, written by crew member Thomas Masham, is in Hakluyt, *Principal Navigations*, 1600 ed., Vol. 11, pp. 8f.

328   **Gilbert returning**: R. Bayly to Colonel William Stanley, November 1598, PRO SP12/227, No. 157; Edwards, Vol. 1, p. 199.

329   **Crying "Anglee"**: Harlow, *Ralegh's Last Voyage*, pp. 128–29.

331   **"Violent calenture"**: This, and his recuperation at Cayenne, from his MS logbook.

331   **Attack on San Thomé**: See Harlow, *Ralegh's Last Voyage*, for eyewitness reports and later depositions.

333   **His severed head**: Rowse, pp. 319–24. Its interment at St. Mary's is claimed in the church's booklets, but there are gaps and inconsistencies in the story. The current incumbent, the Reverend Peter Robinson, has shed no light on the matter.

333   **Others who traveled**: On Gifford: Hasler (s.v.). On Gilbert: Roberts; Rowland Whyte to Sidney, October 26, 1599, HMC Sidney 2, p. 406. On Sparry: information from Stella Sparry.

Sources

1. Documentary Sources

Acronyms in the Notes refer to the following collections:

AGI: Archivo General de Indias, Seville

BM: British Museum, London

CSP: Calendar of State Papers (printed abstracts)

HMC: Historical Manuscripts Commission (Cecil MSS at Hatfield House; Sidney MSS at Penshurst Place)

PRO: Public Record Office, London (SP: State Papers; HCA: High Court of Admiralty proceedings)

2. Ralegh's *Discoverie of Guiana*

The Discoverie of the Large, Rich and Bewtiful Empyre of Guiana, with a Relation of the Great and Golden Citie of Manoa (which the Spaniards call El Dorado) . . . By Sir W. Ralegh, Knight was published by Robert Robinson in early 1596. Registration at Stationers' Hall was on March 15, 1596. Minor variants in extant copies show that at least three further editions were issued in that year.

A facsimile of the 1596 edition (British Library, shelf mark G.7169) is published by Scolar Press (Leeds, 1967).

All page references to the *Discoverie* refer to the 1596 edition. I have not attempted to source every extract I use. Many occur within a narrative sequence, and can be found easily enough by the interested reader.

Other editions referred to are:

DE BRY: *Brevis Descriptio Regni Guianae,* ed. Theodore de Bry (Frankfurt, 1599). This is Part 8 of De Bry's monumental part-work, known variously as *America,* or the *Great and Small Voyages.* A German edition appeared in the same year. There were second editions in Latin (1625) and German (1624).

HULSIUS: *Kurtze Wunderbare Beschreibung Desz Goldreichen Königreichs Guianae,* ed. Levinus Hulsius (Nuremburg, 1599). This is Part 5 of Hulsius's collection, *Sechs und Zwanzig Schiffahrten.* It is a very truncated text, interesting only for the engravings that accompany it.

377

SCHOMBURGK: The first modern edition, by Sir Robert H. Schomburgk (London: Hakluyt Society, 1848), containing notes based on his extensive travels in British Guiana and Venezuela.

HARLOW: The best modern edition, by V. T. Harlow (London: Argonaut Press, 1928), containing a number of previously unpublished documents drawn from AGI and BM.

3. BOOKS AND ARTICLES

Andrews, Kenneth R. *English Privateering Voyages to the West Indies, 1588–95.* London: Hakluyt Society, 1959.

Arber, Edward, ed. *A Transcript of the Registers of the Company of Stationers of London,* 5 vols. London, 1875–94.

Armitage, Christopher. *Sir Walter Ralegh: An Annotated Bibliography.* Chapel Hill, N.C.: University of North Carolina Press, 1987.

Ashmole, Elias, ed. *Theatrum Chemicum Britannicum.* London, 1652.

Aubrey, John. *Brief Lives,* ed. Oliver Lawson Dick. London: Cresset Press, 1949.

Bovill, E.W. "The *Madre de Dios.*" *Mariner's Mirror,* Vol. 54, 1948.

Bry, Theodore de. See Sources/2.

Cattan, Christopher. *The Geomancie,* trans. Francis Sparry. London, 1591.

Chapman, Walker. *The Golden Dream: Seekers of El Dorado.* Indianapolis: Bobbs-Merrill, 1967.

Chute, Anthony. *Tobacco.* London, 1596.

Clissold, Stephen: *Conquistador: The Life of Don Pedro Sarmiento de Gamboa.* London: D. Verschoyle, 1954.

Donne, John. *Poetical Works,* ed. H.J.C. Grierson, 2 vols. Oxford: Clarendon Press, 1912.

Eccles, Mark. "Brief Lives: Tudor and Stuart Authors." *Studies in Philology,* Vol. 79, 1982.

Edwards, Edward. *Life of Sir Walter Ralegh,* 2 vols. London, 1868.

Friel, Ian. "The Three-masted Ship and Atlantic Voyages." *Exeter Studies in History,* Vol. 10, 1985.

Fuller, Mary. "Ralegh's Fugitive Gold." In Greenblatt, *New World Encounters.*

Gillin, John. "Tribes of the Guianas." In *Handbook of South American Indians,* Vol. 3. Washington, D.C.: Smithsonian Institution, 1948.

Gott, Richard. *Land Without Evil: Utopian Journeys Across the South American Watershed.* London: Verso, 1993.

Greenblatt, Stephen. *Sir Walter Ralegh: The Renaissance Man and His Roles.* New Haven, Conn.: Yale University Press, 1973.

———. *Marvellous Possessions.* Oxford: Clarendon Press, 1991.

————. *New World Encounters.* Berkeley, Calif.: University of California Press, 1993.

Hakluyt, Richard. *The Principal Navigations, Voyages, Traffiques and Discoveries of the English Nation.* London, 1589; 2nd ed., 1600.

————. *Original Writing and Correspondence,* ed. E.G.R. Taylor. London: Hakluyt Society, 1935.

Harcourt, Robert. *A Relation of a Voyage to Guiana* (1613), ed. Sir C. Alexander Harris. London: Hakluyt Society, 1928.

Harlow, V.T. See Sources/2.

————. *Colonizing Voyages to the West Indies and Guiana.* London: Hakluyt Society, 1924.

————. *Ralegh's Last Voyage.* London: Argonaut Press, 1932.

Harriot, Thomas. *A Brief and True Report of the New Found Land of Virginia.* London, 1588.

Hasler, P.W. *The House of Commons, 1558–1603,* 3 vols. London: HMSO, 1981.

Haynes, Alan. *Robert Cecil, 1st Earl of Salisbury.* London: P. Owen, 1992.

Heinen, Hans Dieter. *Los Warao.* Caracas: Fundación la Salle, 1987.

Hemming, John. *The Search for El Dorado.* London: Joseph, 1978.

Hulsius, Levinus. See Sources/2.

Hulton, Paul. *America 1585: The Complete Drawings of John White.* Chapel Hill, N.C.: University of North Carolina Press, 1984.

Humboldt, Alexander von. *Personal Narrative of Travels to the Equinoctial Regions,* 6 vols. London, 1821–25.

Jones, H.G., ed. *Raleigh and Quinn: The Explorer and His Boswell.* Chapel Hill, N.C.: University of North Carolina Press, 1987.

Jung, C.G. *Psychology and Alchemy,* Vol. 12 of *Collected Works.* Princeton, N.J.: Princeton University Press, 1968.

————. *Mysterium Coniunctionis,* Vol. 14 of *Collected Works.* Princeton, N.J.: Princeton University Press, 1970.

Keymis, Lawrence. *A Relation of the Second Voyage to Guiana.* London, 1596.

Kirchhoff, Paul. "The Warrau." In *Handbook of South American Indians,* Vol. 3. Washington, D.C.: Smithsonian Institution, 1948.

Knapp, Jeffrey. "Elizabethan Tobacco." In Greenblatt, *New World Encounters.*

Knott, John. "Sir Walter Ralegh's 'Royal Cordial.'" *Dublin Journal of Medical Science,* Vol. 121, 1906.

Lacey, Robert. *Sir Walter Ralegh.* London: Weidenfeld and Nicolson, 1973.

Lee, Sidney. "Caliban's Visits to England." *Cornhill,* Vol. 34, 1913.

Le Fèvre, Nicolas. *A Discourse upon Sir Walter Rawlegh's Great Cordial.* London, 1664.

Levin, Harry. *The Myth of the Golden Age in the Renaissance.* Bloomington, Ind.: Indiana University Press, 1970.

Levillier, Roberto. *El Paititi, El Dorado y Las Amazones.* Buenos Aires: Emece Editores, 1976.

Lorimer, Joyce. *English and Irish Settlement on the River Amazon, 1550–1646.* London: Hakluyt Society, 1989.

———. "Ralegh's First Reconnaissance of Guiana?" *Terrae Incognitae,* Vol. 9, 1977.

"M., R." *Newes of Sir Walter Rauleighe.* London, 1618.

Maier, Michael. *Atalanta Fugiens.* Oppenheim, 1618.

———. *The Laws of the Rosy Cross.* London, 1656.

March, Rosemary. *Sherborne Castle.* Sherborne, England: Sherborne Castle Estates, 1977.

Markham, Sir Clements. *Narratives of the Voyages of Pedro de Sarmiento de Gamboa.* London: Hakluyt Society, 1895.

Mebane, John. *Renaissance Magic and the Return of the Golden Age.* Lincoln, Nebr.: University of Nebraska Press, 1989.

Minta, Stephen. *Aguirre: The Re-creation of a Sixteenth-Century Journey Across South America.* London: Jonathan Cape, 1993.

Montrose, Louis. "The Work of Gender in the Discourse of Discovery." In Greenblatt, *New World Encounters.*

Naipaul, V.S. *The Loss of El Dorado.* London: Deutsch, 1970.

Nashe, Thomas. *Works,* 5 vols., ed. R.B. McKerrow and F.P. Wilson. Oxford: B. Blackwell, 1958.

Oakeshott, Walter. "Sir Walter Ralegh's Library." *The Library,* 5th series, Vol. 23, No. 4 (1968).

Ojer Celigueta, Pablo. *Don Antonio de Berrio: Gobernador del Dorado.* Caracas: Universidad Católica, 1960.

———. *La Formación del Oriente Venezolano.* Caracas: Universidad Católica, 1966.

Porter, Henry C. *The Inconstant Savage: England and the North American Indian, 1500–1600.* London: Duckworth, 1979.

Purchas, Samuel. *Hakluytus Posthumus, or Purchas His Pilgrims.* London, 1625.

Quinn, D.B. *The Voyages and Colonizing Enterprises of Sir Humphrey Gilbert,* 2 vols. London: Hakluyt Society, 1940.

———. *Raleigh and the British Empire.* London: Hodder and Stoughton, 1947.

———. *The Roanoke Voyages,* 2 vols. London: Hakluyt Society, 1955.

———. *Explorers and Colonies: America 1500–1625.* London: Hambledon Press, 1990.

Ralegh, Sir Walter. *The History of the World.* London, 1614.

Ramos Perez, Demetrio. *El Mito del Dorado: Su Génesis y Proceso.* Caracas: Academia Nacional de la Historia, 1973.

———. "Walter Ralegh y la Hispanificación de sus ideas." *Archivo Hispanense,* Vol. 56, 1973.

Rattansi, P.M. "Alchemy and Natural Magic in Ralegh's *History of the World.*" *Ambix,* Vol. 13, 1965.

Roberts, John. "The Younger Sir John Gilbert." *Report and Transactions of the Devonshire Association for the Advancement of Science, Literature and Art,* Vol. 100, 1968.

Rowse, A.L. *Ralegh and the Throckmortons.* London: Macmillan, 1962.

Sarmiento de Gamboa, Pedro. *The History of the Incas,* trans. Sir Clements Markham. London: Hakluyt Society, 1897.

Schomburgk, Sir Robert. See Sources/2.

Shirley, John. *Thomas Harriot.* Oxford: Oxford University Press, 1983.

————. "Sir Walter Raleigh's Guiana Finances." *Huntington Library Quarterly,* Vol. 13, 1949.

————. "The Scientific Experiments of Sir Walter Ralegh in the Tower, 1603–17." *Ambix,* Vol. 4, 1948.

Skelton, R.A. "Ralegh as a Geographer." *Virginia Magazine of History and Biography,* Vol. 72, 1963.

Strathmann, Ernest. *Sir Walter Ralegh: A Study in Elizabethan Skepticism.* New York: Columbia University Press, 1951.

Taylor, Eva G.R. "Hariot's Instructions for Ralegh's Voyage to Guiana." *Journal of the Institute of Navigation,* Vol. 5, 1952.

Waite, Alfred Edward, ed. *The Hermetic Museum Restored and Enlarged* (1678), 2 vols. London, 1893.

Warner, G.F., ed. *The Voyage of Robert Dudley to the West Indies, 1594–5* London: Hakluyt Society, 1899.

Wilbert, Johannes. *Tobacco Shamanism in South America.* London and New Haven, Conn.: Yale University Press, 1981.

————. "Tobacco and Shamanistic Ecstasy Among the Warao Indians of Venezuela." In *Flesh of the Gods,* ed. Peter Furst. New York: Praeger, 1972.

Winton, John. *Sir Walter Ralegh.* London: Joseph, 1975.

4. ILLUSTRATIONS

The author and publisher acknowledge and thank the following sources for permission to use illustrations that appear in the text:

British Museum: Frontispiece, Nos. 1–4, 11, 12, 16, 17, 18–24, 25–34. Collection of Lord Walston, London: 6. Archivo General de Indias, Seville: 7, 15. National Gallery of Ireland, Dublin: 8. Photograph by Peter Burton/Harland Walshaw: 9. Trinity College, Oxford: 10. Tower of London (photograph by author): 13. Collection of Geoffrey Gilbert, Compton Castle, Devon: 14.

INDEX